CW01091604

Yamaha FZ6
Service and Repair Manual

by Phil Mather

Models covered

(4751-304)

FZ6-S/SA Fazer. 600 cc. 2004 to 2007
FZ6-N/NA. 600 cc. 2004 to 2007
FZ6 Fazer S2. 600 cc. 2007 to 2008
FZ6 S2. 600 cc. 2007 to 2008

© Haynes Publishing 2008

ABCDE
FGHIJ
KLMNO
PQRST

A book in the Haynes Service and Repair Manual Series

ISBN: **978 1 84425 751 5**

British Library Cataloguing in Publication Data
A catalogue record for this book is available from the British Library.

Library of Congress Control Number 2007934143

Printed in the USA

Haynes Publishing
Sparkford, Yeovil, Somerset BA22 7JJ, England

Haynes North America, Inc
861 Lawrence Drive, Newbury Park, California 91320, USA

Haynes Publishing Nordiska AB
Box 1504, 751 45 Uppsala, Sweden

Contents

119

120/70 ZR17
180/55 ZR17
BRIDGSTONE 020
WATLING UNIVERSAL TYRES
TOTTENHAM 0208 808 3179
119

Suzuki GSF600 & 1200 Bandit Fours
Service and Repair Manual

by Matthew Coombs & Phil Mather

(3367-288-9AA3)

Models covered
GSF600 (Bandit N 600). 599cc. UK 1995-on
GSF600S (Bandit S 600). 599cc. UK and US 1996-on
GSF1200 (Bandit N 1200). 1157cc. UK 1996-on
GSF1200S (Bandit S 1200). 1157cc. UK 1996-on, US 1997-on

© Haynes Publishing 2001

A book in the **Haynes Service and Repair Manual Series**

ABCDE
FGHIJ
KL

Printed in USA

ISBN **1 85960 784 5**

British Library Cataloguing in Publication Data
A catalogue record for this book is available from the British Library.

Library of Congress Catalogue Card Number 2001135405

Haynes Publishing
Sparkford, Nr Yeovil, Somerset BA22 7JJ, England

Haynes North America, Inc
861 Lawrence Drive, Newbury Park, California 91320, USA

Editions Haynes
Tour Aurore – IBC, 18 Place des Reflets
92975 Paris La Defense 2 Cedex, France

Haynes Publishing Nordiska AB
Box 1504, 751 45 UPPSALA, Sweden

Contents

LIVING WITH YOUR SUZUKI BANDIT

Introduction

Daily (pre-ride) checks

MAINTENANCE

Routine maintenance and servicing

Contents

REPAIRS AND OVERHAUL

Engine, transmission and associated systems

Chassis components

Electrical system

Wiring diagrams

REFERENCE

Index

Yamaha
Musical instruments to motorcycles

**The FS1E -
first bike of many sixteen year olds in the UK**

The Yamaha Motor Company

The Yamaha name can be traced back to 1889, when Torakusu Yamaha founded the Yamaha Organ Manufacturing Company. Such was the success of the company, that in 1897 it became Nippon Gakki Limited and manufactured a wide range of reed organs and pianos.

During World War II, Nippon Gakki's manufacturing base was utilised by the Japanese authorities to produce propellers and fuel tanks for their aviation industry. The end of the war brought about a huge public demand for low cost transport and many firms decided to utilise their obsolete aircraft tooling for the production of motorcycles. Nippon Gakki's first motorcycle went on sale in February 1955 and was named the 125 YA-1 Red Dragonfly. This machine was a copy of the German DKW RT125 motorcycle, featuring a single cylinder two-stroke engine with a four-speed gearbox. Due to the outstanding success of this model the motorcycle operation was separated from Nippon Gakki in July 1955 and the Yamaha Motor Company was formed.

The YA-1 also received acclaim by winning two of Japan's biggest road races, the Mount Fuji Climbing race and the Asama Volcano race. The high level of public demand for the YA-1 led to the development of a whole series of two-stroke singles and twins.

Having made a large impact on their home market, Yamahas were exported to the USA in 1958 and to the UK in 1962. In the UK the signing of an Anglo-Japanese trade agreement during 1962 enabled the sale of Japanese lightweight motorcycles and scooters in Britain. At that time, competition between the many motorcycle producers in Japan had reduced numbers significantly and by the end of the sixties, only the big-four which are familiar with today remained.

Yamaha Europe was founded in 1968 and based in Holland. Although originally set up to market marine products, the Dutch base is now the official European Headquarters and distribution centre. Yamaha motorcycles are built at factories in Holland, Denmark, Norway, Italy, France, Spain and Portugal. Yamahas are imported into the UK by Yamaha Motor UK Ltd, formerly Mitsui Machinery Sales (UK) Ltd. Mitsui and Co. were originally a trading house, handling the shipping, distribution and marketing of Japanese products into western countries. Ultimately Mitsui Machinery Sales was formed to handle Yamaha motorcycles and outboard motors.

Based on the technology derived from its motorcycle operation, Yamaha have produced many other products, such as automobile and lightweight aircraft engines, marine engines and boats, generators, pumps, ATVs, snowmobiles, golf cars, industrial robots, lawnmowers, swimming pools and archery equipment.

Two-strokes first

Part of Yamaha's success was a whole string of innovations in the two-stroke world. Autolube engine lubrication, torque induction, multi-ported engines, reed valves and power valves kept their two-strokes at the forefront of technology. Many advances were achieved with the use of racing as a development laboratory. They went to the USA in the late 1950s with an air-cooled 250cc twin but didn't hit the GPs until the early 1960s when Fumio Ito scored a hat-trick of sixth places in the Isle of Man TT, the Dutch TT and the Belgian GP. This experiment gave rise to the idea of the over-the-counter racer, an idea that became reality in the TD1, the first in an unmatched series of two-stroke racers that were the standard issue for privateers at national and international level for years and helped Yamaha develop their road engines. While privateers raced the twins, Yamaha built the outrageously complicated vee-four 250 for Phil Read and followed it with a vee-four 125 that Bill Ivy lapped the Isle of Man on at over 100mph! When the FIM regulations were changed to limit the smaller GP classes to two cylinders, these exotic bikes died but set the scene for an unparalleled dynasty of mass-produced racers based on the same technology as the road bikes.

In the 1960s and 70s the two-stroke engined YAS3 125, YDS1 to YDS7 250 and YR5 350 formed the core of Yamaha's range. By the mid-70s they had been superseded by the RD (Race-Developed) 125, 250, and 350 range of two-stroke twins, featuring improved 7-port engines with reed valve induction. Braking

was improved by the use of an hydraulic brake on the front wheel of DX models, instead of the drum arrangement used previously, and cast alloy wheels were available as an option on later RD models. The RD350 was replaced by the RD400 in 1976.

Running parallel with the RD twins was a range of single-cylinder two-strokes. Used in a variety of chassis types, the engine was used in the popular 50 cc FS1-E moped, the V50 to 90 step-thrus, RS100 and 125, YB100 and the DT trail range.

The TD racers got water-cooling in 1973 to become the TZs, the most successful and numerous over-the-counter racers ever built. That same year, Jarno Saarinen became the first rider to win a 500cc GP on a four-cylinder two-stroke on the new in-line four which was effectively a pair of TZs side-by-side. TZs won everywhere – including the Daytona 200 and 500 races when overbored to 351cc. A 700cc TZ also appeared, one year later taken out to 750cc. Steve Baker won the first Formula 750 world title – one of the precursors of Superbike – on one in 1977. The following year Kenny Roberts won Yamaha's first world 500 title and would be succeeded by Wayne Rainey and Eddie Lawson before Mick Doohan and the NSR500 took over.

The air-cooled single and twin cylinder RD road bikes were eventually replaced by the LC series in 1980, featuring liquid-cooled engines, radical new styling, spiral pattern cast wheels and cantilever rear suspension (Yamaha's Monoshock). Of all the LC models, the RD350LC, or RD350R as it was later known, has made the most impact in the market. Later models had YPVS (Yamaha Power Valve System) engines, another first for Yamaha – this was essentially a valve located in the exhaust ports which was electronically operated to alter port timing to achieve maximum power output. The RD500LC was the largest two-stroke made by Yamaha and differed from the other LCs by the use of its vee-four cylinder engine.

With the exception of the RD350R, now manufactured in Brazil, the LC range has been discontinued. Two-stroke engined models have given way to environmental pressure, and thus with a few exceptions, such as the TZR125 and TZR250, are used only in scooters and small capacity bikes.

The Four-strokes

Yamaha concentrated solely on two-stroke models until 1970 when the XS1 was produced, their first four-stroke motorcycle. It was perhaps Yamaha's success with two-strokes that postponed an earlier

The distinctive paintwork and trim of the RD models

move into the four-stroke motorcycle market, although their work with Toyota during the 1960s had given them a sound base in four-stroke technology.

The XS1 had a 650 cc twin-cylinder SOHC engine and was later to become known as the XS650, appearing also in the popular SE custom form. Yamaha introduced a three cylinder 750 cc engine in 1976, fitted in a sport-tourer frame and called the XS750, TX750 in the USA . The XS750 established itself well in the sport tourer class and remained in production with very few changes until uprated to 850 cc in 1980.

Other four-strokes followed in 1976, with the introduction of the XS250/360/400 series twins. The XS range was strengthened in 1978 by the four-cylinder XS1100.

The 1980s saw a new family of four-strokes, the XJ550, 650, 750 and 900 Fours. Improvements over the XS range amounted to a slimmer DOHC engine unit due to the relocation of the alternator behind the cylinders, electronic ignition and uprated braking and suspension systems. Models were available mainly in standard trim, although custom-styled Maxims were produced especially for the US market. The XJ650T was the first model from Yamaha to have a turbo-charged engine. Although these early XJ models have now been discontinued, their roots live on in the XJ600S and XJ900S Diversion (Seca II) models.

The FZR prefix encompasses the pure

The XS650 led the way for Yamaha's four-stroke range

sports Yamaha models. With the exception of the 16-valve FZR400 and FZR600 models, the FZ/FZR750 and FZR1000 used 20-valve engines, two exhaust valves and three inlet valves per cylinder. This concept was called Genesis and gave improved gas flow to the combustion chambers. Other features of the new engine were the use of down-draught carburetors and the engine's inclined angle in the frame, plus the change to liquid-cooling.

Yamaha's XS750 was produced from 1976 to 1982 and then uprated to 850 cc

Lightweight Deltabox design aluminium frames and uprated suspension improved the bikes's handling. The Genesis engine lives on in the YZF750 and 1000 models.

The Genesis concept was the basis of Yamaha's foray into four-stroke racing, first with a bike known simply as 'The Genesis', an FZ750 motor in a TT Formula 1 bike with which the factory attempted to steal the Honda RVF750's thunder at important events like the Suzuka 8 Hours and the Bol d'Or although they never fielded it for a whole World Championship season. That had to wait for the advent of the World Superbike Championship, although there was no full works team until 1995, instead it was left to individual importers to support teams. It was the Australian Dealer Team Yamaha which scored the factory's first World Superbike win in the series debut year of 1988. The rider? Mick Doohan. Slightly, embarrassingly, it was the steel framed FZ750 rather than the FZR homologation special that won races. The OW01 was a race winner, mainly in the hands of Fabrizio Pirovano, the factory's most successful Superbike racer with ten victories, but national success in the UK, Japan, and in the Daytona 200 has not been translated into World Championships for any of Yamaha's 750s.

The vee-twin engine has been the mainstay of the XV Virago range. Since 1981 XVs have been produced in 535, 700, 750, 920, 1000 and 1100 engine sizes, all using the same basic air-cooled sohc vee-twin engine. Other uses of vee engines have been in the XZ550 of the early 1980s, the XVZ12 Venture and the mighty VMX-12 V-Max.

Yamaha has always been a sporting-orientated company whose motto could be 'Racing Improves the Breed', so it's no surprise that the latest generation of lightweight sportsters are at the cutting edge of performance on and off the track. The R6 won more races than any other machine in the inaugural year of the World Supersports Championship, the R7 won a race in its debut year in World Superbike in the hands of the mercurial Noriyuki Haga, and the mighty

A new family of four-strokes was released in 1980 with the introduction of the XJ range

1000cc R1 ended Honda's domination of the Isle of Man F1 TT when David Jefferies won three races in a week in 1999.

In Grand Prix racing, the factory took several years to get over the shock of Wayne Rainey's crippling accident. and first 500cc win since the American's enforced retirement didn't come until 1998 when Simon Crafar won at Donington Park. For 1999, Yamaha refocussed their ambitions and signed Italian superstar Max Biaggi plus Spanish trier Carlos Checa for the works team, while dashing young Frenchman Regis Laconi and tough little Aussie Gary McCoy rode for the WCM satellite team. Both teams got a win in the '99 season and with a new TZ250 being developed for 2000 it looks as if Yamaha's spirit of competition will go on unabated into the new Millenium.

Clever Revver

Yamaha's Fazer concept worked right from the time the first model appeared in 1998, and it worked on several levels. The basic idea was to take last year's supersport 600 engine, detune it slightly, house it in a steel chassis and sell it at a price considerably below that of the new cutting-edge supersports model. Thus the first Fazer used a Thundercat motor in a tubular steel chassis with a well-chosen array of components, including stupendous R1 brakes and a very sharp looking half-fairing. The factory was happy; it got to prolong the (cost-amortising) life of a motor that cost a lot to develop and plug a gap in its model range, the customer was happy because he or she bought real-world performance at a bargain price and got a machine that didn't change much and therefore held value better than the supersports model.

Once Yamaha realised that the Fazer formula was a success it was extended to the 1000cc class, with an R1 retuned for more midrange power as the heart of the matter. The old 600cc Thundercat had never been a cutting-edge supersports bike but the R1 most certainly was, so the savings to the factory were certainly more significant. It is in the nature of the supersports bikes that are also homologation models for supersports and superbike racing that they have to be constantly updated and redesigned every few years to keep up with the opposition. That takes money, and extending the life of the motor helped spread those costs. The bigger, sportier Fazer was another success and paved the way for an even sportier 600cc Fazer in the shape of the 2004 model FZ6, based around the 2003 R6 motor.

The XV535 Virago vee-twin

2005 FZ6-N

2008 FZ6 Fazer S2

Yamaha's clever trick with the first Fazer was creating a really useful motorcycle from a selection of parts lying around in their spares department without making the result feel like a mongrel design. For the second-generation model they didn't take any chances. The detuned – sorry, retuned – R6-based motor was alleged to deliver serious midrange punch and the wheels looked like R6 equipment as well. Forks came off the big Fazer and running the exhausts back under the seat gave it that essential MotoGP look. The big upgrade came in the chassis department with a diecast aluminium frame. Yamaha must have got the production engineering costs on that technology under control since introducing it on their sports bikes because the new bike was still very competitively priced. Mind you, it was still possible to see where the factory was saving a few yen. The swinging arm was still fabricated from box-section and the forks

may have also been used on the 1000cc Fazer but were still only conventional 43mm items – multi-adjustable upside-down Ohlins stuff is not on the menu. And as for the brakes – sliding calipers were used.

This time, there were two models, the FZ6-S Fazer with, as usual, a very neat half fairing, plus a naked model known simply as the FZ6-N (strictly speaking, not a Fazer). As you would expect with the change from the Thundercat motor to the R6-derived engine, the bike became reviver in character but obviously not as extreme as the track-orientated donor bike. Not that it did any harm to sales, Europe in particular loved the FZ6-S and bought them in large numbers. It was one of those bikes that really was all things to all riders. It could commute or tour and was quite capable of hustling along when ridden with enthusiasm. Also, it was an obvious and affordable machine for newly qualified bikers.

In keeping with the cost-cutting ethos of all the Fazers, the FZ6 received little change apart from the option of ABS, until its third model year when the S2 versions appeared for 2007. Even then there were precious few significant changes under the restyled bodywork, chief among them was the swinging arm which was now made by the same diecasting method as the frame. Thankfully, Yamaha found that they'd run out of those circa 1970 sliding calipers and fitted proper opposed-piston brakes. Perhaps the cleverest thing about the Fazer concept is that Yamaha had a very clear idea of what the bike should be and who they would be selling to. With the S2 getting modern brakes, there is very little on the spec-sheet that could be described as penny-pinching. With judicious updating, there should be Fazers in the range for many years to come.

Acknowledgements

Our thanks are due to Fowlers Motorcycles of Bristol and to Doug Dearden Motorcycles of Southampton, who supplied the machines featured in the illustrations throughout this manual. We would also like to thank NGK Spark Plugs (UK) Ltd for supplying the colour spark plug condition photographs, the Avon Rubber Company for supplying information on tyre fitting and Draper Tools Ltd for some of the workshop tools shown.

Thanks are also due to Yamaha Motor (UK) Ltd who supplied model photographs, and to Julian Ryder who wrote the introduction 'Musical Instruments to Motorcycles'.

About this Manual

The aim of this manual is to help you get the best value from your motorcycle. It can do so in several ways. It can help you decide what work must be done, even if you choose to have it done by a dealer; it provides information and procedures for routine maintenance and servicing; and it offers diagnostic and repair procedures to follow when trouble occurs.

We hope you use the manual to tackle the work yourself. For many simpler jobs, doing it yourself may be quicker than arranging an appointment to get the motorcycle into a dealer and making the trips to leave it and pick it up. More importantly, a lot of money can be saved by avoiding the expense the shop must pass on to you to cover its labour and overhead costs. An added benefit is the sense of satisfaction and accomplishment that you feel after doing the job yourself.

References to the left or right side of the motorcycle assume you are sitting on the seat, facing forward.

We take great pride in the accuracy of information given in this manual, but motorcycle manufacturers make alterations and design changes during the production run of a particular motorcycle of which they do not inform us. No liability can be accepted by the authors or publishers for loss, damage or injury caused by any errors in, or omissions from, the information given.

Frame and engine numbers

The frame serial number is stamped into the right-hand side of the steering head and is repeated on a sticker on the right-hand side of the frame. The engine number is stamped into the rear of the crankcase. The model code label is on the rear sub-frame under the seat. These numbers should be recorded and kept in a safe place so they can be given to the police in the event of a theft.

The frame serial number, engine serial number, and model code should also be kept in a handy place (such as with your driver's licence) so that they are always available when ordering parts for your machine.

The procedures in this manual identify the bikes by model and year (e.g. FZ6-S (V) 2006). The model codes for all years and models covered are tabled below.

Buying spare parts

Once you have found all the identification numbers, record them for reference when buying parts. Since the manufacturers change specifications, parts and vendors (companies that manufacture various components on the machine), providing the ID numbers is the only way to be reasonably sure that you are buying the correct parts.

Whenever possible, take the worn part to the dealer so direct comparison with the new component can be made. Along the trail from the manufacturer to the parts shelf, there are numerous places that the part can end up with the wrong number or be listed incorrectly.

The two places to purchase new parts for your motorcycle – the accessory store and the franchised dealer – differ in the type of parts they carry. While dealers can obtain virtually every part for your motorcycle, the accessory dealer is usually limited to normal high wear items such as shock absorbers, tune-up parts, various engine gaskets, cables, chains, brake pads, etc. Rarely will an accessory outlet have major suspension components, cylinders, transmission gears, or cases.

Used parts can be obtained for roughly half the price of new ones, but you can't always be sure of what you're getting. Once again, take your worn part to the breaker's yard for direct comparison.

Whether buying new, used or rebuilt parts, the best course is to deal directly with someone who specialises in parts for your particular make.

The frame number is stamped into the right-hand side of the steering head . . .

. . . and is repeated on a sticker on the right-hand side of the frame

FZ6-N models (Europe)	Year	Code
FZ6-N (S)	2004	1B31
FZ6-N (T)	2005	1B33/1B35
FZ6-N (V)	2006	1B3B/1B39
FZ6-NA (V)	2006	not available
FZ6-N (W)	2007	1B3D
FZ6-NA (W)	2007	5S31
FZ6-S2 (W)	2007	5S51
FZ6-SA2 (W)	2007	5S41
FZ6-S2 (X)	2008	5S53
FZ6-SA2 (X)	2008	5S42

FZ6-S models (Europe)	Year	Code
FZ6-S (S)	2004	5VX1
FZ6-S (T)	2005	5VX6
FZ6-S (V)	2006	4P51
FZ6-SA (V)	2006	4P52
FZ6-S (W)	2007	5VXL
FZ6-SA (W)	2007	4P53/4
FZ6 Fazer S2 (W)	2007	4S81
FZ6 Fazer SA2 (W)	2007	5S21
FZ6 Fazer S2 (X)	2008	4S86
FZ6 Fazer SA2 (X)	2008	5S22

FZ6-S models (US)	Year	Code
FZ6-S (S)	2004	5VX3 (49 States)
FZ6-S (S) C	2004	5VX4 (California)
FZ6-S (T)	2005	5VX8 (49 States)
FZ6-S (T) C	2005	5VX9 (California)
FZS6 (V)	2006	FZS6V (49 States)
FZS6 (V) C	2006	FZS6VC (California)
FZS6 (W)	2007	FZS6W (49 States)
FZS6 (W) C	2007	FZS6WC (California)
FZS6 (X)	2008	FZS6X (49 States)
FZS6 (X) C	2008	FZS6XC (California)

The model code label (arrowed) is stuck to the frame

The engine number (arrowed) is stamped into the rear of the crankcase

2004

The FZ-6 Fazer was launched in November 2003 for the 2004 model year.

The engine was based on that used in the Yamaha R6 – a liquid-cooled, in-line four cylinder with two chain driven overhead camshafts actuating on four valves per cylinder. Cam profiles, valve springs and intake ducts were altered, and a new fuel injection system was introduced.

This 'group injection' system split the fuel charge for each cylinder into two, separate injections, which offered the advantage of improved fuel atomisation and fuel/air mixing. The system did away with the camshaft position sensor and, combined with a larger capacity air filter housing and new ECU, offered better mid-range performance.

The exhaust system was a three-section, four-into-two-into-one design, incorporating a catalytic converter in the centre, single pipe, section. Yamaha's air induction system (AIS) fed filtered air into the exhaust ports to improve exhaust end-gas burning.

The clutch was a conventional cable-operated, wet, multi-plate unit and the gearbox had 6-speeds with 'stacked' transmission shafts. Drive to the rear wheel was by chain and sprockets.

The engine was housed in an all-new, lightweight, vacuum cast aluminium frame, bolted together at the headstock. Front suspension was by conventional oil-damped 43 mm forks which were non-adjustable. Rear suspension was by a single shock absorber acting directly on a box-section swingarm.

Seventeen-inch, five-spoke cast aluminium wheels were fitted front and rear, with twin, two-piston sliding caliper disc brakes at the front and a single-piston, sliding caliper brake at the rear.

The FZ-6 Fazer was available in both faired (S model) and unfaired (N model) variants. Twin headlights and a centre stand were fitted to the faired models. In some markets, notably the US, only S models were available.

Colours: S models – silver, dark purple-blue metallic and light grey-blue metallic. N models – silver, dark red metallic and black metallic.

2005

There were no significant changes for 2005.

Colours: S models – silver, dark purple-blue metallic and light silver-blue metallic. N models – silver-blue metallic, dark red and dark grey metallic.

2006

ABS became available as an option on both S and N models. Models equipped with ABS could be identified by the suffix A (e.g. an FZ6-SA was a faired model with ABS. Installation of the ABS modulator behind the engine unit required relocation of the coolant reservoir to a position below the radiator.

Colours: S models – blue-silver, dark grey metallic, purple-blue metallic and dark red metallic. N models – grey-blue metallic, orange metallic and dark grey metallic.

2007

The FZ6 range was expanded with the introduction of two new variants, the faired FZ6 Fazer S2 and the unfaired FZ6 N2 known as the FZ6-SHG and FZ6-NHG respectively.

A new, lower design of fairing and reprofiled front mudguard were complimented by minor cosmetic changes to the handlebar clamp, seat contours, rider's footrest brackets and finish on the front fork sliders. The passenger footrest brackets were detachable from the

rear sub-frame, whereas previously they had been part of the welded assembly.

A new, cast and extruded swingarm was fitted and the new monobloc front brake calipers now housed four opposed pistons, actuated via a modified brake hose layout.

The instrument cluster featured an analogue tachometer with inset warning indicators, all other information being provided by an adjacent LCD.

Internally, the engine remained the same except for the substitution of bolts only for the nuts and bolts used previously to secure the connecting rod big-end caps. The fuel injection system was re-mapped to improve mid-range performance, and an oxygen sensor was located in the mid section of the exhaust pipe together with a honeycomb catalyser matrix.

The forward location of the coolant reservoir became standardised for all models.

The remainder of the range (i.e. the non-S2 and non-N2 models) incorporated the re-mapped fuel injection and uprated exhaust systems, the modified passenger footrests and new seat of the S2 models.

Colours for the S2 models were: FZ6 Fazer models – dark red metallic, purple-blue metallic and black. FZ6 models – light blue, white, silver metallic and black.

Colours for the rest of the range were: silver and black.

2008

There were no significant changes for 2008.

Colours: Fazer models – ocean depth blue, midnight black, silver metallic. FZ6 models – silver metallic, competition white, midnight black.

Engine

Type	Four-stroke 16V in-line four
Capacity	600 cc
Bore	65.5 mm
Stroke	44.5 mm
Compression ratio	12.2 to 1
Cooling system	Liquid cooled
Clutch	Wet multi-plate
Transmission	Six-speed constant mesh
Final drive	Chain and sprockets
Camshafts	DOHC, chain-driven
Throttle bodies	
2004 to 2006 models	2 x Mikuni 36EIDW
2007-on models	
S S2/SA S2 and N S2/NA S2	1 x Mikuni 36EIDW-B1
S/SA (4P53) and N/NA	1 x Mikuni 36EIDW-B7
SA (4P54)	1 x Mikuni 36EIDW-B10
Ignition system	Digital electronic CDI

Chassis

Frame type	Die-cast aluminium
Rake and trail	25°, 97.5 mm
Fuel tank capacity (including reserve)	19.4 litres
Reserve capacity (with fuel light on)	3.5 litres
Front suspension	
Type	43 mm oil-damped conventional telescopic forks
Travel	130 mm
Adjustment	None
Rear suspension	
Type	
2004 to 2006 models	Single shock absorber, box-section aluminium swingarm
2007-on models	
N/NA and S/SA models	Single shock absorber, box-section aluminium swingarm
All S2 models	Single shock absorber, hexagonal-section aluminium swingarm
Travel	130 mm
Adjustment	Spring pre-load
Wheels	17 inch 5-spoke alloys
Tyres	
Front	120/70 x ZR17 M/C (58W) tubeless
Rear	180/55 x ZR17 M/C (73W) tubeless
Front brake	
2004 to 2006 models	Twin 298 mm discs with 2-piston sliding calipers
2007-on models	
S2 models	Twin 298 mm discs with 4 opposed piston calipers
All other models	Twin 298 mm discs with 2-piston sliding calipers
Rear brake	Single 245 mm disc with single piston sliding caliper

Dimensions and weights

Overall length	2095 mm
Overall width	
All FZ6-S models	750 mm
All FZ6-N models	755 mm
Overall height	
FZ6-S/SA models	1215 mm
FZ6-S/SA S2 models	1210 mm
All FZ6-N models	1085 mm
Wheelbase	1440 mm
Seat height	795 mm
Wet weight (with all fluids and full fuel tank)	
FZ6-N/N S2 models	201 kg
FZ6-NA/NA S2 models	206 kg
FZ6-S/S S2 models	207 kg
FZ6-SA/SA S2 models	212 kg

Professional mechanics are trained in safe working procedures. However enthusiastic you may be about getting on with the job at hand, take the time to ensure that your safety is not put at risk. A moment's lack of attention can result in an accident, as can failure to observe simple precautions.

There will always be new ways of having accidents, and the following is not a comprehensive list of all dangers; it is intended rather to make you aware of the risks and to encourage a safe approach to all work you carry out on your bike.

Asbestos

● Certain friction, insulating, sealing and other products - such as brake pads, clutch linings, gaskets, etc. - contain asbestos. Extreme care must be taken to avoid inhalation of dust from such products since it is hazardous to health. If in doubt, assume that they do contain asbestos.

Fire

● Remember at all times that petrol is highly flammable. Never smoke or have any kind of naked flame around, when working on the vehicle. But the risk does not end there - a spark caused by an electrical short-circuit, by two metal surfaces contacting each other, by careless use of tools, or even by static electricity built up in your body under certain conditions, can ignite petrol vapour, which in a confined space is highly explosive. Never use petrol as a cleaning solvent. Use an approved safety solvent.

● Always disconnect the battery earth terminal before working on any part of the fuel or electrical system, and never risk spilling fuel on to a hot engine or exhaust.

● It is recommended that a fire extinguisher of a type suitable for fuel and electrical fires is kept handy in the garage or workplace at all times. Never try to extinguish a fuel or electrical fire with water.

Fumes

● Certain fumes are highly toxic and can quickly cause unconsciousness and even death if inhaled to any extent. Petrol vapour comes into this category, as do the vapours from certain solvents such as trichloro-ethylene. Any draining or pouring of such volatile fluids should be done in a well ventilated area.

● When using cleaning fluids and solvents, read the instructions carefully. Never use materials from unmarked containers - they may give off poisonous vapours.

● Never run the engine of a motor vehicle in an enclosed space such as a garage. Exhaust fumes contain carbon monoxide which is extremely poisonous; if you need to run the engine, always do so in the open air or at least have the rear of the vehicle outside the workplace.

The battery

● Never cause a spark, or allow a naked light near the vehicle's battery. It will normally be giving off a certain amount of hydrogen gas, which is highly explosive.

● Always disconnect the battery ground (earth) terminal before working on the fuel or electrical systems (except where noted).

● If possible, loosen the filler plugs or cover when charging the battery from an external source. Do not charge at an excessive rate or the battery may burst.

● Take care when topping up, cleaning or carrying the battery. The acid electrolyte, evenwhen diluted, is very corrosive and should not be allowed to contact the eyes or skin. Always wear rubber gloves and goggles or a face shield. If you ever need to prepare electrolyte yourself, always add the acid slowly to the water; never add the water to the acid.

Electricity

● When using an electric power tool, inspection light etc., always ensure that the appliance is correctly connected to its plug and that, where necessary, it is properly grounded (earthed). Do not use such appliances in damp conditions and, again, beware of creating a spark or applying excessive heat in the vicinity of fuel or fuel vapour. Also ensure that the appliances meet national safety standards.

● A severe electric shock can result from touching certain parts of the electrical system, such as the spark plug wires (HT leads), when the engine is running or being cranked, particularly if components are damp or the insulation is defective. Where an electronic ignition system is used, the secondary (HT) voltage is much higher and could prove fatal.

Remember...

✗ **Don't** start the engine without first ascertaining that the transmission is in neutral.

✗ **Don't** suddenly remove the pressure cap from a hot cooling system - cover it with a cloth and release the pressure gradually first, or you may get scalded by escaping coolant.

✗ **Don't** attempt to drain oil until you are sure it has cooled sufficiently to avoid scalding you.

✗ **Don't** grasp any part of the engine or exhaust system without first ascertaining that it is cool enough not to burn you.

✗ **Don't** allow brake fluid or antifreeze to contact the machine's paintwork or plastic components.

✗ **Don't** siphon toxic liquids such as fuel, hydraulic fluid or antifreeze by mouth, or allow them to remain on your skin.

✗ **Don't** inhale dust - it may be injurious to health (see Asbestos heading).

✗ **Don't** allow any spilled oil or grease to remain on the floor - wipe it up right away, before someone slips on it.

✗ **Don't** use ill-fitting spanners or other tools which may slip and cause injury.

✗ **Don't** lift a heavy component which may be beyond your capability - get assistance.

✗ **Don't** rush to finish a job or take unverified short cuts.

✗ **Don't** allow children or animals in or around an unattended vehicle.

✗ **Don't** inflate a tyre above the recommended pressure. Apart from overstressing the carcass, in extreme cases the tyre may blow off forcibly.

✔ **Do** ensure that the machine is supported securely at all times. This is especially important when the machine is blocked up to aid wheel or fork removal.

✔ **Do** take care when attempting to loosen a stubborn nut or bolt. It is generally better to pull on a spanner, rather than push, so that if you slip, you fall away from the machine rather than onto it.

✔ **Do** wear eye protection when using power tools such as drill, sander, bench grinder etc.

✔ **Do** use a barrier cream on your hands prior to undertaking dirty jobs - it will protect your skin from infection as well as making the dirt easier to remove afterwards; but make sure your hands aren't left slippery. Note that long-term contact with used engine oil can be a health hazard.

✔ **Do** keep loose clothing (cuffs, ties etc. and long hair) well out of the way of moving mechanical parts.

✔ **Do** remove rings, wristwatch etc., before working on the vehicle - especially the electrical system.

✔ **Do** keep your work area tidy - it is only too easy to fall over articles left lying around.

✔ **Do** exercise caution when compressing springs for removal or installation. Ensure that the tension is applied and released in a controlled manner, using suitable tools which preclude the possibility of the spring escaping violently.

✔ **Do** ensure that any lifting tackle used has a safe working load rating adequate for the job.

✔ **Do** get someone to check periodically that all is well, when working alone on the vehicle.

✔ **Do** carry out work in a logical sequence and check that everything is correctly assembled and tightened afterwards.

✔ **Do** remember that your vehicle's safety affects that of yourself and others. If in doubt on any point, get professional advice.

● If in spite of following these precautions, you are unfortunate enough to injure yourself, seek medical attention as soon as possible.

Note: *The Pre-ride checks outlined in the owner's manual covers those items which should be inspected before riding the motorcycle.*

Engine oil level

Before you start:

✔ Support the motorcycle in an upright position. Make sure it is on level ground.
✔ Start the engine and let it idle for several minutes to allow it to reach normal operating temperature.
Caution: Do not run the engine in an enclosed space such as a garage or workshop.
✔ Leave the motorcycle undisturbed for a few minutes to allow the oil level to stabilise.

Bike care:

● If you have to add oil frequently, you should check whether you have any oil leaks. If there is no sign of oil leakage from the joints and gaskets the engine could be burning oil (see *Fault Finding*).

The correct oil:

● Modern, high-revving engines place great demands on their oil. It is very important that the correct oil for your bike is used.
● Always top up with a good quality oil of the specified type and viscosity and do not overfill the engine.

Oil type	API grade SE, SF or SG
Oil viscosity	SAE 10W30 or 20W40*

*Refer to the viscosity table to select the oil best suited to your conditions.

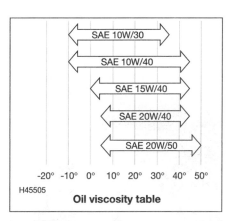

SAE 10W/30
SAE 10W/40
SAE 15W/40
SAE 20W/40
SAE 20W/50
-20° -10° 0° 10° 20° 30° 40° 50°
H45505
Oil viscosity table

2 Insert the clean dipstick back into the engine, but do not screw it in.

1 Remove the dipstick from the right-hand side of the crankcase and use clean rag or paper towel to wipe off all the oil.

3 Remove the dipstick and check the level of the oil, which should be somewhere between the upper and lower level lines (arrowed).

4 If the level is below the lower line, remove the filler cap from the top of the clutch cover.

5 Add the recommended grade and type of oil, to bring the level almost up to the upper line on the dipstick. Do not overfill. Install the filler cap and the dipstick.

Suspension, steering and drive chain

Suspension and Steering:

● Check that the front and rear suspension operates smoothly without binding.
● Check that the rear shock pre-load is adjusted as required.
● Check that the steering moves smoothly from lock-to-lock.

Final drive:

● Check that the drive chain slack isn't excessive, and adjust it if necessary (see Chapter 1).
● If the chain looks dry, lubricate it (see Chapter 1).

Coolant level

Before you start:

✔ Make sure you have a supply of coolant available – a mixture of 50% distilled water and 50% corrosion inhibited ethylene glycol anti-freeze is needed. Note: *Yamaha specify that soft tap water can be used if necessary, but NOT hard water. If in doubt, boil the water first or use only distilled water.*
✔ Always check the coolant level when the engine is cold.
✔ Support the motorcycle in an upright position. Make sure it is on level ground.

> ⚠ **Warning: DO NOT remove the radiator pressure cap to add coolant. Topping up is done via the coolant reservoir tank filler. DO NOT leave open containers of coolant about, as it is poisonous.**

Bike care:

● Use only the specified coolant mixture. It is important that anti-freeze is used in the system all year round, and not just in the winter. Do not top the system up using only water, as the system will become too diluted.
● Do not overfill the reservoir. If the coolant is significantly above the FULL level line at any time, the surplus should be siphoned or drained off to prevent the possibility of it being expelled out of the overflow hose.
● If the coolant level falls steadily, check the system for leaks (see Chapter 1). If no leaks are found and the level continues to fall, it is recommended that the machine be taken to a Yamaha dealer for a pressure test.

1 The reservoir is mounted either behind the engine unit . . .

2 . . . or below the radiator. The coolant FULL and LOW level lines (arrowed) are marked on the reservoir.

3 If the coolant level does not lie between the FULL and LOW level lines, remove the reservoir filler cap and draw the hose out.

4 Remove the fuel tank to access the reservoir filler cap on models with the reservoir mounted behind the engine.

5 Top the coolant level up with the recommended coolant mixture then fit the cap securely.

Brake fluid levels

> ⚠ **Warning: Brake hydraulic fluid can harm your eyes and damage painted surfaces, so use extreme caution when handling and pouring it and cover surrounding surfaces with rag. Do not use fluid that has been standing open for some time, as it absorbs moisture from the air which can cause a dangerous loss of braking effectiveness.**

Before you start:

✔ The front brake fluid reservoir is on the right-hand handlebar. The rear brake fluid reservoir is located below the seat on the right-hand side.
✔ Make sure you have a supply of DOT 4 hydraulic fluid.

✔ Wrap a rag around the reservoir being worked on to ensure that any spillage does not come into contact with painted surfaces.
✔ Support the motorcycle in an upright position. Make sure it is on level ground.

Bike care:

● The fluid in the front and rear brake master cylinder reservoirs may drop as the brake pads wear down. If the fluid level is low, first check the brake pads for wear (see Chapter 1), and replace them with new ones if necessary (see Chapter 6). Do not top the reservoir(s) up until the new pads have been fitted, and then check to see if topping-up is still necessary – as the caliper pistons are pushed back to accommodate the extra thickness of the new pads, some fluid will be displaced back into the reservoir.
● If either fluid reservoir requires repeated topping-up there could be a leak somewhere in the system, which must be investigated immediately.

FRONT BRAKE – Steps 1-6

REAR BRAKE – Steps 7-13

1 The front brake fluid level is visible through a sightglass In the reservoir body – it must be above the LOWER level line (arrowed).

2 If the level is below the LOWER level line, undo the reservoir top screws and remove the top, the diaphragm plate and the diaphragm.

3 Top-up with new DOT 4 hydraulic fluid, until the level is just below the UPPER level line cast on the inside of the reservoir. Take care to avoid spills (see **Warning**) and do not overfill.

4 Wipe any moisture out of the diaphragm using a clean lint-free cloth.

5 Ensure that the diaphragm is correctly seated before installing the plate and top.

6 Tighten the top screws securely.

7 The rear brake fluid level is visible through the reservoir body – it must be between the UPPER and LOWER level lines (arrowed).

8 If the level is below the LOWER level line, hold the reservoir, then unscrew the cap and remove the plate and the diaphragm.

9 If necessary, remove the fuel tank and displace the regulator/rectifier to access the reservoir (see Chapter 6, Section 9).

10 Top-up with new, clean DOT 4 hydraulic fluid, until the level is between the level lines. Take care to avoid spills (see **Warning**) and do not overfill.

11 Wipe any moisture out of the diaphragm using a clean lint-free cloth.

12 Refit the diaphragm, plate and cap.

13 Make sure that the reservoir cap is tightened securely.

Tyres

Loading*/speed	Front	Rear
Up to 90 kg (198 lb) load	33 psi (2.25 Bar)	36 psi (2.5 Bar)
90 kg (198 lb) up to max. load	36 psi (2.5 Bar)	42 psi (3.0 Bar)
High speed riding	33 psi (2.25 Bar)	36 psi (2.5 Bar)
*Load is the total weight of the rider, passenger, luggage and any accessories.		

Recommended max. load	
All non-ABS equipped N models	196 kg (432 lb)
ABS equipped N models	191 kg (421 lb)
All non-ABS equipped S models (except California)	190 kg (419 lb)
All non-ABS equipped S models (California)	189 kg (417 lb)
ABS equipped S models	185 kg (408 lb)

Tyre tread depth:

● At the time of writing UK law requires that the tread depth must be at least 1 mm over the entire tread breadth all the way around the tyre, with no bald patches. Many riders, however, consider 2 mm tread depth minimum to be a safer limit. Yamaha recommend a minimum of 1.6 mm.

● Many tyres now incorporate wear indicators in the tread. Identify the triangular pointer or TWI mark on the tyre sidewall to locate the indicator bar and renew the tyre if the tread has worn down to the bar.

The correct pressures:

● The tyres must be checked when cold, not immediately after riding. Note that low tyre pressures may cause the tyre to slip on the rim or come off. High tyre pressures will cause abnormal tread wear and unsafe handling.

● Use an accurate pressure gauge. Many garage forecourt gauges are wildly inaccurate. If you buy your own, spend as much as you can justify on a quality gauge.

● Correct air pressure will increase tyre life and provide maximum stability, handling capability and ride comfort.

Tyre care:

● Check the tyres carefully for cuts, tears, embedded nails or other sharp objects and excessive wear. Operation of the motorcycle with excessively worn tyres is extremely hazardous, as traction and handling are directly affected.

● Check the condition of the tyre valve and ensure the dust cap is in place.

● Pick out any stones or nails which may have become embedded in the tyre tread. If left, they will eventually penetrate through the casing and cause a puncture.

● If tyre damage is apparent, or unexplained loss of pressure is experienced, seek the advice of a tyre fitting specialist without delay.

1 Remove the cap from the valve – if it's missing, purchase a new one.

2 Check the tyre pressures when the tyres are cold and keep them properly inflated. Fit the cap on completion.

3 Measure tread depth at the centre of the tyre using a tread depth gauge.

4 Tyre tread wear indicator bar and its location marking (usually either an arrow, a triangle or the letters TWI) on the sidewall.

Legal and safety

Lighting and signalling:

● Take a minute to check that the headlight, tail light, brake light, instrument lights and turn signals all work correctly.

● Check that the horn sounds when the switch is operated.

● A working speedometer graduated in mph is a statutory requirement in the UK.

Safety:

● Check that the throttle grip rotates smoothly and snaps shut when released, in all steering positions. Also check for the correct amount of freeplay (see Chapter 1).

● Check that the steering moves freely from lock-to-lock.

● Check that the brake lever and pedal, clutch lever and gearchange lever operate smoothly. Lubricate them at the specified intervals or when necessary (see Chapter 1).

● Check that the engine shuts off when the kill switch is operated.

● Check that the sidestand and centrestand return springs hold the stands up securely when they are retracted.

Fuel:

● This may seem obvious, but check that you have enough fuel to complete your journey. If you notice signs of fuel leakage – rectify the cause immediately.

● Ensure you use the correct grade fuel – see Chapter 4 Specifications.

Chapter 1
Routine maintenance and Servicing

Contents

Degrees of difficulty

Easy, suitable for novice with little experience	Fairly easy, suitable for beginner with some experience	Fairly difficult, suitable for competent DIY mechanic	Difficult, suitable for experienced DIY mechanic	Very difficult, suitable for expert DIY or professional

Engine

Spark plugs	
Type	NGK CR9EK
Electrode gap	0.6 to 0.7 mm
Engine idle speed	1250 to 1350 rpm
Cylinder identification	numbered 1 to 4 from left to right
Throttle body synchronisation – intake vacuum at idle	218 mmHg
Throttle body synchronisation – max. difference between bodies	10 mmHg
Valve clearances (COLD engine)	
Intake valves	0.13 to 0.20 mm
Exhaust valves	0.23 to 0.30 mm

Cycle parts

Drive chain slack	45 to 55 mm
Drive chain type	see Chapter 6
Brake pad friction material wear limit	
Front	
S2 models	0.5 mm
All other models	0.8 mm
Rear	1.0 mm
Rear brake pedal position	25.8 mm
Throttle cable freeplay	3 to 5 mm
Clutch cable freeplay (see text)	10 to 15 mm
Tyre pressures (cold)	see *Pre-ride checks*

Lubricants and fluids

Fuel	see Chapter 4
Engine oil type	see *Pre-ride checks*
Engine oil capacity	
Oil change	2.5 litres
Oil and filter change	2.8 litres
Following engine overhaul – dry engine, new filter	3.4 litres
Coolant type	50% distilled water, 50% ethylene glycol anti-freeze with corrosion inhibitors for aluminium engines. **Note:** *Yamaha specify that soft tap water can be used, but NOT hard water. If in doubt, boil the water first or use only distilled water.*
Coolant capacity	
Radiator	2.0 litres
Reservoir	0.27 litre
Brake fluid	DOT 4
Drive chain	Engine oil or chain lubricant suitable for O-ring chains
Steering head bearings	Lithium-based multi-purpose grease
Swingarm pivot and bearings	Lithium-based multi-purpose grease
Suspension linkage bearings	Lithium-based multi-purpose grease
Bearing seals	Lithium-based multi-purpose grease
Gearchange lever, clutch lever, front brake lever, rear brake pedal, stand pivots	Lithium-based multi-purpose grease
Cables	Aerosol cable lubricant
Throttle twistgrip	Lithium-based multi-purpose grease

Torque wrench settings

Cooling system drain plug	10 Nm
Exhaust manifold nuts	20 Nm
Exhaust system clamp and mounting bolts	20 Nm
Fork clamp bolts	30 Nm
Handlebar clamp bolts	23 Nm
Oil drain plug	43 Nm
Oil filter	17 Nm
Rear axle nut	120 Nm
Spark plugs	18 Nm
Steering head bearing adjuster nut – using Yamaha tool	
Initial setting	52 Nm
Final setting	18 Nm
Steering stem nut	110 Nm
Timing rotor cover bolts	12 Nm

Component locations – left side

1 Clutch cable upper adjuster
2 Steering head bearing adjuster
3 Battery
4 Clutch cable in-line adjuster
5 Idle adjusting screw
6 Air filter element
7 Spring pre-load adjusting ring
8 Drive chain adjuster
9 Gearchange lever adjuster locknuts
10 Engine oil drain bolt
11 Engine oil filter
12 Oil pressure take-off point
13 Spark plugs
14 Fork oil seal

Component locations – right side

1 Rear brake fluid reservoir
2 Coolant reservoir cap (early models)
3 Front brake fluid reservoir
4 Throttle cable adjuster
5 Radiator pressure cap
6 Fork oil seal
7 Coolant reservoir location (later models)
8 Engine oil filler cap
9 Coolant drain bolt
10 Engine oil level dipstick
11 Rear brake light switch
12 Rear brake pedal height adjuster
13 Drive chain adjuster

Pre-ride
- ☐ See *Pre-ride checks* at the beginning of this manual.

After the initial 600 miles (1000 km)
Note: *This check is usually performed by a Yamaha dealer after the first 600 miles (1000 km) from new. Thereafter, maintenance is carried out according to the following intervals of the schedule.*

Every 500 miles (800 km)
- ☐ Check, adjust, clean and lubricate the drive chain (Section 1)

Every 6000 miles (10,000 km)
- ☐ Check and adjust the spark plugs (Section 2)
- ☐ Check and adjust the idle speed (Section 3)
- ☐ Check/adjust throttle body synchronisation (Section 4)
- ☐ Check the fuel system and the air induction system (AIS) (Section 5)
- ☐ Check and adjust the throttle cables (Section 6)
- ☐ Check and adjust the clutch and clutch cable (Section 7)
- ☐ Lubricate the clutch/gearchange/brake lever/brake pedal/stand pivots and cables (Section 8)
- ☐ Check the cooling system (Section 9)
- ☐ Change the engine oil (Section 10)
- ☐ Check the brake system (Section 11)
- ☐ Check the condition of the wheels, wheel bearings and tyres (Section 12)
- ☐ Check the front and rear suspension (Section 13)
- ☐ Check and adjust the steering head bearings (Section 14)
- ☐ Check the sidestand and starter safety circuit (Section 15)
- ☐ Check the tightness of all nuts, bolts and fasteners (Section 16)
- ☐ Check the battery (Section 17)

Every 12,000 miles (20,000 km)
Carry out all the items under the previous interval, plus the following:
- ☐ Fit new spark plugs (see Section 2)
- ☐ Fit a new engine oil filter (Section 10)
- ☐ Re-grease the steering head bearings (see Chapter 5)

Every 25,000 miles (40,000 km)
- ☐ Renew the air filter element and clean the air filter housing (Section 18)
- ☐ Check and adjust the valve clearances (Section 19)

Every 30,000 miles (50,000 km)
- ☐ Re-grease the swingarm bearings (Chapter 5)

Every two years
- ☐ Change the brake fluid, master cylinder seals and caliper seals (Chapter 6)

Every three years
- ☐ Change the coolant (see Chapter 3)

Every four years
- ☐ Fit new brake hoses (see Chapter 6)

Non-scheduled maintenance
- ☐ Fit new fuel hoses (Section 5)
- ☐ Change the front fork oil (see Chapter 5)

Pre-ride

☐ See *Pre-ride checks* at the beginning of this manual.

After the initial 600 miles (1000 km)

Note: *This check is usually performed by a Yamaha dealer after the first 600 miles (1000 km) from new. Thereafter, maintenance is carried out according to the following intervals of the schedule.*

Every 500 miles (800 km)

☐ Check, adjust, clean and lubricate the drive chain (Section 1)

Every 4000 miles (7000 km)

☐ Check and adjust the spark plugs (Section 2)
☐ Check the air filter element (Section 18)
☐ Check and adjust the idle speed (Section 3)
☐ Check/adjust throttle body synchronisation (Section 4)
☐ Check the fuel system and the air induction system (AIS) (Section 5)
☐ Check the crankcase breather system hoses (Section 18)
☐ Check the exhaust system for leaks (Section 16)
☐ Check and adjust the throttle cables (Section 6)
☐ Check and adjust the clutch and clutch cable (Section 7)
☐ Lubricate the clutch/gearchange/brake lever/brake pedal/sidestand pivots and cables (Section 8)
☐ Check the cooling system (Section 9)
☐ Change the engine oil (Section 10)
☐ Check the brake system (Section 11)
☐ Check the condition of the wheels, wheel bearings and tyres (Section 12)
☐ Check the front and rear suspension (Section 13)
☐ Check and adjust the steering head bearings (Section 14)
☐ Check the sidestand and starter safety circuit (Section 15)
☐ Check the tightness of all nuts, bolts and fasteners (Section 16)
☐ Check the battery (Section 17)

Every 8000 miles (13,000 km)

Carry out all the items under the previous interval, plus the following:
☐ Fit new spark plugs (see Section 2)
☐ Fit a new engine oil filter (Section 10)
☐ Re-grease the steering head bearings (see Chapter 5)

Every 12,000 miles (20,000 km)

☐ Renew the air filter element and clean the air filter housing (Section 18)

Every 16,000 miles (25,000 km)

☐ Re-grease the swingarm bearings (Chapter 5)

Every 26,000 miles (42,000 km)

☐ Check and adjust the valve clearances (Section 19)

Every two years

☐ Change the brake fluid, master cylinder and caliper seals (Chapter 6)
☐ Change the coolant (see Chapter 3)

Every four years

☐ Fit new brake hoses (see Chapter 6)

Non-scheduled maintenance

☐ Fit new fuel hoses (Section 5)
☐ Change the front fork oil (see Chapter 5)

Introduction

1 This Chapter is designed to help the home mechanic maintain his/her motorcycle for safety, economy, long life and peak performance.
2 Deciding where to start or plug into the routine maintenance schedule depends on several factors. If the warranty period on your motorcycle has just expired, and if it has been maintained according to the warranty standards, you may want to pick up routine maintenance as it coincides with the next mileage interval. If you have owned the machine for some time but have never performed any maintenance on it, then you may want to start at the beginning and include all frequent procedures to ensure that nothing important is overlooked. If you have just had a major engine overhaul, then you should start the engine maintenance routines from the beginning. If you have a used machine and have no knowledge of its history or maintenance record, you should combine all the checks into one large initial service and then settle into the maintenance schedule prescribed.

3 Before beginning any maintenance or repair, the machine should be cleaned thoroughly, especially around the oil filter, drain plugs and valve cover. Cleaning will help ensure that dirt does not contaminate the engine and will allow you to detect wear and damage that could otherwise easily go unnoticed.
4 Certain maintenance information is sometimes printed on decals attached to the motorcycle. If any information on the decals differs from that included here, use the information on the decal.

⚠️ **Warning: Read the Safety first! section of this manual carefully before starting work.**

Maintenance procedures

1 Drive chain and sprockets

Check

1 A neglected drive chain won't last long and can quickly damage the sprockets. Routine chain adjustment and lubrication isn't difficult and will ensure maximum chain and sprocket life.
Caution: Riding the bike with excess slack in the chain could lead to damage.
2 Yamaha specify that the chain can be checked with the bike supported in various ways – either held upright or supported on its sidestand (there should be no weight on the bike in either case) or supported on the centrestand with the rear wheel off the ground. If available, check with your Owner's Manual for the recommended procedure for your particular machine. In all cases, the chain slack specification remains the same

3 Ensure that the transmission is in neutral.
4 Hold a ruler against the lower edge of the swingarm to the rear of the chain slider. Push down on the bottom run of the chain to take out all the slack up and note the measurement on the lower edge of the chain, then push up on the chain and note the measurement again **(see illustrations)** – don't move the ruler during these checks.
5 To calculate the slack, subtract the second measurement from the first measurement. Compare the result with specification given at the beginning of this Chapter.
6 Since the chain will rarely wear evenly, roll the bike forward (or rotate the wheel) so that another section of chain can be checked; do this several times to check the entire length of chain, and mark the tightest spot.
7 In some cases where lubrication has been neglected, corrosion and dirt may cause the links to bind and kink, which effectively shortens the chain's length and makes it tight **(see illustration)**. Thoroughly clean and work free any such links, then highlight them with a

marker pen or paint. Take the bike for a short ride, then repeat the measurement for slack in the highlighted area.
8 If the chain has kinked again and is still tight, replace it with a new one (see Chapter 6). A rusty, kinked or worn chain will damage the sprockets and can damage transmission bearings. If in any doubt as to the condition of a chain, it is far better to install a new one than risk damage to other components and possibly yourself.
9 Check the entire length of the chain for worn or damaged rollers and side plates, loose links and pins, and missing O-rings and replace it with a new one if necessary.
Caution: Never install a new chain on old sprockets, and never use the old chain if you install new sprockets – renew the chain and sprockets as a set – see Chapter 6.

Adjustment

10 Rotate the rear wheel until the chain is positioned with the tightest spot at the centre of its bottom run (see Step 6). Support the bike as before.

1.4a Push down on the chain and note the measurement against the rule (arrowed) . . .

1.4b . . . then push the chain up and note the measurement against the rule (arrowed)

1.7 Neglect has caused the links in this chain to kink

11 Loosen the rear wheel axle nut.
12 Loosen the locknut on the adjuster on both sides of the swingarm, then turn the adjusters evenly, a small amount at a time, until the specified chain tension is obtained **(see illustrations)**. Following chain adjustment, check that the axle alignment marks on both

sides of the swingarm are equal – if not, the rear wheel will be out of alignment with the front **(see illustrations)**.
13 If there is a discrepancy in the position of the alignment marks, correct it with the adjusters and then check the chain tension as described above. Also check that there is no clearance between the adjusters and the swingarm end caps, or, on S2 models, the front of the adjuster plates. Push the wheel forwards to eliminate any clearance.
14 Tighten the axle nut to the torque setting specified at the beginning of this Chapter, then tighten the adjuster locknuts securely. Recheck the adjustment.
15 If the chain is difficult to adjust satisfactorily, or if it is close to the end of available adjustment, check the chain stretch as described in Chapter 6.

Cleaning and lubrication

16 The best time to lubricate the chain is

after the motorcycle has been ridden. When the chain is warm, the lubricant will penetrate the joints between the side plates better than when cold.
17 If required, wash the chain using a dedicated aerosol cleaner or in paraffin (kerosene), then wipe it off and allow it to dry, using compressed air if available. If the chain is excessively dirty, remove the rear wheel (see Chapter 6) and soak the chain in paraffin.
Caution: Don't use petrol (gasoline), solvent or other cleaning fluids which might damage the internal sealing properties of the chain. Don't use high-pressure water. The entire process shouldn't take longer than five to six minutes – if it does, the O-rings in the chain rollers could be damaged.
18 Apply the lubricant to the area where the side plates overlap – not the middle of the rollers. Protect the tyre from overspray with a rag or piece of cardboard **(see**

1.12a Loosen the locknut (A) and turn the adjuster (B) on both sides

1.12b Locknut (A) and chain adjuster (B) on S2 models

1.12c Location of the axle alignment marks (arrowed)

1.12d Axle alignment marks (arrowed) on S2 models

1.18 Protect the rear tyre from overspray when lubricating the chain

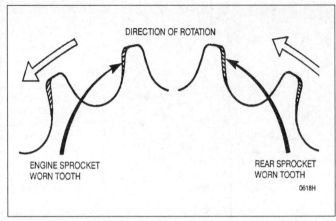

DIRECTION OF ROTATION

ENGINE SPROCKET WORN TOOTH

REAR SPROCKET WORN TOOTH

0618H

1.20 Check the sprockets in the areas indicated to see if they are worn excessively

illustration). **Note:** *Yamaha specifies engine oil or chain lube that is specifically for O-ring chains; do not use chain lube that is not specifically for O-ring chains, as it may contain solvents that could damage the O-rings.*

⚠️ **Warning: Take care not to get any lubricant on the tyres or brake system components. If any of the lubricant inadvertently contacts them, clean it off thoroughly using a suitable solvent or dedicated brake cleaner before riding the machine.**

Sprocket wear check

19 If the drive chain is worn or damaged, it is likely that the sprockets will be worn also (see **Caution** in Step 9).
20 Remove the front sprocket cover (see Chapter 6). Check the teeth on the front sprocket and the rear sprocket for wear **(see illustration)**. If the sprocket teeth are worn excessively, follow the procedure in Chapter 6 and renew the chain and both sprockets as a set.
21 Ensure that the lockwasher is correctly installed on the front sprocket nut and that

the nut is tight. If for any reason the nut is loosened, always fit a new lockwasher **(see illustration)**. Check that the rear wheel sprocket nuts are tight (refer to *Specifications* in Chapter 6 for torque settings).
22 Inspect the drive chain slider on the front of the swingarm for excessive wear and damage and replace it with a new one if necessary (see Chapter 5).

2 Spark plugs

Check and adjustment

1 Make sure your spark plug socket is the correct size (16 mm) before attempting to remove the plugs – a special plug socket is supplied in the motorcycle's tool kit which is stored under the seat.
2 Remove the radiator (see Chapter 3).
3 Clean the area around each spark plug cap to prevent any dirt falling into the spark plug wells. Check that the cylinder location

is marked on each HT lead (numbered 1 to 4 from the left-hand side), then pull the cap off each spark plug **(see illustration)**. If compressed air is available blow away any accumulated dirt lying in the bottom of each plug well to prevent It falling into the engine when the plug is removed.
4 Using either the Yamaha plug socket or a deep socket type wrench, unscrew the plugs from the cylinder head **(see illustrations)**. Lay each plug out in relation to its cylinder so that if any plug shows up a problem, it will be easy to identify the troublesome cylinder.
5 Inspect the electrodes for wear. Both the centre and side electrodes should have square edges and the side electrodes should be of uniform thickness. Look for excessive deposits and evidence of a cracked or chipped insulator around the centre electrode. Compare your spark plugs to the colour spark plug reading chart at the end of this manual. Check the threads, the washer and the ceramic insulator body for cracks and other damage.
6 If the electrodes are not excessively worn,

1.21 Ensure that the lockwasher is folded over against a flat (arrowed) on the sprocket nut

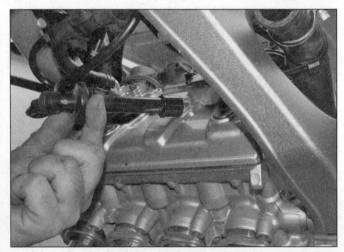

2.3 Pull the caps off the spark plugs

2.4a Insert the plug socket into the spark plug well – Yamaha tool shown . . .

2.4b . . . and unscrew the spark plug

and if the deposits can be easily removed with a wire brush, and there are no cracks or chips visible in the insulator, the plugs can be re-gapped and re-used. If in doubt concerning the condition of the plugs, replace them with new ones, as the expense is minimal. Note that new spark plugs should be fitted at every second service interval.

7 Before installing the plugs, make sure they are the correct type and heat range and check the gap between the side (earth) electrodes and the centre electrode **(see illustrations)**. Compare the gap to that specified and adjust as necessary. If the gap must be adjusted, bend the side electrodes only and be very careful not to chip or crack the insulator nose **(see illustration)**. Make sure the sealing washer is in place on the plug before installing it.

8 Since the cylinder head is made of aluminium, which is soft and easily damaged, thread the plugs into the head and turn the tool by hand **(see illustration 2.4c)**. Once the plugs are finger-tight, the job can be finished with the tool supplied or a socket wrench. If a torque wrench is available, tighten the spark plugs to the torque setting specified at the beginning of this Chapter. Otherwise tighten

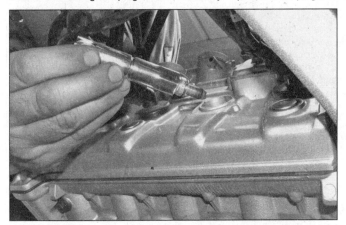

2.4c The spark plug will be retained in the socket

2.7a Using a wire gauge to measure the spark plug electrode gap

2.7b The gaps between the two earth electrodes (A) and the centre electrode (B) must be equal and as specified

2.7c Adjust the electrode gap by bending the side electrodes only

them by 1/4 to 1/2 turn after they have been fully hand tightened and have seated. Do not over-tighten them.

9 Install the plug caps, making sure they locate correctly onto the plugs **(see illustration 2.3)**. Ensure that the caps are connected to the correct cylinder – each HT lead should be marked with its cylinder number (see Step 3).
10 Install the radiator (see Chapter 3).

Renewal

11 At the prescribed interval, whatever the condition of the existing spark plugs, remove them as described above and install new ones.

3 Idle speed

1 Check and adjust the idle speed before and after the throttle bodies are synchronised (balanced), after checking the valve clearances, and when it is obviously too high or too low. Before adjusting the idle speed, make sure the valve clearances were checked at the previous prescribed interval, that the spark plug gaps are correct and that the air filter is clean. Also, turn the handlebars back-and-forth and see if the idle speed changes as this is done. If it does, the throttle cables may not be adjusted or routed correctly, or may be worn out. This is a dangerous condition that can cause loss of control of the bike. Be sure to correct this problem before proceeding.
2 The engine should be at normal operating

3.3 Location of the idle speed adjuster (arrowed)

temperature, which is usually reached after 10 to 15 minutes of stop-and-go riding. Make sure the transmission is in neutral, and place the motorcycle on its centrestand.
3 The idle speed adjuster is located on the left-hand side of the machine below the lower edge of the fuel tank **(see illustration)**. With the engine idling, turn the adjuster until the speed listed in this Chapter's Specifications is obtained. Turn the knob clockwise to increase idle speed, and anti-clockwise to decrease it.
4 Snap the throttle open and shut a few times, then recheck the idle speed. If necessary, repeat the adjustment procedure.
5 If a smooth, steady idle cannot be achieved, the throttle bodies may need synchronising (see Section 4). Also check the operation of the fast idle unit and examine the intake manifolds for loose clamps and cracks which will cause an air leak, resulting in a weak mixture.

4.5a Remove the blanking plugs from the synchronising hoses . . .

4.5c . . . then connect the vacuum gauge hoses

4.5b . . . and press in the adapters . . .

4.5d Connected hoses on the right-hand side – cylinders 3 and 4

4 Throttle body synchronisation

⚠️ **Warning: Petrol (gasoline) is extremely flammable, so take extra precautions when you work on any part of the fuel system. Don't smoke or allow open flames or bare light bulbs near the work area, and don't work in a garage where a natural gas-type appliance is present. If you spill any fuel on your skin, rinse it off immediately with soap and water. When you perform any kind of work on the fuel system, wear safety glasses and have a fire extinguisher suitable for a Class B type fire (flammable liquids) on hand.**

⚠️ **Warning: Do not allow exhaust gases to build up in the work area; either perform the check outside or use an exhaust gas extraction system.**

Special tool: *A set of vacuum gauges or a manometer is necessary for this job.*

1 Throttle body synchronisation ensures each throttle body passes the same amount of fuel/air mixture to each cylinder. This is done by measuring the vacuum produced in each cylinder. Throttle bodies that are out of synchronisation will result in increased fuel consumption, higher engine temperature, less than ideal throttle response and higher vibration levels. Before synchronising the throttle bodies, make sure that the valve clearances and idle speed are properly adjusted.
2 To synchronise the throttle bodies you will need a set of vacuum gauges or a manometer. These instruments measure engine vacuum, and can be obtained from motorcycle dealers or mail order parts suppliers. The equipment used should be suitable for a four cylinder engine and come complete with the necessary adapters and hoses to fit the take-off points.
3 Start the engine and let it run until it reaches normal operating temperature, then shut it off. Support the motorcycle upright on level ground using the centrestand. Remove the fuel tank (see Chapter 4)
4 Locate the synchronising hoses on the left and right-hand sides of the throttle body assembly. Note that the hoses for Nos. 1 and 2 cylinders are on the left-hand side and for Nos. 3 and 4 cylinders are on the right-hand side. Trace each hose to the front of the assembly to check which throttle body it is connected to.
5 Remove the blanking plug from each hose and connect it to the appropriate vacuum gauge or manometer hose with the adapter **(see illustrations)**. Make sure the No. 1 gauge is attached to the hose from the No. 1 (left-hand) throttle body, and so on.
6 Temporarily install the fuel tank, allowing access to the throttle synchronising screws **(see illustration 4.9)**.
7 Start the engine and let it idle, making sure the speed is still correct. If the gauges are fitted with damping adjustment, set this so

4.9 Turn the adjuster screws to synchronise the gauge readings (numbers indicate cylinders)

5.1 Check the breather hoses (arrowed) for blockages

that the needle flutter is just eliminated but so that they can still respond to small changes in pressure.

8 Use the No. 1 cylinder as the base to which all the others are matched. The vacuum readings for the Nos. 2, 3 and 4 cylinders should be the same as the No. 1 cylinder, or at least within the maximum difference specified at the beginning of this Chapter.

9 If the vacuum readings vary, turn the appropriate adjuster screws until the readings are all the same **(see illustration)**. After each adjustment, open and close the throttle quickly to settle the setting and check the reading on the gauges again. **Note:** If an adjuster screw is inadvertently unscrewed, screw it in ¾ of a turn, then make any fine adjustment to its setting according to the gauge readings.

10 When all the throttle bodies are synchronised, open and close the throttle quickly to settle the settings, and recheck the gauge readings, readjusting if necessary.

11 Remove the gauges and ensure that the blanking plugs are installed securely **(see illustration 4.5a)**.

12 Install the fuel tank (see Chapter 4).

13 If necessary, adjust the idle speed (see Section 3).

5 Fuel system, air induction system (AIS) and EVAP system

> ⚠️ *Warning: Petrol (gasoline) is extremely flammable, so take extra precautions when you work on any part of the fuel system. Don't smoke or allow open flames or bare light bulbs near the work area, and don't work in a garage where a natural gas-type appliance is present. If you spill any fuel on your skin, rinse it off immediately with soap and water. When you perform any kind of work on the fuel system, wear safety glasses and have a fire extinguisher suitable for a Class B type fire (flammable liquids) on hand.*

Fuel system

1 Raise the fuel tank (see Chapter 4) and check the underside of the tank, the fuel supply hose and its union, and the tank overflow and breather hoses for signs of leaks, cracking, hardening or damage. Replace any hose that has deteriorated with a new one (see Chap-

ter 4). Don't forget to inspect the lower ends of the overflow and breather hoses for blockages **(see illustration)**.

2 If the joint between the fuel pump mounting plate and the tank is leaking, ensure the mounting bolts are tightened to the specified torque setting (see Chapter 4); if the leak persists, remove the pump and fit a new gasket (see Chapter 4).

3 Remove the tank and the air filter housing (see Chapter 4).

4 Inspect the hoses connected to the synchronising unit and the crankcase breather hose for signs of cracking, hardening or damage **(see illustration)**. Ensure that the hoses are held securely by the spring clips and renew the clips if they are corroded or sprained.

5 Inspect the joints between the fuel rail, the injectors and the throttle bodies. If there are any fuel leaks, remove the fuel rail and fit new seals and O-rings to the injectors (see Chapter 4).

6 Make sure the joints between the air filter housing and the throttle bodies are in good condition and that the clamp screws are not corroded. Note the correct location of the clamps **(see illustration)**.

5.4 Check the hoses connected to the throttle synchronising unit (A). Note the crankcase breather hose (B)

5.6 Clamps locate on tabs (arrowed) to ensure correct position of clamp screws

5.11 Check the AIS hoses (arrowed) and the hose clips

6.3a Use an Allen key . . .

7 Check that the clamp screws on the intake manifolds between the throttle bodies and the cylinder head are tight (see Chapter 4).

Air induction system (AIS)

8 To reduce the amount of unburned hydrocarbons released in the exhaust gases, an air induction system (AIS) is fitted. The system consists of the cut-off valve (mounted in front of the battery housing), the reed valves (fitted in the valve cover) and the hoses linking them. The cut-off valve is actuated electronically by the ECU.

9 The system is not adjustable and requires little maintenance. To gain access for inspection, remove the air filter housing (see Chapter 4), then remove the battery housing (see Chapter 8).

10 Note that carbon deposits inside the air filter housing, particularly on the right-hand side around the union for the AIS hose, indicate a fault with the reed valves (see Section 18).

11 Check that the AIS hoses are not kinked or pinched, are in good condition and are securely connected at each end **(see illustration)**. Replace any hoses that are cracked, split or generally deteriorated with new ones. Renew any spring clips that are corroded or sprained.

12 If the valve clearances are all correct and the throttle bodies have been synchronised and have no other faults, but the idle speed cannot be set properly, it is possible that the AIS is faulty. Refer to Chapter 4 for further information on the system and for checks if it is believed to be faulty.

EVAP system (California models)

13 Raise the fuel tank (see Chapter 4). Visually inspect all the system hoses between the fuel tank and the roll-over valve for kinks and splits and any other damage or deterioration. Make sure that the hoses are securely connected with a clamp on each end. Renew any hoses that are damaged or deteriorated.

14 Refer to your dealer for further information and tests on the system.

6 Throttle cables

1 Make sure the throttle twistgrip rotates easily from fully closed to fully open with the front wheel turned at various angles. The twistgrip should return automatically from fully open to fully closed when released.

2 If the throttle sticks, this is probably due to a cable fault. Remove the cables (see Chapter 4) and lubricate them (see Section 8). If the inner cables still do not run smoothly in the outer cables, replace the cables with new ones.

3 With the cables removed, check that the twistgrip turns smoothly around the handlebar – dirt combined with a lack of lubrication can cause the action to be stiff. If necessary, unscrew the handlebar end-weight with a suitable Allen key and slide the twistgrip off the handlebar **(see illustrations)**. Clean any old grease from the bar and the inside of the tube.

6.3b . . . to unscrew the bar end-weight . . .

6.3c . . . then slide the twistgrip off

6.4 Throttle cable freeplay is measured in terms of twistgrip rotation

6.5 Throttle cable lock ring (A) and adjuster (B)

Smear some new grease of the specified type onto the bar, then refit the twistgrip. Install the lubricated or new cables, making sure they are correctly routed (see Chapter 4). If this fails to improve the operation of the throttle, the fault could lie in the throttle bodies. Remove them and check the action of the throttle linkage and butterflies (see Chapter 4).

4 With the throttle operating smoothly, check for a small amount of freeplay in the opening cable, measured in terms of the amount of twistgrip rotation before the throttle opens, and compare the amount to that listed in this Chapter's Specifications (see illustration). If it is incorrect, adjust the cables as follows:

5 Initially adjust freeplay using the adjuster in the throttle opening cable where it leaves the housing on the handlebar. Loosen the lock ring and turn the adjuster until the specified amount of freeplay is obtained, then retighten the lock ring (see illustration). Turn the adjuster in to increase freeplay and out to reduce it.

6 If the adjuster has reached its limit of adjustment, reset it so that the freeplay is at a maximum, then adjust the cables at the throttle body end as follows.

7 Remove the fuel tank and air filter housing (see Chapter 4). Release the trim clip securing the clutch cable support bracket and displace the bracket (see illustrations).

8 Displace the left-hand corner of the heat shield to access the throttle cable adjusters – the upper cable in the bracket on the throttle bodies is the closing cable, and the lower cable is the opening cable (see illustration).

6.7a Press in the centre of the trim clip (arrowed) . . .

6.7b . . . with a small screwdriver . . .

6.7c . . . so that the clutch cable support bracket can be displaced

6.8 Throttle closing cable (A) and opening cable (B)

6.10 Opening cable adjuster locknut (A) and adjuster (B)

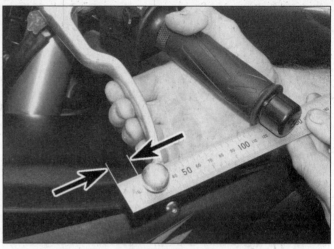

7.5 Measure the amount of freeplay at the clutch lever end as shown (arrowed)

9 There should be no discernable freeplay in the closing cable. If necessary, loosen the locknut on the closing cable adjuster and turn the adjuster until any slack is removed, then tighten the locknut **(see illustration 6.8)**.

10 Now loosen the locknut on the opening cable adjuster and turn the adjuster nut until the specified amount of twistgrip freeplay is obtained, then tighten the locknut **(see illustration)**. Ensure that the adjuster elbow is aligned at the correct angle **(see illustration 6.8)**. Further adjustments can now be made at the handlebar end (see Step 5). If the cables cannot be adjusted as specified, replace them with new ones (see Chapter 4).

 Warning: Turn the handlebars all the way through their travel with the engine idling. Idle speed should not change. If it does, the cables may be routed incorrectly. Correct this condition before riding the motorcycle.

11 Check that the throttle twistgrip operates smoothly and snaps shut when released.

7 Clutch and clutch cable

1 Check that the clutch lever operates smoothly and easily.

2 If the lever action is heavy or stiff, remove the cable (see Chapter 2, Section 12) and lubricate it (see Section 8). If the inner cable still does not run smoothly in the outer cable, replace the cable with a new one. Install the lubricated or new cable (see Chapter 2).

3 If the lever itself is stiff, remove the lever from its bracket (see Chapter 5) and check for damage or distortion, or any other cause, and remedy as necessary. Clean and lubricate the pivot and contact areas (see Section 8).

4 If the lever and cable are good, refer to Chapter 2 and check the release mechanism in the clutch cover and the clutch itself.

5 With the clutch operating smoothly, check that the clutch lever is correctly

adjusted. Periodic adjustment is necessary to compensate for wear in the clutch plates and stretch of the cable. Check that the amount of freeplay at the clutch lever end is within the specifications listed at the beginning of this Chapter **(see illustration)**.

6 If adjustment is required, loosen the lock ring on the adjuster and turn the adjuster in or out of the handlebar bracket until the required amount of freeplay is obtained **(see illustration)**. To increase freeplay, turn the adjuster clockwise (into the lever bracket). To reduce freeplay, turn the adjuster anti-clockwise (out of the lever bracket). Tighten the locking ring securely.

7 If all the adjustment has been taken up at the lever, reset the adjuster to give the maximum amount of freeplay, then set the correct amount of freeplay using the adjuster in the cable underneath the fuel tank.

8 Remove the fuel tank and the air filter housing (see Chapter 4). Slacken the adjuster locknut, then turn the adjuster as required to obtain the correct freeplay **(see illustration)**. When the correct amount of freeplay has been

7.6 Loosen lock ring (A) and turn adjuster (B)

7.8 Location of lower clutch cable adjuster (arrowed)

8.5a Fit the cable into the adapter . . .

8.5b . . . then tighten the screw to seal it in

achieved, hold the adjuster to prevent it rotating and tighten the locknut.

9 Subsequent adjustments can now be made using the clutch lever adjuster.

8 Stand, lever pivots and cable lubrication

Pivot points

1 Since the controls, cables and various other components of a motorcycle are exposed to the elements, they should be checked and lubricated periodically to ensure safe and trouble-free operation.

2 The clutch and brake lever pivots, footrest pivots, brake pedal and gearchange lever pivots and linkage, and stand pivots should be lubricated frequently. In order for the lubricant to be applied where it will do the most good, the component should be disassembled (see Chapter 5).

3 The lubricant recommended by Yamaha for each application is listed at the beginning of the Chapter. If chain or cable lubricant is being used, it can be applied to the pivot joint gaps and will usually work its way into the areas where friction occurs, so less disassembly of the component is needed (however it is always better to do so and clean off all corrosion, dirt and old lubricant first).

4 If motor oil or light grease is being used, apply it sparingly as it may attract dirt (which could cause the controls to bind or wear at an accelerated rate). **Note:** *An alternative lubricant for the control lever pivots is a dry-film lubricant (available from many sources by different names).*

Cables

Special tool: *A cable lubricating adapter is necessary for this procedure.*

5 To lubricate the cables, disconnect the relevant cable at its upper end, then lubricate it with a pressure adapter and aerosol cable lubricant **(see illustrations)**. See Chapter 4 for throttle cable removal procedures, and Chapter 2 for the clutch cable.

8.5c Apply the lubricant using the nozzle provided inserted into the hole in the adapter

Stands

6 The stand return springs must be capable of retracting the stands fully and holding them retracted when the motorcycle is in use. If a spring has sagged or broken, it must be replaced with a new one **(see illustrations)**.

7 If necessary, refer to the procedure in Chapter 5 to remove the stands.

8.6a Check the condition of the sidestand spring . . .

8.6b . . . and the centrestand spring

9.2a Check all the cooling system hoses . . .

9.2b . . . including the pump breather hose (A) and fast idle unit hose (B)

9 Cooling system

Check

Warning: The engine must be cool before beginning this procedure.

1 Check the coolant level in the reservoir (see *Pre-ride checks*).

2 If fitted, remove the fairing (see Chapter 7). Remove the fuel tank (see Chapter 4). Check the entire cooling system for evidence of leaks. Examine each coolant hose along its entire length **(see illustrations)**. Look for cracks, splits, abrasions and other signs of deterioration. Squeeze each hose at various points. They should feel firm, yet pliable, and return to their original shape when released. If they are cracked or hard, replace them with new ones.

3 Check for evidence of leaks at each cooling system joint. If necessary, tighten the hose clips carefully to prevent future leaks **(see illustration)**.

4 Examine the oil cooler inlet and outlet hoses for damage and signs of deterioration – the cooler is on the front of the engine. Ensure that the hose clips are secure and that there are no signs of either coolant or oil leaks at the oil cooler-to-crankcase joint. If there is, refer to Chapter 2 – if coolant is leaking replace the cooler with a new one, and if oil is leaking first make sure the cooler bolt is tightened to the specified torque, and if it is, or if leaks persists, remove the cooler and replace the O-ring with a new one.

5 Check for leaks around the pump on the right-hand side of the engine **(see illustration)**. If it is leaking around the cover, check that the bolts are tight. If they are, remove the cover and replace the O-ring with a new one (see Chapter 3). If it is leaking around the crankcase, remove the pump and replace the body O-ring with a new one (see Chapter 3).

6 To prevent water leaking from the cooling

9.3 Ensure the hose clips are tightened securely

system to the lubrication system and vice versa, two seals are fitted on the water pump shaft. If either seal fails, a drain hole in the underside of the pump body allows the coolant or oil to escape and prevents them mixing. Look for tell-tale signs of leaks where the water pump body enters the crankcase **(see illustration)**.

9.5 Location of the water pump (arrowed)

9.6 Check for signs of leakage from the pump drain hole (arrowed)

9.10a Loosen the cap lock bolt . . .

9.10b . . . then turn the cap anti-clockwise

7 The water seal on the pump shaft is of the mechanical type and bears on the inner face of the pump body and the rear face of the pump impeller. The oil seal, which is mounted in the pump body, is of the normal feathered lip type. If there are signs of coolant leaking, remove the pump and replace the mechanical seal with a new one. If it is oil that is leaking, or if the leaks are white with the texture of emulsion, replace both seals with new ones (the mechanical seal has to be removed in order to remove the oil seal, and it cannot be reused). Refer to Chapter 3 for seal renewal.

8 Check the radiator for leaks and other damage. Leaks in the radiator leave tell-tale scale deposits or coolant stains on the outside of the core below the leak. If leaks are noted, remove the radiator (see Chapter 3) and have it repaired by a specialist.

Caution: Do not use a liquid leak stopping compound to try to repair leaks.

9 Check the radiator fins for mud, dirt and insects, which may impede the flow of air through the radiator. If the fins are dirty, remove the radiator (see Chapter 3) and clean it, using water or low pressure compressed air directed through the fins from the back. If the fins are bent or distorted, straighten them carefully with a screwdriver. Bent or damaged fins will restrict the airflow and impair the efficiency of the radiator causing the engine to overheat. Where there is substantial damage to the radiator's surface area, renew the radiator.

10 Loosen the radiator pressure cap lock bolt, then undo the cap by turning it anti-clockwise until it reaches a stop **(see illustrations)**. If you hear a hissing sound (indicating that there is still pressure in the system), wait until it stops. Now press down on the cap and continue turning until it can be removed **(see illustration)**. Note the location of the locking tab.

11 Check the condition of the coolant in the system. If it is rust-coloured or if accumulations of scale are visible, drain, flush and refill the system with new coolant (see below). Check the cap seal for cracks and other damage. If in doubt about the pressure cap's condition, have it tested by a Yamaha dealer or replace it with a new one.

12 Check the antifreeze content of the coolant with an antifreeze hydrometer. A weak mixture will not provide proper corrosion protection. Sometimes coolant looks like it's in good condition, but might be too diluted to offer adequate protection. If the hydrometer indicates a weak mixture, drain, flush and refill the system (see below). A higher than specified concentration of antifreeze decreases the performance of the cooling system and should only be used when additional protection against freezing is needed. Refer to the manufacturer's specifications when altering the specified ratio of distilled water to antifreeze.

13 Ensure that the locking tab on the pressure cap is in the correct position **(see illustration)** – the cap will not fit correctly if

9.10c Lift the cap off noting the locking tab (A) and cap seal (B)

9.13a Check the position of the locking tab (arrowed) before fitting the cap

9.13b Don't forget to tighten the lock bolt (arrowed) securely

9.18a Location of the radiator pressure cap inside the fairing

the tab is misaligned. Install the cap by turning it clockwise until it reaches the first stop then push down on the cap and continue turning until it will turn no further. Tighten the lock bolt securely **(see illustration)**.

14 Start the engine and let it reach normal operating temperature, then check for leaks again. As the coolant temperature increases beyond normal, the fan should come on automatically and the temperature should begin to drop. If it does not, refer to Chapter 3 and check the fan switch, fan motor and fan circuit carefully.

15 If the coolant level is consistently low, and no evidence of leaks can be found, have the entire system pressure-checked by a Yamaha dealer.

Change the coolant

⚠️ *Warning: Allow the engine to cool completely before performing this maintenance operation. Also, don't allow antifreeze to come into contact with your skin or the painted surfaces of the motorcycle. Rinse off spills immediately with plenty of water. Antifreeze is highly toxic if ingested. Never leave antifreeze lying around in an open container or in puddles on the floor; children and pets are attracted by its sweet smell and may drink it. Check with local authorities (councils) about disposing of antifreeze. Many communities have collection centres where antifreeze can be disposed of safely. Antifreeze is also combustible, so don't store it near open flames.*

Draining

16 Support the motorcycle upright on level ground using the centrestand.

17 Remove the coolant reservoir (see Chapter 3). Empty the contents of the reservoir into a suitable container, rinse the inside with clean water and refit it to the machine.

18 Remove the radiator pressure cap (see Step 10). Note that on machines fitted with a fairing (other than S2 models) it is necessary to remove the fairing trim panel (see Chapter 7) to access the pressure cap **(see illustrations)**.

19 Position a suitable container beneath the drain bolt on the water pump. Remove the bolt, noting that the coolant will spurt out (so hold the container up to it) and allow the coolant to completely drain from the system **(see illustrations)**. Retain the old sealing washer for use during flushing.

Flushing

20 Flush the system with clean tap water by inserting a garden hose in the radiator filler neck. Allow the water to run through the system until it is clear when it flows out of the drain hole. If there is a lot of rust in the water, remove the radiator (see Chapter 3) and have it professionally cleaned. If the drain hole appears to be clogged with sediment, remove the water pump cover and clean the inside of the pump (see Chapter 3).

21 Install the drain bolt using the old sealing washer. Fill the system via the radiator with clean water mixed with a flushing compound.

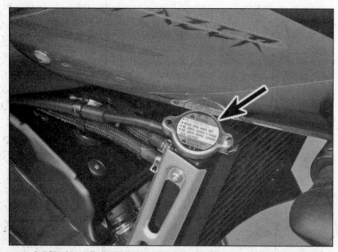

9.18b Location of the radiator pressure cap – S2 models

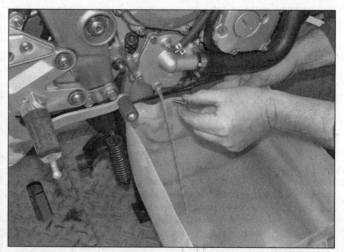

9.19 Draining the coolant from the water pump drain hole

10.3 Remove the oil filler cap from the top of the clutch cover

10.4a Location of the oil drain plug (arrowed)

Make sure the flushing compound is compatible with aluminium components, and follow the manufacturer's instructions carefully. Install the pressure cap. Fill the coolant reservoir to the FULL mark with clean water.

22 Start the engine and allow it to reach normal operating temperature. Let it run for about ten minutes.

23 Stop the engine. Let it cool for a while, then cover the pressure cap with a heavy rag and turn it anti-clockwise to the first stop, releasing any pressure that may be present in the system. Once the hissing stops, push down on the cap and remove it completely. Drain the system once again.

24 Drain the system again.

25 Repeat Steps 20 to 23, filling the system with clean water only.

Refilling

26 Fit a new sealing washer onto the drain bolt and tighten it to the torque setting specified at the beginning of this Chapter.

27 Fill the system via the radiator with the specified coolant mixture (see this Chapter's Specifications). **Note:** *Pour the coolant in slowly to minimise the amount of air entering the system.* When the system appears full, move the bike off its stand and shake it slightly to dissipate the coolant, then place the bike back on the stand and top the system up.

28 When the system is full (all the way up to the top of the radiator filler neck), install the pressure cap. Now fill the coolant reservoir to the FULL mark and fit the cap (see *Pre-ride checks*).

29 Start the engine and allow it to run for several minutes. Flick the throttle open 3 or 4 times, so that the engine speed rises to approximately 4000 – 5000 rpm, then stop the engine. Any air trapped in the system should bleed back to the top of the radiator, and the level will drop.

30 Wait a few minutes for the coolant to settle, then check the coolant level in both the

radiator and the coolant reservoir. If necessary, top up the radiator to the base of the filler neck, then install the pressure cap and tighten the lock bolt securely. Also top up the coolant reservoir to the FULL mark.

31 Check the system for leaks.

32 Do not dispose of the old coolant by pouring it down the drain. Instead pour it into a heavy plastic container, cap it tightly and take it into an authorised disposal site or service station – see **Warning** at the beginning of this Section.

33 Install the remaining components in the reverse order of removal.

---

10 Engine oil and filter

 Warning: Be careful when draining the oil, as the exhaust pipes, the engine, and the oil itself can cause severe burns.

Engine oil

1 Regular oil changes are the single most important maintenance procedure you can perform on a motorcycle. The oil not only lubricates the internal parts of the engine, transmission and clutch, but it also acts as a coolant, a cleaner, a sealant, and a protector. Because of these demands, the oil takes a terrific amount of abuse and should be replaced often with new oil of the recommended grade and type. Saving a little money on the difference in cost between a good oil and a cheap oil won't pay off if the engine is damaged. The oil filter should be changed with every second oil change (see Steps 10 and 11).

2 Before changing the oil, warm up the engine so the oil will drain easily.

3 Support the motorcycle upright on level ground and place a clean drain tray below the engine. Unscrew the oil filler cap from the

clutch cover to vent the engine unit and to act as a reminder that there is no oil in the engine **(see illustration)**.

4 Unscrew the oil drain plug from the left-hand side of the sump and allow the oil to flow into the drain tray **(see illustration)**. Discard the sealing washer and replace it with a new one **(see illustration)**.

5 When the oil has completely drained, fit the plug with its new washer and tighten it to the torque setting specified at the beginning of this Chapter. Avoid overtightening, as you will damage the sump.

6 Refill the engine to the specified level using the recommended type and amount of oil (see *Pre-ride checks*). With the motorcycle upright, the oil level should lie between the maximum and minimum level lines on the dipstick. Install the filler cap **(see illustration 10.3)**. Start the engine and let it run for two or three minutes. Stop the engine, wait a few minutes, then check the oil level. If necessary, add more oil to bring the level almost up to the maximum level line on the dipstick. Check that there are no leaks around the drain plug.

7 The old oil drained from the engine cannot be re-used and must be disposed of properly. Check with your local refuse disposal company, disposal facility or environmental

10.4b Replace the old sealing washer with a new one

10.9 Location of the oil filter (arrowed)

10.10 Ensure the filter removing tool is a good fit on the cartridge

agency to see whether they will accept the used oil for recycling – most will. Don't pour used oil into drains or onto the ground.

OIL CARE
FOLLOW THE CODE

OIL BANK LINE
0800 66 33 66
www.oilbankline.org.uk

Note: it is antisocial and illegal to dump oil down the drain. To find the location of your local oil recycling bank, call this number free.

In the USA, note that any oil supplier must accept used oil for recycling

Oil filter

Special tool: *A filter removing tool is necessary for this job* **(see illustration 10.10)**.

8 Drain the engine oil as described in Steps 2 to 5.

9 The oil filter is located on the lower left-hand side of the engine **(see illustration)**. Place the drain tray below the oil filter. Clean the crankcase around the filter and displace the sidestand switch wiring to allow access to the filter.

10 Unscrew the filter using a filter removing tool **(see illustration)**. **Note:** *Make sure you purchase the correct size of oil filter tool to fit the Yamaha filter cartridge – many sizes are available. A filter tool that can be used with a socket wrench is the best as it allows the new filter to be tightened to the specified torque.* Tip any residual oil into the drain tray.

11 Clean the sealing surface on the crankcase carefully with a suitable solvent. Smear clean engine oil onto the seal on the new filter, then screw the filter onto the engine until the seal just seats **(see illustrations)**. If a suitable oil filter tool is being used, tighten the filter to the torque setting specified at the beginning

of this Chapter. Otherwise, tighten the filter as tight as possible by hand, or by the number of turns specified on the filter or its packaging. **Note:** *Do not use a strap or chain wrench to tighten the filter as you will damage it.*

12 Refill the engine to the specified level (see Step 6).

13 Remember to drain all the old oil from the filter into the drain tray. Note that the old filter should be taken to the oil disposal facility rather than disposed of with the household rubbish.

11 Brake system

Brake system check

1 A routine check of the brake system will ensure that any problems are discovered

10.11a Lubricate the filter seal with clean oil . . .

10.11b . . . then install the filter and tighten it as described

11.5 Inspect the brake connections and hoses for cracks and leaking fluid

11.8 Adjust the rear brake light switch with the nut (arrowed)

and remedied before the rider's safety is jeopardised.

2 Check the brake lever and pedal for looseness, rough action, excessive play, bends, and other damage. Replace any damaged parts with new ones (see Chapter 5). Clean and lubricate the lever and pedal pivots if their action is stiff or rough (see Section 8).

3 Make sure all brake fasteners are tight. Check the fluid level in the reservoirs (see *Pre-ride checks*). Inspect the brake pads for wear (see Steps 11 to 16)

4 If the lever or pedal action is spongy, bleed the brakes (see Chapter 7). Don't forget to change the brake fluid at the specified service interval.

5 Look for leaks at the hose connections and check for cracks in the hoses themselves **(see illustration)**. The hoses should be renewed at the specified service interval – or sooner if they show signs of damage or deterioration (see Steps 18 and 19).

6 Check the brake master cylinder and caliper seals for signs of leaking fluid (see Steps 20 and 21).

7 Make sure the brake light operates when the front brake lever is pulled in. The front brake light switch, mounted on the underside of the master cylinder, is not adjustable. If it fails to operate properly, check it (see Chapter 8).

8 Make sure the brake light is activated just before the rear brake takes effect. The switch is mounted behind the rider's right-hand footrest bracket. If adjustment is necessary, hold the switch and turn the adjuster nut on the switch body until the brake light is activated when required **(see illustration)**. If the brake light comes on too late, turn the nut clockwise. If the brake light comes on too soon or is permanently on, turn the nut anti-clockwise. If the switch doesn't operate the brake light, check it (see Chapter 8).

9 The front brake lever has a span adjuster

which alters the distance of the lever from the handlebar. Each setting is identified by a number on the adjuster which aligns with an arrow on the lever **(see illustration)**. Pull the lever away from the handlebar and turn the adjuster until the setting which best suits the rider is obtained. There are five settings – setting 1 gives the largest span, and setting 5 the smallest. When making adjustment, make sure the marks between the lever and the adjuster align to ensure correct engagement of the adjuster setting.

10 Check the position of the brake pedal. Measure the distance between the top of the brake pedal and the upper edge of the footrest **(see illustration)**. Compare the result with the specification at the beginning of this Chapter. If the pedal height is incorrect, or if the rider's preference is different, loosen the locknut on the master cylinder pushrod, then turn the pushrod using a spanner on the hex at the top of the rod until the pedal is at the correct

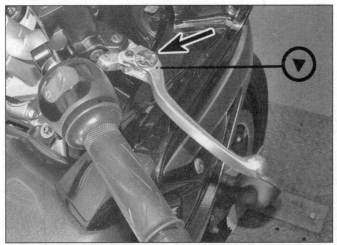

11.9 Set the span adjuster (arrowed) to the most comfortable setting. Note the register mark on the lever

11.10a Measure the brake pedal height between the two points (arrowed)

11.10b Loosen locknut (A) and adjust pushrod at hex (B), making sure rod end is still visible in hole (C)

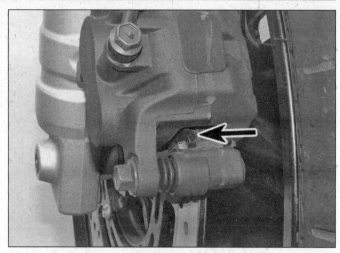

11.11a Front brake pad wear can be checked from the rear of the caliper . . .

11.11b . . . but a better assessment can be made with the caliper displaced

11.12 Checking the front brake pads on S2 models

or desired height **(see illustration)**. After adjustment check that the pushrod end is still visible in the hole in the clevis. On completion tighten the locknut securely. Adjust the rear brake light switch after adjusting the pedal position (see Step 8).

Brake pad wear check

⚠️ *Warning: The dust created by the brake system may contain asbestos, which is harmful to your health. Never blow it out with compressed air and don't inhale any of it. An approved filtering mask should be worn when working on the brakes.*

11 On bikes fitted with two-piston sliding front brake calipers (all except S2 models) the pads can be checked from the rear of the caliper **(see illustration)**. However, if the pads are dirty or if you are in doubt as to the amount of friction material remaining, it is advisable to follow the procedure in Chapter 6 and displace the calipers – the pads can then

be lifted off the caliper brackets and inspected individually **(see illustration)**.
12 On S2 models, the pads must be removed from the calipers for checking **(see illustration)** – follow the procedure in Chapter 6.
13 The rear brake pads on all models can

be checked from the rear of the caliper **(see illustration)**. However, if the pads are dirty or if you are in doubt as to the amount of friction material remaining, it is advisable to follow the procedure in Chapter 6 and remove the pads so that they can be inspected individually **(see illustration)**.

11.13a Rear brake pad wear can be checked from the rear of the caliper (arrowed) . . .

11.13b . . . or they can be removed and checked individually

11.14 Note the wear indicator grooves (arrowed)

11.15 Note the two separate sections of friction material bonded to the backplate

14 Some brake pads have wear indicator grooves – if they are worn to the limit, new ones must be installed **(see illustration)**.
Note: *Some after-market pads may use different wear indicators; always check with your supplier before fitting.*
15 On the S2 model used to illustrate this procedure, the front brake pads featured two separate sections of friction material bonded to each backplate **(see illustration)**. **Warning:** *The gap between the friction material is not a wear indicator groove.*
16 In all cases, it is advisable to measure the thickness of the friction material and compare the result with the Specifications at the beginning of this Chapter **(see illustration)**. If the pads are worn to the limit, new ones must be installed (see Chapter 6). **Note:** *It is not possible to degrease the friction material; if the pads are contaminated in any way they must be renewed.*

Brake fluid change

17 The brake fluid should be changed at the specified service interval or whenever a master cylinder or caliper overhaul is carried out. Refer to Chapter 6 for details. Ensure that all the old fluid is pumped from the system.

Check the level in the fluid reservoir and test the brakes before riding the motorcycle.

Brake hoses

18 The hoses will deteriorate with age and even if they appear to be in good condition they should be replaced with new ones at the specified service interval (see Chapter 6).
19 Always replace the banjo union sealing washers with new ones when fitting new hoses. Refill the system with new brake fluid and bleed the system as described in Chapter 6.

Brake caliper and master cylinder seals

20 Brake system seals will deteriorate over a period of time and lose their effectiveness. Old master cylinder seals will cause sticky operation of the brake lever or pedal; old caliper seals will cause the pistons to stick or fluid leak out. The seals should be renewed at the specified service interval or sooner if defects are evident.
21 Replace all the seals in each caliper as a set – a rebuild kit for each caliper is available. Front and rear master cylinder seals are supplied as a kit along with a new piston and spring assembly (see Chapter 6).

12 Wheels, wheel bearings and tyres

Wheels

1 Cast wheels are virtually maintenance free, but they should be kept clean and checked periodically for cracks and other damage. Also check the wheel runout and alignment (see Chapter 6). Never attempt to repair damaged cast wheels; they must be replaced with new ones.
2 Check the tyre valve rubber for signs of damage or deterioration and have it replaced with a new one if necessary. Also, make sure the valve cap is in place and tight **(see illustration)**. Check that the wheel balance weights are fixed firmly to the wheel rim **(see illustration)**. If the weights have fallen off, have the wheel rebalanced by a motorcycle tyre specialist.

Wheel bearings

Note: *Avoid using a high pressure cleaner around the wheel hubs. Water may penetrate the wheel bearing seals and wash out the grease, leading to corrosion and premature bearing failure.*

11.16 Measuring the thickness of the friction material

12.2a Make sure there is a cap on each valve

12.2b Check the security of any wheel balance weights (arrowed)

12.5 Checking for play in the wheel bearings

13.3 Inspect the fork inner tubes for surface damage and oil leakage

3 Wheel bearings will wear over a period of time and result in handling problems.

4 Support the motorcycle upright using the centrestand. Check for any play in the bearings by pushing and pulling each wheel against the hub **(see illustration)**. Also rotate the wheels and check that they spin smoothly and quietly, but do not mistake brake pad-to-disc noise for noisy bearings.

5 If any play is detected in the hub, or if the wheel does not rotate smoothly (and this is not due to brake or chain drag), the wheel must be removed for thorough inspection of the bearings (see Chapter 6).

Tyres

6 Check the tyre condition and tread depth thoroughly (see *Pre-ride checks*).

13 Suspension

1 The suspension components must be maintained in top operating condition to ensure rider safety. Loose, worn or damaged suspension parts decrease the motorcycle's stability and control.

Front suspension check

2 While standing alongside the motorcycle, apply the front brake and push on the handlebars to compress the forks several times. Check that they move up and down smoothly without binding. If binding is felt, the forks should be disassembled and inspected (see Chapter 5).

3 Inspect the fork inner tubes for signs of scratches, corrosion and pitting, and oil leaks **(see illustration)**. Displace the stone guard from the top of the fork outer tube, then carefully lever the dust seals out using a flat-bladed screwdriver and inspect the area around the fork seals (see Chapter 5). Any scratches, corrosion and pitting will

cause premature seal failure. If the damage is excessive, new tubes should be installed (see Chapter 5).

4 If oil is leaking, new seals must be fitted (see Chapter 5). If there is evidence of corrosion between the seal retaining ring and its groove in the fork outer tube spray the area with a penetrative lubricant, otherwise the ring will be difficult to remove if needed. Press the dust seal back into place on completion.

5 Check the tightness of all suspension nuts and bolts to be sure none have worked loose, referring to the torque settings specified at the beginning of Chapter 5.

Rear suspension check

Note: *Avoid using a high pressure cleaner around the swingarm pivots and the lower shock absorber mounting. Water may penetrate the bearing seals and wash out the grease, leading to corrosion and premature bearing failure.*

6 Inspect the rear shock for fluid leaks and loose mountings. If the shock is leaking, a new one should be installed (see Chapter 5).

7 With the aid of an assistant to support the bike, compress the rear suspension several

times. It should move up and down freely without binding. If any binding is felt, the worn or faulty component must be identified and checked. The problem could be due to either the shock absorber, the suspension linkage components or the swingarm components (see Chapter 5).

8 Support the motorcycle on the centrestand so that the rear wheel is off the ground. Grasp the swingarm and rock it from side to side – there should be no discernible movement at the ends of the swingarm (Yamaha specify a maximum of 1 mm sideplay) **(see illustration)**. If there is a little movement or a slight clicking can be heard, inspect the tightness of all the rear suspension mounting bolts and nuts, referring to the torque settings specified at the beginning of Chapter 5, and re-check for movement.

9 Next, grasp the top of the rear wheel and pull it upwards – there should be no discernible freeplay before the shock absorber begins to compress **(see illustration)**. Any freeplay felt in either check indicates worn bearings in the swingarm, or worn shock absorber mountings. The worn components must be identified and checked (see Chapter 6).

13.8 Checking for play in the swingarm bearings

13.9 Checking for play in the rear shock mountings

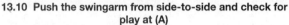

13.10 Push the swingarm from side-to-side and check for play at (A)

13.11 Swingarm should move freely up and down

10 To make an accurate assessment of the swingarm bearings it is necessary to remove the rear wheel (see Chapter 6). Grasp the rear of the swingarm with one hand and place your other hand at the junction of the swingarm and the frame. Try to move the rear of the swingarm from side-to-side **(see illustration)**. Any wear (play) in the bearings should be felt as movement between the swingarm and the frame at the front. If there is any play, the swingarm will be felt to move forward and backward at the front (not from side-to-side).

11 Next, move the swingarm up and down through its full travel – it should move freely, without any binding or rough spots **(see illustration)**. If any play in the swingarm is noted, or if the swingarm does not move freely, remove the swingarm for inspection of the bearings (see Chapter 5).

12 The rear shock is adjustable for spring pre-load (See Chapter 5).

Front fork oil change

13 Although there is no set interval for changing the fork oil, note that the oil will degrade over a period of time and lose its damping qualities. Refer to Chapter 5 for details of front fork removal, oil draining

and refilling. The forks do not need to be completely disassembled to change the oil.

Rear suspension bearing lubrication

14 Over a period of time the grease in the swingarm and lower shock absorber bearings will be washed out (especially if pressure washers are used) or will harden allowing the ingress of dirt and water.

15 The swingarm should be disassembled at the specified service interval and the bearings cleaned and re-greased as necessary (see Chapter 5).

14 Steering head bearings

Freeplay check and adjustment

1 Steering head bearings can become dented, rough or loose during normal use of the machine. In extreme cases, worn or loose steering head bearings can cause steering wobble – a condition that is potentially dangerous.

Check

2 Support the motorcycle in an upright position on the centrestand. Raise the front wheel off the ground either by having an assistant push down on the rear, or by placing a support under the engine.

3 Point the front wheel straight-ahead, and slowly turn the handlebars from side to side. Any dents or roughness in the bearing races will be felt and if the bearings are too tight the bars will not move smoothly and freely. If the bearings are damaged or the action is rough, they should be replaced with new ones (see Chapter 5). If the bearings are too tight they should be adjusted as described below.

4 Again point the wheel straight-ahead, and tap the front of the wheel to one side. The wheel should 'fall' under its own weight to the limit of its lock, indicating that the bearings are not too tight (take into account the restriction that cables and wiring may have). Check for similar movement to the other side.

5 Next, grasp the forks and try to pull and push them forwards and backwards **(see illustration)**. Any looseness in the steering head bearings will be felt as front-to-rear movement of the forks. If play is felt in the bearings, adjust them as follows.

Adjustment

Special tool: *Either the Yamaha service tool described in Step 10 or a suitably sized C-spanner is required for this procedure* **(see illustration 14.11a)**.

6 Support the motorcycle on the centrestand with the front wheel off the ground. Remove the fuel tank (see Chapter 4). If fitted, remove the fairing (see Chapter 7), otherwise displace the headlight and headlight bracket (see Chapter 8). **Note:** *Although it is not strictly necessary to remove the fuel tank and fairing, doing so will prevent the possibility of damage, should a tool slip.*

7 Displace the handlebars (see Chapter 5). Slacken the fork clamp bolts in the top yoke **(see illustration)**.

14.5 Checking for play in the steering head bearings

14.7 Loosen the fork clamp bolts on both sides

14.8a Unscrew the steering stem nut . . .

14.8b . . . and remove the washer

8 Unscrew the steering stem nut and remove it along with its washer, then ease the top yoke upwards off the fork tubes – secure the top yoke with a cable-tie to avoid straining the ignition switch wiring **(see illustrations)**.
9 Remove the tabbed lockwasher, noting how it fits, then unscrew and remove the locknut, using either a C-spanner, though it should only be finger-tight **(see illustrations)**. Remove the rubber washer **(see illustration)**.
10 To adjust the bearings as specified

14.8c Ease the top yoke off

14.9a Remove the tabbed lockwasher . . .

14.9b . . . then unscrew the locknut . . .

14.9c . . . and remove the rubber washer

14.10 Make sure the torque wrench arm is at right-angles (90°) to the service tool

14.11a Alternately loosen . . .

by Yamaha, a special service tool (Pt. No. 90890-01403 for Europe, or YU-33975 for US) and a torque wrench are required. If the tool is available, first slacken the adjuster nut slightly to take pressure off the bearing, then tighten the nut to the initial torque setting specified at the beginning of this Chapter. Make sure the torque wrench handle is at right-angles (90°) to the centre line between the adjuster nut and the service tool wrench socket (see illustration). Now slacken the nut, then tighten it to the final torque setting specified.

11 If the Yamaha tool is not available use a C-spanner to slacken the adjuster nut slightly to take pressure off the bearing then tighten the nut until all freeplay is removed (see illustrations). Now tighten the nut a little more to pre-load the bearings. Now slacken the nut and retighten it, setting it so that all freeplay is just removed from the bearings, yet the steering is able to move freely from side to side. Tighten the nut only a little at a time,

and after each adjustment repeat the checks outlined in Steps 3 to 5.

12 Turn the steering from lock to lock five times to settle the bearings, then recheck the adjustment or the torque setting depending on your method used. The object is to set the adjuster nut so that the bearings are under a very light loading, just enough to remove any freeplay.

Caution: Take great care not to apply excessive pressure because this will cause premature failure of the bearings.

13 With the bearings correctly adjusted, install the rubber washer and the locknut (see illustrations 14.9c and b). Tighten the locknut finger-tight, then tighten it further until its notches align with those in the adjuster nut, making sure the adjuster nut does not turn as well. Install the tabbed lockwasher so that the tabs fit into the notches in both the locknut and adjuster nut (see illustration 14.9a). Recheck the bearing adjustment as described in

Steps 3 to 5 to ensure the adjuster nut hasn't moved.

14 Fit the top yoke onto the steering stem and the fork legs. Install the washer and steering stem nut and tighten it to the torque setting specified at the beginning of this Chapter. Now tighten the fork clamp bolts in the top yoke to the specified torque (see illustration 14.7).

15 Follow the procedure in Chapter 5 to install the handlebars, taking care to align the bars correctly with the lower half of the brackets on the top yoke before installing the upper clamp(s) (see illustration).

Lubrication

16 Over a considerable time the grease in the bearings will be dispersed or will harden allowing the ingress of dirt and water.

17 At the specified interval the steering head should be disassembled and the bearings cleaned and re-greased (see Chapter 5, Section 10).

14.11b . . . and then tighten the adjuster nut as described to remove bearing freeplay

14.15 Align the register mark (arrowed) with the top edge of the lower bracket

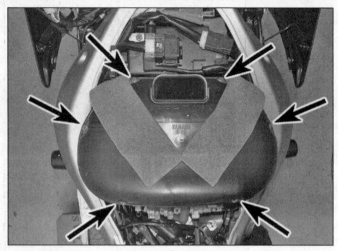

18.2a Remove the air filter housing cover screws . . .

18.2b . . . and lift the cover off

15 Sidestand and starter safety circuit

1 The sidestand switch prevents the motorcycle being started if the transmission is in gear and the stand is down, and cuts the engine if the stand is put down while the engine is running and in gear.
2 Check the operation of the safety circuit (which incorporates the sidestand, clutch and neutral switches, and the starter circuit cut-off relay) by shifting the transmission into neutral, retracting the stand and starting the engine. Pull in the clutch lever and select a gear. Extend the sidestand. The engine should stop as the sidestand is extended.
3 Also make sure that the engine cannot be started while in gear unless the stand is up and the clutch lever is pulled in. If the circuit does not operate as described, check the individual components of the safety circuit (see Chapter 8).

16 Nuts, bolts and fasteners

1 Since vibration of the machine tends to loosen fasteners, all nuts, bolts, screws, etc. should be periodically checked for tightness.
2 Pay particular attention to the following:
Brake caliper and master cylinder mounting bolts
Brake hose banjo bolts and caliper bleed valves
Brake disc bolts
Exhaust system bolts/nuts
Engine oil drain plug
Engine mounting bolts

Spark plugs
Lever and pedal bolts
Handlebar clamp bolts
Footrest, centrestand and sidestand bolts
Shock absorber mounting bolts
Swingarm pivot bolt
Front fork clamp bolts (top and bottom yoke) and fork top bolts
Steering stem nut
Front axle and axle clamp bolt
Rear axle nut
Front and rear sprocket nuts
Chain adjuster locknuts
3 If a torque wrench is available, use it along with the torque settings given at the beginning of this and other Chapters.

17 Battery check

1 All models are fitted with a sealed, gel-type maintenance-free battery. **Note:** *Do not attempt to open the battery as resulting damage will mean it will be unfit for further use.*

18.3 Filter element frame is marked FRONT

2 All that should be done is to check that the terminals are clean and tight and that the casing is not damaged or leaking. See Chapter 8 for further details.

Caution: Be extremely careful when handling or working around the battery. The electrolyte gel is very caustic and an explosive gas (hydrogen) is given off when the battery is charging.

3 If the machine is not in regular use, disconnect the battery and give it a refresher charge every month to six weeks (see Chapter 8, Section 4).

18 Air filter element

Note: *If the machine is continually ridden in dusty conditions, clean the filter more frequently than specified.*

Cleaning – 2004 to 2006 models

Note: *2007-on models are fitted with a disposable oil-impregnated paper element which cannot be cleaned. Renew the element at the specified service interval.*
1 Remove the fuel tank (see Chapter 4).
2 Remove the screws securing the air filter housing cover, then remove the cover **(see illustrations)**. Note the location of the cover gasket, if fitted.
3 The filter element will probably come out with the cover, otherwise lift it out of the housing, noting which way round it fits **(see illustration)**.
4 Check the element for signs of damage. If the element is torn or is obviously beyond further use, replace it with a new one.
5 If the element is undamaged but dirty, tap

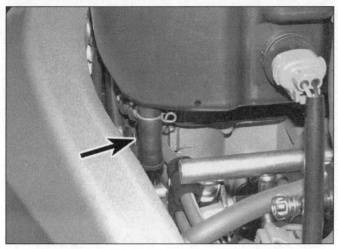

18.6 Drain the air filter housing vent hose (arrowed)

18.7 Location of the AIS hose union (arrowed)

it on a hard surface to dislodge any dirt. Note that in some instances, the filter element can be cleaned with solvent – check with a Yamaha dealer for details

6 Clean out any dirt from the filter housing and cover. Check the housing drain in the bottom left-hand corner **(see illustration)**. If necessary, release the clip and drain off any accumulated moisture.

7 Check for carbon deposits inside the housing, particularly on the right-hand side around the union for the AIS hose **(see illustration)**. Carbon deposits indicate a fault with the AIS reed valves in the engine valve cover (see Chapter 4).

8 Where fitted, install the seal, then fit the filter element into the slot in the housing. Ensure that the element is fitted the correct way round (see illustration 18.3).

9 Fit the cover and check that it is seated all the way round. Ensure that the threads of

the cover screws are clean, then tighten the screws evenly and securely.

10 Check the crankcase breather hose between the engine and the rear of the air filter housing for loose connections, cracks and deterioration, and replace it with a new one if necessary **(see illustration)**. Also check that the short hoses between the throttle synchronising unit and the air filter housing are secure.

11 Check that the air temperature sensor is a tight fit in the housing **(see illustration 18.10)**. If it is loose, renew the sealing grommet.

12 Install the fuel tank (see Chapter 4).

Renewal – all models

13 At the specified service interval, whatever the condition of the existing filter element, remove the element as described above and install a new one.

19 Valve clearances

1 The engine must be completely cool for this maintenance procedure, so let the machine sit overnight before beginning.

2 Where fitted, remove the fairing (see Chapter 7). Remove the radiator (see Chapter 3). Remove the air filter housing (see Chapter 4). Remove the battery housing and displace or remove the ignition coils, then remove the AIS assembly (see Chapter 4).

3 Remove the spark plugs (see Section 2).

4 Follow the procedure in Chapter 2 and remove the valve cover **(see illustration)**.

5 Trace the crankshaft position sensor wiring from the timing rotor cover and disconnect it at the connector **(see

18.10 Location of crankcase breather hose (A) and air temperature sensor (B)

19.4 Valve cover can be lifted off towards the front

19.5a Crankshaft position sensor wiring leaves the cover at (A).
Note the hose guide (B)

19.5b Location of the crankshaft position sensor wiring
connector

illustrations). Feed the wiring back to the cover.

6 Place a drain tray under the timing rotor cover and unscrew the cover bolts (see illustration). Note the guide for the coolant hose (see illustration 19.5a). Ease the cover off – discard the gasket, as a new one must be used and remove the dowels from either the crankcase or the cover if they are loose (see illustration).

19.6a Undo the cover bolts (arrowed)

19.6b Note the location of the dowels (arrowed)

19.8a Align the 'T' mark with the rear facing crankcase mating
surfaces

19.8b Ensure the cam lobes (No. 1 cylinder) are facing away from
each other as shown

19.9a Check the valve clearances on all four valves for the No. 1 cylinder

H46039

19.9b Inset the feeler gauge between the base of the cam lobe and the top of the follower

7 The cylinders are numbered 1 to 4 from left to right, viewed as normally seated on the bike. Make a chart or sketch of all valve positions so that a note of each clearance can be made against the relevant valve.

8 Using a spanner on the timing rotor bolt and rotating in a clockwise direction only, turn the engine until the 'T' mark on the ignition rotor faces to the rear and aligns with the crankcase mating surfaces and the camshaft lobes for the No. 1 (left-hand) cylinder face away from each other **(see illustrations)**. If the cam lobes are facing towards each other, turn the engine clockwise 360° (one full turn) so that the 'T' mark again aligns with the crankcase mating surfaces. The camshaft lobes will now be facing away from each other and the No. 1 cylinder will be at TDC (top dead centre) on the compression stroke.

9 Check the clearances on the No. 1 cylinder intake and exhaust valves. Insert a feeler gauge of the same thickness as the correct valve clearance (see Specifications) between the camshaft lobe and follower of each valve

and check that it is a firm sliding fit – you should feel a slight drag when the you pull the gauge out **(see illustrations)**. If not, use the feeler gauges to measure the exact clearance. Record the measured clearance on your chart.

10 Now turn the engine clockwise 180° (half a turn) so that the camshaft lobes for the No. 2 cylinder are facing away from each other **(see illustration)**. The No. 2 cylinder is now at TDC on the compression stroke. Measure the clearances of the No. 2 cylinder valves using the method described in Step 9.

11 Now turn the engine clockwise 180° (half a turn) so that the camshaft lobes for the No. 4 cylinder are facing away from each other. The No. 4 cylinder is now at TDC on the compression stroke. Measure the clearances of the No. 4 cylinder valves using the method described in Step 9.

12 Now turn the engine clockwise 180° (half a turn) so that the camshaft lobes for the No. 3 cylinder are facing away from each other. The No. 3 cylinder is now at TDC on the

compression stroke. Measure the clearances of the No. 3 cylinder valves using the method described in Step 9.

13 When all clearances have been measured and recorded, identify whether the clearance on any valve falls outside that specified. If it does, the shim between the cam follower and the valve must be replaced with one of a thickness which will restore the correct clearance.

14 Shim replacement requires removal of the camshafts (see Chapter 2). There is no need to remove both camshafts if shims from only one need replacing. Place rags over the spark plug holes and the cam chain tunnel to prevent a shim from dropping into the engine on removal.

15 With the camshaft removed, remove the cam follower of the valve in question, then retrieve the shim from inside the follower **(see illustrations)**. If it is not in the follower, pick it out of the top of the valve using either a magnet, a small screwdriver with a dab of grease on it (the shim will stick to the grease),

19.10 Check the valve clearances on all four valves for the No. 2 cylinder

19.15a Lift out the cam follower . . .

19.15b . . . and retrieve the shim from inside . . .

19.15c . . . or from the top of the valve

19.16 Measuring the shim with a micrometer

or a screwdriver and a pair of pliers. Do not allow the shim to fall into the engine.

16 A size should be marked on the upper face of the shim – a shim marked 175 is 1.75 mm thick. If the mark is not visible, the shim thickness will have to be measured. It is recommended that the shim is measured anyway, to check that it has not worn **(see illustration)**.

17 Using the appropriate shim selection chart, find where the measured valve clearance and existing shim thickness values intersect and read off the shim size required **(see illustrations)**. **Note:** *If the existing shim is marked with a number not ending in* *0 or 5, round it up or down as appropriate to the nearest number ending in 0 or 5, so that the chart can be used. Shims are available in 0.05 mm increments from 1.20 mm to 2.40 mm.* **Note:** *If the required replacement shim is greater than 2.40 mm (the largest available), the valve is probably not seating correctly due to a build-up of carbon deposits and should be checked and cleaned or resurfaced as required (see Chapter 2).*

18 Obtain the replacement shim, then lubricate it with molybdenum disulphide grease and fit it into its recess in the top of the valve, with the size marking facing up **(see**

MEASURED INTAKE VALVE CLEARANCE	EXISTING SHIM SIZE (mm)																								
	1.20	1.25	1.30	1.35	1.40	1.45	1.50	1.55	1.60	1.65	1.70	1.75	1.80	1.85	1.90	1.95	2.00	2.05	2.10	2.15	2.20	2.25	2.30	2.35	2.40
0.00 – 0.02 mm				1.20	1.25	1.30	1.35	1.40	1.45	1.50	1.55	1.60	1.65	1.70	1.75	1.80	1.85	1.90	1.95	2.00	2.05	2.10	2.15	2.20	2.25
0.03 – 0.07 mm			1.20	1.25	1.30	1.35	1.40	1.45	1.50	1.55	1.60	1.65	1.70	1.75	1.80	1.85	1.90	1.95	2.00	2.05	2.10	2.15	2.20	2.25	2.30
0.08 – 0.12 mm		1.20	1.25	1.30	1.35	1.40	1.45	1.50	1.55	1.60	1.65	1.70	1.75	1.80	1.85	1.90	1.95	2.00	2.05	2.10	2.15	2.20	2.25	2.30	2.35
0.13 – 0.20 mm	SPECIFIED CLEARANCE/NO ADJUSTMENT REQUIRED																								
0.21 – 0.25 mm	1.25	1.30	1.35	1.40	1.45	1.50	1.55	1.60	1.65	1.70	1.75	1.80	1.85	1.90	1.95	2.00	2.05	2.10	2.15	2.20	2.25	2.30	2.35	2.40	
0.26 – 0.30 mm	1.30	1.35	1.40	1.45	1.50	1.55	1.60	1.65	1.70	1.75	1.80	1.85	1.90	1.95	2.00	2.05	2.10	2.15	2.20	2.25	2.30	2.35	2.40		
0.31 – 0.35 mm	1.35	1.40	1.45	1.50	1.55	1.60	1.65	1.70	1.75	1.80	1.85	1.90	1.95	2.00	2.05	2.10	2.15	2.20	2.25	2.30	2.35	2.40			
0.36 – 0.40 mm	1.40	1.45	1.50	1.55	1.60	1.65	1.70	1.75	1.80	1.85	1.90	1.95	2.00	2.05	2.10	2.15	2.20	2.25	2.30	2.35	2.40				
0.41 – 0.45 mm	1.45	1.50	1.55	1.60	1.65	1.70	1.75	1.80	1.85	1.90	1.95	2.00	2.05	2.10	2.15	2.20	2.25	2.30	2.35	2.40					
0.46 – 0.50 mm	1.50	1.55	1.60	1.65	1.70	1.75	1.80	1.85	1.90	1.95	2.00	2.05	2.10	2.15	2.20	2.25	2.30	2.35	2.40						
0.51 – 0.55 mm	1.55	1.60	1.65	1.70	1.75	1.80	1.85	1.90	1.95	2.00	2.05	2.10	2.15	2.20	2.25	2.30	2.35	2.40							
0.56 – 0.60 mm	1.60	1.65	1.70	1.75	1.80	1.85	1.90	1.95	2.00	2.05	2.10	2.15	2.20	2.25	2.30	2.35	2.40								
0.61 – 0.65 mm	1.65	1.70	1.75	1.80	1.85	1.90	1.95	2.00	2.05	2.10	2.15	2.20	2.25	2.30	2.35	2.40									
0.66 – 0.70 mm	1.70	1.75	1.80	1.85	1.90	1.95	2.00	2.05	2.10	2.15	2.20	2.25	2.30	2.35	2.40										
0.71 – 0.75 mm	1.75	1.80	1.85	1.90	1.95	2.00	2.05	2.10	2.15	2.20	2.25	2.30	2.35	2.40											
0.76 – 0.80 mm	1.80	1.85	1.90	1.95	2.00	2.05	2.10	2.15	2.20	2.25	2.30	2.35	2.40												
0.81 – 0.85 mm	1.85	1.90	1.95	2.00	2.05	2.10	2.15	2.20	2.25	2.30	2.35	2.40													
0.86 – 0.90 mm	1.90	1.95	2.00	2.05	2.10	2.15	2.20	2.25	2.30	2.35	2.40														
0.91 – 0.95 mm	1.95	2.00	2.05	2.10	2.15	2.20	2.25	2.30	2.35	2.40															
0.96 – 1.00 mm	2.00	2.05	2.10	2.15	2.20	2.25	2.30	2.35	2.40																
1.01 – 1.05 mm	2.05	2.10	2.15	2.20	2.25	2.30	2.35	2.40																	
1.06 – 1.10 mm	2.10	2.15	2.20	2.25	2.30	2.35	2.40																		
1.11 – 1.15 mm	2.15	2.20	2.25	2.30	2.35	2.40																			
1.16 – 1.20 mm	2.20	2.25	2.30	2.35	2.40																				
1.21 – 1.25 mm	2.25	2.30	2.35	2.40																					
1.26 – 1.30 mm	2.30	2.35	2.40																						
1.31 – 1.35 mm	2.35	2.40																							
1.36 – 1.40 mm	2.40																								

19.17a Shim selection chart – intake camshaft

MEASURED EXHAUST VALVE CLEARANCE	EXISTING SHIM SIZE (mm)																								
	1.20	1.25	1.30	1.35	1.40	1.45	1.50	1.55	1.60	1.65	1.70	1.75	1.80	1.85	1.90	1.95	2.00	2.05	2.10	2.15	2.20	2.25	2.30	2.35	2.40
0.00 – 0.02 mm						1.20	1.25	1.30	1.35	1.40	1.45	1.50	1.55	1.60	1.65	1.70	1.75	1.80	1.85	1.90	1.95	2.00	2.05	2.10	2.15
0.03 – 0.07 mm					1.20	1.25	1.30	1.35	1.40	1.45	1.50	1.55	1.60	1.65	1.70	1.75	1.80	1.85	1.90	1.95	2.00	2.05	2.10	2.15	2.20
0.08 – 0.12 mm				1.20	1.25	1.30	1.35	1.40	1.45	1.50	1.55	1.60	1.65	1.70	1.75	1.80	1.85	1.90	1.95	2.00	2.05	2.10	2.15	2.20	2.25
0.13 – 0.17 mm			1.20	1.25	1.30	1.35	1.40	1.45	1.50	1.55	1.60	1.65	1.70	1.75	1.80	1.85	1.90	1.95	2.00	2.05	2.10	2.15	2.20	2.25	2.30
0.18 – 0.22 mm		1.20	1.25	1.30	1.35	1.40	1.45	1.50	1.55	1.60	1.65	1.70	1.75	1.80	1.85	1.90	1.95	2.00	2.05	2.10	2.15	2.20	2.25	2.30	2.35
0.23 – 0.30 mm	STANDARD CLEARANCE/NO ADJUSTMENT REQUIRED																								
0.31 – 0.35 mm	1.25	1.30	1.35	1.40	1.45	1.50	1.55	1.60	1.65	1.70	1.75	1.80	1.85	1.90	1.95	2.00	2.05	2.10	2.15	2.20	2.25	2.30	2.35	2.40	
0.36 – 0.40 mm	1.30	1.35	1.40	1.45	1.50	1.55	1.60	1.65	1.70	1.75	1.80	1.85	1.90	1.95	2.00	2.05	2.10	2.15	2.20	2.25	2.30	2.35	2.40		
0.41 – 0.45 mm	1.35	1.40	1.45	1.50	1.55	1.60	1.65	1.70	1.75	1.80	1.85	1.90	1.95	2.00	2.05	2.10	2.15	2.20	2.25	2.30	2.35	2.40			
0.46 – 0.50 mm	1.40	1.45	1.50	1.55	1.60	1.65	1.70	1.75	1.80	1.85	1.90	1.95	2.00	2.05	2.10	2.15	2.20	2.25	2.30	2.35	2.40				
0.51 – 0.55 mm	1.45	1.50	1.55	1.60	1.65	1.70	1.75	1.80	1.85	1.90	1.95	2.00	2.05	2.10	2.15	2.20	2.25	2.30	2.35	2.40					
0.56 – 0.60 mm	1.50	1.55	1.60	1.65	1.70	1.75	1.80	1.85	1.90	1.95	2.00	2.05	2.10	2.15	2.20	2.25	2.30	2.35	2.40						
0.61 – 0.65 mm	1.55	1.60	1.65	1.70	1.75	1.80	1.85	1.90	1.95	2.00	2.05	2.10	2.15	2.20	2.25	2.30	2.35	2.40							
0.66 – 0.70 mm	1.60	1.65	1.70	1.75	1.80	1.85	1.90	1.95	2.00	2.05	2.10	2.15	2.20	2.25	2.30	2.35	2.40								
0.71 – 0.75 mm	1.65	1.70	1.75	1.80	1.85	1.90	1.95	2.00	2.05	2.10	2.15	2.20	2.25	2.30	2.35	2.40									
0.76 – 0.80 mm	1.70	1.75	1.80	1.85	1.90	1.95	2.00	2.05	2.10	2.15	2.20	2.25	2.30	2.35	2.40										
0.81 – 0.85 mm	1.75	1.80	1.85	1.90	1.95	2.00	2.05	2.10	2.15	2.20	2.25	2.30	2.35	2.40											
0.86 – 0.90 mm	1.80	1.85	1.90	1.95	2.00	2.05	2.10	2.15	2.20	2.25	2.30	2.35	2.40												
0.91 – 0.95 mm	1.85	1.90	1.95	2.00	2.05	2.10	2.15	2.20	2.25	2.30	2.35	2.40													
0.96 – 1.00 mm	1.90	1.95	2.00	2.05	2.10	2.15	2.20	2.25	2.30	2.35	2.40														
1.01 – 1.05 mm	1.95	2.00	2.05	2.10	2.15	2.20	2.25	2.30	2.35	2.40															
1.06 – 1.10 mm	2.00	2.05	2.10	2.15	2.20	2.25	2.30	2.35	2.40																
1.11 – 1.15 mm	2.05	2.10	2.15	2.20	2.25	2.30	2.35	2.40																	
1.16 – 1.20 mm	2.10	2.15	2.20	2.25	2.30	2.35	2.40																		
1.21 – 1.25 mm	2.15	2.20	2.25	2.30	2.35	2.40																			
1.26 – 1.30 mm	2.20	2.25	2.30	2.35	2.40																				
1.31 – 1.35 mm	2.25	2.30	2.35	2.40																					
1.36 – 1.40 mm	2.30	2.35	2.40																						
1.41 – 1.45 mm	2.35	2.40																							
1.46 – 1.50 mm	2.40																								

19.17b Shim selection chart – exhaust camshaft

illustration). Check that the shim is correctly seated, then lubricate the follower with molybdenum disulphide oil (a 50/50 mixture of molybdenum disulphide grease and engine oil) and fit it onto the valve (see illustration 19.15a). Repeat the process for any other valves until the clearances are correct, then install the camshafts (see Chapter 2).

19 Rotate the crankshaft clockwise several turns to seat the new shim(s), then check the clearances again.

20 Install the valve cover (see Chapter 2).

21 Ensure the dowels for the timing rotor cover are in place and fit a new gasket onto the dowels (see illustration 19.6b).

22 Install the cover and secure it with the bolts finger-tight. Don't forget to secure the wiring for the crankshaft position sensor and the coolant hose behind the guide (see illustration 19.5a). Tighten the cover bolts evenly to the torque setting specified at the beginning of this Chapter.

23 Connect the crankshaft position sensor wiring (see illustration 19.5b).

24 Install all remaining components in the reverse order of removal. On completion, check the engine oil level (see Pre-ride checks). Check and adjust the idle speed (see Section 3).

19.18 Fit the shim with the size marking facing up

1•34 Notes

Chapter 2
Engine, clutch and transmission

Contents

Section number

Alternator . . . . see Chapter 8
Cam chain tensioner 7
Cam chain, tensioner blade and guides. 9
Camshafts and followers 8
Camshaft position (CMP) sensor . . . . see Chapter 4
Clutch. 13
Clutch cable 12
Clutch check . . . . see Chapter 1
Component access 2
Connecting rods and bearings. 21
Crankcases and cylinder bores 28
Crankcase separation and reassembly 19
Crankshaft and main bearings 24
Crankshaft position (CKP) sensor . . . . see Chapter 4
Cylinder head and valve overhaul 11
Cylinder head removal and installation 10
Engine overhaul general information 5
Engine removal and installation 4
Engine wear assessment 3
Gearchange mechanism 15
General information 1

Section number

Idle speed. . . . . see Chapter 1
Main and big-end bearing information. 20
Neutral switch. . . . . see Chapter 8
Oil and filter change . . . . see Chapter 1
Oil cooler 16
Oil level check . . . . see Pre-ride checks
Oil level sensor. . . . . see Chapter 8
Oil pump. 18
Oil sump, strainer and pressure relief valve 17
Pistons 22
Piston rings. 23
Running-in procedure. 29
Selector drum and forks. 27
Spark plugs . . . . see Chapter 1
Starter clutch and gears. 14
Starter motor . . . . see Chapter 8
Transmission shaft overhaul. 26
Transmission shaft removal and installation. 25
Valve clearances. . . . . see Chapter 1
Valve cover 6
Water pump . . . . see Chapter 3

Degrees of difficulty

| **Easy,** suitable for novice with little experience | | **Fairly easy,** suitable for beginner with some experience | **Fairly difficult,** suitable for competent DIY mechanic | **Difficult,** suitable for experienced DIY mechanic | **Very difficult,** suitable for expert DIY or professional | |

Specifications

General

Type	Four-stroke in-line four
Capacity	600 cc
Bore	65.5 mm
Stroke	44.5 mm
Compression ratio	12.2 to 1
Cylinder numbering	1 to 4 from left to right
Cooling system.	Liquid cooled
Clutch	Wet multi-plate
Transmission.	Six-speed constant mesh
Final drive	Chain

Cylinder head

Warpage (max)	0.05 mm

Camshafts

Lobe height	
Standard	32.45 to 32.55 mm
Service limit (min)	32.4 mm
Journal diameter	22.967 to 22.980 mm
Holder diameter	23.008 to 23.029 mm
Journal oil clearance	0.028 to 0.062 mm
Service limit (all models)	0.08 mm
Runout (max)	0.06 mm

Valves, guides and springs

Valve clearances . . . .   see Chapter 1
Intake valve
  Stem diameter
    Standard . . . .   3.975 to 3.990 mm
    Service limit (min) . . . .   3.950 mm
  Guide bore diameter
    Standard . . . .   4.000 to 4.012 mm
    Service limit (max) . . . .   4.042 mm
  Stem-to-guide clearance
    Standard . . . .   0.010 to 0.037 mm
    Service limit (max) . . . .   0.08 mm
  Stem runout . . . .   0.04 mm
  Head diameter . . . .   24.9 to 25.1 mm
  Face width . . . .   1.14 to 1.98 mm
  Seat width
    Standard . . . .   0.9 to 1.1 mm
    Service limit (max) . . . .   1.6 mm
  Margin thickness
    Standard . . . .   0.6 to 0.8 mm
    Service limit (min) . . . .   0.5 mm
Exhaust valve
  Stem diameter
    Standard . . . .   3.960 to 3.975 mm
    Service limit (min) . . . .   3.935 mm
  Guide bore diameter
    Standard . . . .   4.000 to 4.012 mm
    Service limit (max) . . . .   4.042 mm
  Stem-to-guide clearance
    Standard . . . .   0.025 to 0.052 mm
    Service limit (max) . . . .   0.10 mm
  Stem runout . . . .   0.04 mm
  Head diameter . . . .   21.9 to 22.1 mm
  Face width . . . .   1.14 to 1.98 mm
  Seat width
    Standard . . . .   0.9 to 1.1 mm
    Service limit (max) . . . .   1.6 mm
  Margin thickness
    Standard . . . .   0.6 to 0.8 mm
    Service limit (min) . . . .   0.5 mm
Valve spring free length
  Intake (inner)
    Standard . . . .   37.0 mm
    Service limit (min) . . . .   35.2 mm
  Intake (outer)
    Standard . . . .   38.4 mm
    Service limit (min) . . . .   36.5 mm
  Exhaust
    Standard . . . .   41.8 mm
    Service limit (min) . . . .   39.7 mm
Valve spring bend (max)
  Intake (inner) . . . .   1.6 mm
  Intake (outer) . . . .   1.7 mm
  Exhaust . . . .   1.8 mm

Lubrication system

Engine oil pressure (at 96°C) . . . .   34.1 psi (2.4 Bar) @ 6600 rpm
Relief valve opening pressure . . . .   65.3 to 79.8 psi (4.5 to 5.5 Bar)
Oil pump
  Inner rotor tip-to-outer rotor clearance
    Standard . . . .   0.03 to 0.09 mm
    Service limit (max) . . . .   0.15 mm
  Outer rotor-to-body clearance
    Standard . . . .   0.03 to 0.08 mm
    Service limit (max) . . . .   0.15 mm

Clutch

Friction plates
  Quantity
    Centre plates (Brown colour code)   6
    Inner and outer plates (Purple colour code)   2
  Thickness
    Standard . . . .   2.9 to 3.1 mm
    Service limit (min) . . . .   2.8 mm
Plain plate
  Outer plates
    Quantity   7
    Thickness . . . .   1.9 to 2.1 mm
    Warpage (max) . . . .   0.1 mm
  Inner plate
    Quantity   1
    Thickness . . . .   2.2 to 2.4 mm
    Warpage (max) . . . .   0.1 mm
Clutch springs
  Free length . . . .   55.0 mm
  Service limit . . . .   52.3 mm

Cylinder bores

Bore . . . .   65.50 to 65.51 mm
Ovality (max) . . . .   0.05 mm
Taper (max) . . . .   0.05 mm
Cylinder compression
  Standard . . . .   220.5 psi (15.5 Bar)
  Maximum . . . .   247 psi (17.4 Bar)
  Minimum . . . .   192 psi (13.5 Bar)
  Max. difference between cylinders . . . .   14.5 psi (1.0 Bar)
Piston-to-bore clearance
  Standard . . . .   0.010 to 0.035 mm
  Service limit . . . .   0.055 mm

Crankshaft and bearings

Main bearing oil clearance
  Standard . . . .   0.034 to 0.058 mm
  Service limit . . . .   0.10 mm
Runout (max) . . . .   0.03 mm

Connecting rods

Piston pin-to-small-end bore clearance . . . .   0.32 to 0.50 mm
Big-end side clearance . . . .   0.160 to 0.262 mm
Big-end oil clearance
  Standard . . . .   0.028 to 0.052 mm
  Service limit (max) . . . .   0.08 mm

Pistons

Piston diameter (measured 4 mm up from skirt, at 90° to piston
  pin axis) . . . .   65.475 to 65.490 mm
Piston-to-bore clearance
  Standard . . . .   0.010 to 0.035 mm
  Service limit . . . .   0.055 mm
Piston pin diameter
  Standard . . . .   15.991 to 16.000 mm
  Service limit (min) . . . .   15.971 mm
Piston pin bore diameter in piston
  Standard . . . .   16.002 to 16.013 mm
  Service limit (max) . . . .   16.043 mm
Piston pin-to-piston pin bore clearance
  Standard . . . .   0.002 to 0.022 mm
  Service limit . . . .   0.072 mm

Piston rings

Top compression ring
  Type . . . . Barrel
  Ring width. . . . . 2.45 mm
  Ring thickness . . . . 0.90 mm
  Ring end gap (installed)
    Standard. . . . . 0.25 to 0.35 mm
    Service limit . . . . 0.60 mm
  Piston ring-to-groove clearance
    Standard. . . . . 0.030 to 0.065 mm
    Service limit . . . . 0.115 mm
2nd compression ring
  Type . . . . Taper
  Ring width. . . . . 2.5 mm
  Ring thickness . . . . 0.8 mm
  Ring end gap (installed)
    Standard. . . . . 0.70 to 0.80 mm
    Service limit . . . . 1.15 mm
  Piston ring-to-groove clearance
    Standard. . . . . 0.030 to 0.065 mm
    Service limit . . . . 0.125 mm
Oil ring
  Ring width. . . . . 2.0 mm
  Ring thickness . . . . 1.5 mm
  Side-rail end gap (installed) . . . . 0.10 to 0.35 mm

Transmission

Gear ratios (no. of teeth)
  Primary reduction. . . . . 1.955 to 1 (86/44T)
  Final reduction . . . . 2.875 to 1 (46/16T)
  1st gear. . . . . 2.846 to 1 (37/13T)
  2nd gear. . . . . 1.947 to 1 (37/19T)
  3rd gear. . . . . 1.555 to 1 (28/18T)
  4th gear. . . . . 1.333 to 1 (32/24T)
  5th gear. . . . . 1.190 to 1 (25/21T)
  6th gear. . . . . 1.083 to 1 (26/24T)
Shaft runout (max) . . . . 0.02 mm

Gearchange mechanism

Gearchange linkage rod installed length . . . . 290 mm
Selector fork shaft runout (max). . . . . 0.05 mm

Torque wrench settings

Alternator cover bolts. . . . . 10 Nm
Cam chain tensioner cap bolt . . . . 7 Nm
Cam chain tensioner mounting bolts . . . . 12 Nm
Camshaft holder bolts . . . . 10 Nm
Camshaft sprocket bolts . . . . 20 Nm
Clutch centre nut . . . . 90 Nm
Clutch cover bolts . . . . 12 Nm
Clutch pressure plate bolts . . . . 8 Nm
Connecting rod cap nuts
  Initial setting . . . . 15 Nm
  Final setting (see Section 21) . . . . + 150°
Connecting rod cap bolts
  Initial setting . . . . 15 Nm
  Final setting (see Section 21) . . . . + 120°
Crankcase bolts (see Section 19)
  8 mm bolts
    Nos. 1 to 10
      1st stage. . . . . 12 Nm
      2nd stage . . . . 25 Nm
      3rd stage. . . . . 27 Nm
    Nos. 11 and 12 . . . . 24 Nm
  6 mm bolts
    Nos. 13 and 14 . . . . 14 Nm
    Nos. 15 to 27 . . . . 12 Nm

Torque wrench settings (continued)

Cylinder head bolts
  10 mm bolts
    1st stage . . . . 19 Nm
    2nd stage . . . . 50 Nm
  6 mm bolts . . . . 12 Nm
Engine mounting bolts/nuts . . . . 55 Nm
Front sprocket cover bolts . . . . 10 Nm
Gearchange shaft centralising spring locating pin . . . . 22 Nm
Gearchange linkage arm pinch bolt . . . . 10 Nm
Oil baffle plate bolts . . . . 12 Nm
Oil cooler bolt . . . . 63 Nm
Oil filter fitting bolt . . . . 70 Nm
Oil level sensor bolts . . . . 10 Nm
Oil gallery bolt . . . . 8 Nm
Oil pipe (U-shaped) bolts . . . . 12 Nm
Oil pump drive chain guide bolts . . . . 12 Nm
Oil pump housing bolts . . . . 12 Nm
Oil pump mounting bolts . . . . 12 Nm
Oil sump bolts . . . . 12 Nm
Selector drum retaining plate bolts . . . . 10 Nm
Starter clutch bolts . . . . 32 Nm
Timing rotor bolt . . . . 35 Nm
Timing rotor cover bolts . . . . 12 Nm
Transmission input shaft bearing housing Torx screws . . . . 12 Nm
Valve cover bolts . . . . 12 Nm

1 General information

The engine is a liquid-cooled in-line four, with four valves per cylinder. The valves are operated by double overhead camshafts which are chain driven off the right-hand end of the crankshaft. The engine assembly is constructed from aluminium alloy. The crankcase is divided horizontally.

The crankcase incorporates a wet sump, pressure-fed lubrication system which uses a chain-driven, dual-rotor oil pump, an oil filter, a relief valve and an oil level switch. The pump is chain-driven from the back of the clutch housing. The oil is circulated through a cooler which is located on the front of the crankcases.

The alternator is on the left-hand end of the crankshaft, and the starter clutch is on the back of the alternator.

Power from the crankshaft is routed to the transmission via the clutch. The clutch is of the wet, multi-plate type and is gear-driven off the crankshaft. The transmission is a six-speed constant-mesh unit. Final drive to the rear wheel is by chain and sprockets.

Read the *Safety first!* section of this manual carefully before starting work.

2 Component access

Operations possible with the engine in the frame

The components and assemblies listed below can be removed without having to remove the engine assembly from the frame. If however, a number of areas require attention at the same time, removal of the engine is recommended.
Valve cover
Camshafts
Cam chain
Cylinder head
Water pump and thermostat
Clutch and starter clutch
Gearchange mechanism
Alternator
Starter motor
Crankshaft position (CKP) sensor
Oil filter and cooler
Oil sump, oil strainer and oil pressure relief valve
Oil pump

Operations requiring engine removal

It is necessary to remove the engine from the frame to gain access to the following components.
Crankshaft and bearings
Connecting rods and bearings
Cylinder bores, pistons and piston rings
Transmission shafts
Selector drum and forks

3 Engine wear assessment

Warning: Be careful when working on the hot engine – the exhaust pipes, the engine and engine components can cause severe burns.

Cylinder compression test

Special tools: *A compression gauge with a 10 mm adapter* **(see illustration 3.6)** *is necessary for this procedure.*

1 Among other things, poor starting and engine performance may be caused by leaking valves, a leaking head gasket or worn pistons, rings and/or cylinder walls. A cylinder compression check will help pinpoint these conditions.
2 Before carrying out the test, check that the valve clearances are correct (see Chapter 1).
3 Run the engine until it reaches normal operating temperature, then turn the ignition OFF. Support the machine on its centrestand.
4 Follow the procedure in Chapter 1, Section 2, and remove the spark plugs.
5 Install the plugs back into their caps and arrange the plugs so that their metal bodies are earthed against the valve cover.
6 Working on the first cylinder to be tested, thread the adapter into the spark plug hole then install the compression gauge **(see illustration)**. Yamaha provide a gauge (part

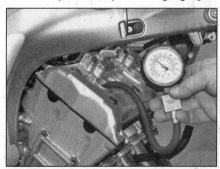

3.6 Connect the compression gauge as described

no. 90890-03081 in Europe, YU-33223 in the US) and gauge adapter (part no. 90890-04136) for this purpose.

7 Open the throttle fully and crank the engine over on the starter motor until the gauge reading stabilises after a few revolutions the pressure should build up to a maximum figure and then remain stable. Make a note of the pressure reading and then repeat the procedure on the other cylinders. Turn the ignition OFF when the test has been completed.

8 Compare the results with the specifications at the beginning of this Chapter (see *Cylinder bores*). If they are all within the specified range and relatively equal, the engine is in good condition.

9 If there is a marked difference between the readings, or if the readings are lower than specified, it is likely components in the engine top-end are worn. Pour a small quantity of clean engine oil through the spark plug hole of the cylinder being checked, then test for compression again. An increase in pressure indicates worn or broken piston rings. No change in the pressure indicates a problem with the valves or cylinder head gasket.

10 Readings that are higher than specified are unlikely, but if found indicate excessive carbon build-up in the combustion chamber and on the top of the piston. If this is the case, remove the cylinder head and clean the carbon deposits off.

11 When the test is complete, follow the procedure in Chapter and install the spark plugs.

Engine oil pressure check

Special tools: *An oil pressure gauge with a 16 mm threaded adapter* **(see illustration 3.15)** *is necessary for this procedure.*

12 If there is any doubt about the performance of the engine lubrication system an oil pressure check must be carried out. The check provides useful information about the state of wear of the engine. **Note:** *This engine is fitted with an oil level sensor and warning light. The function of the circuit is described in Chapter 8.*

13 Check the engine oil level and top up if necessary (see *Pre-ride checks*).

14 Run the engine until it reaches normal operating temperature, then turn the ignition OFF. Support the machine on its centrestand.

15 Place a drain tray under the alternator cover. Unscrew the oil gallery bolt in the crankcase below the alternator cover, then quickly screw the adapter into the threads. Connect the pressure gauge to the adapter **(see illustration)**. Yamaha provide a gauge (part no. 90890-03153 in Europe, YU-03153 in the US) and gauge adapter (part no. 90890-03139) for this purpose.

⚠️ **Warning:** *Take great care not to burn your hand on the hot engine unit, exhaust pipe or with engine oil when accessing the gauge take-off point on the crankcase. Do not allow*

exhaust gases to build up in the work area; either perform the check outside or use an exhaust gas extraction system.

16 Start the engine and increase the engine speed to 6600 rpm whilst watching the pressure gauge reading. The oil pressure should be similar to that given in the specifications at the beginning of this Chapter.

17 If the pressure is significantly lower than the standard, either the pressure relief valve is stuck open, the oil pump is faulty, the oil strainer or filter is blocked, or there is considerable engine wear. Begin diagnosis by checking the oil filter, strainer and relief valve, then the oil pump (see Sections 17 and 18). If those items check out okay, the engine bearing oil clearances are likely to be excessive and the engine needs to be overhauled.

18 If the pressure is too high, either an oil passage is clogged, the relief valve is stuck closed or the wrong grade of oil is being used.

19 Stop the engine.

20 Fit a new O-ring onto the oil gallery bolt and lubricate it with clean engine oil.

21 Unscrew the gauge and adapter from the crankcase, then install the oil gallery bolt and tighten it to the specified torque setting. Check the engine oil level (see *Pre-ride checks*).

22 Refer to the appropriate Sections within this Chapter and rectify any problems before running the engine again.

4 Engine removal and installation 🔧

Caution: The engine is very heavy. Engine removal and installation should be carried out with the aid of at least one assistant. Personal injury or damage could occur if the engine falls or is dropped. An hydraulic or mechanical floor jack should be used to support and lower or raise the engine, if possible.

Removal

Note: *If you intend to remove the alternator, timing rotor or clutch with the engine removed from the frame, it is best to slacken the*

3.15 Using a suitable pressure gauge to check engine oil pressure

alternator rotor bolt, timing rotor bolt and clutch nut while the engine is still in the frame – they are tight and the engine needs to be held securely while they are undone. Refer to Chapter 8 for the alternator, Section 9 for the timing rotor and Section 13 for the clutch.

1 Support the motorcycle securely in an upright position using the centrestand. Work can be made easier by raising the machine to a suitable working height on an hydraulic ramp or a suitable platform. Make sure the motorcycle is secure and will not topple over (see Section 1 of *Tools and Workshop Tips* in the *Reference* section). When disconnecting any wiring, cables and hoses, it is advisable to mark or tag them as a reminder of where they connect.

2 Remove the seat and, where fitted, remove the fairing (see Chapter 7).

3 Remove the fuel tank and the air filter housing (see Chapter 4). Remove the battery and the battery housing (see Chapter 8).

4 If the engine is dirty, particularly around its mountings, wash it thoroughly before starting any major dismantling work. This will make work much easier and rule out the possibility of dirt falling inside.

5 Drain the engine oil and the coolant (see Chapter 1).

6 Disconnect the coolant hoses from the radiator and remove the radiator (see Chapter 3). On machines fitted with ABS, undo the bolt securing the brake pipes to the left-hand radiator bracket before removing the radiator **(see illustrations)**.

4.6a ABS pipe assembly is secured to radiator bracket through this union (arrowed)

4.6b Hold the union to prevent it twisting while undoing the mounting bolt

4.6c Displace the ABS pipe assembly to access the radiator top mounting bolt (arrowed)

4.7a Note the location of the heat shield . . .

4.7b . . . then lift the shield out

7 Note the routing of all cables and wiring over and around the heat shield, then lift the shield out **(see illustration)**. Note which way round the shield is fitted **(see illustration)**.
8 Remove the ignition coils, then remove the AIS control valve along with the hoses (see Chapter 4).
9 Remove the throttle body assembly (see

Chapter 4). Plug the intake manifolds with clean rag.
10 Detach the inner clutch cable from the release mechanism arm and pull the cable out of the bracket on the top of the clutch cover (see Section 12).
11 Pull back the boot on the wiring at the back of the engine unit. Disconnect the connectors for the alternator, speed sensor,

sidestand switch and oil level sensor **(see illustrations)**. Disconnect the neutral switch wiring connector on the right-hand side of the frame **(see illustration)**. Secure the wiring clear of the engine unit.
12 Remove the exhaust system (see Chapter 4).
13 Detach the coolant hoses to the thermostat housing on the rear of the cylinder

4.11a Disconnect the alternator wiring connector . . .

4.11b . . . the speed sensor wiring connector . . .

4.11c . . . the sidestand switch wiring connector . . .

4.11d . . . and the oil level warning switch wiring connector

4.11e Disconnect the neutral switch wiring connector

4.13a Release the clip (A) securing the hose to the thermostat housing (B) . . .

4.13b . . . and pull the hose off

4.13c Disconnect the pump breather hose . . .

head and from the water pump cover **(see illustrations)**. If required, mark the hoses as an aid to installation. Remove the coolant reservoir and the radiator mounting bracket on the front of the engine, noting how it fits (see Chapter 3).

14 Peel back the boot on the starter motor terminal, then unscrew the starter motor terminal nut and detach the lead **(see illustration)**.

15 Unscrew the bolt securing the crankcase earth (ground) lead and detach the lead **(see**

illustration). Secure the lead clear of the engine.

16 Trace the crankshaft position sensor wiring from the timing rotor cover on the right-hand side of the engine and disconnect it at the connector **(see illustration)**. Secure the wiring so that it does not impede engine removal.

17 Make sure the transmission is in neutral. Loosen the gearchange linkage rod locknuts, then unscrew the rod and separate it from the lever and the arm (see Section 15). Withdraw the rod from the frame.

18 Remove the front sprocket and disengage the chain from the gearbox output shaft (see Chapter 6).

19 On machines fitted with ABS, undo the bolt securing the brake pipes to the bracket on the gearchange mechanism cover **(see illustrations)**.

4.13d . . . and the feed hose from the radiator

4.14 Detach the lead from the starter motor terminal (arrowed)

20 At this point, position an hydraulic or mechanical jack under the engine with a block of wood between the jack head and crankcase **(see illustration)**. Make sure the jack is centrally positioned so the engine will not topple in any direction when the last mounting bolt is removed and the engine is supported only by the jack. Take the weight of the engine on the jack. It is also advisable to place a block of wood between the rear wheel and the ground in case the bike tilts back onto the rear wheel when the engine is removed.

21 Check around the engine and frame to make sure that all the necessary wiring, cables and hoses have been disconnected, and that any that remain connected to the engine are

4.15 Unscrew the bolt securing the crankcase earth lead (arrowed)

4.19a Counter-hold the nut (arrowed) . . .

4.16 Disconnect the crankshaft position sensor wiring connector

4.19b . . . and undo the bolt securing the ABS system pipes

4.20 Support the engine using a jack

4.22 Unscrew the right-hand front mounting bolt

4.23a Unscrew the two left-hand front mounting bolts . . .

4.23b . . . noting the location of the frame protector assembly

not retained by any clips, guides or brackets on the frame. When removing the engine mounting bolts note which fits where as there are different lengths and sizes.

22 Unscrew and remove the single front engine mounting bolt and washer on the right-hand side **(see illustration)**. Where fitted, note the location of the frame protector and spacer assembly **(see illustration 4.23b)**.

23 Unscrew and remove the two front mounting bolts on the left-hand side, noting the location of the frame protector and spacer assembly, where fitted **(see illustrations)**.

24 Unscrew the nuts from the right-hand end of the upper and lower rear mounting bolts, but do not withdraw the bolts **(see illustrations)**. **Note:** *The nuts are of the self-locking type – discard them and fit new nuts on reassembly.* Make sure the engine is properly supported on the jack, and have an assistant support it as well, then withdraw the mounting bolts **(see illustration)**.

25 Carefully lower the engine and bring it forward, then manoeuvre it out of the frame from the right-hand side.

Installation

26 Installation is the reverse of removal, noting the following points:

- With the aid of an assistant, place the engine unit onto the jack and block of wood and carefully raise it into position so that the mounting bolt holes align. Make sure no wires, cables or hoses become trapped between the engine and the frame.

- Lubricate the threads of the upper and lower rear mounting bolts with engine oil and slide them into place **(see illustration 4.24c)**. Install the new self-locking nuts finger-tight.

- Install the front mounting bolt on the right-hand side, then install the two front mounting bolts on the left-hand side **(see illustrations 4.22, 23a and 23b)**. The bolts should only be finger-tight at this stage. Don't forget to fit the frame protectors as applicable.

- Counter-hold the lower rear mounting bolt and tighten the nut to the torque setting specified at the beginning of this Chapter, then tighten the nut on the upper rear mounting bolt to the specified torque.

- Tighten the front mounting bolts on the left-hand side to the specified torque, then tighten the mounting bolt on the right-hand side.

- Make sure all wires, cables and hoses are correctly routed and connected, and secured by any clips or ties.

- Refill the engine with oil and coolant to the correct levels (see Chapter 1 and *Pre-ride checks*).

- Check the throttle and clutch cable freeplay (see Chapter 1).

- Adjust the drive chain tension (see Chapter 1).

- Tighten all nuts and bolts to the specified torque settings where given.

- Start the engine and check that there are no oil or coolant leaks.

- Adjust the engine idle speed (see Chapter 1).

5 Engine overhaul general information

1 Before beginning the engine overhaul, read through the related procedures to familiarise yourself with the scope and requirements of the job. Overhauling an engine is not all that difficult, but it is time consuming. Check on the availability of parts and make sure that any necessary special tools are obtained in advance.

2 Most work can be done with a decent set of typical workshop hand tools, although a number of precision measuring tools are required for inspecting parts to determine if they are worn.

3 To ensure maximum life and minimum trouble from a rebuilt engine, everything must be assembled with care in a spotlessly clean environment, using the correct lubricant where directed.

Disassembly

4 Before disassembling the engine, thoroughly clean and degrease its external surfaces. This will prevent contamination of the engine internals, and will also make the job a lot easier and cleaner. A high flash-point solvent, such as paraffin (kerosene) can be used, or better still, a proprietary engine degreaser such as Gunk. Use old paintbrushes and toothbrushes to work the solvent into the various recesses of the casings. Take care to exclude solvent or water from the electrical components and intake and exhaust ports.

4.24a Unscrew nut from the upper (arrowed) . . .

4.24b . . . and lower (arrowed) rear mounting bolts . . .

4.24c . . . then withdraw the bolts (arrowed)

6.3a Unscrew the bolts (arrowed) . . .

6.3b . . . noting the location of the sealing washers . . .

6.3c . . . then lift the cover off

 Warning: The use of petrol (gasoline) as a cleaning agent should be avoided because of the risk of fire.

5 When clean and dry, position the engine on the workbench, leaving suitable clear area for working. Gather a selection of small containers, plastic bags and some labels so that parts can be grouped together in an easily identifiable manner. Also get some paper and a pen so that notes can be taken. You will also need a supply of clean rag, which should be as absorbent as possible.

6 Before commencing work, read through the appropriate section so that some idea of the necessary procedure can be gained. When removing components note that great force is seldom required, unless specified (checking the specified torque setting of the particular bolt being removed will indicate how tight it is, and therefore how much force should be needed). In many cases, a component's reluctance to be removed is indicative of an incorrect approach or removal method; if in any doubt, re-check with the text.

7 When disassembling the engine, keep 'mated' parts together (including gears, pistons, connecting rods, valves, etc, that have been in contact with each other during engine operation). These 'mated' parts must be reused or replaced as an assembly.

8 A complete engine disassembly should be done in the following general order with reference to the appropriate Sections (or Chapters, where indicated).

Remove the valve cover
Remove the cam chain tensioner
Remove the camshafts
Remove the cylinder head
Remove the clutch
Remove the alternator and starter clutch
Remove the starter motor (see Chapter 8)
Remove the gearchange mechanism
Remove the water pump (see Chapter 3)
Remove the oil cooler
Remove the oil sump
Remove the oil pump
Separate the crankcase halves
Remove the crankshaft
Remove the connecting rods and pistons
Remove the transmission output shaft
Remove the selector drum and forks
Remove the transmission input shaft

Reassembly

9 Reassembly is accomplished by reversing the general disassembly sequence.

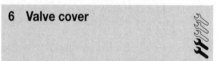

6 Valve cover

Note: *This procedure can be carried out with the engine in the frame. If the engine has been removed, ignore the steps that do not apply.*

Removal

1 Where fitted, remove the fairing (see Chapter 7). Remove the radiator (see Chapter 3).

2 Remove the air filter housing (see Chapter 4). Remove the battery housing (see Chapter 8). Displace or remove the ignition coils, then remove the AIS assembly (see Chapter 4).

3 Unscrew the bolts securing the valve cover and remove them, noting the location of the sealing washers **(see illustrations)**. Lift the cover off the cylinder head **(see illustration)**. If It is stuck, break the gasket seal by tapping gently around the edge with a soft-faced hammer or block of wood. Do not lever the cover off as this will damage the sealing surface.

4 Remove the gasket. Note the four AIS system air passage dowels and remove them if they are loose **(see illustration)**.

Installation

5 Examine the valve cover gasket rim and circular spark plug seals for signs of damage or deterioration and fit new ones if necessary. Similarly check the sealing washers on the cover bolts for cracks, hardening and deterioration and use new ones if necessary.

6 Clean the mating surfaces of the cylinder head and the valve cover with a suitable solvent.

7 Apply a smear of a suitable sealant to the valve cover and into the cut-outs in the cylinder head. Make sure the AIS system dowels are pushed fully into place **(see illustration 6.4)**. Fit the gasket onto the valve cover, making sure It locates correctly **(see illustrations)**. If the gasket has a bridge piece between the cam chain end and the adjacent

6.4 Take care not to lose the dowels (arrowed)

6.7a Fit the gasket into the groove in the rim of the cover . . .

6.7b . . . making sure it locates correctly (arrowed)

6.7c Cut the bridge piece (arrowed) away

6.8 Use new sealing washers with the bolts if necessary

7.1 Location of the cam chain tensioner (arrowed)

spark plug seal cut it away using a sharp knife **(see illustration)**.

8 Position the valve cover on the cylinder head, making sure the gasket stays in place. Fit the sealing washers with the cover bolts and tighten the bolts to the torque setting specified at the beginning of this Chapter **(see illustration)**.

9 Install the remaining components in the reverse order of removal.

7 Cam chain tensioner

Note: *This procedure can be carried out with the engine in the frame. If the engine has been removed, ignore the steps that do not apply.*

1 The cam chain tensioner is located on the rear, right-hand side of the cylinder head, forward of the clutch mechanism arm **(see illustration)**.

Removal

2 To access the cam chain tensioner, it may be necessary to displace the water pump breather hose as follows. First loosen the rotor cover bolt securing the hose guide **(see illustration)**. Position a suitable container below the pump, then release the clip and pull the hose off, being prepared to catch any residual coolant **(see illustration)**. Place a suitable blanking plug over the end of the breather hose union. Secure the hose clear of the tensioner body. Also, if necessary, follow the procedure in Section 12 and disconnect the lower end of the clutch cable from the clutch mechanism arm **(see illustration)**.

3 Unscrew the tensioner cap bolt and remove the bolt and the sealing washer **(see illustration)**. Note the 'UP' mark on the tensioner body.

4 Slacken the tensioner mounting bolts slightly **(see illustration)**. Insert a small flat-bladed screwdriver into the tensioner so that it engages the slotted plunger **(see illustration)**. Turn the screwdriver clockwise until the plunger is fully retracted and hold it in this position while unscrewing the tensioner mounting bolts and removing the tensioner.

5 Release the screwdriver. The plunger will spring back out once the screwdriver is removed, but can be easily reset on installation.

6 Discard the gasket, as a new one must be used on reassembly. Do not dismantle the tensioner.

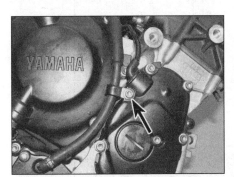

7.2a Free the hose from its guide (arrowed)

7.2b Detach the breather hose from the union on the water pump

7.2c Detach the clutch cable from the mechanism arm

7.3 Unscrew the cap bolt (arrowed) and remove the washer

7.4a Slacken the mounting bolts (arrowed) slightly . . .

7.4b . . . then insert the screwdriver and retract the plunger and unscrew the mounting bolts

7.7 Check the action of the plunger as described

7.9 Fit a new gasket onto the tensioner . . .

7.10 . . . then install the tensioner, all the time holding the screwdriver to keep the plunger retracted

Inspection

7 Apply hand pressure to the end of the tensioner plunger and wind it into the tensioner body by turning the screwdriver **(see illustration)**. Hold the plunger under pressure and remove the screwdriver, then slowly release the plunger. Check that the plunger

moves smoothly and springs out freely when released.

8 If the tensioner is worn or damaged, or if the plunger does not run smoothly in the body, the tensioner must be replaced with a new one; individual components are not available.

Installation

9 Ensure the tensioner and cylinder head surfaces are clean and dry. Lightly smear the new gasket with grease. Insert a small flat-bladed screwdriver into the tensioner so that it engages the slotted plunger, then turn it clockwise until the plunger is fully retracted **(see illustration 7.7)**. Fit the gasket onto the tensioner **(see illustration)**. Fit the bolts into their holes in the tensioner.

10 Hold the screwdriver so the plunger remains retracted and fit the tensioner into the cylinder head with the 'UP' mark facing up **(see illustration 7.3)**, and tighten its bolts to the torque setting specified at the beginning of this Chapter **(see illustration)**.

11 Release the tension on the screwdriver and remove it; the plunger will spring out

(which you should hear) and tension the chain. Install the tensioner cap bolt with a new sealing washer and tighten it to the specified torque **(see illustration)**.

12 Install the remaining components in the reverse order of removal. Don't forget to check the coolant level in the radiator (see Chapter 3).

8 Camshafts and followers

Note: *This procedure can be carried out with the engine in the frame. If the engine has been removed, ignore the steps that do not apply.*

Removal

1 Remove the valve cover (see Section 6). Remove the spark plugs (see Chapter 1). Place rags in the spark plug holes and the cam chain tunnel to prevent anything dropping into the engine.

2 Note the crankshaft position sensor wiring where it leaves the timing rotor cover **(see illustration)**. Disconnect the wiring at the

7.11 Fit the cap bolt using a new sealing washer

8.2 Crankshaft position sensor wiring leaves the cover at (A). Note the hose guide (B)

8.3a Undo the cover bolts (arrowed)

8.3b Note the location of the dowels (arrowed)

connector (see illustration 4.16). Feed the wiring back to the cover.

3 Place a drain tray under the timing rotor cover and unscrew the cover bolts (see illustration). Note the guide for the coolant hose (see illustration 8.2). Ease the cover off – discard the gasket, as a new one must be used and remove the dowels from either the crankcase or the cover if they are loose (see illustration).

4 The engine must now be turned to position the No. 1 (left hand) cylinder at TDC (top dead centre) on the compression stroke. Using a spanner on the ignition rotor bolt, turn the engine clockwise until the 'T' mark on the ignition rotor faces to the rear and aligns with the crankcase mating surfaces (see illustrations). The camshaft lobes for the No. 1 cylinder should face away from each other (see illustrations); if the cam lobes are facing towards each other, rotate the engine clockwise 360° (one full turn) so that the 'T' mark again faces to the rear and aligns with the crankcase mating surfaces. The camshaft lobes should now be facing away from each

8.4a Turn the engine clockwise using the rotor bolt . . .

8.4b . . . to align the T mark with the rear facing crankcase mating surfaces

other and the No. 1 cylinder will be at TDC (top dead centre) on the compression stroke.

5 Before disturbing the camshafts, ensure that the timing marks on the camshaft sprockets face away from each other and align with the cylinder head mating surface (see illustration). If you are in any doubt as to the alignment of the markings, or if they are not visible, make your own alignment marks

between all components, and also between a tooth on each sprocket (including the timing sprocket) and its corresponding link on the chain, before disturbing them. These markings ensure that the valve timing can be correctly set up on assembly. As it is easy to be a tooth out on installation, marking between a tooth on each sprocket and its link in the chain is especially useful.

8.4c The camshaft lobes should face away from each other as shown

8.5 Ensure that the camshaft sprocket marks (arrowed) are as shown

8.7a There are three holders (arrowed) for each camshaft

8.7b Note the arrows pointing to the right-hand side of the engine, and the E1 marks for the two right-hand exhaust camshaft holders . . .

8.7c . . . and the E2 mark for the left-hand holder

8.8 Camshaft markings 'E' for exhaust and 'I' for intake

6 Remove the cam chain tensioner (see Section 7).

7 There are three camshaft holders for each camshaft **(see illustration)**. Each has an identity mark (I1 or I2 on the intake side and E1 or E2 on the exhaust side) and an arrow which points to the right-hand side of the engine **(see illustrations)**. Note the position

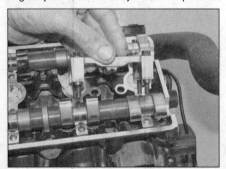

8.10 Unscrew the bolts as described and remove the holders

of each holder for correct installation later. If the marks are unclear make your own.

8 Note the camshaft identification markings on the centre of each shaft; the intake camshaft is marked 'I' and the exhaust camshaft is marked 'E' **(see illustration)**.

9 Working on one camshaft at a time and starting with the intake shaft if removing both, unscrew the camshaft holder bolts evenly and a little at a time in a criss-cross pattern, starting from the outside and working towards the centre. Slacken the bolts above any cam lobes that are pressing onto a valve last in the sequence so that the pressure from the open valves cannot cause the camshaft to bend.

Caution: If the bolts are loosened carelessly and the holders do not come away from the head squarely, a holder is likely to break. If this happens the complete cylinder head assembly must be replaced with a new one as the holders are matched to the head and cannot be obtained separately. Also, the camshaft could be damaged if the holder

bolts are not slackened evenly and the pressure from a depressed valve causes a shaft to bend.

10 Remove the bolts, then lift off the camshaft holders **(see illustration)**. Retrieve the dowels from either the holder or the cylinder head if they are loose.

11 Disengage the chain from the camshaft sprocket and lift the camshaft out of the head **(see illustrations 8.35a and 8.34a)**. With both camshafts removed secure the cam chain with a length of wire to prevent it dropping into the crankcase, and avoid rotating the crankshaft in case the chain jams between the timing sprocket and the case.

12 If required remove the cam chain front guide blade, the tensioner blade and the cam chain (see Section 9).

13 If the followers and shims are being removed from the cylinder head, obtain a container which is divided into sixteen compartments, and label each compartment with the location of its corresponding valve

8.13a Carefully lift out the follower using your fingers, grips, a lapping tool or a magnet . . .

8.13b . . . and retrieve the shim from inside it . . .

8.13c . . . or from the top of the valve

in the cylinder head. If a container is not available, use labelled plastic bags (egg cartons also work very well). Remove the cam follower of the valve in question, then retrieve the shim from the inside of the follower **(see illustrations)**. If it is not in the follower, pick it out of the top of the valve using either a magnet, a small screwdriver with a dab of grease on it (the shim will stick to the grease), or a screwdriver and a pair of pliers **(see illustration)**. Do not allow the shim to fall into the engine.

Inspection

14 Inspect the bearing surfaces of the cylinder head and camshaft holder and the corresponding journals on the camshaft **(see illustration)**. Look for score marks, deep scratches and evidence of spalling (a pitted appearance). If damage is noted or wear is excessive, the relevant parts must be renewed. The cylinder head and holder must be replaced as a new matched set –individual parts are not available.

15 Check the camshaft lobes for heat discoloration (blue appearance), score marks, chipped areas, flat spots and spalling **(see illustration)**. Measure the height of each lobe with a micrometer **(see illustration)** and compare the results to the minimum lobe height listed in this Chapter's Specifications. If damage is noted or wear is excessive, the camshaft must be replaced with a new one. Also check the condition of the cam followers.

16 Check the amount of camshaft runout by supporting each end of the camshaft on V-blocks, and measuring any runout at the journals using a dial gauge. If the runout exceeds the specified limit the camshaft must be replaced with a new one.

17 The camshaft journal oil clearance should now be checked. There are two possible ways of doing this, either by direct measurement (see Steps 18 to 21) or by the use of a product known as Plastigauge (see Steps 22 to 27).

18 If the direct measurement method is to be used, make sure the camshaft holder dowels are fitted then install the holders in their correct location (see Step 7). Lubricate the threads of

8.14 Check all related bearing surfaces as described

the holder bolts with clean engine oil, then tighten the bolts evenly and a little at a time in a criss-cross pattern to the torque setting specified at the beginning of this Chapter. Using telescoping gauges and a micrometer (see *Tools and Workshop Tips*), measure the inside diameter of the holder journals.

19 Now measure the diameter of the corresponding camshaft journals with a micrometer **(see illustration)**. To determine the journal oil clearance, subtract the journal diameter from the holder diameter and compare the result to the clearance specified. If any clearance is greater than specified, it is an indication of wear on the camshaft, the holder, or both.

20 First check to see if the camshaft journals are worn below the service limit. If they are, a new camshaft must be fitted. However, since

8.15b Measure the height of the camshaft lobes with a micrometer

8.15a Check the camshaft lobes as described – damage as shown requires immediate attention

it is likely that the holder is also worn, ensure that the specified journal diameter for a new camshaft will restore the oil clearance to within specification before buying a new camshaft.

21 If the camshaft journals are good, or if fitting a new camshaft will not restore the oil clearance to within specification, the holders and cylinder head will have to be replaced as a new matched set.

22 If the Plastigauge method is to be used, clean the camshaft being checked (work on one at a time), the bearing surfaces in the cylinder head and camshaft holder with a suitable solvent and a clean, lint-free cloth, then lay the camshaft in place in the cylinder head, making sure the timing marks are correctly aligned (see Step 4 and 5).

23 Cut some strips of Plastigauge and lay one piece on each journal, parallel with the

8.19 Measure the journals with a micrometer

8.23 Lay a strip of Plastigauge across each bearing journal parallel with the centreline

8.25 Compare the width of the crushed Plastigauge with the scale printed on the container

8.29 Camshaft sprocket bolts (arrowed)

camshaft centreline (see illustration). Make sure the camshaft holder dowels are fitted then install the holders in their correct location (see Step 7) (see illustrations 8.7a, b and c, 8.10 and 8.37). Lubricate the threads of the holder bolts with clean engine oil, then tighten the bolts evenly and a little at a time in a criss-cross pattern to the torque setting specified at the beginning of this Chapter. Work from the centre of the camshafts outwards (i.e. starting with the bolts that are above valves that will be opened when the camshafts are tightened down). Whilst tightening the bolts, make sure each holder is being pulled down squarely and is not binding on the dowels. Whilst doing this, don't let the camshaft rotate.

24 Now unscrew the bolts evenly and a little at a time in a criss-cross pattern, starting from the outside and working towards the centre, and carefully lift off the camshaft holders.

25 To determine the oil clearance, compare the crushed Plastigauge (at its widest point) on each journal to the scale printed on the Plastigauge container (see illustration). Compare the results to this Chapter's Specifications. Carefully clean away all traces of Plastigauge using a fingernail or other object which will not score the bearing surfaces. If any clearance is greater than specified, it is an indication of wear on the camshaft, the holder, or both.

26 First check to see if the camshaft journals are worn below the service limit by measuring them with a micrometer (see illustration 8.19). If they are, a new camshaft must be

fitted. However, since it is likely that the holder is also worn, ensure that the specified journal diameter for a new camshaft will restore the oil clearance to within specification before buying a new camshaft.

27 If the camshaft journals are good, or if fitting a new camshaft will not restore the oil clearance to within specification, the holders and cylinder head will have to be replaced as a matched set.

28 Inspect the cam chain guide blade, tensioner blade and cam chain (see Section 9).

29 Inspect the camshaft sprockets; if they show signs of wear, cracks or other damage, replace them and the cam chain with a new set. The camshaft sprockets are retained by two bolts (see illustration); unscrew the bolts and remove the sprockets, noting how they fit. Install the new sprockets on their respective camshafts with the marks facing out, and tighten the bolts to the specified torque setting.

30 Inspect the outer surfaces of the cam followers for evidence of wear, scoring or other damage. If the side of a follower is in poor condition, it is probable that the bore in which it works is also damaged. Check for clearance between the followers and their bores. Whilst no specifications are given, if slack is excessive, replace the followers with new ones. If the bores are seriously out-of-round or tapered, then replace the cylinder head and followers with new ones.

Installation

31 If removed, lubricate each valve shim

and follower with molybdenum disulphide oil (a 50/50 mixture of molybdenum disulphide grease and engine oil) and fit each shim into its recess on the top of the valve, with the size marking on the shim facing up (see illustration). Make sure the shim is correctly seated, then install the follower, making sure it fits squarely in its bore (see illustration 8.13a). Note: It is important that the shims and followers are returned to their original valves, otherwise the valve clearances will be inaccurate.

32 Make sure the camshaft journals and the bearing surfaces in the cylinder head are clean, then apply molybdenum disulphide oil to them and to the camshaft lobes.

33 If removed, install the cam chain, the tensioner blade and the front guide blade (see Section 9).

34 Ensure that the 'T' mark on the ignition rotor still aligns with the crankcase mating surfaces (see Step 4). Fit the exhaust camshaft, making sure the timing mark on the sprocket faces forward and aligns with the cylinder head mating surface (see illustrations). Fit the cam chain around the sprocket as you install the camshaft, pulling up on the chain to remove all slack in the front run between the crankshaft and the camshaft. If alignment marks were made prior to disassembly (see Step 5), check that the marks on the cam chain and sprocket align.

35 Now fit the intake camshaft, making sure the timing mark on the sprocket faces to the rear and aligns with the cylinder head mating

8.31 Fit each shim into its recess

8.34a Install the exhaust camshaft as described . . .

8.34b . . . and fit the chain round the sprocket

8.35a Install the intake camshaft as described . . .

8.35b . . . and fit the chain round the sprocket

8.37 Install the holders making sure the dowels and rim locate correctly (arrowed)

surface **(see illustrations)**. Fit the cam chain around the sprocket, aligning the marks (if made) between sprocket and chain. When fitting the chain, pull it tight to make sure there is no slack between the two camshaft sprockets; any slack in the chain must lie in the rear run, so that it is taken up by the tensioner.

36 Fit the camshaft holder dowels into the holders or cylinder head if removed. Make sure the bearing surfaces in the holders are clean, then lubricate them with molybdenum disulphide oil.

37 Lubricate the threads of the holder bolts with clean engine oil and fit them into the holders. Install the holders in their correct location (see Step 7). Ensure that the holders locate correctly over the rims of the locating bosses on the camshafts **(see illustration)**. Tighten the bolts evenly and a little at a time in a criss-cross pattern to the torque setting specified at the beginning of this Chapter. Work from the centre of the holder outwards (i.e.

starting with the bolts that are above valves that will be opened when the camshafts are tightened down). Whilst tightening the bolts, make sure each holder is being pulled down squarely and is not binding on the dowels.

Caution: The camshaft holder is likely to break if it is not tightened down evenly and squarely and the camshaft is likely to bend if it is tightened down onto the closed valves before the open ones.

38 Using a piece of wooden dowel, press on the back of the cam chain tensioner blade via the tensioner bore in the crankcase to take up any slack in the cam chain. Check that all the timing marks are still in **exact** alignment as described in Steps 4 and 5. If it is necessary to turn the engine slightly to align the marks with the engine mating surfaces, keep the wooden dowel pressed onto the tensioner blade as without the tensioner in place, the chain may slip on the sprockets. Note that it is easy to be slightly out (by one tooth on a sprocket) without the marks appearing drastically out of alignment.

39 If the camshaft marks are out, release the tension on the chain and remove the cam chain front guide, slip the chain around the relevant sprocket to correct the alignment, install the guide and recheck the timing marks.

Caution: If the marks are not aligned exactly as described, the valve timing will be incorrect and the valves may strike the pistons, causing extensive damage to the engine.

40 With everything correctly aligned, install the cam chain tensioner (see Section 7). Turn the engine clockwise through two full turns and check again that all the timing marks still align (see Steps 4 and 5).

41 Check the valve clearances and adjust them if necessary (see Chapter 1).

42 Ensure the dowels for the timing rotor cover are in place and install the cover using a new gasket **(see illustration 8.3b)**. Install the guide for the coolant hose and tighten the cover bolts to the torque setting specified at the beginning of this Chapter **(see illustrations 8.3a and 2)**.

43 Install the valve cover (see Section 6).

9 Cam chain, tensioner blade and guides

Note: *This procedure can be carried out with the engine in the frame. If the engine has been removed, ignore the steps that do not apply.*

Tensioner blade and guides

Removal

1 Remove the valve cover (see Section 6), the timing rotor cover (see Section 8) and the cam chain tensioner (see Section 7). The cam chain top guide is fixed in the valve cover and should not be removed **(see illustration)**.

2 To remove the cam chain front guide, lift it out of the front of the cam chain tunnel, noting which way round it fits and how it locates; it is a fairly tight fit but can be removed with the exhaust camshaft in place **(see illustration)**.

3 To remove the cam chain tensioner blade, first remove the intake camshaft (see Section 8). Withdraw the tensioner blade pivot pin, then draw the blade out of the top of the engine, noting which way round it fits **(see illustrations)**.

9.1 The top guide (arrowed) is fixed in the valve cover

9.2 Lift the front guide blade out of the engine

9.3a Withdraw the pivot pin . . .

9.3b . . . and draw the blade out of the engine

9.6a Make sure the blade locates correctly in its seat . . .

9.6b . . . and in the head (arrowed)

9.9a Remove the bolt and the washer . . .

9.9b . . . then remove the rotor, noting how its keyway (A) locates in the rotor slot (B)

Inspection

4 Check the sliding surfaces of the tensioner blade and guides for excessive wear, deep grooves, cracking and other obvious damage, and replace them with new ones if necessary.

Installation

5 Apply some clean engine oil to the tensioner blade pivot pin, then install the tensioner blade and insert the pin **(see illustrations 9.3b and a)**. Install the intake camshaft (see Section 8).
6 Slide the front guide into the front of the cam chain tunnel, making sure it locates correctly

onto its seat at its lower end and its lugs at the top locate in their cut-outs **(see illustrations)**.
7 Install the cam chain tensioner and the valve and timing rotor covers.

Cam chain

Removal

8 Remove the camshafts (see Section 8).
9 Unscrew the bolt securing the timing rotor **(see illustration)**. To prevent the crankshaft turning, either select a gear and apply the rear brake (if the engine is in the frame), or remove the alternator cover (see Chapter 8) and use

a rotor holding strap to counter-hold the crankshaft. Remove the bolt, washer and the rotor, noting how it fits **(see illustrations)**.
10 Lift the cam chain off the crankshaft sprocket and out of the engine. The sprocket is an integral part of the crankshaft.

Inspection

11 Except in cases of oil starvation, the cam chain wears very little. If the chain is stiff or the links are binding, or if the links are loose, discard the chain. A chain in poor condition will wear the sprocket teeth and ideally a chain and sprockets should be replaced as a set. The camshaft sprockets are easily renewed, but if the crankshaft sprocket is unfit for further use the crankshaft will have to be renewed.

Installation

12 Installation of the chain is the reverse of removal. Make sure the marked side of the ignition rotor faces out and that the key on the rotor locates in the keyway on the crankshaft. Tighten the rotor bolt to the torque setting specified at the beginning of this Chapter, counter-holding the crankshaft as on removal.

10 Cylinder head removal and installation

Note: *To remove the cylinder head with the engine in the frame you need an Allen bit that is 75 mm long to reach the rear 6 mm bolt on the right-hand end.*

Removal

1 Remove the valve cover (see Section 6), the camshafts (see Section 8) and cam chain (see Section 9).
2 Remove the forward engine front mounting bolt on the left-hand side **(see illustration)**.
3 The cylinder head is secured by twelve bolts **(see illustration)**. First unscrew and remove

10.2 Remove the mounting bolt (arrowed)

10.3a Cylinder head 6 mm bolts (A) and 10 mm bolts (B)

10.3b Unscrew the 6 mm bolts (arrowed) first

10.4 Lift the head up off the block and remove it

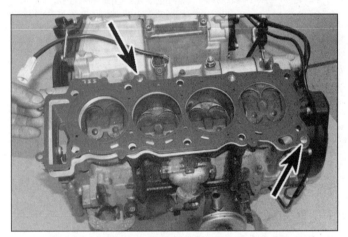

10.9 Fit the dowels (arrowed) then lay the new gasket on the block

10.11 Tightening sequence for the cylinder head 10 mm bolts

the 6 mm bolts on the right-hand end of the head (see illustration). Now unscrew the 10 mm bolts evenly and no more than a half turn at a time in the *reverse* of the tightening sequence (see illustration 10.11). When all the bolts are loose, remove them.

4 Pull the cylinder head up off the cylinder block (see illustration). If it is stuck, tap around the joint faces of the head with a soft-faced hammer or block of wood to free it. Do not attempt to free the head by inserting a lever between it and the cylinder block or you might damage the sealing surfaces.

5 If they are loose, remove the dowels from the cylinder block (see illustration 10.9). If they appear to be missing they are probably stuck in the underside of the cylinder head.

6 Check the cylinder head gasket and the mating surfaces on the cylinder head and block for signs of leaks from the cylinders, or the oil or coolant passages, which could indicate that the head is warped. Refer to Section 11 and check the flatness of the cylinder head.

7 Remove the old cylinder head gasket and discard it as a new one must be fitted on reassembly. Lay a clean cloth over the cylinders and pistons while the head is off to prevent any dirt getting in.

Installation

8 Clean all traces of old gasket material from the cylinder head and block with a suitable solvent. If you need to use a scraper, take care not to scratch or gouge the soft aluminium. Be careful not to let any of the gasket material fall into the crankcase, the cylinder bores or the oil or coolant passages. Check that the oil nozzle on the right-hand underside of the head is clear (see illustration 11.11).

9 Lubricate the cylinder bores with clean engine oil. If removed, fit the dowels into the crankcase, then lay the new head gasket in place, making sure it locates correctly over the dowels, and all the holes are correctly aligned (see illustration).

10 Carefully fit the cylinder head onto the crankcase, making sure it locates correctly onto the dowels (see illustration 10.4).

11 Lubricate the threads and seating surfaces of the 10 mm cylinder head bolts with clean engine oil. Install the bolts and tighten them finger-tight (see illustrations 10.3a). Now tighten the 10 mm bolts evenly and in two stages, to the torque settings specified at the beginning of this Chapter. Tighten all the bolts in the sequence shown to the first torque setting, then tighten then in the same sequence to the second torque setting (see illustration).

12 Install the 6 mm bolts and tighten them to the specified torque setting (see illustration 10.3b).

13 Install the remaining components in the reverse order of removal.

11 Cylinder head and valve overhaul

1 Because of the complex nature of this job and the special tools and equipment required, most owners leave servicing of the valves, valve seats and valve guides to a professional. However, you can make an initial assessment of whether the valves are seating correctly, and therefore sealing, by pouring a small amount of solvent into each of the valve ports. If the solvent leaks past any valve into the combustion chamber area the valve is not seating correctly and sealing.

2 With the correct tools (a valve spring compressor is essential – make sure it is

11.7a Compressing the valve springs using a valve spring compressor

11.7b Make sure the compressor is a good fit on the top . . .

11.7c . . . and the bottom of the valve

11.8a Remove the collets taking care not to drop them into the engine

11.8b If the valve stem (2) won't pull through the guide, deburr the area above the collet groove (1)

7 Compress the valve spring on the first valve with a spring compressor, making sure it is correctly located onto each end of the valve assembly **(see illustrations)**. On the underside of the head, make sure the plate on the compressor only contacts the valve and not the soft aluminium of the head; if the plate is too big for the valve, use a spacer between them **(see illustration)**. Do not compress the springs any more than is absolutely necessary.

8 Remove the collets, using either needle-nose pliers, tweezers, a magnet or a screwdriver with a dab of grease on it **(see illustration)**. Carefully release the valve spring compressor and remove the spring retainer, noting which way up it fits, the spring(s) and the valve **(see illustrations 11.30c, b and a)**. If the valve binds in the guide (won't pull through), push it back into the head and deburr the area around the collet groove with a very fine file or whetstone **(see illustration)**. **Note:** *There are two springs fitted with each intake valve and one with each exhaust valve. Note the difference in length between the exhaust and intake valve springs and do not mix them up* **(see illustration)**.

9 Pull the valve stem seal off the top of the valve guide with pliers and discard it (the old seals should never be reused) **(see illustration)**. Remove the spring seat, noting which way up it fits; using a magnet is the easiest way to lift the seat off the head **(see illustration 11.29a)**.

suitable for motorcycle work), you can also remove the valves and associated components from the cylinder head, clean them and check them for wear to assess the extent of the work needed, and, unless seat cutting or guide replacement is required, grind in the valves and reassemble them in the head.

3 A dealer service department or engine specialist can replace the guides and re-cut the valve seats.

4 After the valve service has been performed, be sure to clean it very thoroughly before installation on the engine to remove any metal particles or abrasive grit that may still be present from the valve service operations. Use compressed air, if available, to blow out all the holes and passages.

Disassembly

5 Before proceeding, arrange to label and store the valves along with their related components in such a way that they can be returned to their original locations without getting mixed up. Either use the same container as the valve shims and followers are stored in (see Section 8), or obtain a separate container which is divided into sixteen compartments, and label each compartment with the identity of the valve which will be stored in it. Alternatively, labelled plastic bags will do just as well.

6 Clean all traces of old gasket material from the cylinder head with a suitable solvent. If you need to use a scraper, take care not to scratch or gouge the soft aluminium.

11.8c Exhaust (A) and intake (B) valve springs differ in length. Springs are fitted with the closer-wound coils into the head

11.9 Pull the stem seal off with long nosed pliers

11.11 Blow compressed air through the oil nozzle (arrowed) to ensure it is clear

11.14 Checking the head for warpage with a straight-edge

11.15 Measure the valve seat width with a ruler (or for greater accuracy use a Vernier caliper)

10 Repeat the procedure for the remaining valves. Remember to keep the parts for each valve together and labelled so they can be reinstalled in the correct location.

11 Next, clean the cylinder head with solvent and dry it thoroughly. Compressed air will speed the drying process and ensure that all holes and recessed areas are clean. Check that the oil nozzle on the right-hand underside of the head is clear **(see illustration)**.

12 Clean all the valve springs, collets, retainers and spring seats with solvent and dry them thoroughly. Clean the parts from one valve at a time so that no mixing of parts between valves occurs. Scrape off any deposits that may have formed on the valves, then use a motorised wire brush to remove deposits from the valve heads and stems. Again, make sure the valves do not get mixed up.

Inspection

13 Inspect the head very carefully for cracks and other damage. If cracks are found, a new head will be required. Check the cam bearing surfaces for wear and evidence of seizure. Check the camshafts for wear as well (see Section 8).

14 Using a precision straight-edge and a feeler gauge, check the head gasket mating surface for warpage **(see illustration)**. Refer to *Tools and Workshop Tips* (Section 3) in the *Reference* section for details of how to use the straight-edge. If the head is warped beyond the limit specified at the beginning of this Chapter, consult your Yamaha dealer or take it to an engineer for rectification.

15 Examine the valve seats in the combustion chamber. If they are pitted, cracked or burned, the head will require work beyond the scope of the home mechanic. Measure the valve seat width and compare it to this Chapter's Specifications **(see illustration)**. If it exceeds the service limit, or if it varies around its circumference, consult your Yamaha dealer or take the head to an engineer for rectification.

16 Examine each valve face for cracks, pits and burned spots **(see illustration)**. **Note:** *Slight imperfections between the valve face and seat may be overcome by grinding the valve (see Steps 24 to 28).*

17 Rotate the valve and check for any obvious indication that it is bent. Using V-blocks and a dial gauge if available, measure the valve stem runout and compare the results to the specifications at the beginning of this Chapter **(see illustration)**. If the measurement exceeds the service limit specified, the valve must be replaced with a new one. Note that a slightly bent valve stem will prevent the valve from seating properly in the head.

18 Measure the various aspects of the valve head and compare them with the listed specifications **(see illustration)**. If the valve is worn it should be replaced with a new one.

19 Measure the valve stem diameter **(see illustration)**. Clean the valve guides to remove any carbon build-up, then measure the inside diameters of the guides (at both ends and the centre of the guide) with a small hole gauge and micrometer (see *Tools and Workshop Tips* (Section 3) in the *Reference* section). The guides are measured at the

11.16 Check the valve face (A), stem (B) and collet groove (C) for wear and damage

ends and at the centre to determine if they are worn in a bell-mouth pattern (more wear at the ends). Subtract the stem diameter from the valve guide diameter to obtain the valve stem-to-guide clearance. If the stem-to-guide clearance is greater than listed in this Chapter's Specifications, replace whichever

11.17 Measure valve stem runout with V-blocks and a dial gauge

11.18 Valve head measurement points

A Head diameter   B Face width   C Seat width   D Margin thickness

11.19 Measuring valve stem diameter with a micrometer

11.21 Measuring spring free length with a Vernier caliper

11.25 Apply small dabs of grinding compound to the valve face only

11.26a Rotate the valve grinding tool back and forth between the palms of your hands (arrowed)

components are worn beyond their specified limits with new ones. If the valve guide is within specifications, but is worn unevenly, it should be renewed.

20 Inspect the valve stem and collet groove area for scuffing and cracks (see illustration 11.16). Check the end of the stem for pitting and wear. The presence of any of the above conditions indicates the need for fitting new valves.

21 Check the end of each valve spring for wear. Measure the free length of each spring, making sure you identify each one correctly as to its location, and compare it to that listed in the specifications (see illustration). If any spring is shorter than specified it has sagged and must be replaced with a new one. Also place the spring upright on a flat surface and check it for bend by placing a ruler or

engineer's square against it. If the bend in any spring exceeds the specified limit, it must be replaced with a new one.

22 Check the spring retainers and collets for obvious wear and cracks. Any questionable parts should not be reused, as extensive damage will occur in the event of failure during engine operation.

23 If the inspection indicates that no overhaul work is required, the valve components can be reinstalled in the head.

Reassembly

24 Unless a valve service has been performed, before installing the valves in the head they should be ground in (lapped) to ensure a positive seal between the valves and seats. Note: Do not grind in the valves after the seats have been re-cut. The valve seat must be soft and unpolished for final seating to occur when

the engine is first run. This procedure requires coarse and fine valve grinding compound and a valve grinding tool (either hand-held or drill driven – note that some drill-driven tools specify using only a fine grinding compound). If a grinding tool is not available, a piece of rubber or plastic hose can be slipped over the valve stem (after the valve has been installed in the guide) and used to turn the valve.

25 Apply a small amount of coarse grinding compound to the valve face (see illustration). Smear some molybdenum disulphide oil (a 50/50 mixture of molybdenum disulphide grease and engine oil) to the valve stem, then slip the valve into the guide (see illustration 11.30a). Note: Make sure each valve is installed in its correct guide and be careful not to get any grinding compound on the valve stem.

26 Attach the grinding tool to the valve and rotate the tool between the palms of your hands. Use a back-and-forth motion (as though rubbing your hands together) rather than a circular motion (i.e. so that the valve rotates alternately clockwise and anti-clockwise rather than in one direction only) (see illustration). If a motorised tool is being used, take note of the correct drive speed for it – if your drill runs too fast and is not variable, use a hand tool instead. Lift the valve off the seat and turn it at regular intervals to distribute the grinding compound properly. Continue the grinding procedure until the valve face and seat contact area is of uniform width, and unbroken around the entire circumference (see illustrations).

27 Carefully remove the valve from the guide and wipe off all traces of grinding compound. Use solvent to clean the valve and wipe the seat area thoroughly with a solvent soaked cloth.

28 Repeat the procedure with fine valve grinding compound, then repeat the entire procedure for the remaining valves.

29 Working on one valve at a time, lay the spring seat in place in the cylinder head so that its shouldered side faces upwards (see illustration). Fit a new valve stem seal onto the guide and use an appropriate size deep socket to press the seal over the end of the valve guide until it is felt to clip into place (see illustration). Don't twist or cock the seal, or it will not seal properly against the valve stem. Also, don't remove it again or it will be damaged.

11.26b The valve face (arrowed) and seat should appear as a uniform, unbroken ring . . .

11.26c . . . and the seat (arrowed) should be the specified width all the way round

11.29a Install the valve spring seat

11.29b Press the new stem seal into place with a suitable deep socket

11.30a Lubricate the valve stem then install the valve

11.30b Install the valve spring(s) . . .

11.30c . . . and the spring retainer

11.31 A small dab of grease will help to keep the collets in place on the valve while the spring is released

11.33 Tap the valve stem gently to seat the collets in the groove

31 Apply a small amount of grease to the inside of the collets; this will help to help hold them in place when fitting them on the valve stem (see illustration). Compress the spring with the valve spring compressor and install the collets (see illustrations 11.7a, b and c and 11.8a). When compressing the spring, do so only as far as is necessary to slip the collets into place. Make certain that the collets are securely located in the collet groove and release the spring compressor.

32 Repeat the procedure for the remaining valves. Remember to keep the parts for each valve together and separate from the other valves so they can be reinstalled in their original locations.

33 Support the cylinder head on blocks so the valves can't contact the workbench top, then very gently tap the top of each valve stem to seat the collets in the groove (see illustration).

30 Coat the valve stem with molybdenum disulphide oil, then install it into its guide, rotating it slowly to avoid damaging the seal (see illustration). Check that the valve moves up and down freely in the guide. Next, install the spring(s)

(two springs on the intake valves), with the closer-wound coils facing down into the cylinder head (see illustration). Fit the spring retainer, with its shouldered side facing down so that it fits into the top of the spring (see illustration).

12 Clutch cable

Removal

1 Remove the fuel tank and air filter housing (see Chapter 4).
2 Release the trim clip securing the clutch cable support bracket and displace the bracket (see illustrations). Release the cable clip on the bracket and lift off the bracket (see illustrations).

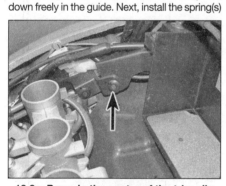

12.2a Press in the centre of the trim clip (arrowed) . . .

12.2b . . . with a small screwdriver . . .

12.2c . . . so that the clutch cable support bracket can be displaced

12.2d Release the cable clip . . .

12.2e . . . and remove the bracket

12.3a Turn the adjuster (arrowed) . . .

12.3b . . . to obtain freeplay in the inner cable (arrowed)

12.4a Bend back the tab on the cable retainer . . .

12.4b . . . and release the inner cable end (A). Slip the cable out of the bracket (B)

12.5a Screw the adjuster (A) into the bracket (B)

3 Slacken the adjuster locknut, then turn the adjuster to obtain freeplay in the inner cable (see illustrations).

4 Bend back the tab in the cable retainer on the end of the clutch release mechanism arm, then release the cable end from the retainer, noting how it fits (see illustrations). Slip the cable out of the bracket on the clutch cover.

5 Screw the adjuster at the handlebar end of the cable fully into the lever bracket (see illustration). Align the slot in the adjuster with that in the lever bracket, then pull the outer cable from the socket in the adjuster and release the inner cable end from the lever (see illustrations).

6 Release the ties securing the clutch cable to the left-hand radiator hose (see illustration). Remove the cable from the machine, noting its routing.

Installation

7 Installation is the reverse of removal. Apply grease to the cable ends and make sure the cable is correctly routed and clipped into place.

8 Adjust the clutch lever freeplay (see Chapter 1). With the cable installed, turn the adjuster on the lever bracket so that the slots are not aligned. Bend the retainer on the release mechanism arm to secure the cable end (see illustration 12.4a).

9 Check the clutch release mechanism for smooth operation and any signs of wear or damage. Remove it for cleaning and re-greasing if required (see Section 13).

10 Install the fuel tank and air filter housing (see Chapter 4).

12.5b Align the slots in the adjuster and the bracket and pull the cable out

12.5c Release the inner cable end from the lever

12.6 Clutch cable is secured to the coolant hose by ties (arrowed)

13.5a Unscrew the clutch cover bolts (arrowed) . . .

13.5b . . . noting the location of the cable bracket (arrowed)

13.7 Note how the pull-rod (A) engages with the actuating shaft (B)

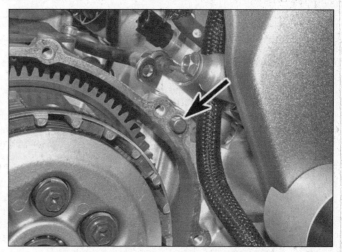

13.8a Note the location of the upper (arrowed) . . .

13 Clutch

Note: *This procedure can be carried out with the engine in the frame. If the engine has been removed, ignore the steps that do not apply.*
Special tool: *A clutch centre holding tool is useful, although not essential – see Step 12.*

Removal

1 To allow clearance for removing the clutch cover, unscrew the bolt on the timing rotor cover that retains the coolant hose guide and release the guide **(see illustration 8.2)**.
2 Position a suitable container below the water pump, then release the clip and pull the pump breather hose off, being prepared to catch any residual coolant **(see illustration 4.13c)**. Place a suitable blanking plug over the

end of the breather hose union. Secure the hose clear of the tensioner body.
3 Detach the clutch cable from the release mechanism arm (see Section 12).
4 Ensure that the engine casing below the clutch cover and around the oil dipstick is clean. Place a drain tray under the clutch cover.
5 Working evenly in a criss-cross pattern, unscrew the clutch cover bolts, noting the location of the clutch cable bracket **(see illustrations)**.
6 Remove the oil dipstick and plug the hole with a clean rag.
7 Remove the cover, being prepared to catch any residual oil. If the cover will not lift away easily, break the gasket seal by tapping gently around the edge with a soft-faced hammer or block of wood. Note how the teeth on the clutch pull-rod engage on the actuating shaft in the clutch cover **(see illustration)**.
8 Remove the cover gasket and discard it

as a new one must be fitted on reassembly. Note the position of the two locating dowels and remove them for safe-keeping if they are loose; they could be in either the cover or the crankcase **(see illustrations)**.
9 Working in a criss-cross pattern, gradually

13.8b . . . and lower (arrowed) locating dowels

13.9 Remove the clutch bolts and springs

13.10a Note the alignment marks (arrowed)

13.10b Remove the pull-rod from its bearing

slacken the clutch spring bolts until the spring pressure is released, counter-holding the clutch using a rag. Remove the bolts and springs (see illustration).

10 Remove the clutch pressure plate, noting the alignment marks on the pressure plate and the clutch centre (see illustration). Remove the pull-rod from the pressure plate, noting the bearing (see illustration).

11 Grasp the complete set of clutch plates and remove them as a pack. Unless the plates are being replaced with new ones, keep them in their original order. Note that the innermost plain plate is thicker than the rest; the inner and outer friction plates have a purple colour-code and different friction material segments to the rest which are colour-coded brown (see Step 37).

12 Bend back the tabs on the clutch centre nut lockwasher (see illustration). To remove the clutch centre nut, the transmission input shaft must be locked. This can be done in several ways. If the engine is in the frame, engage 1st gear and have an assistant hold the rear brake on hard with the rear tyre in firm contact with the ground. Alternatively, the Yamaha service tool Pt. No. 90890-04086 (European models) or YM-91042 (US models) or a similar commercially available tool, can be used to stop the clutch centre from turning while the nut is loosened. Protect the engine casing with a piece of wood if the clutch holding tool bears against it (see illustration).

13 With the transmission input shaft locked, unscrew the nut and remove the lockwasher, noting how it fits (see illustration 13.36b).

Discard the lockwasher, as a new one must be fitted on reassembly.

14 Slide the clutch centre and the thrust washer off the input shaft (see illustrations 13.36a and 13.35).

15 Note how the primary driven gear on the clutch housing engages with the primary drive gear on the crankshaft. Note also the position of the oil pump drive chain which engages on a sprocket on the back of the clutch housing (see illustration).

16 Ease out the bearing centre and needle bearing from between the clutch housing and the input shaft; this can be done using a magnet and by sliding the housing on the shaft to help push them along (see illustrations).

17 There is now enough clearance to pull the clutch housing out along the input shaft

13.12a Bend back the lockwasher tabs

13.12b Remove the clutch nut as described

13.15 Note the primary drive gear engagement (A) and the position of the oil pump drive chain (B)

13.16a Use a tool to dislodge the bearing centre from the clutch housing . . .

13.16b . . . then remove the bearing centre . . .

13.16c . . . and the needle roller cage

13.17a Withdraw the clutch housing to expose the oil pump drive chain

13.17b Rotate the crankshaft to obtain clearance from the connecting rod (A) and crankshaft web (B)

and expose the oil pump drive chain behind it **(see illustration)**. Disengage the chain from the drive sprocket and remove the clutch housing, the thrust washer and spacer. **Note:** *It may be necessary to rotate the crankshaft to obtain clearance between the primary driven gear and the connecting rod of No. 4 cylinder or the right-hand web on the crankshaft* **(see illustration)**. *To rotate the crankshaft, unscrew the inspection plug in the ignition rotor cover and turn the rotor bolt on the end of the crankshaft in a clockwise direction only.*

18 If required, unscrew the bolts that retain the oil pump drive chain guide to the crankcase and remove the guide **(see illustration)**.

Inspection

19 After an extended period of service the clutch friction plates will wear and promote clutch slip. Measure the thickness of each friction plate using a Vernier caliper **(see illustration)**. If any plate has worn to or beyond the service limit given in the Specifications at the beginning of this Chapter, the friction plates must be replaced with a new set. Also, if any of the plates smell burnt or are glazed, they must be replaced as a set.

20 The plain plates should not show any signs of excess heating (bluing). Check for warpage using a flat surface and feeler gauges **(see illustration)**. If any plate exceeds the maximum permissible amount of warpage, or shows signs of bluing, all the plain plates must be renewed as a set.

21 Measure the free length of each clutch spring **(see illustration)**. If any spring is below the service limit specified, renew all the springs as a set.

22 Inspect the clutch assembly for burrs and indentations on the edges of the protruding tangs of the friction plates and/or slots in the edge of the housing with which they engage. Similarly check for wear between the inner teeth of the plain plates and the slots in the clutch centre. Wear will cause clutch drag and slow disengagement during gear changes, as

the plates will snag when the pressure plate is lifted. With care, a small amount of wear can be corrected by dressing with a fine file, but if it is excessive the worn components should be replaced with new ones.

23 Inspect the needle roller bearing in conjunction with the internal bearing surface of the clutch housing and the external surface of the bearing centre. If there are any signs of wear, pitting or other damage the affected parts must be replaced with new ones.

24 Check the teeth of the primary driven gear on the clutch housing and the corresponding teeth of the primary drive gear on the end of the crankshaft. Replace the clutch housing

with a new one if any teeth are worn or chipped. The primary drive gear is an integral part of the crankshaft (see Section 24 for removal of the crankshaft).

25 Check the teeth of the oil pump drive sprocket on the back of the clutch housing. If any are worn or chipped, replace the housing with a new one and remove the oil pump and chain for inspection (see Section 18).

26 The clutch housing incorporates a cush-drive mechanism; check that the springs are not loose and that there is no backlash between the centre of the housing and the primary driven gear.

27 Check the pressure plate and its bearing

13.18 Remove the oil pump drive chain guide if required

13.19 Measuring clutch friction plate thickness

13.20 Checking the plain plates for warpage

13.21 Measure the free length of the clutch springs as shown

13.28a Remove the E-clip (arrowed) and washer securing the clutch actuating shaft

13.28b Note the position of the spring (A) and the alignment marks (B)

for signs of wear or damage and roughness. Check the pull-rod for signs of wear or damage. Replace any parts, as necessary, with new ones.

28 Check the clutch release mechanism shaft pinion and the pull-rod teeth for signs of wear and damage. Check that the shaft turns smoothly in the clutch cover. If necessary, remove the E-clip and washer securing the shaft and withdraw the shaft **(see illustration)**. Note the position of the return spring and the alignment marks on the clutch cover and release mechanism arm **(see illustration)**.

29 Check the condition of the shaft, oil seal and two bearings, and fit new parts if

necessary **(see illustration)**. If the bearings need to be removed, first remove the oil seal **(see illustrations)**, then heat the cover in very hot water to ease removal and drive the bearings out (see *Tools and Workshop Tips* (Sections 5 and 6) in the *Reference* section). Discard the oil seal as a new one must be fitted on reassembly.

30 If required, remove the E-clip and washer securing the arm on the end of the shaft. Note the position of the arm and return spring, then slide the arm off the shaft and remove the spring.

31 Clean all components and lubricate the seal and bearings with grease. Installation is

the reverse of removal. Before installing the arm on the shaft, fit the spring and ensure that the 'UP' mark on the arm is facing up when the shaft is installed in the cover.

Installation

32 Remove all traces of old gasket from the crankcase and clutch cover surfaces. If removed, install the oil pump chain guide, applying a suitable non-permanent thread locking compound to its bolts and tightening them to the torque setting specified at the beginning of this Chapter **(see illustration 13.18)**.

33 Slide the spacer and the thrust washer onto the transmission input shaft **(see illustration)**. Slide the clutch housing along the shaft to a position where the oil pump drive chain can be located onto the drive sprocket on the back of the clutch housing. Slowly rotate the housing and feed the chain onto the sprocket **(see illustration)**. Ensure that the chain is correctly routed between the guides on the inside of the crankcase.

34 Lubricate the needle roller bearing with clean engine oil. Support the clutch housing and engage the primary driven and drive gears, then slide the bearing and the bearing centre into place on the input shaft **(see illustrations 13.16c and 16b)**.

13.29a Examine the actuating shaft pinion (arrowed) and bearing surfaces

13.29b Lever the oil seal out . . .

13.29c . . . before removing the actuating shaft bearing

13.33a Install the spacer (A) and thrust washer (B)

13.33b Rotate the clutch housing to engage the oil pump drive chain

13.35 Install the thrust washer . . .

13.36a . . . and the clutch centre

13.36b Align the new lockwasher tabs with the flats on the clutch centre boss

35 Lubricate the thrust washer with clean engine oil and slide it onto the shaft **(see illustration)**.

36 Slide the clutch centre onto the shaft splines, then fit the new lockwasher. Note how two of the lockwasher tabs locate on flats on the clutch centre boss **(see illustrations)**. Install the clutch centre nut with the shouldered side on the inside, and tighten the nut to the torque setting specified at the beginning of this Chapter using the method employed on removal to lock the input shaft (see Step 12) **(see illustration)**. **Note:** *Check that the clutch centre rotates freely after tightening.* Bend up the tabs of the lockwasher to secure the nut **(see illustration 13.12a)**.

37 Coat each clutch plate with clean engine oil prior to installation. Build up the plates as follows: first fit the thick plain plate, then a purple-coded friction plate, then a standard plain plate, then a brown-coded friction plate **(see illustrations)**.

38 Continue to alternate plain plates and brown-coded friction plates until all are installed, then install the second purple-coded friction plate.

39 Lubricate the bearing in the pressure plate with clean engine oil. Fit the pull-rod into the back of the pressure plate **(see illustration)**.

40 Align the reference marks on the clutch pressure plate and the clutch centre and fit the pressure plate, making sure the castellations in its rim locate into the slots in the clutch centre **(see illustration 13.10a)**.

41 Install the clutch springs and bolts, then

13.36c Tighten the clutch nut to the specified torque and secure it with the lockwasher tabs

tighten the bolts evenly and a little at a time in a criss-cross sequence to the specified torque setting **(see illustration)**. Counter-hold the clutch housing to prevent it turning when

13.37a First install the thick plain plate . . .

tightening the spring bolts. Set the pull-rod so that its teeth point towards the rear and are angled up slightly.

42 If removed, insert the dowels in the

13.37b . . . then a purple-coded friction plate . . .

13.37c . . . then a standard plain plate . . .

13.37d . . . followed by a brown-coded friction plate

13.39 Fit the pull-rod into the back of the pressure plate

13.41 Tighten the bolts in a criss-cross sequence to the specified torque

13.42 Fit a new gasket onto the dowels

13.43 Pull-rod teeth should face rearwards

13.44 Release arm should turn rearwards as the cover is installed

crankcase and fit the new gasket onto them **(see illustration)**.
43 When installing the clutch cover, getting the release shaft to engage correctly with the pull-rod teeth can be tricky. First set the pull-rod teeth facing rearwards **(see illustration)**.
44 Set the release arm so that it is pointing to the front, then as the cover is installed and the teeth engage, the arm should turn back **(see illustration)**. With the cover fully installed, the alignment marks on the cover and the clutch arm should be in line when any backlash in the mechanism is taken up by light finger pressure

14.3a Note the wiring guides (arrowed) secured by the alternator cover bolts

(see illustration 13.28b). If the marks do not line-up, pull the cover off, reposition the clutch arm and refit the cover. Check that both ends of the return spring are correctly located.
45 Install the cover bolts and the clutch cable bracket and tighten the bolts evenly in a criss-cross sequence to the specified torque setting **(see illustration 13.5a and 5b)**.
46 Check the engine oil level (see *Pre-ride checks*) and install the dipstick.
47 Fit the clutch cable onto the bracket and release arm and adjust the cable as necessary (see Section 12).
48 Install the coolant hose and guide (see Steps 1 and 2). Check the coolant level in the radiator (see Chapter 3).

14 Starter clutch and gears

Note: *This procedure can be carried out with the engine in the frame. If the engine has been removed, ignore the steps which do not apply.*
1 Remove the fuel tank (see Chapter 4).
2 Pull back the boot on the wiring at the back of the engine unit. Trace the wiring from the top of the alternator cover on the left-hand side of the engine and disconnect it at the

white, three-pin connector **(see illustration 4.11a)**. Feed the wiring through to the alternator cover, noting its routing.
3 Place a drain tray under the alternator cover. Unscrew and remove the bolts securing the cover, noting the wiring guides **(see illustration)**. Remove the cover, being prepared to catch any residual oil. If the cover will not lift away easily, break the gasket seal by tapping gently around the edge with a soft-faced hammer or block of wood, or by levering carefully with a screwdriver on the tab as shown **(see illustration)** – do not try to lever between the cover/crankcases mating surfaces as they could be damaged. Discard the gasket as a new one must be used. Remove the dowels from either the cover or the crankcase if they are loose.

Check

4 The operation of the starter clutch can be checked while it is in place. Check that the idler gear is able to rotate freely anti-clockwise as you look at it from the left-hand side of the bike, but locks when rotated clockwise **(see illustration)**. If not, the starter clutch is faulty and should be removed for inspection.

Removal

5 Withdraw the idler gear shaft from the

14.3b Some leverage can be applied to the purpose made tab if required

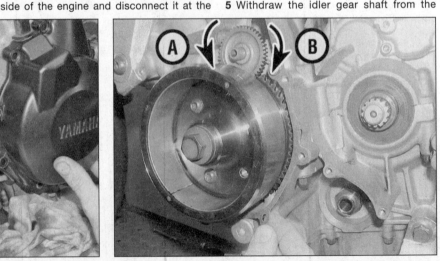

14.4 Idler gear should rotate freely anti-clockwise (A), and lock when turned clockwise (B)

14.5a Withdraw the shaft and the idler gear

14.5b Remove the bolts to separate the starter clutch from the alternator rotor

14.7 Examine the idler gear teeth for wear and damage

crankcase and remove the gear **(see illustration)**. Remove the alternator rotor; the starter clutch is mounted on the back of it (see Chapter 8). **Note:** *Before removing the alternator rotor, slacken the three starter clutch bolts while holding the rotor centre bolt. If the rotor has already been removed from the bike, hold the rotor with a strap wrench to slacken the bolts* **(see illustration)**.

6 Lay the alternator rotor face down on the work surface and withdraw the starter driven gear from the starter clutch. If the gear appears stuck, rotate it anti-clockwise as you withdraw it to free it from the starter clutch. If the starter driven gear does not come away with the alternator rotor, slide it off the crankshaft.

Inspection

7 Inspect the teeth on the idler gear and replace it with a new one if any are chipped or worn **(see illustration)**. Check the idler shaft bearing surfaces for signs of wear or damage, and replace with a new one if necessary.

8 Fit the starter driven gear into the starter clutch, rotating it anti-clockwise to spread the sprags and allow the gear hub to enter. With the alternator rotor face down, check that the starter driven gear rotates freely in an anti-clockwise direction and locks against the rotor in a clockwise direction **(see illustration)**.

14.8 Check that the driven gear turns freely anti-clockwise

If it doesn't, the starter clutch should be dismantled.

9 Unscrew the three bolts and remove the clutch housing from the back of the alternator rotor **(see illustration)**. Depress the spring lock on the outside edge of the clutch sprag assembly and withdraw it from the housing **(see illustration)**.

10 Inspect the condition of the sprags and their cage inside the clutch assembly **(see illustration)**. If they are damaged or worn at any point, the starter clutch should be replaced with a new one.

11 Inspect the driven gear bearing surfaces

14.9a Remove the clutch housing from the back of the rotor

for signs of wear and scoring. If the bearing surfaces show signs of excessive wear, replace the gear with a new one and inspect the surface of the crankshaft for damage. Inspect the teeth of the driven gear and replace the gear with a new one if they are worn or damaged.

Installation

12 Fit the clutch sprag assembly into its housing and ensure that the spring lock engages **(see illustration 14.9b)**. Clean the starter clutch bolts and apply a drop of locking compound to their threads. Fit the

14.9b Depress the spring lock (arrowed) to release the clutch assembly from its housing

14.10 Inspect the starter clutch sprags (A), cage (C) and housing (B)

14.12 Apply locking compound to the starter clutch bolts and tighten them securely

14.16a Fit a new gasket onto the dowels (arrowed) . . .

14.16b . . . and make sure the cover locates correctly on the idler gear shaft

housing onto the back of the alternator rotor, then install the bolts and tighten them to the specified torque setting **(see illustration)**. **Note:** *If a strap wrench is not available to hold the alternator rotor, final tightening of the bolts can take place once the rotor has been fitted to the crankshaft.*

13 Lubricate the starter driven gear hub with clean engine oil, then fit it into the starter clutch, rotating it anti-clockwise to spread the sprags and allow the hub to enter **(see illustration 14.8)**. Check the operation of the starter clutch as described in Step 8.

14 Install the alternator (see Chapter 8).

15 Lubricate the idler gear shaft with clean engine oil. Slide the gear onto the shaft, making

sure the smaller pinion faces inwards, and the teeth of the larger pinion mesh with the teeth of the starter motor shaft **(see illustration 14.5a)**.

16 If removed, insert the dowels in the crankcase, then install the alternator cover using a new gasket, making sure the cover locates correctly onto the dowels and the idle gear shaft **(see illustrations)**. Install the cover bolts, not forgetting the wiring guides, and tighten the bolts evenly in a criss-cross sequence to the torque setting specified at the beginning of this Chapter **(see illustration 14.3a)**.

17 Install the remaining components in the reverse order of removal.

18 Refill the engine with oil to the correct level (see Chapter 1 and *Pre-ride checks*).

15 Gearchange mechanism

Note: *This procedure can be carried out with the engine in the frame. If the engine has been removed, ignore the steps which do not apply.*

Removal

1 Make sure the transmission is in neutral. Note how far the gearchange linkage rod is threaded into the lever and arm, as this determines the height of the lever relative to the footrest. Loosen the rod locknuts – the locknut on the lever end is reverse threaded **(see illustrations)**.

2 Unscrew the rod and separate it from the lever and the arm – the rod is reverse-threaded on the lever end, so will unscrew from both lever and arm simultaneously when turned in the one direction. Withdraw the rod from the frame.

3 Note the alignment of the punch marks on the gearchange shaft and gearchange arm **(see illustration)**. Unscrew the pinch bolt on the gearchange arm and slide the arm off the shaft. **Note:** *If no marks are visible, make your own before removing the arm so that it can be correctly aligned with the shaft on installation.*

4 Remove the front sprocket cover (see Chapter 6).

15.1a Slacken the locknuts (arrowed) . . .

15.1b . . . at the upper and lower ends of the rod . . .

15.1c . . . then unscrew the rod and withdraw it from the frame

15.3 Note the alignment of the punch marks on the shaft (A) and the arm (B)

15.5 Unscrew the bolts (arrowed) and remove the cover

15.6a Note the location of the centralising spring ends (A) and the stopper arm spring (B)

15.6b Note the position of the selector arm pawls (A) and the stopper arm roller (B)

15.7 Remove the complete gearchange shaft assembly and collar (arrowed)

5 Unscrew the bolts securing the gearchange mechanism cover and remove it **(see illustration)**. Discard the gasket, as a new one must be used. Remove the dowels from either the cover or the crankcase if they are loose.

6 Note how the gearchange shaft centralising spring ends fit on each side of the locating pin

in the crankcase, and where the stopper arm spring locates **(see illustration)**. Note how the pawls on the selector arm locate onto the pins on the end of the selector drum and how the roller on the stopper arm locates in the neutral detent on the selector drum **(see illustration)**.

7 Unhook the stopper arm spring from its

anchor pin, then withdraw the gearchange shaft assembly **(see illustration)**. Ensure the washer is on the inner end of the shaft as you remove the assembly – it may stick to the crankcase wall.

8 Slide the washer off the gearchange shaft, then remove the circlip, the second washer and the stopper arm **(see illustrations)**.

15.8a Slide the collar and the washer . . .

15.8b . . . then the circlip . . .

15.8c . . . and the second washer . . .

15.8d . . . and the stopper arm off the shaft

15.9 Check the selector pins for wear

15.13 Examine the oil seal (A) and bearing (B) for wear and damage

Inspection

9 Inspect the splines on the gearchange shaft; if they are worn or damaged, or if the shaft is bent, replace the shaft with a new one. Check the shaft selector arm for cracks, distortion and wear of its pawls, and check for any corresponding wear on the selector pins on the selector drum **(see illustration)**.
10 Check the stopper arm roller and the detents in the selector drum for any wear or damage, and make sure the roller turns freely. Replace any components that are worn or damaged with new ones.
11 Inspect the centralising spring, the pawl spring and the stopper arm return spring for fatigue, wear or damage. If any faults are found, replace the components with new ones. Note how the ends of the centralising spring locate each side of the tab on the selector arm.
12 Check that the centralising spring locating

pin in the crankcase is securely tightened. If it is loose, remove it and apply a non-permanent thread locking compound to its threads, then tighten it to the torque setting specified at the beginning of this Chapter.
13 Check the condition of the gearchange shaft oil seal and bearing in the cover. If the oil seal is damaged, deteriorated or shows signs of a leak it must be replaced with a new one. Lever out the old seal with a flat-bladed screwdriver. If the bearing is damaged or does not run smoothly and freely, it must be replaced with a new one (see Section 5 of *Tools and Workshop Tips* in the *Reference* section) **(see illustration)**. Drive the new seal squarely into place, with its lip facing inward, using a seal driver or suitable socket.

Installation

14 Lubricate the gearchange shaft with clean engine oil. If removed, slide the centralising

spring onto the gearchange shaft, making sure the ends are correctly positioned each side of the selector arm tab **(see illustration)**.
15 Slide the stopper arm onto the shaft, making sure it is the correct way round, then fit the washer and the circlip **(see illustration)**.
16 Fit the washer onto the shaft, and the stopper arm spring onto the stopper arm, then install the gearchange shaft assembly into the crankcase.
17 Ensure that the centralising spring ends fit on each side of the locating pin and that the selector arm pawls engage the pins on the selector drum. Locate the stopper arm roller onto the neutral detent on the selector drum **(see illustrations 15.6a and b)**.
18 Hook the stopper arm spring over its anchor pin **(see illustration)**.
19 If removed, fit the dowels into the crankcase and lubricate the gearchange shaft oil seal with grease. Install the gearchange mechanism cover using a new gasket, ensuring the gasket and cover locate correctly onto the dowels, and tighten the cover bolts securely **(see illustration)**.
20 Install the remaining components in the reverse order of removal. To adjust the gearchange lever position, first loosen both locknuts on the linkage rod. Rotate the rod in one direction or the other to either raise or lower the lever height. Make sure the linkage rod length is within specification (see beginning of this chapter), then tighten both locknuts securely.

15.14 Centralising spring ends locate on each side of tab (arrowed)

15.15 Gearchange shaft stopper arm components

16 Oil cooler

Note: *This procedure can be carried out with the engine in the frame. If the engine has been removed, ignore the steps that do not apply.*

⚠️ **Warning: Allow the engine to cool completely before starting work.**

Removal

1 The cooler is located on the front of the engine. Drain the engine oil and the coolant (see Chapter 1). Leave a drain tray under the cooler to catch residual oil and coolant as the cooler is removed.

15.18 Hook the stopper arm spring over its anchor pin

15.19 Make sure the cover locates over the dowels (arrowed)

16.3a Loosen the clips on the water pump outlet hose (arrowed) . . .

16.3b . . . the front water jacket hose (arrowed) . . .

16.3c . . . the oil cooler inlet hose . . .

16.3d . . . and the oil cooler outlet hose . . .

16.3e . . . and detach the hoses

2 Remove the radiator (see Chapter 3) and the exhaust system (see Chapter 4).
3 Loosen the clips securing the coolant inlet and outlet hoses to the oil cooler and detach the outlet hose from the top **(see illustrations)**.
4 Unscrew the oil cooler centre bolt and remove the bolt, washer and oil cooler, detaching it from the inlet hose as you do. Note how the tab on the cooler body locates between the lugs on the crankcase **(see illustration)**.
5 Discard the washer and the O-ring from the cooler body as new ones must be fitted on reassembly.

6 Check the cooler body for cracks and dents and any evidence of coolant leaking and replace it with a new one if necessary. Also check the hoses for splits, cracks, hardening and deterioration and fit new ones if required.

Installation

7 Installation is the reverse of removal, noting the following:
● Clean the mating surfaces of the crankcase and the cooler with a rag and solvent.
● Before reassembly, lubricate the new O-ring with clean engine oil and ensure it

seats correctly on the cooler body **(see illustration)**.
● Locate the tab on the cooler body between the lugs on the crankcase **(see illustration 16.4)**.
● Use a new washer on the centre bolt and lubricate its threads, and tighten it to the torque setting specified at the beginning of this Chapter.
● Make sure the coolant hoses are pressed fully onto their unions and tighten the clips securely.
● Refill the engine with oil and refill the cooling system, both to the correct levels (see Chapter 1 and *Pre-ride checks*).
● Start the engine and check that there are no leaks before taking the machine on the road.

16.4 Remove the oil cooler, noting how the tab (arrowed) locates against the crankcase

16.7 Use a new O-ring on the oil cooler body

17 Oil sump, oil strainer and pressure relief valve

Note: *This procedure can be carried out with the engine in the frame. If the engine has been removed, ignore the steps which do not apply.*

 Warning: Allow the engine to cool completely before starting work.

17.3a Unscrew the bolts (arrowed) and remove the sump

17.3b Note the position of the wiring clamp (A) and lower fairing brackets (B)

Removal

1 Raise or remove the fuel tank. Remove the radiator (see Chapter 3). Remove the exhaust system (see Chapter 4).

2 Drain the engine oil (see Chapter 1). Trace the wire from the oil level sensor underneath the sump and disconnect it at the connector (see illustration 4.11d). Feed the wire through to the underside of the engine, noting its routing.

3 Unscrew the sump bolts, noting there is one in the middle as well (13 in all), slackening them evenly in a criss-cross sequence to prevent distortion, and remove the sump

(see illustration). Note: *Do not unscrew the two bolts retaining the oil level sensor*. If necessary, break the gasket seal by tapping gently around the edge of the sump with a soft-faced hammer or block of wood; do not lever the sump off as this will damage the sealing surface. Note the position of the oil level sensor wiring clamp and the two lower fairing fixing brackets (see illustration). Discard the gasket, as a new one must be used. Note the positions of the dowels and remove them if they are loose.

4 Pull the oil strainer out of its socket in the oil pump, noting how the tab on the strainer locates between the lugs on the

pump. Remove the seal and discard it as a new one must be fitted on reassembly (see illustration).

5 Pull the pressure relief valve out of the crankcase (see illustration). Discard the O-ring, as a new one must be fitted on reassembly.

Inspection

6 Remove all traces of gasket from the sump and crankcase mating surfaces, and clean the inside of the sump with a suitable solvent (see illustration). Do not remove the oil level sensor unless it is necessary for testing the unit (see Chapter 8).

7 Clean the strainer in solvent, flushing it through from the inside, and remove any debris caught in the strainer mesh. Inspect the mesh for any signs of wear or damage and replace the strainer with a new one if necessary.

8 Push the relief valve plunger into the valve body and check that it moves smoothly and freely against spring pressure (see illustration). If not, remove the circlip, noting that it is under spring pressure, and remove the spring seat, spring and plunger (see illustrations). Clean all the components in solvent and check them for scoring, wear or damage. If any is found, replace the relief valve with a new one – individual components

17.4 Pull out the strainer and the seal (arrowed)

17.5 Pull the pressure relief valve out of its socket

17.6 Clean the inside of the sump thoroughly

17.8a Press down on the spring seat to remove the circlip

17.8b Disassemble the relief valve and examine the components

are not available. Otherwise, coat the inside of the valve body and the plunger with clean engine oil, then insert the plunger, spring and spring seat and secure them with the circlip. Check the action of the valve plunger again – if it is still suspect, replace the valve with a new one.

Installation

9 Fit a new O-ring onto the relief valve and smear it with grease **(see illustration)**. Push the valve into its socket in the crankcase **(see illustration 17.5)**.

10 Lubricate the new seal for the oil strainer with grease and fit it into the pump **(see illustrations)**. Fit the strainer into the seal and onto the pump, making sure the tab locates between the lugs and the arrow points to the front of the engine **(see illustration 17.4)**.

11 If removed, fit the sump dowels into the crankcase. Lay a new gasket onto the sump (if the engine is in the frame) or onto the crankcase (if the engine has been removed and is upside down on the work surface) **(see illustration)**. Make sure the holes in the gasket align correctly with the bolt holes.

17.9 Fit an new O-ring and lubricate it

17.10a Lubricate the new seal . . .

12 Position the sump on the crankcase, then install the bolts, the oil level sensor wiring clamp and the lower fairing fixing brackets **(see illustration and 17.3b)**. Apply a suitable non-permanent thread locking compound to the central bolt and tighten all bolts evenly and a little at a time in a criss-cross pattern to the specified torque setting **(see illustration)**.

13 Connect the oil level sensor wire at the connector **(see illustration 4.11d)**.

14 Install the exhaust system and the fuel tank (see Chapter 4), and the radiator (see Chapter 3).

15 Fill the engine with the correct type and quantity of oil and coolant (see Chapter 1 and *Pre-ride checks*).

16 Start the engine and check that there are no leaks around the sump before taking the machine on the road.

17.10b . . . and fit it into the pump

17.11 Ensure the new gasket aligns with the dowels (arrowed) and sump bolt holes

17.12a Fit the sump . . .

17.12b . . . and apply a thread lock to the central bolt

18.3 Unscrew the bolts (arrowed) and remove the U-shaped oil pipe . . .

18.4 . . . and the oil return pipe

18 Oil pump

Note: *This procedure can be carried out with the engine in the frame. If the engine has been removed, ignore the steps which do not apply.*

18.5 Unscrew the bolts . . .

> **Warning: Allow the engine to cool completely before starting work.**

Removal

1 Remove the water pump (see Chapter 3).
2 Remove the sump and the oil strainer (see Section 17). If the engine is upside down on

18.6 . . . then disengage the chain and remove the pump

the bench, from here on take care not to drop any bolts as you remove them.
3 Unscrew the U-shaped oil pipe retaining bolts and pull the pipe out of its sockets in the crankcase **(see illustration)**. Discard the O-rings as new ones must be fitted on reassembly.
4 Unscrew the bolt retaining the oil return pipe and pull out the pipe **(see illustration)**.
5 Unscrew and remove the bolts securing the oil pump **(see illustration)**.
6 Tilt the pump to disengage the drive chain from the driven sprocket, then remove the pump from the engine **(see illustration)**. If the engine is upside down on the work surface, secure the chain with a length of wire to prevent it dropping into the crankcase. Note the dowels in the pump mounting lugs and remove them if they are loose.

Inspection

7 Unscrew the bolts securing the two halves of the oil pump body, then separate the body halves and remove the dowels **(see illustrations)**.

18.7a Unscrew the pump body bolts (arrowed) . . .

18.7b . . . and separate the body halves. Remove the dowels (arrowed)

18.8a First slide the outer . . .

18.8b . . . and then the inner rotor off the pump shaft

18.9a Withdraw the drive pin . . .

8 Remove the outer and inner pump rotors from the housing, noting how they fit **(see illustrations)**. The outer rotor is not marked but it should be installed in the pump the same way round on reassembly.

9 Withdraw the drive pin from the shaft, noting how it locates in the slots in the inner rotor, then slide the washer off the shaft and pull the shaft out of the pump body **(see illustrations)**.

10 Clean all components in solvent. Check that the oilways in the body are clear by blowing them through with compressed air.

11 Inspect the components for scoring and wear. If any damage, scoring or uneven or excessive wear is evident, replace the pump with a new one – individual components are not available.

12 Reassemble the pump rotors in the housing and measure the clearance between the outer rotor and the pump body with a feeler gauge and compare it to the maximum clearance listed in the specifications at the beginning of this Chapter **(see illustration)**. If the clearance measured is greater than the maximum listed, replace the pump with a new one.

13 Measure the clearance between the inner rotor tip and the outer rotor with a feeler gauge and compare it to the maximum clearance

18.9b . . . and then remove the washer . . .

listed in the specifications at the beginning of the Chapter **(see illustration)**. If the clearance measured is greater than the maximum listed, replace the pump with a new one.

14 Check the pump driven sprocket and the chain for wear or damage, and replace them with new ones if necessary. **Note:** *When replacing the chain and driven sprocket, also check the condition of the drive sprocket on the back of the clutch housing (see Section 13).*

15 If the pump is good, make sure all the components are clean, then lubricate them with clean engine oil. Fit the pump shaft through the pump body and install the washer

18.9c . . . and pull the shaft out of the pump body

and drive pin **(see illustration 18.9c, b and a)**. Slide the inner rotor onto the shaft so that the slots in the rotor locate over the drive pin then fit the outer rotor onto the inner rotor, remembering to install it the same way round as noted on removal **(see illustrations 18.8b and a)**.

16 Fit the dowels into the body, then fit the other half of the pump body over the rotors and the shaft **(see illustration 18.7b)**.

17 Install the bolts and tighten them to the torque setting specified at the beginning of this Chapter. Rotate the pump shaft by hand and check that the rotors turn freely. If not, strip and reassemble the pump.

18.12 Measure the outer rotor to body clearance as shown

18.13 Measure the inner rotor tip to outer rotor clearance as shown

18.21a Fit the oil return pipe . . .

18.21b . . . then fit new O-rings onto the U-shaped pipe . . .

18.21c . . . and fit it into the crankcase

Installation

18 Before installing the pump, prime it with clean engine oil and ensure that the dowels are in place on the mounting lugs.

19 Install the pump, tilting it to engage the driven sprocket with the drive chain (see illustration 18.6). Ensure the chain is correctly routed between the guides on the inside of the crankcase (see illustration 13.15).

20 Apply a suitable non-permanent thread locking compound to the pump bolts and tighten them to the torque setting specified at the beginning of this Chapter (see illustration 18.5).

21 Fit the oil return pipe and tighten its bolt (see illustration). Smear the new O-rings

19.4 Remove the oil filter and fitting to access crankcase bolt No. 12 (arrowed)

for the U-shaped oil pipe with grease and fit them onto the pipe (see illustration). Fit the U-shaped pipe, then apply a suitable non-permanent thread locking compound to its bolts and tighten them to the specified torque (see illustration).

22 Install the oil strainer and the sump (see Section 17), then the water pump (see Chapter 3).

23 Fill the engine with the specified quantity and type of new engine oil and coolant (see Chapter 1 and Pre-ride checks).

19 Crankcase separation and reassembly

Note: To separate the crankcase halves, the engine must be removed from the frame.

Separation

1 To gain access to the connecting rods, pistons and rings, crankshaft, bearings, transmission shafts and selector drum and forks, the crankcase must be split into two parts.

2 Remove the engine from the frame (see Section 4). Note: To reduce the weight of the engine, where possible remove as many of the components listed below before removing the engine from the frame.

3 Before the crankcases can be separated

the following components must be removed:
Camshafts and cam chain tensioner (Sections 7 and 8).
Cylinder head (Section 10).
Alternator rotor (Chapter 8).
Thermostat (Chapter 3).
Starter motor (Chapter 8).
Cam chain (Section 9).
Clutch (Section 13).
Gearchange mechanism (Section 15).
Oil cooler (Section 16).
Water pump (Chapter 3)
Oil sump, strainer and pressure relief valve (Section 17).
Oil pump and drive chain (Section 18).

4 Remove the oil filter and unscrew the filter fitting from the crankcase to gain access to crankcase bolt No. 12 (see illustration).

5 Turn the engine upside down. The crankcases are joined by twelve 8 mm bolts (Nos. 1 to 12) and fifteen 6 mm bolts (Nos. 13 to 27). Unscrew the bolts a quarter turn at a time in a reverse of the numerical sequence shown and as marked on the crankcase (the number of each bolt is cast into the crankcase), until they are finger-tight, then remove them and store them in a template to ensure correct installation of the crankcase (see illustrations). Note the washers fitted to bolts Nos. 1 to 10.

6 Carefully lift the lower crankcase half off the upper half, using a soft-faced hammer or block of

19.5a Crankcase bolt location and TIGHTENING sequence. Loosen bolts in REVERSE order

19.5b Bolt numbers (arrowed) are cast into the crankcase

19.6 Lift the lower half of the crankcase off the upper half

19.7 Remove the three locating dowels (arrowed) shown in the upper crankcase

wood to tap around the joint to initially separate the halves, if necessary **(see illustration)**. **Note:** *If the halves do not separate easily, make sure all fasteners have been removed. Do not try and separate the halves by levering between the sealing surfaces as they are easily damaged and will leak oil on reassembly.*

7 Remove the three locating dowels from the crankcase (they could be in either half) **(see illustration)**.

8 Refer to Sections 20 to 28 for the removal and installation of the components housed within the crankcases.

Reassembly

9 Remove all traces of sealant from the crankcase mating surfaces.

10 Ensure that all components and their bearings are in place in the upper and lower crankcase halves. If the transmission shafts have not been removed, check the condition of the oil seal on the left-hand end of the output shaft and replace it with a new one if it is damaged, deformed or deteriorated – it is

wise to fit a new seal whatever the perceived condition of the existing one (you wouldn't want to discover a leak after the engine has been rebuilt and put back in the frame) **(see illustration)**. Apply some grease to the inside of the new seal on installation. Check that the selector drum is in the neutral position.

11 Generously lubricate the crankshaft, transmission shafts and selector drum and forks, particularly around the bearings, with clean engine oil, then use a rag soaked in high flash-point solvent to wipe over the mating surfaces of both crankcase halves to remove all traces of oil.

12 Apply a small amount of suitable sealant (such as Yamaha Bond 1215) to the mating surface of one crankcase half as shown **(see illustration)**.

Caution: Do not apply an excessive amount of sealant as it will ooze out when the case halves are assembled and may obstruct oil passages. Do not apply the sealant on or too close (within 2 to 3 mm) to any of the bearing shells or surfaces.

13 If removed, fit the three locating dowels into the crankcase **(see illustration 19.7)**.

14 Check again that all components are in position, particularly that the bearing shells are located in their seats in the lower crankcase half, then fit the lower crankcase half onto the upper crankcase half, making sure the dowels locate correctly.

15 Check that the lower crankcase half is seated correctly. **Note:** *The crankcase halves should fit together without being forced. If the casings are not correctly seated, remove the lower crankcase half and investigate the problem. Do not attempt to pull them together using the crankcase bolts as the casing will crack and be ruined.* Rotate the transmission selector drum to ensure that the gears select correctly and investigate any problems before bolting the crankcase halves together.

16 Clean the threads of the crankcase bolts and lubricate the threads of all except bolt No. 18 **(see illustration 19.5a)** with clean engine oil. Lubricate the underside of the heads and washers of bolt Nos. 1 to 10. Apply

19.10 It is best to fit a new output shaft oil seal before reassembly

19.12 Apply sealant to the shaded area

H46042

19.17a Ensure the bolts are refitted in their correct locations, with washers as required . . .

19.17b . . . and then tightened in sequence to the specified torques

21.2 Measuring the connecting rod side clearance with a feeler gauge

a suitable thread locking compound to the threads of bolt No. 18.

17 Install the bolts in their correct locations and secure them finger-tight **(see illustration)**. First tighten bolt Nos. 1 to 10 in the correct numerical sequence as marked and as shown **(see illustration 19.5a)** to the first stage torque setting specified at the beginning of the Chapter, then tighten them in the same sequence to the 2nd stage torque setting. Now reverse the sequence (i.e. 10 to 1) and loosen the bolts. Now tighten them in the correct sequence (1 to 10) to the 3rd stage torque setting specified. Now tighten bolts 11 to 27, evenly and a little at a time, in the correct numerical sequence as marked on the crankcase and as shown **(see illustration 19.5a)**, to the torque settings specified at the beginning of this Chapter **(see illustration)**.

18 With all crankcase bolts tightened, check that the crankshaft and transmission shafts rotate smoothly and easily. Check that all gears can be selected and that the shafts rotate freely in every gear. If there are any signs of undue stiffness, rough spots, or of any other problem, the fault must be rectified before proceeding further.

19 Install all the removed assemblies in the reverse order of removal, according to your procedure (see Steps 2 and 3).

20 Main and big-end bearing information

1 Even though main and connecting rod bearings are generally replaced with new ones during an engine overhaul, the old bearings should be carefully examined as they can reveal valuable information about the condition of the engine.

2 Bearing failure occurs mainly because of lack of lubrication, the presence of dirt or other foreign particles, overloading the engine and/or corrosion. Regardless of the cause of bearing failure, it must be corrected before the engine is reassembled to prevent it from happening again.

3 When examining the bearings, match

them with their corresponding journal on the crankshaft to help identify the cause of any problem.

4 Dirt and other foreign particles get into the engine in a variety of ways. They may be left in the engine during assembly or they may pass through filters or breathers, then get into the oil and from there into the bearings. Metal chips from machining operations and normal engine wear are often present. Abrasives are sometimes left in engine components after reconditioning operations, especially when parts are not thoroughly cleaned using the proper cleaning methods. Whatever the source, foreign objects often end up imbedded in the soft bearing material and are easily recognised. Large particles will not imbed in the bearing and will score or gouge the bearing and journal. The best prevention for this type of bearing failure is to clean all parts thoroughly and keep everything spotlessly clean during engine reassembly. Regular oil and filter changes are also essential.

5 Lack of lubrication or lubrication breakdown have a number of interrelated causes. Excessive heat (which thins the oil), overloading (which squeezes the oil from the bearing face) and oil throw-off (from excessive bearing clearances, a worn oil pump or high engine speeds) all contribute to a breakdown of the protective lubricating film. Blocked oil passages will starve a bearing of lubrication and destroy it. When lack of lubrication is the cause of bearing failure, the bearing material is wiped or extruded from the steel backing of the bearing. Temperatures may increase to the point where the steel backing and the journal turn blue from overheating.

6 Riding habits can have a definite effect on bearing life. Full throttle, low speed operation, or labouring the engine, puts very high loads on bearings, which tend to squeeze out the oil film. These loads cause the bearings to flex, which produces fine cracks in the bearing face (fatigue failure). Eventually the bearing material will loosen in pieces and tear away from the steel backing. Short trip riding leads to corrosion of bearings, as insufficient engine heat is produced to drive off the condensed water and corrosive gases produced. These products collect in the engine oil, forming acid

and sludge. As the oil is carried to the engine bearings, the acid attacks and corrodes the bearing material.

7 Incorrect bearing installation during engine assembly will lead to bearing failure as well. Tight fitting bearings which leave insufficient bearing oil clearances result in oil starvation. Dirt or foreign particles trapped behind a bearing shell result in high spots on the bearing which lead to failure.

8 To avoid bearing problems, clean all parts thoroughly before reassembly, double check all bearing clearance measurements and lubricate the new bearings with clean engine oil during installation.

21 Connecting rods and bearings

Note: *To remove the connecting rods the engine must be removed from the frame. On installation new rod bolts and nuts (or bolts only, where no nuts are used) must be used, so it is wise to obtain them before commencing work.*

Removal

1 Remove the engine from the frame (see Section 4) and separate the crankcase halves (see Section 19).

2 Before separating the rods from the crankshaft, measure the side clearance on each rod with a feeler gauge **(see illustration)**. If the clearance on any rod is greater than the service limit listed in this Chapter's Specifications, replace that rod with a new one.

3 Using paint or a marker pen, mark the cylinder identity on the top of each piston and on each connecting rod and cap. Cylinders are numbered 1 to 4 from the left-hand side of the motorcycle (as seated). Note that the number and letter already written on the rod and cap are the rod size code and weight grade respectively, not the cylinder number.

4 Unscrew the connecting rod cap nuts/bolts and separate the caps, complete with the lower bearing shells from the crankpins (see

21.4a Unscrew the nuts/bolts (arrowed) . . .

21.4b . . . and pull the cap off the connecting rod

21.6 Remove each piston and connecting rod from the top of its bore

illustrations). If a cap appears stuck, tap it on one end with a hammer while pulling it. **Note:** *The rod caps are secured by either nuts and bolts, or bolts only, depending upon market model and year of manufacture.*

5 Detach the connecting rods, complete with the upper bearing shells, from the crankpins, then lift the crankshaft out of the upper crankcase half, taking care not to dislodge the main bearing shells **(see illustration 24.2)**. If required, remove the main bearing shells from the crankcase halves by pushing their centres to the side, then lifting them out **(see illustration 24.3)** – it is imperative that the shells are kept in order so that they can be returned to their original locations.

6 Raise the front of the crankcase and rest it on some wood, or turn it onto its side. Push each piston/connecting rod assembly to the top end of the cylinder bore and remove it, making sure the connecting rod does not mark the bore walls **(see illustration)**. Note the 'Y' mark on each connecting rod that must face to the left-hand side of the engine **(see illustration 21.27)**, and the arrow on the top of each piston which points to the front of the engine **(see illustration 22.2)**. If this is not visible, mark the piston accordingly so that it can be installed the correct way round.

Caution: Do not try to remove the piston/ connecting rod from the bottom of the cylinder bore. The piston will not pass the crankcase main bearing webs. If the piston is pulled right to the bottom of the bore the oil control ring will expand and lock the

piston in position. If this happens it is likely the ring will be broken.

7 Fit the related bearing shells (if removed), bearing cap, and bolts on each piston/ connecting rod assembly so that they are all kept together as a matched set. **Note:** *New big-end nuts and bolts must be used on final assembly. Use the old nuts and bolts for the oil clearance check and for seating the bearing shells, then discard them.*

8 Separate the pistons from the connecting rods (see Section 22).

Inspection

9 Check the connecting rods for cracks and other obvious damage.

10 Apply clean engine oil to the piston pin, insert it into its connecting rod small-end and check for any freeplay between the two **(see illustration)**. If freeplay is excessive, measure the external diameter at the centre of the pin **(see illustration)**. Compare the result to the specifications at the beginning of this Chapter. Replace the pin with a new one if it is worn beyond its specified limits. If the pin diameter is within specifications, replace the connecting rod with a new one. Repeat the measurements for all the pins and rods.

11 Refer to Section 20 and examine the connecting rod bearing shells. If they are scored, badly scuffed or appear to have seized, new shells must be installed. Always renew the shells in the connecting rods as a set. If they are badly damaged, check the

corresponding crankpin. Evidence of extreme heat, such as bluing, indicates that lubrication failure has occurred. Be sure to thoroughly check the oil pump and pressure relief valve as well as all oil holes and passages before reassembling the engine.

12 Have the rods checked by a Yamaha dealer if you are in doubt about their straightness.

Oil clearance check

Note: *It is essential that, throughout this procedure, the connecting rod does not rotate on the crankshaft. If the procedure is being carried out on a bench find some way of clamping the crankshaft so it cannot move, and also the connecting rod once it has been fitted onto its journal. The alternative is to fit the rod and piston back into its bore and lay the crankshaft in the crankcase to keep them held steady.*

13 Whether new bearing shells are being fitted or the original ones are being re-used, the connecting rod big-end bearing oil clearance should be checked prior to reassembly. Bearing oil clearance is measured with a product known as Plastigauge.

14 Remove the bearing shells from the rods and caps, keeping them in order **(see illustration)**. Clean the backs of the shells, the bearing locations in both the connecting rod and cap, and the crankpin journal with a suitable solvent.

15 Press the bearing shells into their locations, ensuring that the tab on each shell engages the notch in the connecting rod or

21.10a Rock the piston pin back and forth in the small-end to check for looseness (arrowed)

21.10b Measure the diameter at the centre of the pin

21.14 To remove a big-end bearing shell, push it sideways and then lift it out

cap **(see illustration)**. Make sure the shells are fitted in the correct locations and take care not to touch any shell's bearing surface with your fingers.

16 Working on one rod at a time, apply molybdenum disulphide grease to the shanks and threads of the bolts, and to the seats of the nuts if applicable. Fit the connecting rod and cap together, ensuring that the cap is fitted the correct way around so the previously made markings align (see Step 3). Tighten the cap nuts/bolts to 24.5 Nm and check that there is no gap between the mating surfaces of the rods and the caps caused by misalignment of the bearing shells. Now carefully undo the cap nuts/bolts without disturbing the shells.

17 Cut an appropriate size length of Plastigauge (it should be slightly shorter than the width of the crankpin) and place it on the crankpin journal to be checked **(see illustration 24.12)**. Do not place Plastigauge over the oil holes in the journal. Fit the connecting rod and cap onto the crankpin **(see illustration 21.34)**. Make sure the cap is fitted the correct way around so the previously made markings align (see Step 3), and that the 'Y' mark on the rod is facing to the left-hand end of the crankshaft (see Step 6). Fit the nuts/bolts and tighten them finger-tight. **Note:** *It is essential that, throughout this procedure, the connecting rod does not rotate on the crankshaft.*

18 Tighten the nuts/bolts to the initial torque setting specified at the beginning of this Chapter with a torque wrench **(see illustration 21.36a)**. Now tighten each nut/bolt in turn and in one continuous movement through the specified angle using a torque angle gauge **(see illustration 21.36b)**. **Note:** *The torque angles are different for cap nuts and cap bolts.* If tightening is paused between the initial and final settings, slacken the nut/bolt to below the initial setting and repeat the procedure.

Note 1 (cap nuts): *If a torque angle gauge is not available, tighten the cap nuts as follows.*

21.18b After initial tightening, mark the bolts and rod cap as shown. Turn the bolt clockwise through 120° for final tightening

21.15 Ensure tab (A) locates in notch (B)

Paint a small reference mark on one point of the nut hex after tightening the nut to the initial torque setting, then go clockwise around the nut a distance of two and a half flats and paint another mark corresponding to this on the connecting rod cap – the angle between two flats is 60°, so going around two and a half flats equals 150°. Now, using a ring spanner so that you can see the two marks, tighten the nut clockwise in one continuous movement until the marks align **(see illustration)**.

Note 2 (cap bolts): *If a torque angle gauge is not available, tighten the cap bolts as follows. Paint a small reference mark on one point of the bolt bi-hex after tightening the bolt to the initial torque setting, then go clockwise around the bolt a distance of four points and paint another mark corresponding to this on the connecting rod cap – the angle between two points is 30°, so going around four points equals 120°. Now, using a ring spanner so that you can see the two marks, tighten the bolt clockwise in one continuous movement until the marks align* **(see illustration)**.

19 Slacken the nuts/bolts and remove the cap and rod from the crankshaft.

20 Compare the width of the crushed Plastigauge on the crankpin to the scale printed on the Plastigauge envelope to obtain the connecting rod bearing oil clearance **(see illustration 24.16)**. Compare the reading to the specifications at the beginning of this Chapter. If the clearance is within the range specified and the bearings are in perfect condition, they can be reused.

21 Carefully clean away all traces of the Plastigauge from the crankpin journal and

21.18a After initial tightening, mark the nuts and rod cap as shown. Turn the nut clockwise through 150° for final tightening

bearing shells using a fingernail or other object which will not score the bearing surfaces.

22 If the clearance is beyond the service limit, replace the bearing shells with new ones (see Steps 25 and 26) and check the oil clearance once again. Always renew all of the shells at the same time.

23 If the clearance is still greater than the service limit listed in this Chapter's Specifications, the big-end bearing journal is worn and the crankshaft should be replaced with a new one.

24 Repeat the procedure for the remaining connecting rods, then discard the old big-end bolts and nuts.

Bearing shell selection

25 Replacement bearing shells for the big-end bearings are supplied on a selected fit basis. Code numbers for the crankshaft journals are stamped on the outside of the crankshaft web on the left-hand end of the crankshaft **(see illustration)**. The right-hand block of four numbers are the size codes for the big-end bearing journals (the left-hand block of five numbers are the size codes for the main bearing journals). The first number of the block is for the left-hand (No. 1 cylinder) journal, and so on. Each connecting rod size code number is marked in ink on the flat face of the connecting rod and cap **(see illustration)**.

21.25a Main bearing journal numbers (A) and big-end bearing journal numbers (B)

21.25b Connecting rod size code number

21.27 Align the bolt head with the recess in the rod. Note the Y mark (arrowed)

21.32a With the ring ends staggered, fit the ring compressor over the piston . . .

21.32b . . . then insert the rod assembly into the top of the bore . . .

26 A range of bearing shells are available. To select the correct shells for a particular journal, subtract the big-end bearing journal number from the connecting rod number and compare the result with the table below to find the colour coding of the replacement shells, e.g. connecting rod number 4 minus journal number 2 = 2; No. 2 bearing shells are colour-coded black. The colour code is marked on the side of each bearing shell.

Number	Colour
1	blue
2	black
3	brown
4	green

Installation

Note: New big-end bolts and nuts must be used on final assembly.

27 If the rod caps are secured by nuts and bolts, note the alignment of each bolt head with the recess in the connecting rod, then press the old bolts out of the rods. Align the heads of the new bolts with the recesses in the rods and press the bolts into place **(see illustration)**.

28 Fit the pistons onto the connecting rods (see Section 22).

29 Ensure that the backs of the bearing shells, the bearing seats in the caps and rods and the crankpin journals are clean. If new shells are being fitted, ensure that all traces of protective grease are removed using paraffin (kerosene). Dry the shells, caps, rods and journals with a clean, lint-free cloth. Install the shells, making sure the tab on each shell engages the notch in the cap or rod **(see illustration 21.15)**. If the original bearing shells are to be fitted, make sure that they are in their correct locations. Take care not to touch any bearing surfaces with your fingers.

30 Follow the procedure in Step 16 to ensure that the bearing shells are correctly seated.

31 Lubricate the pistons, rings and cylinder bores with clean engine oil. Insert the piston/connecting rod assembly into the top of its bore, taking care not to allow the connecting rod to mark the bore. Make sure the arrow on the top of the piston points to the front and the 'Y' mark on the rod faces the left-hand side of the engine (see Step 6).

32 Stagger the piston ring end gaps (see Section 23) and carefully compress and feed each piston ring into the bore until the piston crown is flush with the top of the bore. If available, a piston ring compressor makes installation a lot easier **(see illustrations)**.

33 Lower the crankshaft into position in the

21.32c . . . and carefully press the piston into the bore

upper crankcase, making sure all the main bearing shells are in place (see Section 24).

34 Working on one connecting rod at a time, lubricate the crankpin and the shells in the connecting rod and cap with clean engine oil. Apply molybdenum disulphide grease to the shanks and threads of the new big-end bolts. Pull the rod onto the crankpin and fit the cap onto the rod **(see illustration)**. Make sure the cap is fitted the correct way around so the previously made markings align (see Step 3).

35 If the rod caps are secured by nuts and bolts, apply molybdenum disulphide grease to the seats of the new nuts, then fit the nuts and tighten them finger-tight **(see illustration)**. If the rod caps are secured by bolts only, install

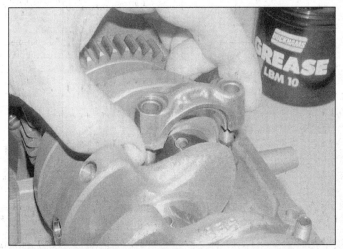

21.34 Align the markings and fit the big-end cap onto the rod . . .

21.35 . . . then install the cap nuts or bolts finger-tight

21.36a Tighten the nuts/bolts to the initial torque setting with a torque wrench . . .

21.36b . . . and then to the final setting with a torque angle gauge

21.36c Alternatively, make reference marks (arrowed) with a dab of paint . . .

21.36d . . . and tighten them finally with a ring spanner as described

the bolts and tighten them finger-tight Check that all components have been returned to their original locations using the marks made on disassembly.

36 Tighten the nuts/bolts to the initial

22.2 Note the arrow that points to the front of the engine

22.3a Prise out the circlip . . .

22.3b . . . then push out the pin and remove the piston

22.4a Removing the piston rings using a ring removal and installation tool

torque setting specified at the beginning of this Chapter with a torque wrench **(see illustration)**. Now tighten each nut in turn and in one continuous movement through the specified angle using a torque angle gauge

(see illustration). If tightening is paused between the initial and final settings, slacken the nut to below the initial setting and repeat the procedure. Fit the remaining rods onto the crankshaft in the same way. If a torque angle gauge is not available, follow the procedure in Step 18 and mark the nuts or bolts with a dab of paint in order to tighten them to the specified angle **(see illustrations)**.

37 Lubricate the bores liberally with clean engine oil and check that the crankshaft rotates smoothly and freely. If there are any signs of roughness or tightness, detach the rods and recheck the assembly. Sometimes tapping the bottom of the connecting rod cap will relieve tightness.

38 Reassemble the crankcase halves (see Section 19).

22 Pistons

Note: *To remove the pistons the engine must be removed from the frame.*

Removal

1 Remove the engine from the frame (see Section 4), separate the crankcase halves (see Section 19). Remove the piston/connecting rod assemblies (see Section 21).

2 Before removing the piston from the connecting rod, ensure it is marked with its cylinder identity. If the piston is going to be cleaned, scratch the identity lightly on the inside of the piston skirt. Each piston must be installed in its original cylinder on reassembly. Note the arrow on the top of each piston that points to the front of the engine **(see illustration)**. If this is not visible, mark the piston accordingly so that it can be installed the correct way round.

3 Carefully prise out the circlips on each side of the piston pin using needle-nose pliers or a small flat-bladed screwdriver inserted into the notch **(see illustration)**. Check for burring around the circlip grooves and remove any with a very fine file or knife blade, then push the piston pin out to free the piston from the connecting rod **(see illustration)**. Discard the circlips as new ones must be used on reassembly. When the piston has been removed from the rod, keep the piston and its pin together so that related parts do not get mixed up.

4 Using your thumbs or a piston ring removal and installation tool, carefully remove the rings from the pistons, working on one piston at a time **(see illustration)**. Do not nick or gouge the pistons in the process. Note which way up each ring fits and in which groove, as they must be installed in their original positions if being re-used. The upper surface of the two top rings (compression rings) should have a manufacturer's mark or letter at one end – if the mark on each ring is different, note which

22.4b Note the mark on the end of the two top rings (compression)

22.7a Ensure that the oil return holes (arrowed) are clear . . .

22.7b . . . and that the piston is still clearly marked

mark is for the top ring and which is for the second **(see illustration)**.

5 Scrape all traces of carbon from the tops of the pistons. A hand-held wire brush or a piece of fine emery cloth can be used once most of the deposits have been scraped away. Do not, under any circumstances, use a wire brush mounted in a drill motor; the piston material is soft and is easily damaged.

6 Use a piston ring groove cleaning tool to remove any carbon deposits from the ring grooves. If a tool is not available, a piece broken off an old ring will do the job. Be very careful to remove only the carbon deposits. Do not remove any metal and do not nick or gouge the sides of the ring grooves.

7 Once the carbon has been removed, clean the pistons with a suitable solvent and dry them thoroughly. Make sure the oil return holes at the back of the oil ring groove are clear **(see illustration)**. If the identification mark previously applied to the piston is cleaned off, be sure to re-mark it correctly **(see illustration)**.

Inspection

8 Inspect each piston for cracks around the skirt, at the pin bosses and at the ring lands. Normal piston wear appears as even, vertical wear on the thrust surfaces of the piston and slight looseness of the top ring in its groove. If the skirt is scored or scuffed, the engine may have been suffering from overheating and/or abnormal combustion, resulting in excessively high operating temperatures.

9 A hole in the top of the piston (only likely in extreme circumstances), or burned areas around the edge of the piston crown, indicate that pre-ignition or knocking under load have occurred. If you find evidence of any problems the cause must be corrected or the damage will occur again (see *Fault Finding* in the *Reference* section).

10 Check the piston-to-bore clearance by measuring the bore (see Section 28) and the piston diameter. Make sure each piston is matched to its correct cylinder. Measure the piston 4 mm up from the bottom of the skirt and at 90° to the piston pin axis **(see illustration)**. Subtract the piston diameter from the bore diameter to obtain the clearance. If it is greater than the figure specified at the

22.10 Measuring the piston diameter with a micrometer

beginning of this Chapter, check whether it is the bore or piston that is worn beyond its service limit. If the bores are good, install new pistons and rings. If the bores are worn, replace the crankcases, pistons and rings.

11 Measure the piston ring-to-groove clearance by laying each compression ring in its groove and slipping a feeler gauge in beside it **(see illustration)**. Make sure you have the correct ring for the groove (see Step 4). Check the clearance at three or four locations around the groove. If the clearance is greater than specified, renew both the piston and rings as a set. If new rings are being used, measure the clearance using the new rings. If the clearance is greater than that specified, the piston is worn and must be replaced with a new one.

12 Apply clean engine oil to the piston pin, insert it part way into the piston and check for any freeplay between the two

22.12a Insert the pin (A) into the piston (B) and try to rock it back and forth. If the pin is loose . . .

22.11 Measuring the piston ring-to-groove clearance with a feeler gauge

(see illustration). Measure the pin external diameter at each end, and the pin bores in the piston **(see illustration)**. Subtract the pin diameter from the bore diameter to obtain the clearance. If it is greater than the specified figure, check whether it is the bore or pin that is worn beyond its service limit and replace them with new ones as required. Check for excessive play between the pin and the connecting rod small-end (see Section 21).

Installation

13 Inspect and install the piston rings (see Section 23).

14 Install a **new** circlip into one side of the piston (never re-use old circlips), then lubricate the piston pin, the piston pin bore and the connecting rod small-end bore with clean engine oil.

15 Line up the piston on its connecting rod

22.12b . . . measure the pin external diameter and the pin bore in the piston

so that the arrow on the top of the piston will point to the front and the 'Y' mark on the rod will face the left-hand side of the engine when they are installed. Insert the piston pin from the side without the circlip **(see illustration 22.3b)**. Secure the pin with the other **new** circlip. When installing the circlips, compress them only just enough to fit them in the piston, and make sure they are properly seated in their grooves with the open end away from the removal notch **(see illustration)**.
16 Install the connecting rods (see Section 21).

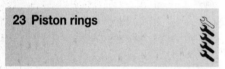

23 Piston rings

1 It is good practice to fit new piston rings when an engine is being overhauled. Before installing the rings on the pistons, the ring end gaps must be checked with the rings installed in the cylinder.

Inspection

2 Lay out each piston with its new ring set so the rings will be matched with the same piston and cylinder during the measurement procedure and engine reassembly. The upper surface of the two top rings (compression rings) should have a manufacturer's mark or letter at one end – if the mark on each ring is different, note which mark is for the top ring and which is for the second **(see illustration 22.4b)**. The rings are also identifiable by their different profiles.

22.15 Fit the circlip with the open end away from the removal notch

3 To measure the ring end gap, fit the ring into the top of the cylinder and square it up with the cylinder walls by pushing it in with the top of the piston. The ring should be about 5 mm below the top edge of the cylinder. Slip a feeler gauge between the ends of the ring and compare the measurement to the specifications at the beginning of this Chapter **(see illustration)**.
4 If the gap is larger or smaller than specified, double check to make sure that you have the correct rings before proceeding.
5 Excess end gap is not critical unless it exceeds the service limit. Check that the bore is not worn (see Section 28).
6 Repeat the procedure for each ring and each cylinder in turn. Note that the end gaps differ between the top, second and oil ring. When checking the oil ring, only the side-rails can be checked as the ends of the expander ring should contact each other. Remember to

keep the rings together with their matched pistons and cylinders.

Installation

7 Once the ring end gaps have been checked and corrected as necessary, the rings can be installed on the pistons.
8 The oil control ring (lowest on the piston) is installed first. It is composed of three separate components, namely the expander and the upper and lower side rails. Slip the expander into the ring groove, then install the lower side rail **(see illustrations)**. Do not use a piston ring installation tool on the oil ring side rails as they may be damaged. Instead, place one end of the side rail into the groove between the expander and the ring land. Hold it firmly in place and slide a finger around the piston while pushing the rail into the groove. Next, install the upper side rail in the same manner **(see illustration)**. Make sure the ends of the expander touch but do not overlap.
9 After the three oil ring components have been installed, check to make sure that both the upper and lower side rails can be turned smoothly in the ring groove.
10 The upper surface of each compression ring should have a mark or letter at one end which must face up when the ring is installed on the piston (see Step 2). Fit the second ring into the middle groove in the piston. Do not expand the ring any more than is necessary to slide it into place **(see illustration)**. To avoid breaking the ring, use a piston ring installation tool **(see illustration 22.4a)**, or pieces of old feeler gauge blades **(see illustration)**.

23.3 Measuring piston ring end gap

23.8a Fit the oil ring expander in its groove . . .

23.8b . . . then fit the lower side rail . . .

23.8c . . . and the upper side rail as described

23.10a Carefully feed the second ring into its groove

23.10b Old pieces of feeler gauge blade can be used to guide the ring over the piston

11 Finally, fit the top ring in the same manner into the top groove in the piston **(see illustration)**.

12 Once the rings are correctly installed, check they move freely without snagging and stagger their end gaps as shown **(see illustration)**.

24 Crankshaft and main bearings

Note: *To remove the crankshaft the engine must be removed from the frame.*

Removal

1 Remove the engine from the frame (see Section 4), separate the crankcase halves (see Section 19) and disconnect the piston/connecting rod assemblies from the crankshaft (see Section 21). There is no need to remove the piston/connecting rod assemblies from the cylinders; push them up the bores so that the connecting rod ends are clear of the crankshaft and wrap clean rag around the rod ends to prevent damage to the bores. **Note:** *New big-end bolts and nuts must be used on reassembly.*

2 Lift the crankshaft out of the upper crankcase half, taking care not to dislodge the main bearing shells **(see illustration)**.

3 If required, remove the main bearing shells from the crankcase halves by pushing their centres to the side, then lifting them out **(see illustration)**. Keep the shells in order so that they can be fitted in their original locations for the oil clearance check.

Inspection

4 Clean the crankshaft with a suitable solvent, paying particular attention to flush out the oil passages. If available, blow the crank dry with compressed air, and also blow through the oil passages. Check the primary drive gear for wear or damage. If any of the teeth are excessively worn, chipped or broken, the crankshaft must be replaced with a new one. Check the primary driven gear on the clutch housing for corresponding wear or damage. Also check the cam chain sprocket, the sprockets on the camshafts and the cam

23.11 Finally, install the top ring . . .

chain itself and replace them with new ones, if necessary.

5 Refer to Section 20 and examine the main bearing shells. If they are scored, badly scuffed or appear to have seized, new bearings must be installed. Always renew the main bearings as a set. If they are badly damaged, check the corresponding crankshaft journals. Evidence of extreme heat, such as bluing, indicates that lubrication failure has occurred. Be sure to thoroughly check the oil pump and pressure relief valve as well as all oil holes and passages before reassembling the engine.

6 Give the crankshaft journals a close visual examination, paying particular attention where damaged bearings have been discovered. If the journals are scored or pitted in any way, a new crankshaft will be required. Note that undersized bearing shells are not available, precluding the option of re-grinding the crankshaft.

7 Place the crankshaft on V-blocks and check the runout at the main bearing journals using a dial gauge (see *Tools and Workshop Tips* in the *Reference* section). Compare the reading to the maximum specified at the beginning of this Chapter. If the runout exceeds the limit, the crankshaft must be replaced with a new one.

Oil clearance check

8 Whether new bearing shells are being fitted or the original ones are being re-used, the main bearing oil clearance should be checked before the engine is reassembled. Main bearing oil clearance is measured with a product known as Plastigauge.

23.12 . . . and then stagger the ring end gaps as shown

1 *Top ring*
2 *Oil ring lower side rail*
3 *Oil ring upper side rail*
4 *Second ring*

9 If not already done, remove the bearing shells from the crankcase halves (see Step 3). Clean the backs of the shells and the bearing seats in both crankcase halves, and the main bearing journals on the crankshaft.

10 Press the bearing shells into their seats, ensuring that the tab on each shell engages in the notch in the crankcase **(see illustration)**. Make sure the bearings are fitted in the correct locations and take care not to touch the bearing surfaces with your fingers.

11 Ensure the shells and crankshaft are clean and dry. Lay the crankshaft in position in the upper crankcase.

12 Cut five appropriate size lengths of Plastigauge (they should be slightly shorter than the width of the crankshaft journals). Place a strand of Plastigauge on each journal **(see illustration)**. Do not place Plastigauge over the oil holes in the crankshaft. Make sure the crankshaft is not rotated.

13 If removed, fit the dowels into the crankcase **(see illustration 19.7)**. Carefully fit the lower crankcase half onto the upper half, making sure the dowels locate correctly and the Plastigauge is not disturbed. Check that the lower crankcase half is correctly seated. **Note:** *Do not tighten the crankcase bolts if the casing is not correctly seated.*

14 Clean and lubricate the threads and underside of the heads and washers of the crankcase bolts Nos. 1 to 10 **(see illustration**

24.2 Lift the crankshaft out of the crankcase carefully

24.3 To remove a main bearing shell, push it sideways and lift it out

24.10 Ensure tab (A) locates in notch (B)

24.12 Place a strip of Plastigauge on each bearing journal

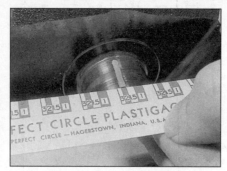

24.16 Measure the crushed Plastigauge using the scale on the pack

the crankcase number, and then subtract 1. Compare the result with the table below to find the colour code of the replacement shells, e.g. crankcase number 5 minus crankshaft journal number 2 minus 1 = 2; No. 2 bearing shells are colour coded black. The colour code is marked on the side of each bearing shell.

Number	Colour
0	white
1	blue
2	black
3	brown
4	green

19.5a) with clean engine oil. Install the bolts in their correct locations and secure them finger-tight. Now tighten bolt Nos. 1 to 10 in the correct numerical sequence as marked and as shown **(see illustration 19.5a)** to the first stage torque setting specified at the beginning of the Chapter, then tighten them in the same sequence to the 2nd stage torque setting. Now reverse the sequence (i.e. 10 to 1) and loosen the bolts. Now tighten them in the correct sequence (1 to 10) to the 3rd stage torque setting specified.

15 Unscrew the bolts a quarter turn at a time in a **reverse** of the numerical sequence shown in illustration **19.5a** and as marked on the crankcase, until they are loose, then remove them. **Note:** *As each bolt is removed, store it in its relative position in the cardboard template of the crankcase halves.* Carefully lift off the lower crankcase half, making sure the Plastigauge is not disturbed.

16 Compare the width of the crushed Plastigauge on each crankshaft journal to the scale printed on the Plastigauge envelope to obtain the main bearing oil clearance **(see illustration)**. Compare the reading to the specifications at the beginning of this Chapter. If the clearance is within the range specified and the bearings are in perfect condition, they can be reused.

17 Carefully clean away all traces of the Plastigauge from the journals and bearing shells using a fingernail or other object which

will not score the bearing surfaces.
18 If the clearance is beyond the service limit, replace the bearing shells with new ones (see Steps 20 to 22) and check the oil clearance once again. Always renew all of the shells at the same time.
19 If the clearance is still greater than the service limit listed in this Chapter's Specifications, the crankshaft journal is worn and the crankshaft should be renewed.

Bearing shell selection

20 Replacement bearing shells for the main bearings are supplied on a selected fit basis. Code numbers for the crankshaft journals are stamped on the outside of the crankshaft web on the left-hand end of the crankshaft **(see illustration 21.25a)**. The left-hand block of five numbers are the size codes for the main bearing journals (the right-hand block of four numbers are the size codes for the big-end bearing journals). The first number of the block is for the left-hand (No. 1) journal, and so on.
21 The main bearing size codes are stamped into the back of the lower crankcase half **(see illustrations)**. The first number of the five is for the left-hand (No. 1) bearing, and so on. **Note:** *If there is only one number stamped into the crankcase, it means that all the bearings are the same size code.*
22 A range of bearing shells are available. To select the correct shells for a particular journal, subtract the crankshaft journal number from

Installation

23 Ensure the backs of the bearing shells, the bearing seats in both crankcase halves, and the main bearing journals on the crankshaft are clean. If new shells are being fitted, ensure that all traces of the protective grease are cleaned off using paraffin (kerosene). Wipe the shells and crankcase halves dry with a lint-free cloth. Make sure all the oil passages and holes are clear, and blow them through with compressed air if it is available.
24 Press the bearing shells into their seats. Make sure the tab on each shell engages in the notch in the casing **(see illustration 24.10)**. Make sure the bearings are fitted in the correct locations and take care not to touch any bearing surfaces with your fingers. Lubricate the shells with clean engine oil.
25 Fit new bolts into the connecting rods – note the alignment of the bolt head with the recess in the connecting rod, then press the old bolt out of the rod. Align the head of the new bolt with the recess in the rod and press the bolt into place. Lower the crankshaft into position in the upper crankcase, making sure all bearing shells remain in place **(see illustration 24.2)**.
26 Refer to Section 21, Steps 34 to 37, and fit the connecting rods onto the crankshaft using new big-end nuts/bolts.
27 Reassemble the crankcase halves (see Section 19).

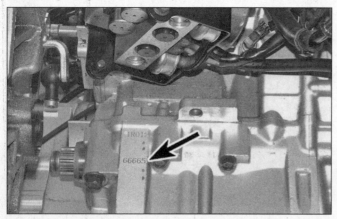

24.21a Main bearing size codes (arrowed)

24.21b Single number denotes one size code for all five bearings

25.2a Note the locating pin (arrowed) on the output shaft bearing

25.2b Lift the output shaft out of the crankcase

25 Transmission shaft removal and installation

Note: *To remove the transmission shafts the engine must be removed from the frame.*
Special tool: Although not strictly a tool, this procedure requires the use of two M6 x 1.0 bolts of 30 mm thread length and three M6 x 1.0 bolts of 25 mm thread length with plain washers – see Steps 5 and 7.

Removal

1 Remove the engine from the frame (see Section 4). Temporarily install the gearchange linkage arm and shift the transmission into neutral. Remove the gearchange mechanism (see Section 15) and separate the crankcase halves (see Section 19).
2 Note how the pin on the output shaft bearing locates in the upper crankcase half, and how the output shaft selector forks locate in the grooves on the 5th and 6th gear pinions and how the guide pins on the forks locate in the grooves in the selector drum **(see illustration)**. Lift the output

25.3a Remove the bearing retainer . . .

25.3b . . . and discard the shaft oil seal

shaft out of the crankcase **(see illustration)**; if it is stuck, use a soft-faced hammer and gently tap on the ends of the shaft to free it.
3 Remove the bearing half-ring retainer from the crankcase or bearing, noting how it fits **(see illustration)**. Discard the oil seal from the left-hand end of the shaft as a new one must be fitted on reassembly **(see illustration)**.
4 Remove the selector drum and forks (see Section 27).
5 Undo the Torx screws securing the input

shaft bearing housing. Discard the screws as new ones must be fitted on reassembly. Obtain two 6 mm bolts, 30 mm long excluding the bolt head, and with a 1 mm thread pitch, and screw them into the two holes in the bearing housing as shown **(see illustration)**. Tighten the bolts until they contact the surface of the crankcase, then continue tightening them evenly and a little at a time until the bearing housing is displaced **(see illustration)**. Withdraw the input shaft from the crankcase.

25.5a Displace the bearing housing by screwing in two bolts (arrowed) . . .

25.5b . . . and turning them against the crankcase surface

25.7a Locate the end of the input shaft in the bearing (arrowed)

25.7b Using bolts and washers . . .

6 To remove the inner input shaft bearing, see *Tools and Workshop Tips* in the *Reference* section.

Installation

7 Slide the input shaft into the crankcase far enough for the left-hand end of the shaft to locate in its bearing **(see illustration)**. Obtain three 6 mm bolts, 25 mm long excluding the bolt head, and three flat washers. Insert the bolts and washers through the bearing housing screw holes and screw them into the crankcase. Tighten the bolts evenly and a little at a time to draw the bearing housing into its location in the crankcase **(see illustrations)**. When the housing is fully installed, unscrew the bolts.

8 Apply a suitable thread locking compound to the new Torx screws and tighten them to the torque setting specified at the beginning of this Chapter. Stake the edge of each screw into the indent in the housing using a suitable punch **(see illustration)**.

9 Install the selector drum and forks (see Section 27).

10 Fit the output shaft bearing half-ring retainer into its slot in the upper crankcase **(see illustration 25.3a)**. Smear the inside of the new output shaft seal with grease. Slide the seal onto the left-hand end of the shaft **(see illustration 25.3b)**.

11 Lower the output shaft into position in the upper crankcase, making sure the groove in the bearing engages correctly with the half-ring retainer and the pin on the bearing locates correctly in the crankcase **(see illustrations 25.2b and a)**.

Caution: If the half-ring retainer is not correctly engaged, the crankcase halves will not seat correctly.

12 Make sure output shaft is correctly seated and that the selector forks are located in the grooves in the appropriate gear pinions (see Section 27).

13 Position the gears in the neutral position and check the shafts are free to rotate easily and independently (i.e. the input shaft can turn whilst the output shaft is held stationary) before proceeding further.

14 Reassemble the crankcase halves (see Section 19).

26 Transmission shaft overhaul

1 Remove the transmission shafts from the crankcase (see Section 25). Always disassemble the transmission shafts separately to avoid mixing up the components.

Input shaft disassembly

2 Slide the 2nd gear pinion off the left-hand end of the shaft, noting which way around it is fitted – mark its outer face with a marker pen as an aid to reassembly **(see illustration 26.26)**.

3 Note how the tabs on the lock washer fit into the slotted splined washer and remove the lockwasher **(see illustration 26.25)**.

4 Turn the slotted splined washer to align it with the splines on the shaft and slide it off the shaft **(see illustration 26.24)**.

5 Slide the 6th gear pinion and its splined bush off the shaft, followed by the splined washer **(see illustrations 26.23c, b and a)**.

6 Remove the circlip securing the combined

25.7c . . . draw the bearing housing into the crankcase

25.8 Tighten the new Torx screws as specified and then stake them in place

26.8 The 1st gear pinion (arrowed) is integral with the shaft

26.9 Remove the bearing and housing if required

3rd/4th gear pinion, then slide the pinion off the shaft noting which way round it fits **(see illustrations 26.22b and a)**. Discard the circlip as a new one must be fitted on reassembly.

7 Remove the circlip securing the 5th gear pinion, then slide the splined washer, the pinion and its bush off the shaft **(see illustrations 26.21b and a and 26.20b and a)**. Discard the circlip as a new one must be fitted on reassembly.

8 The 1st gear pinion is integral with the shaft **(see illustration)**.

9 If required, remove the bearing and its housing from the right-hand end of the shaft, referring to *Tools and Workshop Tips* (Section 5) in the *Reference* section **(see illustration)**.

Shaft inspection

10 Wash all the components in solvent and dry them off.

11 Check the gear teeth for cracking, chipping, pitting and other obvious wear or damage. Any pinion that is damaged must be replaced with a new one.

12 Inspect the dogs and the dog holes in the gears for cracks, chips, and excessive wear especially in the form of rounded edges. Make sure mating gears engage properly. Replace mating gears as a set if necessary.

13 Check for signs of scoring or bluing on the pinions, bushes and shaft. This could be caused by overheating due to inadequate lubrication. Check that all the oil holes and passages are clear. Replace any worn or damaged parts with new ones.

14 Check that each pinion moves freely on the shaft or bush but without undue freeplay. Check that each bush moves freely on the shaft but without undue freeplay.

15 The shaft is unlikely to sustain damage unless the engine has seized, placing an unusually high loading on the transmission, or the machine has covered a very high mileage. Check the surface of the shaft, especially where a pinion turns on it, and replace the shaft with a new one if it has scored or picked up, or if there are any cracks. Check the shaft runout using V-blocks and a dial gauge and replace the shaft with a new one if the runout exceeds the limit specified at the beginning of this Chapter.

16 Check the washers and replace any that are bent or worn with new ones.

17 Check the bearings referring to *Tools and Workshop Tips* (Section 5) in the *Reference* section. Do not forget the input shaft left-hand bearing, which is housed in the crankcase.

Input shaft reassembly

18 During reassembly, apply clean engine oil or molybdenum disulphide oil (a 50/50 mixture of molybdenum disulphide grease and engine oil) to the mating surfaces of the shaft, pinions and bushes. Use new circlips and do not expand their ends any further than is necessary to slide them along the shaft. Install them so that their chamfered side faces the pinion they secure (see *Correct fitting of a stamped circlip* illustration in *Tools and Workshop Tips* (Section 2) in the *Reference* section).

19 If removed, fit the bearing and its housing onto the right-hand end of the shaft, referring to *Tools and Workshop Tips* (Section 5) in the *Reference* section **(see illustration 26.9)**.

20 Slide the 5th gear pinion bush onto the left-hand end of the shaft then fit the 5th gear pinion onto the bush with its dog holes facing away from the integral 1st gear **(see illustrations)**.

26.20a Slide the 5th gear pinion bush . . .

26.20b . . . the 5th gear pinion . . .

26.21a ... and the splined washer onto the shaft ...

26.21b ... and secure them with the circlip

26.22a Slide the 3rd/4th gear pinion onto the shaft ...

26.22b ... and secure it with the circlip

26.23a Install the splined washer ...

26.23b ... align the oil holes (arrowed) and fit the 6th gear pinion bush ...

26.23c . . . and slide on the 6th gear pinion

21 Slide the splined washer onto the shaft, then fit the new circlip, making sure that it locates correctly in the groove in the shaft **(see illustrations)**.
22 Slide the combined 3rd/4th gear pinion onto the shaft with the smaller 3rd gear pinion facing the 5th gear pinion. Ensure the oil hole in the pinion aligns with the oil holes in the shaft. Fit the new circlip, making sure it locates correctly in its groove in the shaft **(see illustrations)**.
23 Slide the splined washer onto the shaft, followed by the splined 6th gear pinion bush, aligning the oil hole in the bush with the hole in the shaft. Fit the 6th gear pinion, making sure its dog holes face the 3rd/4th gear pinion **(see illustrations)**.
24 Slide the slotted splined washer onto the shaft and locate it in its groove, then turn it in the groove, so that the splines on the washer locate against the splines on the shaft and secure the washer in the groove **(see illustration)**.
25 Slide the lockwasher onto the shaft, so that the tabs on the lockwasher locate in the slots on the outside edge of the splined washer **(see illustration)**.
26 Slide the 2nd gear pinion onto the shaft, the correct way around as noted on removal **(see illustration)**.
27 Check that all components have been correctly installed. The assembled shaft should look as shown **(see illustration)**.

Output shaft disassembly

28 Slide the bearing off the right-hand end of the shaft **(see illustration 26.49)**.
29 Slide the thrust washer off the shaft, followed by the 1st gear pinion and its bush **(see illustrations 26.48c, b and a)**.
30 Slide the 5th gear pinion off the shaft **(see illustration 26.47)**.
31 Remove the circlip securing the 3rd gear pinion, then slide the splined washer, the pinion and its splined bush off the shaft **(see illustrations 26.46d, c, b and a)**. Discard

26.24 Install the slotted splined washer as described . . .

26.25 . . . then slide on the tabbed lockwasher . . .

26.26 . . . and the 2nd gear pinion

26.27 The assembled gearbox input shaft

26.37 Remove the collar (A) and bearing (B) if required

26.41a Slide the 2nd gear pinion bush . . .

the circlip as a new one must be fitted on reassembly.

32 Note how the tabs on the lock washer fit into the slotted splined washer and remove the lockwasher **(see illustration 26.45)**.

33 Turn the slotted splined washer to align it with the splines on the shaft and slide it off the shaft **(see illustrations 26.44)**.

34 Slide the 4th gear pinion and its splined bush, followed by the splined washer, off the shaft **(see illustrations 26.43c, b and a)**.

35 Remove the circlip securing the 6th gear pinion, then slide the pinion off the shaft **(see illustrations 26.42b and a)**. Discard the circlip as a new one must be fitted on reassembly.

36 Remove the circlip securing the 2nd gear pinion, then slide the splined washer, the pinion and its bush off the shaft **(see illustrations 26.41d, c, b and a)**.

37 If required, remove the collar and bearing from the left-hand end of the shaft, referring to *Tools and Workshop Tips* (Section 5) in the *Reference* section **(see illustration)**.

Shaft inspection

38 Refer to Steps 10 to 17 above.

Output shaft reassembly

39 During reassembly, apply engine oil or molybdenum disulphide oil (a 50/50 mixture

of molybdenum disulphide grease and engine oil) to the mating surfaces of the shaft, pinions and bushes. When installing the new circlips, do not expand their ends any further than is necessary to slide them along the shaft. Install them so that their chamfered side faces the pinion they secure (see *Correct fitting of a stamped circlip* illustration in *Tools and Workshop Tips* (Section 2) in the *Reference* section).

40 If removed, fit the bearing and collar onto the left-hand end of the shaft, referring to *Tools and Workshop Tips* (Section 5) in the *Reference* section.

41 Slide the 2nd gear pinion bush onto the shaft, then slide on the 2nd gear pinion (dog holes facing away from the bearing) and the splined washer. Fit the new circlip, making sure it is locates correctly in its groove on the shaft **(see illustrations)**.

42 Align the oil holes in the shaft and the 6th gear pinion, and slide the pinion onto the shaft with its selector fork groove facing away from the 2nd gear pinion, then fit the new circlip, making sure it locates correctly in its groove on the shaft **(see illustrations)**.

43 Slide the splined washer and the splined 4th gear pinion bush onto the shaft, making sure the oil hole in the bush aligns with the hole in the shaft, then fit the 4th gear pinion so that its dished side and

26.41b . . . the 2nd gear pinion . . .

26.41c . . . and the splined washer onto the shaft . . .

26.41d . . . and secure them with the circlip

26.42a Align the oil holes (arrowed) and slide the 6th gear pinion onto the shaft . . .

26.42b . . . and secure it with the circlip

26.43a Install the splined washer . . .

26.43b . . . then align the oil holes (arrowed) and fit the 4th gear pinion bush . . .

26.43c . . . and slide on the 4th gear pinion

26.44 Install the slotted splined washer as described . . .

26.45 . . . then slide on the tabbed lockwasher

dog holes face the 6th gear pinion (see illustrations).

44 Slide the slotted splined washer onto the shaft and locate it in its groove, then turn it in the groove so that the splines on the washer align against the splines on the shaft and secure the washer in the groove (see illustration).

45 Slide the lockwasher onto the shaft, so that the tabs on the lockwasher locate into the slots in the outer rim of the splined washer (see illustration).

46 Slide the splined 3rd gear pinion bush onto the shaft, making sure the oil hole in the bush aligns with the hole in the shaft, then fit the 3rd gear pinion (dished side and dog holes facing away from the 4th gear pinion) and the splined washer. Fit the new circlip, making

26.46a Align the oil holes (arrowed) and fit the 3rd gear pinion bush . . .

26.46b . . . then slide on the 3rd gear pinion . . .

sure it locates correctly in its groove in the shaft (see illustrations).

47 Align the oil holes in the shaft and the 5th

gear pinion, and slide the pinion onto the shaft with its selector fork groove facing the 3rd gear pinion (see illustration).

26.46c . . . and the splined washer . . .

26.46d . . . and secure them with the circlip

26.47 Align the oil holes (arrowed) and slide the 5th gear pinion onto the shaft

26.48a Install the 1st gear pinion bush . . .

26.48b . . . then slide the 1st gear pinion . . .

26.48c . . . and the thrust washer onto the shaft . . .

48 Slide the 1st gear pinion bush onto the shaft, followed by the 1st gear pinion (dished side facing the 5th gear pinion) and the thrust washer **(see illustrations)**.
49 Fit the bearing onto the end of the shaft with its open side facing the 1st gear pinion **(see illustration)**.
50 Check that all components have been correctly installed. The assembled shaft should look as shown **(see illustration)**.

27 Selector drum and forks

Note: *To remove the selector drum and forks the engine must be removed from the frame.*

Removal

1 Position the transmission in neutral. Remove the engine from the frame (see Section 4). Remove the gearchange mechanism (see Section 15), then separate the crankcase halves (see Section 19).
2 Note how the output shaft selector forks locate in the grooves on the 5th and 6th gear pinions and how the guide pins on the forks locate in the grooves in the selector drum, then remove the output shaft (see Section 25).
3 Note the position of the selector drum as an aid for installation; note the position of the neutral detent on the left-hand end of the selector drum **(see illustration)**.
4 Note that each selector fork is lettered for identification. The right-hand fork has an 'R',

the centre fork a 'C', and the left-hand fork an 'L' **(see illustration)**. These letters face the right-hand side (clutch side) of the engine. If no letters are visible, mark the forks yourself using a felt pen before removing the forks.
5 Note how the input shaft selector fork locates in the groove on the 3rd/4th gear pinion and how the guide pin on the fork locates in the groove in the selector drum.
6 Unscrew the bolts securing the selector drum retainer plate and remove the plate, noting how it fits **(see illustration)**. Support the output shaft selector forks (L and R) and withdraw the fork shaft from the crankcase **(see illustration)**. Note the springs in the ends of the shaft and remove them for safekeeping, if loose.
7 Remove the selector forks and slide them

26.49 . . . and fit the bearing

26.50 The assembled gearbox output shaft

27.3 Note the position of the neutral detent (arrowed) on the end of the selector drum

27.4 Note the letter on each fork denoting its position

27.6a Remove the selector drum retainer plate . . .

27.6b . . . then withdraw the shaft for the output shaft selector forks

back onto the shaft in the correct order and the right way round **(see illustration)**.

8 Support the input shaft selector fork (C) and withdraw the fork shaft from the crankcase **(see illustration)**. Remove the springs from the ends of the shaft for safekeeping, if loose. Move the fork guide pin out of its track in the selector drum, then withdraw the selector drum from the left-hand side of the casing **(see illustration)**.

9 Move the selector fork around in its groove in the 3rd/4th gear pinion and remove it **(see illustration)**. Slide the fork back onto the shaft.

Inspection

10 Inspect the selector forks for any signs of wear or damage, especially around the fork ends where they engage with the grooves in the pinions. Check that each fork fits correctly in its pinion groove. Check closely to see if the forks are bent. If the forks are in any way damaged they must be replaced with new ones.

11 Check that the forks fit correctly on their shaft. They should move freely with a light fit but no appreciable freeplay. Check that the fork shaft holes in the casing are not worn or damaged.

12 Check the selector fork shaft runout using V-blocks and a dial gauge and replace the shaft with a new one if the runout exceeds the limit specified at the beginning of this Chapter. A bent shaft will cause difficulty in selecting gears and make the gearchange action heavy.

13 Inspect the selector drum grooves and selector fork guide pins for signs of wear or damage. If either show signs of wear or damage they must be replaced with new ones.

14 Check the selector drum bearing referring to *Tools and Workshop Tips* (Section 5) in the *Reference* section. If the bearing is worn a new selector drum will have to be fitted as the bearing is not available separately. Also check that the neutral switch contact on the right-hand end of the drum is not damaged or worn away. If required, remove the contact and replace it with a new one.

Installation

15 Locate the input shaft selector fork (C) in

27.16a Lubricate the end of the selector drum before assembly

27.7 Install the forks on the shaft for safekeeping. Note the springs (arrowed)

27.8b ... then disengage the fork guide pin and withdraw the selector drum ...

27.16b Neutral contact on the drum (arrowed) should align with the neutral switch

27.8a Withdraw the shaft for the input shaft selector fork ...

27.9 ... and the fork

27.18 Slide the fork shaft (A) through the fork (B)

its groove in the 3rd/4th gear pinion, making sure the letter faces the right-hand (clutch) side of the engine, then slide the fork around and below the input shaft so that it does not get in the way when installing the selector drum.

16 Lubricate the end of the selector drum with clean engine oil, then align the selector drum so that the neutral detent points to the upper rear engine mounting and slide the drum into the crankcase **(see illustration)**. Make sure the drum end locates in its bore in the crankcase, and that the neutral contact on the drum locates against the neutral switch contact on the inside back of the crankcase **(see illustration)**.

17 If removed, fit the springs into the ends of the selector fork shafts and lubricate the shafts with clean engine oil.

18 Move the input shaft selector fork around

in its groove and locate the fork guide pin into its track in the selector drum, then slide the fork shaft into the crankcase and through the fork **(see illustration)**.

19 Position the output shaft forks (R and L) in the crankcase, making sure the letters face the right-hand (clutch) side of the engine and the fork guide pins locate in their tracks in the drum. Slide the fork shaft into the crankcase and through the forks **(see illustration 27.6b)**.

20 Apply a suitable non-permanent thread locking compound to the selector drum retainer plate bolts. Install the plate and tighten the bolts to the torque setting specified at the beginning of this Chapter.

21 Lower the transmission output shaft into the crankcase. Ensure that the fork marked 'R' locates in the groove in the 5th gear pinion, and that the fork marked 'L' locates in the groove in the 6th gear pinion (see Step 2).

28.2a Withdraw the oil feed pipe (arrowed) from the crankcase . . .

28.2b . . . and check the condition of the O-rings (arrowed)

28.3 Remove the external oil pipe . . .

22 Check that the output shaft is correctly seated and that the transmission shafts rotate easily and independently (see Section 25).

28 Crankcases and cylinder bores

Crankcase halves

1 After the crankcases have been separated, remove the crankshaft, connecting rods and pistons, bearings, transmission shafts, selector drum and forks, and any other components or assemblies, referring to the relevant Sections of this and other Chapters (see Step 3 of Section 19).
2 Withdraw the oil feed pipe from the upper crankcase – it is a push-fit (see illustration). Check the condition of the pipe O-rings and replace them with new ones if they are in any way damaged, deformed or deteriorated (see illustration).
3 Unscrew the bolts retaining the external U-shaped oil pipe on the front of the lower crankcase and pull the pipe out of its sockets (see illustration). Discard the O-rings as new ones must be fitted on reassembly.
4 Unscrew the main oil gallery plug from each side of the lower crankcase and discard the O-rings as new ones must be fitted on reassembly (see illustration).
5 Unscrew the bolts securing the oil baffle plate in the clutch housing and remove it

28.4 . . . and the oil passageway plug and discard the O-rings

noting how it fits (see illustration). Unscrew the bolts securing the crankcase breather cover. Remove the cover and discard its gasket.
6 Clean the crankcases thoroughly with solvent and dry them with compressed air. Blow out all oil passages and pipes with compressed air (see illustrations).
7 Remove all traces of old gasket sealant from the mating surfaces. Minor damage to the surfaces can be cleaned up with careful use of a fine sharpening stone.
Caution: Be very careful not to nick or gouge the crankcase mating surfaces, or oil leaks will result. Check both crankcase halves very carefully for cracks and other damage.
8 Before proceeding further, check the cylinder bores (see Steps 18 to 21).
9 Inspect the bearing seats for signs of damage, especially if an engine or transmission

28.5 Oil baffle plate is in the back of the clutch housing (arrowed)

bearing has overheated or seized (see Section 20) (see illustration). If bearing shells or a ball bearing cage are not a precise fit in their seats, ask your Yamaha dealer for a suitable bearing locking compound which will overcome small amounts of wear. Otherwise the crankcase halves will have to be replaced with a new set.
10 Small cracks or holes in aluminium castings can be repaired with an epoxy resin adhesive as a temporary measure. Permanent repairs can only be effected by argon-arc welding, and only a specialist in this process is in a position to advise on the economy or practical aspect of such a repair. Note that low temperature aluminium welding kits are available for minor repairs. If any damage is found that can't be repaired, renew the crankcase halves as a set.
11 Damaged threads can be economically reclaimed by using a diamond section wire

28.6a Clean the crankcases thoroughly . . .

28.6b . . . and blow through the oil passageways with compressed air

28.9 Inspect the bearing seats and oilways (arrowed)

28.18 Examine the cylinder walls carefully

28.19 Measure the cylinder bore in the directions shown with a telescoping gauge

insert which is easily fitted after drilling and re-tapping the affected thread.

12 Sheared studs or screws can usually be removed with stud or screw extractors; if you are in any doubt consult your Yamaha dealer or specialist motorcycle engineer.

13 Install the oil baffle plate, then apply a suitable non-permanent thread locking compound to the threads of the bolts and tighten them to the torque setting specified at the beginning of this Chapter. Fit the crankcase breather cover using a new cover and tighten its bolts.

14 Lightly grease the new O-rings for the oil gallery plugs and install the plugs, tightening them to the specified torque setting.

15 Lightly grease the new O-rings for the external U-shaped oil pipe and install the pipe, then tighten the retaining bolts securely.

16 Lightly grease the O-rings on the oil feed pipe and install the pipe, locating the tab on the outer end in the cut-out in the crankcase. Ensure the outer end of the pipe is a flush fit with the crankcase; the pipe is retained by the lip of the input shaft bearing housing.

17 Install the remaining components in the reverse order of removal.

Cylinder bores

18 Check the cylinder walls carefully for scratches and score marks **(see illustration)**.

19 Using telescoping gauges and a micrometer (see *Tools and Workshop Tips*), check the dimensions of each cylinder to assess the amount of wear, taper and ovality. Measure near the top (but below the level of

the top piston ring at TDC), the centre and bottom (but above the level of the oil ring at BDC) of the bore. Measure both parallel to and across the crankshaft axis in each case and calculate the average cylinder dimension at each point **(see illustration)**. Compare the results to the specifications at the beginning of this Chapter.

20 If the precision measuring tools are not available, take the crankcase to a Yamaha dealer or specialist motorcycle engineer for assessment and advice.

21 If the cylinders are worn beyond the service limit, or badly scratched, scuffed or scored, replace the crankcases with a new set. The cylinders cannot be rebored. If new crankcases are fitted, new pistons and rings must be used.

29 Running-in procedure

1 Make sure the engine oil and coolant levels are correct (see *Pre-ride checks*).

2 Make sure there is fuel in the tank.

3 Turn the ignition 'ON' and check that the oil level warning light and the engine management warning light come on for a few seconds and then go off. Ensure that the transmission is in neutral and that the neutral light is illuminated.

4 Start the engine, then allow it to run at a moderately fast idle until it reaches normal operating temperature.

5 As no oil pressure warning light is fitted, an oil pressure check is advised (see Section 3).

6 If a lubrication failure is suspected, stop the engine immediately and try to find the cause. If an engine is run without oil, even for a short period of time, severe damage will occur. After running the rebuilt engine for 600 miles (1000 km), change the engine oil and filter (see Chapter 1).

7 Check carefully that there are no oil or coolant leaks and make sure the transmission and controls, especially the brakes and clutch, work properly before road testing the machine.

8 Treat the machine gently for the first few miles to allow the oil to circulate throughout the engine and any new parts installed to seat.

9 Great care is necessary if the engine has been extensively overhauled – the bike will have to be run in as when new. This means more use of the transmission and a restraining hand on the throttle until at least 600 miles (1000 km) have been covered. There is no point in keeping to any set road speed, the main idea is to keep from labouring the engine and to gradually increase performance up to the 1000 mile (1600 km) mark. These recommendations apply less when only a partial overhaul has been done, though it does depend to an extent on the nature of the work carried out and which components have been renewed. Experience is the best guide, since it is easy to tell when an engine is running freely. If in any doubt, consult a Yamaha dealer. The following maximum engine speed limitations, which Yamaha provide for new motorcycles, can be used as a guide.

Up to 600 miles (1000 km)
Do not exceed 7000 rpm
600 to 1000 miles (1000 to 1600 km)
Vary throttle position/speed. Do not exceed 8400 rpm for long periods
Over 1000 miles (1600 km)
Normal riding. Do not exceed tachometer red line

10 Upon completion of the road test, and after the engine has cooled down completely, recheck the valve clearances (see Chapter 1) and check the engine oil and coolant levels (see *Pre-ride checks*).

Chapter 3
Cooling system

Contents

Degrees of difficulty

Easy, suitable for novice with little experience	**Fairly easy,** suitable for beginner with some experience	**Fairly difficult,** suitable for competent DIY mechanic	**Difficult,** suitable for experienced DIY mechanic	**Very difficult,** suitable for expert DIY or professional 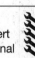

Specifications

Coolant

Coolant type. . . . .   50% distilled water, 50% ethylene glycol anti-freeze with corrosion inhibitors for aluminium engines. **Note:** *Yamaha specify that soft tap water can be used, but NOT hard water. If in doubt, boil the water first or use only distilled water.*

Coolant capacity
     Radiator . . . .   2.0 litres
     Reservoir. . . . .   0.25 litre

Radiator

Cap valve opening pressure. . . . .   13.2 to 17.5 psi (0.9 to 1.2 Bar)

Coolant temperature sensor

Resistance @ 0°C. . . . .   5.21 to 6.37 K-ohms
Resistance @ 10°C. . . . .   approx. 4 K-ohms
Resistance @ 20°C. . . . .   approx 3 K-ohms
Resistance @ 80°C. . . . .   290 to 350 ohms

Thermostat

Opening temperature. . . . .   71 to 85°C
Valve lift . . . .   8 mm @ 85°C

Water pump

Impeller shaft tilt (max.) . . . .   0.15 mm

Torque wrench settings

Coolant temperature sensor. . . . .   18 Nm
Radiator mounting bolts. . . . .   7 Nm
Thermostat cover bolts . . . .   12 Nm
Water pump cover/drain bolts . . . .   10 Nm
Water pump mounting bolts. . . . .   12 Nm

1 General information

The cooling system uses a water/antifreeze mixture to carry excess heat away from the engine. The cylinders are surrounded by a water jacket, through which the coolant is circulated by thermo-syphonic action in conjunction with a water pump. The water pump drives off the oil pump which is driven by chain and sprockets off the back of the clutch.

Heated coolant rises through the system to a thermostat and then to the radiator. It flows across the radiator, where it is cooled by the air flow, then down to the water pump and back into the engine, where the cycle is repeated. The thermostat is fitted in the system to prevent the coolant flowing through the radiator when the engine is cold, therefore accelerating the speed at which the engine reaches normal operating temperature.

A coolant temperature sensor is fitted into the back of the cylinder head which provides signals for the coolant temperature display on the instrument panel and for the ECU as part of the engine management system.

A relay-controlled cooling fan is fitted behind the radiator, to aid cooling in extreme conditions. The relay is controlled by a signal from the ECU.

Some coolant is routed from the engine through the fast idle unit on the throttle bodies then back to the radiator – when the coolant is cold the unit increases engine idle speed for fast warm-up.

The complete cooling system is partially sealed and pressurised, the pressure being controlled by a spring-loaded valve contained in the radiator cap. By pressurising the coolant the boiling point is raised, preventing premature boiling in adverse conditions. The overflow hose from the system is connected to a reservoir mounted behind the engine or below the radiator, into which excess coolant is expelled under pressure. The discharged coolant automatically returns to the radiator when the engine cools.

⚠ **Warning: Do not remove the pressure cap from the radiator when the engine is hot. Scalding hot coolant and steam may be blown out under pressure and could cause serious injury. When the engine has cooled, place a thick rag such as a towel over the pressure cap; slowly rotate the cap anti-clockwise to the first stop. This procedure allows any residual pressure to escape. When the pressure has stopped escaping, press down on the cap while turning it anti-clockwise, and remove it.**

Do not allow antifreeze to come into contact with your skin, or painted surfaces of the motorcycle. Rinse off any spills immediately with plenty of water. Antifreeze is highly toxic if ingested. Never leave antifreeze lying around in an open container or in puddles on the floor; children and pets are attracted by its sweet smell and may drink it. Check with the local authorities about disposing of used antifreeze. Many communities will have collection centres which will see that antifreeze is disposed of safely.

Caution: At all times use the specified type of antifreeze, and always mix it with distilled water in the correct proportion. The antifreeze contains corrosion inhibitors which are essential to avoid damage to the cooling system. A lack of these inhibitors could lead to a build-up of corrosion which will block the coolant passages inside the engine, resulting in overheating and severe engine damage. Distilled water must be used as opposed to tap water to avoid a build-up of scale which would also block the passages.

Read the *Safety first!* section of this manual carefully before starting work.

2 Radiator

Removal

⚠ **Warning: The engine must be completely cool before carrying out this procedure.**

1 If fitted, remove the fairing (see Chapter 7).
2 Remove the fuel tank and the air filter housing (see Chapter 4). Remove the battery and the battery housing (see Chapter 8).
3 Drain the cooling system (see Chapter 1).
4 Trace the wiring from the fan motor on the back of the radiator and disconnect it at the black connector **(see illustration)**.
5 Release the clips securing the radiator overflow hose, the water pump breather hose and the fast idle unit hose, then detach the hoses, noting which fits where **(see illustrations)**.
6 Slacken the clamps securing the radiator inlet and outlet hoses and the oil cooler outlet hose, and detach the hoses from the radiator unions, noting which fits where **(see illustrations)**.
7 Unscrew the radiator lower mounting bolt and remove the bolt and washer **(see**

2.4 Disconnect the fan motor wiring connector (arrowed)

2.5a Detach the radiator overflow hose . . .

2.5b . . . the pump breather hose (A) and fast idle unit hose (B)

2.6a Detach the oil cooler hose (A), the radiator outlet hose (B) . . .

2.6b . . . and the radiator inlet hose from their unions

2.7 Unscrew the radiator lower mounting bolt (arrowed)

2.8a ABS pipe assembly is secured to radiator bracket through this union (arrowed)

2.8b Hold the union to prevent it twisting while undoing the mounting bolt

2.8c Displace the ABS pipe assembly to access the radiator top mounting bolt (arrowed)

2.8d Remove the ABS brake pipes support bracket

illustration). Note the spacer that fits in the bush in the radiator mounting tab and remove it if it is loose.

8 Unscrew the upper (left-hand) mounting bolt and remove the bolt and washer. Note the spacer that fits in the bush in the radiator mounting tab and remove it if it is loose. On machines fitted with ABS, undo the bolt securing the brake pipes to the left-hand radiator bracket to gain access to the radiator mounting bolt (see illustrations). Unscrew the bolt and remove the support bracket (see illustration).

9 Carefully manoeuvre the radiator clear of the lower bracket, then draw it off the upper right-hand frame lug and remove it (see illustration).

10 If necessary, separate the cooling fan from the radiator (see Section 4).

11 Check the radiator for signs of damage and clear any dirt or debris that might obstruct airflow and inhibit cooling. Radiator fins can be straightened carefully with a flat-bladed screwdriver, but if the fins are badly damaged or broken the radiator must be replaced with a new one. Also check the mounting bushes,

and replace them with new ones if necessary (see illustrations).

Installation

12 Installation is the reverse of removal, noting the following.

● Make sure the spacers, bushes and washers are correctly installed with the mounting bolts (see illustration 2.11a and b). Tighten the bolts to the torque setting specified at the beginning of this Chapter.

● Ensure the coolant hoses are in good condition (see Chapter 1), and are securely

2.9 Manoeuvre the radiator clear of its brackets

2.11a Check the condition of the mounting bushes. Note the spacer (arrowed)

2.11b Ensure the spacers are fitted before assembly

3.2 Remove the cap and draw out the end of the overflow hose (arrowed)

3.3a Release the clip (arrowed) securing the hoses . . .

retained by their clamps or clips, using new ones if necessary (see Steps 5 and 6).
● Make sure that the wiring connector Is secure (see illustration 2.4).
● Refill the cooling system as described in Chapter 1.

Radiator pressure cap

13 If problems such as overheating or loss of coolant occur, check the entire system as described in Chapter 1. The radiator cap opening pressure should be checked by a Yamaha dealer with the special tester required for the job. If the cap is defective, replace it with a new one.

3 Coolant reservoir

Removal

2004 to 2006 non-ABS models

1 Remove the fuel tank (see Chapter 4).
2 Remove the reservoir cap and draw out the radiator overflow hose (see illustration).
3 Release the clip securing the fuel tank breather hoses to the bottom of the reservoir, then unscrew the reservoir mounting bolts and lift the reservoir off the motorcycle (see

3.3b . . . and unscrew the mounting bolts (arrowed)

3.4 Release the hose clip (arrowed)

illustrations). Draw the reservoir breather hose out, noting its routing. Tip the coolant out of the reservoir into a suitable container.

All ABS models and 2007-on non ABS models

4 Release the clip securing the radiator outlet hose to the reservoir bracket (see illustration).
5 Remove the reservoir cap and draw out the end of the radiator overflow hose (see illustration). Note the short breather hose in the cap.
6 Unscrew the reservoir mounting bolt and lift the reservoir off the motorcycle (see illustration). Tip the coolant out of the reservoir into a suitable container.

7 If required, release the clip securing the radiator overflow hose from the union on the filler neck (see illustration 2.5a). Release the overflow hose from the clip secured by the timing rotor cover bolt, then carefully draw the hose off, noting its routing.

Installation

8 Installation is the reverse of removal, noting the following:
● Ensure the breather hose and the overflow hose are correctly routed and secured.
● Fill the reservoir with the specified coolant up to the correct level (see Pre-ride checks).

3.5 Remove the cap (A) and draw out the end of the overflow hose (B)

3.6 Location of the reservoir mounting bolt (arrowed)

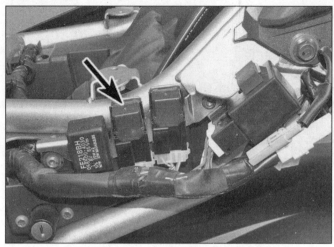

4.2 Location of the cooling fan relay (arrowed)

4.6 Fan assembly mounting bolts (arrowed)

4 Cooling fan and cooling fan relay

Cooling fan

Check

1 If the engine is overheating and the coolant temperature display flashes (or coolant temperature warning light is on – S2 models), yet the cooling fan isn't cutting in, first check the fan fuse in the fusebox (see Chapter 8). If the fuse is good, make sure there is battery voltage at the red wire to the fuse with the ignition OFF.

2 If the fuse is good, remove the left-hand side panel (see Chapter 7). Check that voltage is present at the brown/black wire to the fan relay, with the ignition OFF, and at the red/white wire to the relay when the ignition is ON (see illustration). If there is voltage, the fault lies in either the wiring and connectors between the relay and the fan, the cooling fan motor or the fan relay. If not check the circuit between the cooling fan relay and the ignition switch, referring to the wiring diagram for your model (see Chapter 8).

3 To test the cooling fan motor, first remove the fuel tank and the air filter housing (see Chapter 4), then remove the battery and the battery housing (see Chapter 8).

4 Trace the wiring from the fan motor and disconnect it at the connector (see illustration 2.4). Using a 12 volt battery and two jumper wires, connect the positive (+) battery lead to the blue wire terminal on the fan side of the wiring connector and the negative (–) lead to the black wire terminal. Once connected, the fan should operate. If it does not, and the wiring is all good, then the fan motor is faulty. Replace the fan assembly with a new one – individual components are not available.

Removal and installation

⚠️ Warning: The engine must be completely cool before carrying out this procedure.

5 Remove the radiator (see Section 2).

6 Unscrew the bolts securing the fan assembly to the radiator and remove it (see illustration).

7 Installation is the reverse of removal.

Cooling fan relay

Check

8 Remove the seat and the left-hand side panel (see Chapter 7). If not already done, refer to Step 2 and check the power to the relay.

9 If the voltage is good, disconnect the fan relay wiring connector. Set a multimeter to the ohms x 1 scale and connect the positive (+) probe to the brown/black wire terminal on the relay, and the negative (-) probe to the blue wire terminal. There should be no continuity (infinite resistance).

10 Using a fully-charged 12 volt battery and two insulated jumper wires, connect the positive (+) battery terminal to the red/white wire terminal on the relay, and the negative (–) battery terminal to the green/yellow wire terminal. At this point the relay should be heard to click and the multimeter should read 0 ohms (continuity).

11 If this is the case, the relay is proved good. If there is continuity through the relay at all times, or if the relay does not click when battery voltage is applied and indicates no continuity (infinite resistance) across its terminals, it is faulty and must be replaced with a new one.

12 If the relay is good, and the wiring between the relay, the fan motor and the ECU is good, test the fan motor (if not already done), and the coolant temperature sensor (see Section 5).

Removal and installation

13 Remove the seat and the left-hand side panel (see Chapter 7). Note the location of the relay (see illustration 4.2).

14 Release the relay from its mounting, then disconnect the wiring connector.

15 Check that the terminals inside the connector are clean and free from corrosion, then install the new relay.

5 Coolant temperature display and sensor

Temperature display

Check

1 The circuit consists of the sender mounted in the back of the cylinder head and the coolant temperature indicated on the multi-function display in the instrument cluster.

2 The temperature display should function as follows. When the ignition main switch is turned ON, all the segments of the temperature display should appear in sequence as a test of the circuit. Then, if the engine is cold, only the 'L' segment will be shown. If the engine has been running, either the appropriate segment of the display will be shown, or the actual temperature will be displayed, depending on the style of instrument cluster fitted to your machine (see Chapter 8).

3 If the 'H' segment of the display is shown, or the temperature display begins flashing, the coolant is over-heating – turn the engine OFF immediately. When the engine has cooled, check the coolant level (see Pre-ride checks). If the level is low, check the cooling system for leaks (see Chapter 1, Section 9). If insufficient coolant is not the cause of the over-heating, check the thermostat (see Section 6).

4 If the temperature display malfunctions, first check the ignition fuse in the fusebox (see Chapter 8). If the fuse is good, check the sensor wiring and connections

5.4 Location of the coolant temperature sensor (arrowed)

(see illustration). If required, the operation of the temperature sensor can be checked as described below.

5 If no problems are found, take the instrument cluster to a Yamaha dealer for further assessment – Yamaha provide no specific test data for the instruments themselves. If there are any faults, a new cluster will have to be fitted, as no individual components are available.

Removal and installation

6 Refer to Chapter 8, Section 16, for removal and installation details.

Coolant temperature sensor

Check

7 Remove the fuel tank (see Chapter 4). Disconnect the engine breather hose from the air filter housing and displace the hose to gain access to the temperature sensor located on the back of the cylinder head.

8 Disconnect the sensor wiring connector, then check for continuity between the sensor body and earth (ground) **(see illustration)**. There should be continuity. If there is no continuity, check that the sensor is tight in the cylinder head (see torque Specifications at the beginning of this Chapter).

9 To check the operation of the sensor, remove it from the engine as described below, then fill a small heatproof container with cold coolant (see Specifications) and place it on a stove. Using an ohmmeter, connect the probes to the terminals on the sensor. Suspend the sensor in the coolant so that just the sensing portion and the threads are submerged. Also place a thermometer

5.8 Disconnect the temperature sensor wiring connector (arrowed)

capable of reading temperatures of up to 100°C in the water so that its bulb is close to the sensor **(see illustration)**. **Note:** *None of the components should be allowed to directly touch the container.*
10 Check the temperature of the cold coolant and compare the reading on the meter with the resistances specified at the beginning of the Chapter according to the temperature.

> ⚠️ *Warning: This must be done very carefully to avoid the risk of personal injury.*

11 Heat the coolant, stirring it gently and note the resistance readings at the temperatures specified. If the meter readings obtained are widely different, or they are obtained at different temperatures, then the sensor is faulty and must be replaced with a new one.

Removal and installation

> ⚠️ *Warning: The engine must be completely cool before carrying out this procedure.*

12 Follow the procedure in Step 7 to access the temperature sensor. Drain the cooling system (see Chapter 1).
13 Disconnect the sensor wiring connector, then unscrew the sensor from the head **(see illustration)**. Discard the sealing washer as a new one must be used.
14 On reassembly, apply a suitable sealant (Yamaha advise Three Bond Sealock 10) to the sensor threads, then install the sensor using a new sealing washer and tighten it to the torque setting specified at the beginning of this Chapter.
15 Fill the cooling system (see Chapter 1) and install the remaining components in the reverse order of removal.

H45560

5.9 Set-up for testing the coolant temperature sensor

6 Thermostat

> ⚠️ *Warning: The engine must be completely cool before carrying out this procedure.*

1 The thermostat is automatic in operation and should give many years' service without requiring attention. In the event of a failure, the valve will probably jam open, in which case the engine will take much longer than normal to warm up. Conversely, if the valve jams shut, the coolant will be unable to circulate and the engine will quickly overheat. Neither condition is acceptable, and the fault must be investigated promptly.

Removal

2 Drain the cooling system (see Chapter 1). Remove the throttle bodies (see Chapter 4).
3 Slacken the clamp securing the radiator inlet hose to the thermostat housing and detach the hose **(see illustration)**. Unscrew the bolts securing the cover to the cylinder head and remove the cover, being prepared to catch any residual coolant.
4 Lift the thermostat out of its recess in the cylinder head, noting how it fits **(see illustration)**.

5.13 Unscrew the temperature sensor (arrowed) from the rear of the cylinder head

6.3 Disconnect the hose (A) and unscrew the thermostat housing bolts (B)

6.4 Withdraw the thermostat from the back of the cylinder head

6.7 Set-up for testing the thermostat

6.10 Install thermostat with breather hole (arrowed) at top

7.1 Location of the water pump (arrowed)

5 Inspect the cover for cracks and corrosion, especially around the hose union. Clean off any corrosion with a wire brush or steel wool.

Check

6 Examine the thermostat visually before carrying out the test. If it remains in the open position at room temperature, it should be replaced with a new one.
7 To check the operation of the thermostat, suspend it in a container of cold water. Place a thermometer capable of reading temperatures up to 100°C in the water so that the bulb is close to the thermostat (see illustration).
8 Heat the water whilst stirring it gently, noting the temperature when the thermostat opens, and compare the result with the specifications given at the beginning of this Chapter. Also check the amount the valve opens after it has been heated at 85°C for a few minutes and compare the measurement to the specifications. If the readings obtained differ from those given, the thermostat is faulty and must be replaced with a new one.
9 In the event of the thermostat jamming closed, *as an emergency measure only*, it can be removed and the machine used without it. **Note:** *Take care when starting the engine from cold, as it will take much longer than usual to warm up.* Ensure that a new unit is installed as soon as possible.

Installation

10 Smear the thermostat seal lightly with lithium-based grease and fit the thermostat into the cylinder head, making sure that it seats correctly and that the breather hole is at the top (see illustration).
11 Install the cover and tighten the bolts to the specified torque setting. Make sure the radiator inlet hose is pushed fully onto its union and tighten the clamp securely (see illustration 6.3).
12 Fill the cooling system (see Chapter 1) and install the remaining components in the reverse order of removal.

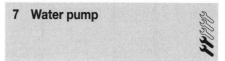

7 Water pump

Check

1 The water pump is located on the right-hand side of the engine and is driven by the oil pump (see illustration).
2 To prevent water leaking from the cooling system into the lubrication system and vice versa, two seals are fitted on the pump shaft (see illustration 7.15). The seal inside the water pump is of the mechanical type which bears on the rear face of the impeller. The other seal, which is located in the pump housing, is of the normal feathered lip type.

3 If either seal fails, a drain hole in the pump body allows the coolant or oil to escape and prevents them mixing (see illustration). If on inspection there are signs of leaks, the pump must be removed and new seals installed (see Steps 14 to 21). If you are not sure about the condition of the seals, remove the pump and check them visually.

Removal

4 Drain the coolant (see Chapter 1).
5 Slacken the clamps securing the large bore hoses on the pump cover and detach the hoses, noting which fits where (see illustration). Release the clip securing the pump breather hose, then pull the hose off its union.
6 Unscrew the pump mounting bolts and draw the pump out of the crankcase (see illustration).

7.3 Water pump drain hole (arrowed)

7.5 Release the clamps and pull the hoses off their unions

7.6 Unscrew the bolts (arrowed) and withdraw the pump

7.7 Discard the pump body O-ring (arrowed)

7.8 Note how the seal fits in the cover

7.10 Withdraw the impeller from the pump

7 Discard the O-ring on the back of the pump body as a new one must be fitted on reassembly (see illustration).

8 If required unscrew the pump cover bolts and lift off the cover. Discard the cover seal as a new one must be fitted on reassembly (see illustration).

Inspection

9 To check the pump impeller bearing, wiggle the impeller back-and-forth and spin it by hand. If there is excessive movement, or the bearing is noisy or rough when turned, the bearing must be replaced with a new one. Also check the bearing referring to *Tools and Workshop Tips* (Section 5) in the *Reference* section.

10 Withdraw the impeller from the pump body to check the condition of the impeller shaft (see illustration). If there are signs of wear or other damage, the impeller must be

replaced with a new one. Check that the shaft is straight – if it tilts by more than the specified limit, replace it with a new one.

11 Check the condition of the rubber damper on the rear (inside) face of the impeller. If it is damaged or deteriorated, fit a new impeller – Yamaha do not list the damper as being available separately.

12 Inspect the pump body for corrosion or a build-up of scale and clean with steel wool as necessary, then rinse the pump body in running clean water.

13 Lubricate the impeller shaft and damper with coolant and slide the impeller into the pump body prior to installation.

Seal and bearing renewal

14 Remove the pump from the engine and the cover from the pump (Steps 4 to 8), then withdraw the impeller from the pump body (see illustration 7.10).

15 To remove the mechanical seal, tap it out towards the inside of the pump body from the outside using a suitable punch, noting which way round it fits (see illustration).

16 To remove the oil seal, first remove the mechanical seal (see Step 15) then remove the circlip retaining the bearing in the pump body (see illustration). Tap the oil seal and bearing out from the inside of the body using a suitable sized bearing driver or socket (see illustration 7.15). Note which way round the seal fits.

17 Clean any traces of sealant from around the mechanical seal seat with a suitable solvent.

18 Press or drive the bearing into the pump body until it is properly seated, then install the circlip (see illustration 7.15).

19 Apply a smear of coolant to the outside of the new oil seal. Press or drive the seal into the body from the inside until it fits against the bearing. The marked side of the seal should be facing the bearing.

20 Smear Yamaha Bond 1215 or a suitable equivalent onto the mechanical seal seat. Press or carefully drive the new mechanical seal into the pump body using a suitable sized socket or seal driver which bears only on the outer rim of the seal and not on the centre. Yamaha produce a special tool, Part No. 90890-04078 (European models) or YM-33221 (US models), for installing the seal if required.

21 Lubricate the impeller shaft with coolant and slide it into the pump body.

Installation

22 Fit the new cover O-ring into its groove (see illustration 7.8). Fit the cover and install the cover bolt and drain bolt, fitting a new sealing washer to the drain bolt (see illustration). Tighten the bolts to the torque setting specified at the beginning of this Chapter.

23 Fit a new pump body O-ring and smear it lightly with grease (see illustration). Install the pump in the crankcase, ensuring that the impeller shaft engages the drive peg on the oil pump spindle, and tighten the mounting bolts to the specified torque.

24 Install the remaining components in the reverse order of removal

7.15 Mechanical seal (1), oil seal (2), bearing (3) and circlip (4)

7.16 To remove the bearing, first remove the circlip

7.22 Fit a new sealing washer to the drain bolt

7.23 Fit a new O-ring to the pump body

8.4a Detach the hose from the coolant inlet union . . .

8.4b . . . then unscrew the union bolts (arrowed)

8.4c Note the location of the sealing O-ring

8 Coolant hoses, pipes and unions

Removal

⚠ **Warning: Allow the engine to cool completely before disconnecting a coolant hose.**

1 Before removing a hose, pipe or union, drain the coolant (see Chapter 1). **Note:** *When removing components of the cooling system, be prepared to catch any residual fluids.*

2 Use a screwdriver to slacken the larger-bore hose clamps **(see illustration 2.6b)**. Slide the clamp back along the hose and clear of the union spigot, then pull the hose off the union. The smaller-bore hoses are secured by spring clips which can be expanded by squeezing their ears together with pliers **(see illustration 2.5b)**.

Caution: The radiator unions are fragile. Do not use excessive force when attempting to remove the hoses.

3 If a hose proves stubborn, release it by rotating it on its union before working it off. If all else fails, cut the hose with a sharp knife then slit it at each union so that it can be peeled off in two pieces. Whilst this means renewing the hose, it is preferable to buying a new radiator.

4 Remove the union on the front of the engine by detaching the hose, then unscrewing the union retaining bolts **(see illustrations)**. Discard the O-ring, as a new one must be fitted on reassembly **(see illustration)**.

Installation

5 Slide the clip onto the hose and then work the hose onto its union.

6 Rotate the hose on its union to settle it in position before sliding the clip into place and tightening it securely.

7 If the union on the engine has been removed, fit a new O-ring and smear it with grease, then install the union and tighten the mounting bolts securely.

Notes

Chapter 4
Engine management system

Contents

Degrees of difficulty

Easy, suitable for novice with little experience	Fairly easy, suitable for beginner with some experience	Fairly difficult, suitable for competent DIY mechanic	Difficult, suitable for experienced DIY mechanic	Very difficult, suitable for expert DIY or professional

Specifications

General information

Cylinder numbering	1 to 4 from left to right
Ignition timing	5° BTDC @ 1300 rpm
Spark plugs	see Chapter 1

Component test data

AIS cut-off valve solenoid resistance	18.0 to 22.0 ohms @ 20°C
AIS reed valve bending limit	0.4 mm (max)
Crankshaft position sensor resistance	248 to 372 ohms @ 20°C
Coolant temperature sensor	
Resistance @ 0°C	5.21 to 6.37 K-ohms
Resistance @ 80°C	290 to 350 ohms
Fuel level sensor resistance	
Fuel tank full	20 to 26 ohms
Fuel tank empty	134 to 140 ohms
Fuel pump resistance	0.2 to 3.0 ohms @ 20°C
Fuel pump pressure	36.3 psi (2.5 Bar)
Intake air pressure sensor output voltage	3.75 to 4.25V
Intake air temperature sensor resistance	2.2 to 2.7 K-ohms @ 20°C
Speed sensor output voltage	
On	4.8V
Off	0.6V
Throttle position sensor	
Resistance (max)	4 to 6 K-ohms @ 20°C
Resistance range (for position adjustment)	3.5 (or less) to 6.5 K-ohms
Output voltage (at idle)	0.63 to 0.73V
Tip-over sensor output voltage	
Sensor upright	approx. 1.0V
Sensor tilted at 65°	approx. 4.0V

Fuel

Grade	Unleaded, minimum 95 RON (Research Octane Number)
Fuel tank capacity (including reserve)	19.4 litres
Reserve	3.6 litres

Throttle bodies

Type	
2004 to 2006 models	2 x Mikuni 36EIDW
2007-on models	
S S2/SA S2 and N S2/NA S2	1 x Mikuni 36EIDW-B1
S/SA (4P53) and N/NA	1 x Mikuni 36EIDW-B7
SA (4P54)	1 x Mikuni 36EIDW-B10
Throttle valve size.	# 50
Intake vacuum	see Chapter 1

Fuel injector

Manufacturer	DENSO
Type/quantity	0290/4

Ignition coils

Primary resistance	1.53 to 2.07 ohms @ 20°C
Secondary resistance.	12.0 to 18.0 K-ohms @ 20°C
Minimum spark gap	6 mm
Spark plug cap resistance	10.0 K-ohms @ 20°C

Torque wrench settings

Crankshaft position sensor bolts	10 Nm
Exhaust header pipe nuts.	20 Nm
Exhaust system clamp and mounting bolts	20 Nm
Fuel tank mounting bolts	7 Nm
Fuel pump screws	4 Nm
Oxygen sensor.	45 Nm
Silencer heat shield screws	9 Nm
Timing rotor cover bolts	12 Nm

1 General information and precautions

General information

All models are fitted with a fully electronic engine management system which controls both the fuelling and ignition from one engine control unit, or ECU.

Fuel system

The fuel system consists of the fuel tank inside which is located the fuel pump with integral filter and fuel level sensor, the fuel supply hose, the fuel injectors located in the throttle body assembly, and the control cables. Air is drawn into the throttle bodies via an air filter, which is housed under the fuel tank.

The fuel pump is activated initially by the ignition switch, and fuel pressure is controlled by a regulator in the pump.

To aid cold starting and engine warm-up, a fast idle unit is fitted to the throttle body assembly.

In the event of the machine falling over, a tip-over sensor cuts power to the fuel and ignition systems.

The fuel injection system is controlled by the engine control unit (ECU) which monitors data sent from the various system sensors and adjusts fuel delivery to the engine and ignition timing accordingly. The ECU has its own fault diagnosis function and displays fault codes and diagnostic codes on the LCD display in the instrument cluster.

The exhaust is a four-into-two-into-one design. An air induction system (AIS) introduces filtered air into the exhaust ports to promote the burning of excess fuel in the exhaust gases to reduce harmful emissions. A catalytic converter is located in a mid-section of the exhaust system. 2007-on Europe models have an oxygen sensor on the right-hand side of the exhaust pipe, below the transmission.

Many of the fuel system service procedures are considered routine maintenance items and for that reason are included in Chapter 1.

Ignition system

The ignition system comprises a timing rotor, crankshaft position sensor (CKP sensor), the engine control unit (ECU) and ignition coils.

The timing rotor on the right-hand end of the crankshaft generates a signal in the CKP sensor as the crankshaft rotates. The CKP sensor sends that signal to the ECU which, in conjunction with data sent from the various other system sensors, calculates the best ignition timing and supplies the ignition coils with the power necessary to produce a spark at the plugs. There is no provision for adjusting the ignition timing.

The system incorporates a starter safety circuit which will cut the ignition if the sidestand is extended whilst the engine is running and in gear, or if a gear is selected whilst the engine is running and the sidestand is extended. It also prevents the engine from being started if the engine is in gear unless the clutch lever is pulled in and the stand is up.

Models sold in certain markets are fitted with an immobiliser system which will not allow the engine to be started unless the correct key is used. The immobiliser system has its own fault diagnosis function. An alarm system is available as an optional extra.

Note: Individual engine management system components can be checked but not repaired if faulty. If system troubles occur, and the faulty component can be isolated, the only cure for the problem in most cases is to replace the part with a new one. Keep in mind that most electronic parts, once purchased, cannot be returned. To avoid unnecessary expense, make very sure the faulty component has been positively identified before buying a new part.

Precautions

⚠️ *Warning: Petrol (gasoline) is extremely flammable, so take extra precautions when you work on any part of the fuel system. Don't smoke or allow open flames or bare light bulbs*

2.2 Loosen the bolt (arrowed) at the rear of the tank

2.3 Unscrew the two bolts (arrowed) at the front

2.5 Detach the breather hose (A) and drain hose (B)

near the work area, and don't work in a garage where a natural gas-type appliance is present. If you spill any fuel on your skin, rinse it off immediately with soap and water. When you perform any kind of work on the fuel system, wear safety glasses and have a fire extinguisher suitable for a class B type fire (flammable liquids) on hand.

● Always perform service procedures in a well-ventilated area to prevent a build-up of fumes.
● Never work in a building containing a gas appliance with a pilot light, or any other form of naked flame. Ensure that there are no naked light bulbs or any sources of flame or sparks nearby.
● Do not smoke (or allow anyone else to smoke) while in the vicinity of petrol (gasoline), or of components containing petrol. Remember the possible presence

of vapour from these sources and move well clear before smoking.
● Check all electrical equipment belonging to the house, garage or workshop where work is being undertaken (see the Safety First! section of this manual). Remember that certain electrical appliances such as drills, cutters, etc, create sparks in the normal course of operation and must not be used near petrol (gasoline) or any component containing it. Again, remember the possible presence of fumes before using electrical equipment.
● Always mop up any spilt fuel and safely dispose of the rag used.
● Any stored fuel that is drained off during servicing work must be kept in sealed containers that are suitable for holding petrol (gasoline), and clearly marked as such; the containers themselves should

be kept in a safe place. Note that this last point applies equally to the fuel tank if it is removed from the machine; also remember to keep its filler cap closed at all times.
● Read the Safety first! section of this manual carefully before starting work.

2 Fuel tank

⚠ **Warning: Refer to the precautions given in Section 1 before starting work.**

Removal

Note: *To reduce the weight of the tank remove it when it is nearly empty, or if the tank is full siphon the fuel into a suitable container using a hand pump (available from tool suppliers).*

1 Make sure the fuel filler cap is secure. Remove the seat (see Chapter 7).
2 Loosen but do not remove the bolt securing the rear of the tank **(see illustration)**.
3 Unscrew the bolts securing the front of the tank, noting the location of the washers **(see illustration)**.
4 Raise the tank at the front to access the hoses and wiring connectors.
5 Release the clamps securing the drain hose and, on all except California models, the breather hose to their unions on the underside of the tank and detach the hoses, noting which fits where **(see illustration)**. On California models, detach the EVAP hose from its union.
6 Disconnect the fuel pump (green) and fuel level sensor (white) wiring connectors **(see illustration)**.
7 Remove the security clip on the fuel supply hose connector, then press in the two tabs on the connector and pull it off the union **(see illustrations)**. Have a rag ready to catch any residual fuel from the hose.
8 Remove the bolt securing the rear of the tank, then carefully lift the tank off the frame **(see illustration)**. **Note:** A U-shaped bracket on the fuel pump retaining ring is designed to protect the fuel hose union and wiring connectors when the tank is off the bike – take care not to rest the tank on the underside of the fuel pump.

2.6 Disconnect the fuel pump and level sensor wiring connectors

2.7a Remove the security clip . . .

2.7b . . . then disconnect the fuel hose

2.8 Remove the rear bolt and lift off the tank

2.10 Make sure that the tank mounting rubbers (arrowed) are in place

3.10a Unscrew the bolts (arrowed) . . .

3.10b . . . and remove the ring

9 Inspect the tank support and mounting bolt rubbers for signs of damage or deterioration and replace them with new ones if necessary.

Installation

10 Installation is the reverse of removal, noting the following:
- Make sure the hoses are properly attached and secured by their clamps. Make sure the wiring connectors are secure.
- Make sure the mounting rubbers are securely attached to the left and right-hand edges of the tank (see illustration).
- Tighten the mounting bolts to the torque settings specified at the beginning of this Chapter.
- Start the engine and check that there are no fuel leaks. If the tank has been emptied, ensure it is refilled before turning the ignition switch ON.

Repair

11 All repairs to the fuel tank should be carried out by a professional who has experience in this critical and potentially dangerous work. Even after cleaning and flushing of the fuel system, explosive fumes can remain and ignite during repair of the tank.

12 If the fuel tank is removed from the bike, it should not be placed in an area where sparks or open flames could ignite the fumes coming out of the tank. Be especially careful inside garages where a natural gas-type appliance is located, because the pilot light could cause an explosion.

3 Fuel pump and pressure regulator

> **⚠ Warning:** *Refer to the precautions given in Section 1 before starting work.*

Check

1 The fuel pump is located inside the fuel tank. When the ignition is switched ON, it should be possible to hear the pump run for a few seconds until the system is up to pressure – the pressure regulator will then switch the pump off. If you can't hear anything, first check that the battery is fully-charged, then

check the main, ignition and fuel injection system fuses.

2 Next, check the ignition switch and engine stop switch (see Chapter 8), and the fuel pump relay (see Section 8). If they are good, check the wiring and terminals in the circuit for physical damage or loose or corroded connections and rectify as necessary (see the *Wiring Diagrams* at the end of Chapter 8).

3 If the pump still will not run, check the pump resistance as follows. Make sure the ignition switch is OFF. Raise the fuel tank and disconnect the pump (green) wiring connector (see Section 2). Using an ohmmeter or multimeter set to the ohms scale, measure the resistance between the terminals on the pump side of the connector. Connect the positive (+) probe to the red/blue wire terminal in the connector and the negative (-) probe to the black wire terminal. Compare the result to the specification at the beginning of the Chapter; if the result is not as specified fit a new fuel pump. If it is as specified, and you are certain all the wiring and connectors are good, have the ECU checked by a Yamaha dealer.

Fuel pressure check

Special tools: *A fuel pressure gauge with an appropriate adapter is required for this procedure.*

4 Fuel pressure is governed by a regulator that is an integral part of the fuel pump.

5 Raise the fuel tank (see Section 2). Disconnect the fuel supply hose from the fuel rail on the throttle body assembly. Install the adapter and fuel pressure gauge between the

supply hose and the fuel rail. Yamaha provide a gauge (Pt. No. 90890-03153 in Europe, YU-03153 in the US) and gauge adapter (Pt. No. 90890-03176) for this purpose.

6 Start the engine and note the pressure recorded on the gauge. The fuel pressure should be similar to that given in the specifications at the beginning of this Chapter. Stop the engine.

7 If the pressure is significantly lower than the standard, either the fuel hose has become kinked and is restricting fuel flow, or the regulator is faulty. If the hose is in good condition, a new pump will have to be fitted – individual components are not available. Note that the fuel filter is an integral part of the fuel pump.

Removal and installation

8 Siphon the fuel from the tank into a suitable container using a hand-pump, available from good tool and DIY stores.

9 Remove the fuel tank (see Section 2), and lay it upside down on plenty of clean rag.

10 Unscrew the bolts securing the pump retaining ring and remove the ring, noting how it fits (see illustrations).

11 Carefully lift the pump and manoeuvre it out of the tank, noting that there is little clearance and delicate bits can easily catch the rim (see illustration).

12 Remove the pump O-ring and discard it as a new one must be fitted.

13 Install the pump O-ring, fitting its flat side down onto the pump base (see illustration).

3.11 Carefully lift the pump out of the tank

3.13 Fit a new O-ring to the pump on reassembly

3.14 Position the pump as shown when fitting it into the tank

3.15 Cut-out in retaining ring must align with stud (arrowed)

14 Manoeuvre the pump into the aperture in the tank – sit the wider diameter section of the rear on the rim of the aperture as shown so there is clearance for the protruding parts at the front **(see illustration)**.

15 Align the pump so the fuel supply hose union points to the back, and fit the retaining ring with the U-shaped support bracket at the front **(see illustration 3.10b)**. Align the cut-out in the retaining ring with the stud on the underside of the pump **(see illustration)**. Tighten the screws evenly and in a criss-cross sequence to the torque setting specified at the beginning of this Chapter.

4 Fuel level display and sensor

Fuel level display

Check

1 The circuit consists of the sensor mounted on the fuel pump inside the tank and the fuel level indicated on the multi-function display in the instrument cluster.

2 The fuel level display should function as follows. When the ignition switch is turned ON, all the segments of the display should appear in sequence as a test of the circuit. Then, depending upon how much fuel is in the tank, the requisite number of segments between 'F' (full) and 'E' (empty) will be shown.

3 When the fuel content in the tank falls to approx. 3.6 litres, the E segment on the display begins flashing and the odometer display automatically changes to fuel reserve tripmeter mode.

4 If required, the tripmeter can be reset using the SELECT button on the instrument cluster (see Chapter 8). Once the tank has been topped-up, the fuel reserve tripmeter should reset automatically after the machine has travelled approx. 3 miles.

5 If the fuel level display malfunctions, first check the ignition fuse in the fusebox (see Chapter 8). If the fuse is good, check the sensor wiring and connections **(see illustration 2.6)**. If required, the sensor can be checked as described below.

6 If no problems are found, take the instrument cluster to a Yamaha dealer for further assessment – Yamaha provide no specific test data for the instruments themselves. If

there are any faults, a new cluster will have to be fitted, as no individual components are available.

Removal and installation

7 Refer to Chapter 8, Section 16, for removal and installation details.

Fuel level sensor

8 Remove the fuel pump from the tank (see Section 3).

9 Using an ohmmeter or multimeter set to the ohms x 10 scale, measure the resistance between the sensor terminals on the underside of the pump. Connect the positive (+) probe to the green/white wire terminal and the negative (-) probe to the black wire terminal.

10 Note the resistance reading with the pump the right way up (fuel tank empty), and then with the pump upside down (fuel tank full), and compare the results to the specifications at the beginning of this Chapter. If the results are not as specified, the sensor is faulty and a new pump will have to be fitted – individual components are not available (see Section 3).

5 Air filter housing

Removal

1 Remove the fuel tank (see Section 2). Remove the battery (see Chapter 8).

2 Pull the air temperature sensor out of the filter housing, then use pliers to release the clips securing the crankcase breather hose and throttle synchronising unit hoses and detach the hoses from the housing **(see illustrations)**.

3 Slacken the clamps on the underside of the housing securing the outlets to the throttle

5.2a Detach the temperature sensor (A) synchronising unit hoses (B) and crankcase breather hose (C)

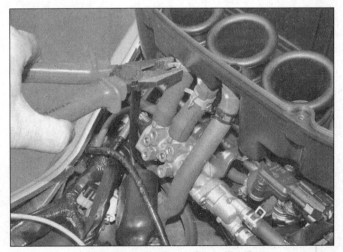

5.2b Release the hose clips with pliers

5.3 Intake clamps (arrowed) on the underside of the housing are accessible from the rear

5.4 Location of the AIS hose (arrowed)

5.6 Clamps locate on tabs (arrowed) to ensure correct position of clamp screws

body intakes (see illustration). A long Allen key or extension drive will be needed to reach the clamps (see Section 9).

4 Lift the housing up off the throttle bodies, then when accessible release the clamp securing the AIS hose on the right-hand side and detach it from the housing (see illustration).

Installation

5 Installation is the reverse of removal.

6 Ensure that the clamps are correctly positioned over the tabs on the housing outlets (see illustration).

7 Lubricate the inside of the housing outlets with a squirt of WD40 or a smear of grease to aid installation on the throttle bodies. Check the condition of the various hoses and their clamps and replace them with new ones if necessary.

6 Fuel injection system description

1 The fuel injection system consists of two main component groups, the fuel circuit and the electronic control circuit (see illustration).

2 The fuel circuit consists of the tank, pump and filter, pressure regulator, throttle bodies and injectors. Fuel is pumped under pressure from the tank to the fuel rail, from which the individual injectors are fed. Operating pressure is maintained by the pressure regulator. The injectors spray pressurised fuel into the throttle bodies where it mixes with air and vaporises, before entering the cylinder where it is compressed and ignited.

3 The electronic control circuit consists of the engine control unit (ECU), which operates and co-ordinates both the fuel injection and ignition systems, and the various sensors which provide the ECU with information on engine operating conditions.

4 The ECU monitors signals from the following sensors:

Intake air temperature sensor
Intake air pressure sensor
Throttle position sensor
Crankshaft position sensor
Coolant temperature sensor
Oxygen sensor (2007-on models)
Speed sensor

5 Based on the information it receives, the ECU calculates the appropriate ignition and fuel requirements of the engine. By varying the length of the electronic pulse it sends to each

1 Engine warning light
2 Ignition coils
3 Battery
4 Air filter
5 Intake air temperature (IAT) senor
6 Throttle position (TP) sensor
7 Intake air pressure (IAP) sensor
8 Fuel pump
9 Fuel pressure regulator
10 Engine control unit (ECU)
11 Tip-over sensor
12 Relay assembly (fuel pump relay and starter circuit cut-off relay)
13 Catalytic converter
14 Oxygen sensor
15 Crankshaft position (CKP) sensor
16 Coolant temperature sensor
17 Fuel injectors
18 Spark plugs

6.1 Fuel injection and engine management system component location

injector, the ECU controls the length of time the injectors are held open and thereby the amount of fuel that is supplied to the engine. Fuel supply varies according to the engine's needs for starting, warming-up, idling, cruising and acceleration.

6 In the event of an abnormality in any of the sensor signals, the ECU will determine whether the engine can still be run safely. If it can, a back-up mode substitutes the sensor signal with a fixed signal, restricting performance but allowing the bike to be ridden home or to a dealer. When this occurs, the engine management warning light in the instrument cluster will come on and stay on. If the fault is serious, the fuel injection system will be shut down and the engine will not run. When this occurs, the engine management warning light will flash when the ignition switch is ON and the start button is being pressed. **Note:** *The warning light should come on for 1.4 seconds after the ignition switch has been turned ON and while the starter button is being pressed. If the warning light does not come on, check its LED circuit in the instrument cluster (see Chapter 8).*

7 After the engine has been stopped, the appropriate self-diagnostic fault code will appear on the clock LCD. If more than one fault has occurred, the lowest code numerically will be displayed. See Section 7 for fault diagnosis.

7 Fuel injection system fault diagnosis

1 The system incorporates a self-diagnostic function whereby most faults, when they occur, are identified by a fault code which is displayed on the clock LCD after the engine has been stopped. The codes are stored in the ECU memory until a deletion operation is performed. In the case of a minor fault in the injection system, the engine management warning light in the instrument cluster will come on and stay on and the engine will continue to run enabling the machine to be ridden, although performance will be significantly reduced. In the case of a major fault the warning light will flash when the ignition switch is turned ON and the start button is pressed, and it will not be possible to run the engine. Certain faults will not activate the warning light and are not subject to a fault code, but will be recorded as a diagnostic code. If the engine does not run correctly but no warning light and fault code are shown, enter diagnostic mode (see Step 3 onwards), check the code given and refer to the table.

2 Compare the fault code displayed with those in Table 1 to identify the faulty component and the appropriate diagnostic code (where given). Next, follow the appropriate steps according to your machine and set the instrument cluster to diagnostic mode to confirm the appropriate test information. If a diagnostic code is not given for a particular fault code (i.e. 12 or 24), refer to Section 8 and check the component as described.

Table 1 Fuel system fault codes

Fault code	Faulty component – symptoms	Possible causes	Diagnostic code
12	Crankshaft position sensor – engine will stop and will not restart	Faulty wiring or wiring connector Damaged or improperly installed sensor or timing rotor Faulty ECU	-
13	Intake air pressure sensor – engine will run	Faulty wiring or wiring connector Damaged or faulty sensor Faulty ECU	03
14	Intake air pressure sensor hose system – engine will run	Kinked, clogged or detached hose Faulty ECU	03
15	Throttle position sensor – engine will run	Faulty wiring or wiring connector Damaged or improperly installed sensor Faulty ECU	01
16	Throttle position sensor – engine will run	Throttle position sensor stuck Faulty ECU	01
19	Sidestand switch – engine will not run	Faulty wiring or wiring connector Faulty ECU	20
21	Coolant temperature sensor – engine will run	Faulty wiring or wiring connector Damaged or improperly installed sensor Faulty ECU	06
22	Intake air temperature sensor – engine will run	Faulty wiring or wiring connector Damaged or improperly installed sensor Faulty ECU	05
24	Oxygen sensor (2007-on models) – engine will run	Faulty wiring or wiring connector Damaged or improperly installed sensor Faulty ECU	-
30	Tip-over sensor – engine will not run, fuel system turned OFF	Machine overturned Damaged or improperly installed sensor Faulty ECU	08
33	Ignition coil, Nos. 1 and 4 cylinders – engine will run dependent on how many cylinders are affected	Faulty primary wiring or wiring connector Damaged ignition coil Faulty component in ignition cut-off safety circuit Faulty ECU	30
34	Ignition coil, Nos. 2 and 3 cylinders – engine will run dependent on how many cylinders are affected	Faulty primary wiring or wiring connector Damaged ignition coil Faulty component in ignition cut-off safety circuit Faulty ECU	31

Table 1 Fuel system fault codes (continued)

-	Fuel injector, Nos. 1 and 4 cylinders	Faulty wiring or wiring connector	36
-	Fuel injector, Nos. 2 and 3 cylinders	Faulty wiring or wiring connector	37
-	Air induction system cut-off valve	Faulty wiring or wiring connector	48
-	Starter safety cut-off relay	Faulty wiring or wiring connector Damaged relay	50
-	Radiator cooling fan relay	Faulty wiring or wiring connector Damaged relay	51
-	Headlight relay	Faulty wiring or wiring connector Damaged relay	52
41	Tip-over sensor – engine will not run	Faulty wiring or wiring connector Damaged sensor Faulty ECU	08
42	Speed sensor/neutral switch – engine will run	Damaged speed sensor/neutral switch Faulty wiring or wiring connector Faulty ECU	07/21
43	Power supply to the fuel pump or injectors – engine will run	Faulty wiring or wiring connector Faulty ECU	09
44	Carbon monoxide (CO) density reading/writing error – engine will run	Error writing CO adjustment value to EEPROM Faulty ECU	60
46	Power supply to fuel injection system – engine will run	Faulty charging system	-
50	ECU malfunction, fault code may not be displayed – engine will not run	ECU internal memory malfunction	-
Start unable warning	Engine warning light flashes when the ignition switch is ON and the start button is pushed	Error detected – refer to fault codes 12, 19, 30, 41, 43 or 50	-
Er-1 Er-2 Er-3 Er-4	No communication or unreadable communication between ECU and instrument cluster – engine will not run	Faulty wiring or wiring connector Damaged instrument cluster Damaged ECU	-

Diagnostic mode set-up 2004 to 2006

3 To set-up the diagnostic mode, first ensure that the ignition switch is OFF and that the engine stop switch is OFF, then disconnect the fuel pump wiring connector (see Section 2).

4 Press the SELECT and RESET buttons on the instrument cluster simultaneously, then turn the ignition switch ON, keeping the SELECT and RESET buttons pressed for at least 8 seconds – all displays on the meter should disappear except for the clock and tripmeter.

5 Select the diagnostic mode by pressing the SELECT button until DIAG appears on the clock LCD. **Note:** *The CO adjustment mode will appear as an option at this stage.* Confirm the selection of DIAG by pressing the SELECT and RESET buttons simultaneously for 2 seconds.

6 Referring to Table 1 above, verify the diagnostic code that corresponds with the fault code originally displayed. Now press the SELECT or RESET button until the appropriate diagnostic code is displayed on the clock LCD. The SELECT button scrolls through the code numbers in ascending order, the RESET button scrolls through the numbers in descending order. The corresponding operating data, as found, is displayed on the trip LCD.

7 Refer to the diagnostic code on Table 2, and the corresponding operating data, to identify the test action required. Note that in some instances it will be necessary to turn the engine stop switch ON to verify the operating data.

8 After each check the ignition switch must be turned OFF and the set-up procedure repeated for subsequent checks.

9 To cancel the diagnostic mode, turn the ignition switch OFF.

Diagnostic mode set-up 2007-on

10 To set-up the diagnostic mode, first ensure that the ignition switch is OFF and that the engine stop switch is ON, then disconnect the fuel pump wiring connector (see Section 2).

11 Press the SELECT and RESET buttons on the instrument cluster simultaneously, then turn the ignition switch ON, keeping the SELECT and RESET buttons pressed for at least 8 seconds – all displays on the meter should disappear except for the clock and tripmeter.

12 Select the diagnostic mode by pressing the SELECT button until DIAG appears on the clock LCD. **Note:** *The CO adjustment mode will appear as an option at this stage.* Confirm the selection of DIAG by pressing the SELECT and RESET buttons simultaneously for 2 seconds.

13 Turn the engine stop switch OFF.

14 Referring to Table 1 above, verify the diagnostic code that corresponds with the fault code originally displayed. Now press the SELECT or RESET button until the appropriate diagnostic code is displayed on the clock LCD. The SELECT button scrolls through the code numbers in ascending order, the RESET button scrolls through the numbers in descending order. The corresponding operating data, as found, is displayed on the trip LCD.

15 Select the diagnostic code on Table 2, and the corresponding operating data, to identify the test action required. Note that in some instances it will be necessary to turn the engine stop switch ON to verify the operating data.

16 After each check the ignition switch must be turned OFF and the set-up procedure repeated for subsequent checks.

17 To cancel the diagnostic mode, turn the ignition switch OFF.

Table 2 Fuel system diagnostic codes and data

Diagnostic code	Action required	Data displayed
01	Check angle data displayed with throttle fully closed Check angle data displayed with throttle fully open	Fully closed – 15 to 17 Fully open – 97 to 100
03	Turn the engine stop switch ON and crank the engine using the starter motor to generate a pressure difference	10 to 200 mmHg
05	Check the temperature* in the air filter housing and compare with data displayed	-
06	Check the temperature** of the coolant and compare with data displayed – see Chapter 3 to check the operation of the sensor	-
07	Turn the rear wheel in the normal direction of rotation and check pulses generated are displayed. On machines fitted with ABS, check the rear wheel ABS wiring connector and sensor-to-rotor clearance (see Chapter 6)	0 to 999 -
08	Check the operation of the tip-over sensor	Sensor upright – 0.4 to 1.4V Tilted more than 65° – 3.8 to 4.2V
09	Turn the engine stop switch ON and check for battery voltage Check the operation of the fuel pump relay	0 to 18.7V. Normally 12V
20	Check the operation of the sidestand switch. Select a gear position other than neutral – see Chapter 8 for access and further checks	Stand retracted – ON Stand down – OFF
21	Check the operation of the neutral switch – see Chapter 8 for access and further checks	Gearbox in neutral – ON In gear – OFF
30 and 31	Check the operation of the appropriate ignition coil (see Sections 17 and 18) – turning the engine stop switch ON will generate five sparks in the appropriate plug and the engine warning light will come on.	-
36 and 37	Check the operation of the appropriate fuel injector (see Section 10) – turning the engine stop switch ON will generate five pulses in the appropriate injector and the engine warning light will come on. Check for the pulses using a sounding rod.	-
48	Check the operation of the air induction system solenoid – turning the engine stop switch ON will actuate the solenoid five times and the engine warning light will come on. You should be able to hear the solenoid click – (see Section 15)	-
50	Check the operation of the fuel injection system (starter safety cut-off) relay – turning the engine stop switch ON will actuate the relay five times and the engine warning light will flash. You should be able to hear the relay click – see Chapter 8 for access and further checks	-
51	Check the operation of the radiator cooling fan relay – turning the engine stop switch ON will actuate the relay five times and the engine warning light will come on. You should be able to hear the relay click – see Chapter 3 for access and further checks	-
52	Check the operation of the headlight relay – turning the engine stop switch ON will actuate the relay five times and the engine warning light will come on. When the relay is ON the headlight should be ON. You should be able to hear the relay click – see Chapter 8 for access and further checks	-
60	Check the carbon monoxide density in the exhaust gas Check the AIS cut-off valve (see Section 14)	01– faulty cylinders 1 and 4 02– faulty cylinders 2 and 3 -
61	Fault history code display – once corrected, delete the fault codes No history History	 00 12 to 50 as appropriate
62	Fault history – codes erased	00 to 17
63	Fault history – reinstate codes	Turn the engine stop switch ON
70	Programme control number displayed	00 to 255

* If possible, check the temperature next to the sensor, otherwise use the ambient temperature as the standard
** Check the temperature of the coolant as close as possible to the sensor

8.5a Trace the crankshaft position sensor wiring (arrowed) . . .

8.5b . . . to the connector inside the frame

8.8a Undo the timing rotor cover screws (arrowed)

18 Once the fault has been corrected, confirm that the fault code is no longer displayed by turning the ignition switch OFF and then ON again. If the code is no longer displayed on the clock LCD the repair is complete.

19 To delete a fault code from the ECU memory, follow the appropriate procedure above to set-up the diagnostic mode, then enter code 62 on the clock LCD. The total number of stored codes will be displayed on the trip LCD (00 to 17). Turn the engine stop switch ON to delete the stored codes – the LCD should display 00 codes.

8 Fuel injection system components

1 If a fault is indicated in any of the system components, first check the wiring and connectors between the appropriate component and the ECU (see *Wiring Diagrams* at the end of Chapter 8). A continuity test of all wires will locate a break or short in any circuit. Inspect the terminals inside the wiring connectors and ensure they are not loose, bent or corroded. Spray the inside of the connectors with a proprietary electrical terminal cleaner before reconnection.

2 It is possible to undertake most checks on system components using a multimeter and comparing the results with the specifications at the beginning of the Chapter. **Note:** *Different meters may give slightly different results to those specified even though the component being tested is not faulty – do not consign a component to the bin before having it double-checked.*

However, some faults will only become evident when a component is tested with specialised equipment, in which case the checks should be undertaken by a Yamaha dealer.

3 If after a thorough check the source of a fault has not been identified, it is possible that the ECU itself is faulty. Yamaha provides no test specifications for the ECU. In order to determine conclusively that the unit is defective, it should be substituted with a known good one. If the problem is rectified, the original unit is confirmed faulty.

Crankshaft position sensor

Check

4 Make sure the ignition is OFF. Remove the fuel tank (see Section 2).

5 The crankshaft position sensor is located inside the timing rotor cover on the right-hand side of the engine. Trace the wiring from the cover and disconnect it at the connector (see illustrations).

6 Using an ohmmeter or multimeter set to the ohms x 100 scale, measure the resistance between the terminals on the sensor side of the connector. Connect the positive (+) meter probe to the grey wire terminal in the connector and the negative (-) probe to the black wire terminal. Compare the result with the specification at the beginning of this Chapter. If the result is not as specified, replace the sensor with a new one.

Removal and installation

7 Follow Steps 4 and 5, then feed the wiring back to the rotor cover, noting its routing.

8 Place a drain tray under the rotor cover and unscrew the cover bolts (see illustration). Note the guide for the coolant hose retained by one of the bolts. Ease the cover off – discard the gasket, as a new one must be used and remove the dowels from either the crankcase or the cover if they are loose (see illustration).

9 Undo the bolts securing the sensor and the screw securing the wiring guide to the inside of the cover, then free the wiring grommet from the cut-out in the cover and remove the sensor (see illustration).

10 Prior to installation, apply a suitable sealant to the wiring grommet. Fit the sensor and the wiring grommet into their locations in the cover and tighten the bolts to the torque setting specified at the beginning of this Chapter (see illustration). Install the wiring guide and tighten the screw securely.

11 Ensure the dowels for the rotor cover are in place and install the cover using a new gasket (see illustration 8.8b). Install the guide for the coolant hose and tighten the cover bolts to the torque setting specified at the beginning of this Chapter (see illustration 8.8a).

12 Feed the wiring up to the connector and reconnect it (see illustration 8.5b).

13 Install the remaining components in the reverse order of removal.

Intake air pressure sensor

Check

14 Make sure the ignition is OFF. Remove the air filter housing (see Section 5).

15 The intake air pressure sensor is located on the right-hand end of the fuel rail (see

8.8b Note the location of the cover dowels (arrowed)

8.9 Undo the bolts (A) and the wiring guide screw (B)

8.10 Apply sealant to the wiring grommet (arrowed)

8.15 Location of the intake air pressure sensor (arrowed)

8.16 Measuring the sensor output voltage

8.18 Sensor wiring connector (A) and mounting screws (B)

illustration). Check the condition of the vacuum hose between the underside of the sensor and the throttle bodies. If the hose is cracked or perished replace it with a new one. Ensure the hose is a tight fit on the sensor union, the hose connectors and the throttle bodies. Note that in order to carry out a thorough inspection of the vacuum hoses it is necessary to remove the throttle body assembly (see Section 9).

16 Using a voltmeter or multimeter set to the volts (DC) scale, measure the sensor output voltage as follows – do not disconnect the wiring connector for this test. Insert the positive (+) probe of the meter into the pink/white wire terminal in the back of the sensor wiring connector, and the negative (-) probe into the black/blue wire terminal **(see illustration)**. Turn the ignition switch ON and note the output voltage. Turn the ignition OFF.

17 If the voltage is not as specified, replace

the sensor with a new one. Note that the wiring for the air pressure sensor is connected to the main wiring loom via a sub loom (see Section 9) – ensure that the sub loom connector is clean and secure.

Removal and installation

18 Follow Step 14, then disconnect the sensor wiring connector and undo the screws securing the sensor to its bracket **(see illustration)**. Lift the sensor and disconnect the vacuum hose.

19 Prior to installation, check the condition of the vacuum hose. Ensure that the hose is a tight fit on the sensor union and that the wiring connector terminals are clean.

Throttle position sensor

Check

20 Make sure the ignition is OFF. Remove the air filter housing (see Section 5).

21 The throttle position sensor is on the right-hand end of the throttle body assembly **(see illustration 8.25)**. Since the sensor is not accessible while the assembly is in place, disconnect the sensor sub loom wiring connector on the left-hand side of the machine **(see illustration)**.

22 Using an ohmmeter or multimeter set to the K-ohms scale, connect the meter positive (+) probe to the blue wire terminal and the negative (-) probe to the black/blue wire terminal on the sensor side of the connector and measure the sensor maximum resistance. Next, connect the positive (+) probe to the yellow wire terminal and the negative (-) probe to the black/blue wire terminal and measure the resistance range while slowly opening and closing the throttle twistgrip. The resistance should change gradually within the specified range.

23 If the resistance in either test is not as specified, or if it changes abruptly, replace the sensor with a new one.

Removal and installation

24 Remove the throttle body assembly (see Section 9).

25 The sensor is secured by two Torx security screws **(see illustration)**. Undo the Torx screws and lift off the sensor, noting how the slot in the sensor fits over the throttle shaft.

26 To install the sensor, position the slot in the sensor onto the throttle shaft and tighten the screws finger-tight.

27 To adjust the position of the sensor, first temporarily connect the sensor wiring connector. Using a voltmeter or multimeter set to the volts (DC) scale, insert the positive (+) probe of the meter into the yellow wire terminal in back of the connector and the negative (-) probe into the black/blue wire terminal. Turn the ignition switch ON and carefully adjust the position of the sensor until the output voltage is within the specified range, then tighten the fixing screws. Turn the ignition OFF. Install the throttle body assembly (see Section 9).

Intake air temperature sensor

28 Make sure the ignition switch is OFF.

29 Remove the fuel tank (see Section 2).

30 The sensor is mounted in the left-hand side of the air filter housing **(see illustration)**. Pull the sensor out of the housing, then disconnect the wiring connector **(see illustration)**.

8.21 Disconnect the throttle position sensor wiring connector

8.25 Throttle position sensor is secured by Torx screws (arrowed)

8.30a Location of the intake air temperature sensor (arrowed)

8.30b Remove the intake air temperature sensor

8.31 Measuring the air temperature sensor resistance

8.34 Location of the oxygen sensor

8.39 Location of the tip-over sensor (arrowed)

31 Using an ohmmeter or multimeter set to the ohms x 100 scale, connect the meter positive (+) probe to the brown/white wire terminal on the sensor and the negative (-) probe to the black/blue wire terminal and measure the resistance (see illustration).

32 If the result is not as specified, replace the sensor with a new one.

33 Ensure that the wiring connector terminals are clean and that the sensor is a firm fit in the grommet in the air filter housing.

Oxygen sensor (2007-on)

34 Make sure the ignition is OFF. Remove the fuel tank (See Section 2). The sensor, where fitted, is located in the exhaust pipe on the right-hand side below the transmission (see illustration).

35 Inspect the sensor for damage, then trace the wiring to the connector and ensure that the wiring is not damaged or trapped, and that the connector is secure.

36 If a suitable adapter is available, check that the sensor is tightened to the torque setting specified at the beginning of this Chapter.

37 No test specifications for the sensor are available – if no physical damage can be found, it must be assumed that the sensor is defective.

Tip-over sensor

Check

38 Make sure the ignition is OFF. Remove the right-hand side panel (see Chapter 7).

39 The tip-over sensor is located next to the fusebox – undo the mounting bolts and washers and lift the sensor off (see illustration). Do not disconnect the wiring connector.

40 Using a voltmeter or multimeter set to the volts (DC) scale, insert the positive meter (+) probe into the yellow/green wire terminal in back of the connector and the negative (-) probe into the black/blue wire terminal.

41 Hold the sensor in its normal position with the UP mark facing up, then turn the ignition switch ON and note the output voltage. Now tilt the sensor 65° to one side and then 65° to the other, noting the output voltage (see illustration). Turn the ignition OFF.

42 If the output voltage is not as specified when the sensor is tilted over, replace it with a new one.

Removal and installation

43 Follow the procedure in Steps 36 and 37 to remove the sensor, then disconnect the wiring connector. Note the top surface of the sensor is marked UP (see illustration) – make sure this is uppermost when the sensor is installed.

Speed sensor

Check

44 Support the machine on the centrestand with the rear wheel off the ground. Make sure the ignition is OFF. Remove the fuel tank (see Section 2).

45 The speed sensor is located on the top of the crankcase to the rear of the starter motor (see illustration).

46 Trace the wiring from the sensor to the white three-pin connector inside the wiring boot at the back of the engine unit (see illustration). Do not disconnect the wiring connector.

47 Using a voltmeter or multimeter set to the volts (DC) scale, insert the positive meter (+) probe into the white/yellow wire terminal in the connector, and the negative (-) probe into the black/blue terminal. Turn the ignition switch ON. Turn the rear wheel in its normal direction of rotation and check the reading on the meter – it should be seen to fluctuate between 0.6 and 4.8 volts as the wheel is turned. Turn the ignition switch OFF.

48 If the voltage is not as specified, replace the sensor with a new one.

Removal and installation

49 To remove the sensor, first disconnect the wiring connector (see illustration 8.45). Undo the screw securing the sensor to the crankcase and withdraw the sensor (see

8.41 Tilt the tip-over sensor both ways to check its operation

8.43 Note the top surface of the sensor is marked UP

8.45 Location of the starter motor terminal (A) and speed sensor (B)

8.46 Location of the speed sensor wiring connector (arrowed)

8.49 Undo the screw (arrowed) to remove the speed sensor

8.51 Location of the relay assembly (arrowed)

8.52a Ease the relay assembly off the bracket . . .

8.52b . . . then disconnect the wiring connector

1 Positive tester probe
2 Negative tester probe
3 Positive battery terminal
4 Negative battery terminal
R Red
R/U Red/blue
R/B Red/black
U/Y Blue/yellow

H46469

8.53 Test connections for the fuel pump relay

illustration). Discard the sealing washer as a new one must be fitted.

50 On installation, ensure the wiring connector terminals are clean and that the pins are not damaged.

Fuel pump relay

51 Make sure the ignition is OFF. Remove the left-hand side panel (see Chapter 7). The relay assembly is mounted on the left-hand side of the rear sub-frame and contains the fuel pump relay and starter circuit safety cut-off relay (see illustration).

52 Lift the relay assembly off its bracket and disconnect the wiring connector (see illustrations).

53 Using an ohmmeter or continuity tester, connect the positive (+) probe to the red wire terminal on the relay and the negative (-) probe to the red/blue wire terminal (see illustration). There should be no continuity.

54 Using a fully-charged 12V battery and some insulated jumper leads, connect the positive (+) battery terminal to the red/black wire terminal on the relay, and the negative (–) battery terminal to the blue/yellow wire terminal (see illustration 8.53). There should now be continuity between the red and red/blue wire terminals.

55 If the relay does not operate as described, replace it with a new one.

Exhaust gas oxygen content

56 Follow the procedure in Section 14 to check the AIS.

57 Have the exhaust gases analysed by a Yamaha dealer.

9 Throttle bodies

⚠ **Warning: Refer to the precautions given in Section 1 before starting work.**

Special tool: *Access to the clamp screws is extremely restricted and requires the use of a long reach 3 mm Allen key.*

Removal

1 Remove the air filter housing (see Section 5). On California models, detach the synchronising hose from the throttle body assembly.

2 Partially drain the cooling system to avoid coolant leaking when the hoses are disconnected from the fast idle unit (see Chapter 3).

3 Disconnect the throttle position sensor sub loom wiring connector (see illustration 8.21).

4 Disconnect the throttle body assembly sub loom wiring connector (see illustration).

5 Disconnect the coolant temperature sensor wiring connector – the sensor is located on the back of the cylinder head (see illustration).

6 Disconnect the throttle cables (see Section 12).

7 Place some rag under the fast idle unit to

9.4 Release the catch and disconnect the sub-loom wiring connector

9.5 Disconnect the coolant temperature sensor wiring connector

9.7 Disconnect the hoses from the fast idle unit

9.8 An extension drive is required to slacken the intake manifold clamps

9.9 Ease the throttle body assembly off

catch any residual coolant. Release the clips and disconnect the coolant hoses from the unit, noting which fits where **(see illustration)**. If required, plug the hoses to prevent further loss of coolant.

8 Slacken the clamps on the cylinder head intake manifolds – you will need a long 3 mm Allen bit and a socket extension to access them **(see illustration)**. Slacken the right-hand clamps from under the left-hand side of the frame and the left-hand clamps from the right-hand side **(see illustration 9.10)**.

9 Ease the throttle body assembly off the intake manifolds **(see illustrations)**.

10 Note how the clamps locate on the intake manifolds **(see illustration)**.

Caution: Stuff clean rag into each intake manifold to prevent anything from falling inside.

Disassembly

11 Refer to Section 11 and remove the throttle synchronising/fast idle unit.

12 Refer to Section 10 and remove the fuel rail and injectors.

13 Note the arrangement of the vacuum hoses and where they connect on the throttle body assembly, then pull them off their unions **(see illustration)**.

14 If required, remove the throttle position sensor (see Section 8).

Cleaning

Caution: Use only a petroleum-based solvent for cleaning. Do not use caustic cleaners.

15 Ensure that only metal components come into contact with the cleaning solvent and always follow manufacturer's

recommendations as to cleaning time. If a spray cleaner is used, direct the spray into all passages.

16 After the cleaner has loosened and dissolved most of the varnish and other deposits, use a nylon-bristle brush to remove the stubborn deposits. Rinse the throttle bodies, then dry them with compressed air.

17 Use compressed air to blow out all of the fuel and air passages.

Caution: Never clean the jets or passages with a piece of wire or a drill bit, as they will be enlarged, causing the fuel and air metering rates to be upset.

Inspection

18 Check the throttle bodies for cracks, distorted sealing surfaces and other damage. If any defects are found, fit a new throttle body assembly.

19 Operate the throttle pulley and ensure that the throttle butterfly valves open and close smoothly **(see illustration)**. If they don't, clean the throttle linkage, and check the throttle bodies for wear where butterfly valves close against them **(see illustrations)**.

20 Check all the vacuum hoses for cracks, splits and kinks and replace them with new ones if necessary.

Reassembly

21 Reassemble the throttle bodies in the reverse order of disassembly. Ensure that the assembly screws are tightened securely. Ensure that all the hoses are securely clipped in place.

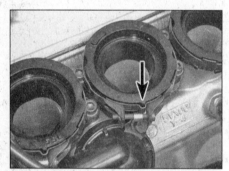

9.10 Note how the clamps locate on the intake manifolds

9.13 Note the location of the vacuum hoses (arrowed)

9.19a Check the operation of the throttle pulley

9.19b Ensure that the throttle linkage is clean (arrowed)

9.19c Check that the butterfly valves (arrowed) close properly against the throttle bodies

10.6 Undo the screws (A) securing the fast idle unit. Screws (B) secure the fuel rail

10.7 Location of the fuel injector wiring connectors (arrowed)

22 If removed, follow the procedure in Section 8 to install the throttle position sensor.

Installation

23 Installation is the reverse of removal, noting the following.
● Check for cracks or splits in the intake manifolds and replace them with new ones if necessary. Unscrew the two bolts to release each manifold – they are marked L (left) and R (right) to ensure correct installation.
● Make sure the clamps are correctly aligned with the tabs on the manifolds **(see illustration 9.10)**.
● Lubricate the inside lip of each manifold with a squirt of WD40 or a smear of grease to aid installation of the throttle body assembly.
● Once the assembly is correctly aligned, press it firmly into place and tighten the clamps securely.
● Refer to Section 12 for installation of the throttle cables.
● Ensure the terminals in the wiring connectors are clean and ensure that the connectors are secure (see Steps 3 to 5).
● Top-up the cooling system (see Chapter 1 and Pre-ride checks).
● Check idle speed and throttle body synchronisation and adjust as necessary (see Chapter 1).

10 Fuel rail and injectors

Warning: Refer to the precautions given in Section 1 before proceeding.

Check

1 Remove the fuel tank (see Section 2).
2 Follow the procedure in Section 7 to set-up the diagnostic mode on your machine. Confirm that the diagnostic codes for checking the fuel

injectors are 36 (injectors No. 1 and 4) and 37 (injectors No. 2 and 3).
3 Check the operation of each injector in turn, using a stethoscope or sounding rod. Turn the engine stop switch ON – if the injector is good it will click five times. If any injector is silent, either the injector or its wiring harness is faulty.
4 Disconnect the wiring connector from the injector. Using the wiring diagrams at the end of Chapter 8, check for continuity in the wiring and connectors between the injectors, the sub loom and the ECU, and between the injectors and earth (ground).

Removal

5 Remove the throttle body assembly (see Section 9).
6 Disconnect the intake air pressure sensor wiring connector (see Section 8). Undo the screws securing the throttle synchronising/fast idle unit and displace the unit **(see illustration)**. Release the clips securing the synchronising unit hoses to the unions on the throttle bodies and detach the hoses, then lift the unit off.
7 Disconnect the wiring connectors from the fuel injectors and throttle position sensor, then remove the throttle body assembly wiring sub loom, noting its routing and releasing it from any ties **(see illustration)**.
8 Undo the screws securing the fuel rail **(see illustration 10.6)**. Carefully lift the fuel rail off the throttle body assembly – the injectors will come away with the rail. Note the seals on the lower end of each injector.
9 Pull each injector out of the fuel rail, noting which way round it fits. Note the O-ring on the upper end of each injector. Discard the injector seals and O-ring as new ones must be fitted on reassembly.
10 Modern fuels contain detergents which should keep the injectors clean and free of gum or varnish from residue fuel. If an injector is suspected of being blocked, clean it through with injector cleaner.
11 The fuel rail incorporates a fuel pressure

damper that is designed to smooth-out any changes in pressure in the rail caused by the injectors opening and closing. On early models, the damper is detachable – do not remove it, but check that there are no fuel leaks between the damper and the rail. If necessary, renew the fuel rail and damper as a single unit.

Installation

Note: Apply a smear of clean engine oil to all new seals and O-rings before reassembly.
12 Fit a new seal onto the lower end of each injector and a new O-ring onto the upper end. Align each injector with the throttle body assembly (wiring connector at the rear), then carefully press the injectors into position. **Note:** Avoid twisting the injectors as this may damage the seals.
13 Align the fuel rail with the injectors, then press the fuel rail into place evenly. Ensure that the fuel rail is correctly seated on all four injectors before installing the screws – do not use the screws to correctly seat and align the fuel rail.
14 Install the fuel rail screws and tighten them securely **(see illustration 10.6)**.
15 Connect the individual injector wiring connectors and the TP sensor connector **(see illustration 10.7)**. Secure the sub loom.
16 Install the remaining components in the reverse order of removal. Run the engine and make sure there are no fuel leaks before riding the bike.

11 Fast idle unit

Warning: Refer to the precautions given in Section 1 before proceeding.

Operation

1 The fast idle unit is located on the right-hand side of the assembly that incorporates the

11.1 Location of the fast idle unit (arrowed)

12.3 Throttle closing cable (A) and opening cable (B)

12 Throttle cables

 Warning: Refer to the precautions given in Section 1 before proceeding.

throttle body synchronising screws and the idle speed adjuster **(see illustration)**.

2 The unit allows extra air to pass from the air filter housing into the throttle body assembly which in turn draws more fuel through the injectors, raising the idle speed even though the throttle twistgrip is closed.

3 Operation of the unit is dependant upon the temperature of coolant that circulates through it between the cylinder head and the radiator. As the coolant temperature rises, a wax element inside the unit expands, gradually closing the intake airways to the throttle body assembly.

4 The intake airways should be fully open when the engine is cold, and fully closed when the engine reaches normal operating temperature, which is usually reached after 10 to 15 minutes of stop-and-go riding. If a

smooth, steady idle cannot be achieved, and all other components have been checked, the fast idle unit may be faulty. Have the operation of the unit checked by a Yamaha dealer. **Note:** *Where fitted, the oxygen sensor may try to compensate for an incorrect fuel/air mixture caused by a faulty fast idle unit. A fuel injection system fault code based upon incorrect carbon monoxide density in the exhaust gas will result.*

Removal and installation

5 Follow the procedure in Section 10 to remove the throttle synchronising/fast idle unit. The two units are not available separately

6 Installation is the reverse of removal. Make sure all hoses are in good condition, correctly routed and secured and not trapped or kinked.

Removal

1 Remove the air filter housing (see Section 5).

2 Follow the procedure in Chapter 2, Section 12, and displace the clutch cable support bracket.

3 Note the location of the throttle closing (upper) and throttle opening (lower) cables in the bracket on the left-hand end of the throttle body assembly **(see illustration)**. Mark each cable according to its location at both ends. If new cables are being fitted, match them to the old cables to ensure they are correctly installed.

4 Loosen the locknut on the upper cable adjuster, then slide the adjuster out of the bracket and detach the inner cable end from the throttle pulley, noting how it fits **(see illustration)**.

5 Loosen the locknut on the lower cable adjuster, then slide the adjuster out of the bracket and detach the inner cable end from the throttle pulley, noting how it fits **(see illustration)**.

6 Note the difference between the adjusters on the upper and lower cables **(see illustration)**.

7 Undo the front (short) and rear (long) screws securing the cable cover on the underside of the twistgrip housing and lift the cover off, noting the locating tab **(see illustrations)**.

12.4 Detach the throttle closing cable from the bracket and pulley

12.5 Detach the throttle opening cable from the bracket and pulley

12.6 Note the different adjusters on the closing cable (A) and opening cable (B)

12.7a Undo the front . . .

12.7b . . . and rear cable cover screws . . .

12.7c . . . and remove the cover. Note the locating tab (arrowed)

12.8 Note how the opening (A) and closing (B) cables locate

12.9a Undo the screw . . .

12.9b . . . and separate the housing halves

12.10a Detach the inner cable ends from the pulley. Note the locating pin (arrowed)

12.10b Draw the cable elbows from the housing

12.12 Ensure that the opening (A) and closing (B) cables are correctly arranged

8 Note the arrangement of the throttle opening and closing cable elbows in the lower half of the twistgrip housing **(see illustration)**.
9 Undo the long screw securing the two halves of the twistgrip housing and pull the halves apart **(see illustrations)**.
10 Detach the inner cable ends from the pulley then draw the cable elbows from the housing, noting how they fit **(see illustrations)**.
11 Withdraw the cables from the machine, noting the correct routing of each cable.

Installation

12 Feed the cables from the handlebar through to the throttle bodies, making sure they are correctly routed and arranged **(see illustration)**. The cables must not interfere with any other component and should not be kinked or bent sharply.
13 Lubricate the cable ends with

multi-purpose grease, then fit the cable elbows into the housing, making sure the opening cable fits into the front and the closing cable fits into the rear **(see illustration 12.10b)**.
14 Fit the cable ends into their sockets in the throttle twistgrip pulley, then join the housing halves, making sure the pin locates in the hole in the handlebar **(see illustration 12.10a)**. Ensure that the twistgrip is free to rotate, then install the fixing screw **(see illustration 12.9a)**.
15 Ensure that the opening and closing cable elbows are correctly located in the lower half of the twistgrip housing **(see illustration 12.8)**.
16 Install the cable cover and secure it with the front (short) and rear (long) screws **(see illustrations 12.7c, a and b)**.
17 Fit the opening cable end into the throttle pulley, then locate the adjuster into the lower holder on the cable bracket and tighten it against the bracket **(see illustration 12.5)**.

18 Fit the closing cable end into the throttle pulley, then locate the adjuster into the upper holder on the cable bracket and secure it with the locknut **(see illustration 12.4)**.
19 Follow the procedure in Chapter 1, Section 6, to adjust the cable freeplay.
20 Install the remaining components in the reverse order of removal. Start the engine and check that the idle speed does not rise as the handlebars are turned. If it does, the throttle cables are routed incorrectly. Correct the problem before riding the motorcycle.

13 Exhaust system

Warning: If the engine has been running the exhaust system will be very hot. Allow the system to cool before carrying out any work.

Silencer

Removal

1 Remove the seat cowling, silencer cowling and rear number plate assembly (see Chapter 7).
2 Slacken the clamp bolt securing the mid-section of the exhaust system to the single pipe section at the rear of the header pipe assembly **(see illustration)**.
3 Slacken the clamp bolt securing the mid-section of the exhaust system to the single pipe at the front of the silencer **(see illustration)**.

13.2 Slacken the clamp bolt (arrowed) at the rear of the header pipe assembly

13.3 Slacken the clamp bolt (arrowed) between the mid-section and the silencer front pipe

13.4a Displace the rear brake fluid reservoir . . .

13.4b . . . then unscrew the exhaust bracket bolt (arrowed) . . .

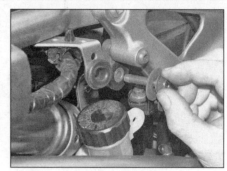

13.4c . . . and remove the bolt and washer from the bracket

4 Undo the bolt securing the rear brake fluid reservoir and displace the reservoir to access the exhaust system bracket bolt (see illustrations). Undo the bolt and remove the bolt and washer (see illustration).
5 Undo the bolt securing the cover plate and lift the plate off (see illustrations).
6 Undo the silencer mounting bolts (see illustration).
7 Support the silencer/mid section assembly, then manoeuvre it out from underneath the rear sub-frame (see illustration). Note: The exhaust mid-section contains the catalytic converter – handle it carefully to avoid damage to the cat.
8 If required, separate the mid-section from the silencer; note the location of the sealing rings in the silencer front pipe and the lower end of the exhaust mid-section (see

illustrations). Discard the sealing rings as new ones should be used on reassembly.

Installation

9 Check the condition of the rubber bush in the exhaust mounting bracket and replace it with a new one if it is damaged, deformed or deteriorated (see illustration 13.4c). Check that the collar is fitted inside the bush.
10 Fit the new sealing rings as required (see illustrations 13.8a and 8b). If separated, assemble the silencer and exhaust mid-section.
11 Manoeuvre the silencer/mid section assembly into position, ensuring that the lower end of the mid-section is pushed firmly into the rear of the header pipe assembly (see illustration 13.2). Install the silencer mounting

bolts and exhaust system bracket bolt and washer finger-tight
12 Tighten the clamp bolts to the torque setting specified at the beginning of this Chapter (see illustrations 13.2 and 3). Tighten the bracket bolt and silencer mounting bolts to the specified torque (see illustration 13.4b and 6).
13 Install the rear brake fluid reservoir (see illustration 13.4a). Install the cover plate (see illustration 13.5a).
14 Install the remaining components in the reverse order of removal.
15 Run the engine and check that there are no exhaust gas leaks.

Header pipe assembly

Removal

16 Remove the radiator (see Chapter 3).

13.5a Undo the bolt (arrowed) . . .

13.5b . . . and lift the cover plate off

13.6 Undo the silencer mounting bolts (arrowed)

13.7 Manoeuvre the silencer assembly out

13.8a Note the location of the sealing ring in the silencer front pipe (arrowed) . . .

13.8b . . . and the lower end of the mid-section (arrowed)

13.18a Unscrew the flange nuts (arrowed) . . .

13.18b . . . and draw the flanges off

13.20a Undo the header pipe assembly mounting bolt (arrowed)

17 If the exhaust system is fitted with an oxygen sensor, first remove the seat (see Chapter 7), then trace the wiring from the oxygen sensor and disconnect it at the connector **(see illustration 8.34)**. Feed the wiring back to the sensor, noting any clips or ties.
18 Unscrew the eight header pipe flange nuts and draw the flanges off the studs **(see illustrations)**.
19 Slacken the clamp bolt securing the mid-section of the exhaust system to the single pipe section at the rear of the header pipe assembly **(see illustration 13.2)**.
20 Unscrew the bolt and washer securing the rear of the header pipe assembly to its mounting bracket **(see illustration)**. On systems fitted with an oxygen sensor, the mounting bracket bolt is on the left-hand side **(see illustration)**.

21 Supporting the system, detach the header pipes from the cylinder head and pull the rear of the assembly out of the mid-section, then manoeuvre the assembly off **(see illustrations)**.
22 Remove the gasket from each exhaust port in the cylinder head and discard them, as new ones must be fitted **(see illustration)**.
23 Note the location of the sealing ring in the lower end of the exhaust mid-section **(see illustration 13.8b)**. Discard the sealing ring as a new one should be used on reassembly.

Installation

24 Check the condition of the rubber bush in the mounting bracket and replace it with a new one if it is damaged, deformed or deteriorated **(see illustrations 13.20a and b)**. Check that the collar is fitted inside the bush.
25 Fit a new gasket into each exhaust port

(see illustration). If necessary, apply a smear of grease to the gaskets to keep them in place whilst fitting the header pipe. Fit a new sealing ring into the lower end of the exhaust mid-section **(see illustration 13.8b)**.
26 Manoeuvre the assembly into position, ensuring that each header pipe is located in its port in the cylinder head **(see illustration 13.21a)**, then push the rear pipe firmly into the mid-section and install the mounting bracket bolt and washer finger-tight **(see illustration 13.20a or b)**.
27 Locate the header pipe flanges onto the studs, then fit the nuts and tighten them to the torque setting specified at the beginning of the Chapter **(see illustration 13.18b and 18a)**.
28 Tighten the clamp bolt and the mounting bracket bolt to the specified torque **(see illustrations 13.2, 20a or b)**.

13.20b Left-hand side location of mounting bolt (arrowed)

13.21a Detach the header pipes from the cylinder head . . .

13.21b . . . and from the mid-section (arrowed) . . .

13.21c . . . then manoeuvre the assembly off

13.22 Remove and discard the old exhaust port gaskets

13.25 Secure the new exhaust port gaskets with a smear of grease

29 If the exhaust system is fitted with an oxygen sensor, reconnect the wiring connector (see Step 17).

30 Install the radiator (see Chapter 3).

31 Run the engine and check that there are no exhaust gas leaks.

14 Air induction system (AIS)

Function

1 The air induction system uses exhaust gas pulses to suck fresh air into the exhaust ports, where it mixes with hot combustion gases. The extra oxygen causes continued combustion, allowing unburnt hydrocarbons to burn off, thereby reducing emissions.

2 Reed valves located in the engine valve cover ensure a one-way flow of air into the ports, only opening when there is negative pressure in the ports. The reed valves also prevent exhaust gases flowing back into the AIS.

3 An air cut-off valve, controlled electronically by signals from the ECU, allows air to flow from the air filter housing when the engine is cold and when it is at idle. The valve shuts off the flow of air when the engine reaches normal operating temperature. If, however, the coolant temperature drops, the valve opens and air is added to aid combustion and raise the gas temperature inside the exhaust system.

4 A general inspection of the AIS should be carried out at the specified service interval (see Chapter 1, Section 5).

Testing, removal and installation

Air cut-off valve

5 If not already done, remove the air filter housing (see Section 5), then remove the battery housing (see Chapter 8).

6 Release the clips securing the AIS hoses to the unions on the reed valves and pull the hoses off **(see illustration)**.

7 Undo the bolt securing the cut-off valve assembly to its mounting bracket, then disconnect the valve wiring connector and lift the assembly off **(see illustrations)**.

8 Using an ohmmeter or multimeter set to the

14.6 Release the clip before pulling the hose off the union (arrowed)

14.7b Disconnect the cut-off valve solenoid wiring connector

ohms x 1 scale, connect the meter positive (+) probe to the brown/red wire terminal and the negative (-) probe to the red/white wire terminal and measure the resistance.

9 If the result is not as specified, replace the cut-off valve assembly with a new one.

Reed valves

10 If not already done, remove the air filter housing (see Section 5) and the battery housing (see Chapter 8).

11 Lift out the heat shield, nothing how it fits **(see illustration)**.

12 Disconnect the hose from both reed valve housings **(see illustration 14.6)**. Attach a length of clean auxiliary hose to one of the unions.

13 Check the valve by blowing and sucking on the auxiliary hose end. Air should flow through the hose only when blown down it (valve open) and not when sucked back up

14.7a Cut-off valve mounting bolt (arrowed)

14.11 Lift out the heat shield

(valve closed). If this is not the case, the reed valve is faulty, though it is worth removing it (see below) and cleaning it in case it is just sticking due to a build-up of debris. Check the other valve in the same way.

14 To remove either reed valve, unscrew the bolts securing the valve cover and remove the cover **(see illustration)**. Lift out the reed valve and the base plates, noting which way around they are fitted **(see illustrations)**.

15 Inspect the reed and its seat for carbon deposits or gum that might impair its operation. If necessary, clean the surface or the reed carefully with a rag and a suitable solvent – do not bend the reed.

16 The reed should sit flat against its seat to act as a seal against back pressure in the exhaust port. Use a feeler gauge to measure any gap between the reed and its seat and compare the result with the specification at the

14.14a Unscrew the bolts and remove the cover

14.14b Lift out the reed valve . . .

14.14c . . . and the two base plates

14.16 Checking the reed valve bending limit

1 Stopper plate
2 Reed
3 Valve seat
4 Bending limit measurement

beginning of this Chapter **(see illustration)**. If the gap is greater than the service limit, fit a new valve.

17 Installation is the reverse of removal.

15 Catalytic converter

General information

1 A catalytic converter is incorporated in the mid-section of the exhaust system to minimise the level of exhaust pollutants released into the atmosphere.
2 The catalytic converter consists of a canister containing a fine ceramic honeycomb impregnated with a catalyst material, over which the hot exhaust gases pass. The catalyst speeds up the oxidation of harmful carbon monoxide, unburned hydrocarbons and soot, effectively reducing the quantity of harmful products released into the atmosphere via the exhaust gases.
3 On 2004 to 2006 models, the catalytic converter is of the open-loop design – there is no exhaust gas content feedback to the ECU. 2007-on models are fitted with a closed-loop design – an oxygen sensor in the exhaust system enables the ECU to vary the intake fuel/air mixture dependant upon engine operating conditions (see Section 8).

Precautions

4   The catalytic converter is a reliable and simple device which needs no maintenance in itself, but there are some facts of which an owner should be aware if the converter is to function properly for its full service life.
● DO NOT use leaded or lead replacement petrol (gasoline) – the additives will coat the precious metals, reducing their converting efficiency and will eventually destroy the catalytic converter.
● Always keep the ignition and fuel systems well-maintained in accordance with the manufacturer's schedule – if the fuel/air

16.3 Ensure that the HT leads are numbered before removing the plug caps

mixture is suspected of being incorrect have the exhaust gas CO content checked by a Yamaha dealer.
● If the engine develops a misfire, do not ride the bike at all (or at least as little as possible) until the fault is cured.
● DO NOT use fuel or engine oil additives – these may contain substances harmful to the catalytic converter.
● DO NOT continue to use the bike if the engine burns oil to the extent of leaving a visible trail of blue smoke.
● Remember that the catalytic converter is FRAGILE – handle the exhaust mid-section carefully if removing it from the machine.

16 Ignition system check

⚠ Warning: The energy levels in electronic systems can be very high. On no account should the ignition be switched on whilst the plugs or plug caps are being held. Shocks from the HT circuit can be most unpleasant. Secondly, it is vital that the engine is not turned over or run with any of the plug caps removed and isolated, and that the plugs are soundly earthed (grounded) when the system is checked for sparking. The ignition system components can be seriously damaged if the HT circuit becomes isolated.

1 As no means of adjustment is available, any failure of the system can be traced to failure of a system component or a simple wiring fault. Of the two possibilities, the latter is by far the most likely. In the event of failure, check the system in a logical fashion, as described below.
2 Remove the radiator (see Chapter 3).
3 Clean the area around each spark plug cap to prevent any dirt falling into the spark plug wells. Check that the cylinder location is marked on each HT lead (numbered 1 to 4 from the left-hand side), then pull the cap off each spark plug **(see illustration)**.
4 The ignition system must be able to produce a spark which is capable of jumping a particular size gap. Yamaha specify that

16.4 Using an adjustable spark gap test tool

a healthy system should produce a spark capable of jumping at least 6 mm. An ignition spark gap test tool (which should have an adjustable gap) can be purchased to check the strength of the spark **(see illustration)**.
5 Set the tool gap to 6 mm, following the manufacturer's instructions. Connect the spark plug cap of No. 1 cylinder to the test tool, and contact the tool to a good earth (ground) on the engine **(see illustration 16.4)**. Connect the remaining plug caps to spare plugs and lay the plugs on the engine with the threads earthed (grounded).
6 Check that the kill switch is in the RUN position, turn the ignition switch ON and turn the engine over on the starter motor. If the system is in good condition a regular, fat blue spark will be seen to jump the gap on the test tool. Turn the ignition OFF.
7 Repeat the test for the other cylinders. If the test results are good, the entire ignition system can be considered good. If any of the sparks appears thin or yellowish, or are non-existent, further investigation will be necessary.

⚠ Warning: Do not remove any of the spark plugs from the engine to perform this check – atomised fuel being pumped out of the open spark plug hole could ignite, causing severe injury!

8   Ignition faults can be divided into two categories, namely those where the ignition system has failed completely, and those which are due to a partial failure. The likely faults are listed below, starting with the most probable source of failure. Work through the list systematically, referring to the appropriate Section of this Chapter and/or the specified Chapter for full details of the necessary checks and tests. **Note:** Before checking the following items ensure that the battery is fully charged and that all fuses are in good condition.

Loose, corroded or damaged wiring connections; broken or shorted wiring between any of the component parts of the ignition system (see Chapter 8).
Faulty spark plug, dirty, worn or corroded plug electrodes, or incorrect gap between electrodes (Chapter 1).
Faulty ignition switch or engine stop switch (see Chapter 8).
Faulty neutral, clutch or sidestand switch (see Chapter 8).

Faulty tip-over sensor or starter safety cut-off relay (see Section 8 and Chapter 8).

Faulty crankshaft position sensor (Section 8) or damaged timing rotor trigger (Chapter 2).

Faulty ignition coil(s) (Section 17).

Faulty ECU (Section 18).

9 If the above checks don't reveal the cause of the problem, have the ignition system tested by a Yamaha dealer.

17.2a Ensure that the HT leads (arrowed) are secure

17.2b Check that the wiring connectors are clean and tight

17 Ignition coils

17.3a Unscrew the plug cap from the HT lead . . .

17.3b . . . and check the plug cap resistance

Check

1 Remove each coil (see Steps 7 to 12). Note that the HT leads on the upper coil (as fitted) are connected to cylinders 1 and 4, and the leads on the lower coil are connected to cylinders 2 and 3. Note the location of the wiring connectors on the primary circuit terminals.

2 Inspect the coils for cracks and other damage. Ensure that the HT leads are securely connected to the coil body and that the wiring terminals are clean and secure **(see illustrations)**.

3 Unscrew the plug caps from the HT leads and check the cap resistance with a multimeter as follows **(see illustration)**. Set the meter to the K-ohm scale and measure the resistance between the terminals in either end of the cap **(see illustration)**. If the reading obtained differs from the one shown in the Specifications, fit a new cap.

4 Next, measure the ignition coil primary circuit resistance as follows. Set the meter to the ohms x 1 scale, then connect the positive (+) meter probe to the red/black wire terminal on the coil and the negative (-) probe to the

orange/black (cyls 1 and 4) or grey/black (cyls 2 and 3) wire terminal **(see illustration)**. If the reading obtained is not within the range shown in the Specifications, it is likely that the coil is defective.

5 Finally, measure the secondary circuit resistance as follows. Set the meter to the K-ohm scale. Connect one meter probe to one HT lead and the other meter probe to the other HT lead, ensuring that the probes make good contact with the core wire inside the leads **(see illustration)**. If the reading obtained is not within the range shown in

the Specifications, it is likely that the coil is defective.

6 If a coil is confirmed to be faulty, it must be replaced with a new one – the coils are sealed units and cannot therefore be repaired.

Removal and installation

7 Remove the radiator (see Chapter 3).

8 Pull the cap off each spark plug (see Section 16, Step 3).

9 Remove the air filter housing (see Section 5). Displace the battery housing (see Chapter 8).

10 Unscrew the bolt securing the right-hand

17.4 Checking the coil primary resistance between the wiring terminals

17.5 Checking the coil secondary resistance between the HT leads

17.10a The coils are secured by bolts (arrowed) on the right-hand ends

17.10b Ease out the centre of the trim clip . . .

17.10c . . . then prise the whole clip out

end of the upper ignition coil (see illustration). The left-hand end of the coil is secured by a trim clip – ease out the centre of the trim clip, then prise out the whole clip, noting how it fits (see illustrations). If the trim clip is damaged on removal, use a new one on installation.

11 Note the routing of the HT leads and ignition coil wiring around the heat shield. Disconnect the wiring connectors from the coil primary circuit terminals and lift the coil off (see illustration).

12 Follow the same procedure to remove the lower ignition coil. Note that on this coil, the primary circuit terminals are on the left and the HT leads are on the right-hand side, directly opposite to the layout on the upper coil (see illustration).

13 Installation is the reverse of removal. Ensure that the coils are fitted in their correct locations and that the wiring connectors are secure.

14 Make sure the HT leads are connected to the spark plugs in the correct order.

18 Engine Control Unit (ECU)

Check

1 If the tests shown in the preceding Sections have failed to isolate the cause of an ignition fault, it is possible that the ECU itself is faulty. No details are available for testing the ECU – it must taken to a Yamaha dealer for assessment.

2 On machines not fitted with an immobiliser system, it is possible to substitute a known good ECU in place of the suspect one for testing purposes. If an immobiliser system is fitted, the only solution in the event of an ECU failure is to fit a new unit. If a new ECU is fitted, the (red) immobiliser code re-registering key must be registered to the unit (see Section 19).

Removal and installation

3 Remove the rider's seat (see Chapter 7). Disconnect the battery negative (–) lead.

17.11 Lift out the upper ignition coil. Note the numbered HT leads (arrowed)

17.12 Note the location of the primary circuit terminals (A) and HT leads (B) – lower ignition coil

4 The ECU is located inside the frame on the left-hand side (see illustrations). On machines equipped with ABS, first unclip the strap securing the ABS control

unit and displace the unit to access the right-hand ECU mounting bolt (see illustrations).

5 Undo the two mounting bolts, then lift the

18.4a Location of the ECU (arrowed) – 2004 to 2006 models (non-ABS equipped)

18.4b Location of the ECU – 2007-on models (non-ABS equipped)

18.4c Where fitted, displace the ABS control unit (arrowed) . . .

18.4d . . . before removing the ECU

18.5a Undo the mounting bolts . . .

18.5b . . . then lift the ECU . . .

18.5c . . . and disconnect the wiring
connector

ECU and disconnect the multi-pin wiring connector **(see illustrations)**.

6 Installation is the reverse of removal. Make sure the wiring terminals inside the connector are clean and ensure that the connector is pushed firmly onto the ECU.

19 Immobiliser system

General information

1 The immobiliser system will only allow the machine to be started if a registered key is used to turn the ignition switch ON. The system consists of a transponder which is part of the ignition key, a transceiver which is fitted on the front of the ignition switch, and the engine control unit (ECU).
2 When the ignition is switched ON, the ECU sends power through the immobiliser transceiver to the transponder. The transponder sends a coded signal back through the transceiver to the ECU. If the code sent by the transponder matches the code stored in the ECU memory, the immobiliser indicator light in the instrument cluster comes on for about a second, then goes out, and the ECU allows the engine to be started.
3 If the key code is not recognised, or if there is a fault in the system, the indicator light flashes. If the light flashes, refer to the *Fault diagnosis* and *Troubleshooting* Sections below. Likewise if the light does not come on at all.

4 The ECU can store the codes for up to three registered keys, two of which are standard-use keys with black casings, the other being the code re-registering key with a red casing. The three keys should be kept separately i.e. not on the same key-ring. The proximity of another key to the one being used in the switch can lead to the signal from the switch key transponder being jammed, and the bike will not start.
5 The transponder in the ignition key can be damaged if the key is dropped or knocked, gets too hot, is too close to a magnetic object, or is submerged in water. If this happens, a new key can be obtained from a Yamaha dealer and registered using the (red) code re-registering key. It is important, therefore, to keep the (red) code re-registering key in a safe place and never to use it on a daily basis.
6 Always make sure you have a spare standard-use key. If an existing key is damaged or lost, obtain a new key and register it with the immobiliser system as soon as possible.
7 If all the keys are lost, or if the ignition switch is faulty, all the components in the immobiliser system must be renewed.

Standard-use key registration procedure

Note: *This must be done when a standard-use key is lost and a new one is obtained.*
8 Obtain a new key from a Yamaha dealer, and have it cut to match the original key.
9 Have all three keys ready to hand – when a new standard-use key is registered, the code in the remaining standard-use key is cancelled, so this will also have to be registered.
10 Using the (red) code re-registering key, turn the ignition switch ON, then turn it OFF and remove the key. Within 5 seconds, turn the ignition ON with the new key. **Note:** *The immobiliser indicator light should flash on and off every half second. This indicates that the system is in registration mode. If at any time during the procedure the light stops flashing, more than 5 seconds have elapsed and the system is no longer in registration mode, in which case start again to register both keys.*
11 While the light is still flashing, turn the

ignition OFF, remove the new key (placing it well away from the transceiver) and within 5 seconds turn the ignition ON with the remaining standard-use key. When the light stops flashing the registration is complete. Turn the ignition OFF and remove the key.
12 Check that both standard-use keys can start the motorcycle.

Code re-registering key registration procedure

Note: *This must be done when a new ECU has been fitted, or when a new immobiliser system has been installed.*
13 Turn the ignition switch ON using the (red) code re-registering key. The immobiliser light will come on for about one second, then go out, indicating that the key has been registered.
14 Check that the key can start the motorcycle.
15 Now register the standard-use keys as described in Steps 8 to 12.

Installing a new ECU

16 Install the ECU (see Section 18).
17 Turn the ignition switch ON using the code re-registering key. This registers the key to the new ECU.
18 Check that the key can start the motorcycle.
19 Now register the standard-use keys as described in Steps 8 to 12.

Installing a new immobiliser transceiver

20 Remove the old immobiliser transceiver/ ignition switch assembly and fit the new one (see Chapter 8).
21 Turn the ignition switch ON using the code re-registering key. This registers the key to the transceiver.
22 Check that the key can start the motorcycle.
23 Now register the standard-use keys as described in Steps 8 to 12

Fault diagnosis

24 If there is a fault in the system, the immobiliser indicator light in the instrument cluster flashes and a fault code is shown in the LCD display.

Fault code	Symptoms	Possible causes
51	Signal from key not being received by immobiliser transceiver	Interference from other keys or magnet Faulty key transponder Faulty immobiliser transceiver
52	Code from key not recognised by immobiliser transceiver	Interference from other key Unregistered key being used
53	Signal from immobiliser transceiver not being received by ECU	Faulty wiring or wiring connector Faulty immobiliser transceiver Faulty ECU
54	Codes do not match between immobiliser and ECU	Code re-registering key not registered Faulty wiring or wiring connector Faulty immobiliser transceiver Faulty ECU
55	Key registration error	Same key being registered twice
56	Code not recognised by ECU	Interference Faulty wiring or wiring connector Faulty immobiliser transceiver Faulty ECU

Troubleshooting procedure

25 If fault code 51 or 52 is shown, first check that none of the other registered keys are close to the receiver. If they are, remove them and try the ignition again. The key transponder may be faulty – try starting the bike with another key.

26 If any fault code is shown, first check the fuses, wiring and connectors between the immobiliser receiver, ignition switch and the ECU (see *Wiring diagrams* at the end of Chapter 8). A continuity test of all wires will locate a break or short in any circuit. Inspect the terminals inside the wiring connectors and ensure they are not loose, bent or corroded. Spray the inside of the connectors with a proprietary electrical terminal cleaner before reconnection. Also make sure the battery is in good condition and that the ignition switch is not faulty (see Chapter 8).

27 Remove the air filter housing (see Section 5). Trace the wiring from the immobiliser transceiver to the wiring connector and disconnect the connector. Using a voltmeter, connect the positive (+) probe to the red/white wire terminal on the loom side of the connector and the negative (–) probe to the black (No. 1) wire terminal **(see illustration)**. Turn the ignition ON – there should be battery voltage. Now repeat the test with the positive (+) probe connected to the red/green wire terminal. If no voltage was recorded in either test refer to the wiring diagrams and check the red/white and red/green circuits to their power sources, and check the black wire for continuity to earth. If there is voltage, the immobiliser transceiver is probably faulty and must be replaced with a new one.

28 If the immobiliser LED or the LCD display in the instrument cluster do not come on, refer to Chapter 8 and check the instrument cluster.

29 If all indications are that either the immobiliser transceiver or the ECU are faulty, it is worth having them checked by a Yamaha dealer before buying new parts.

Removal and installation

30 Follow the procedure in Section 18 to remove and install the ECU.

31 Refer to Steps 20 to 23 to remove and install the immobiliser transceiver/ignition switch assembly.

19.27 Wire terminal identification for the immobiliser transceiver connector

1 Black wire terminal
2 Black wire terminal
3 Red/green wire terminal
4 Yellow/blue wire terminal
5 Green/blue wire terminal
6 Red/white wire terminal

Chapter 5
Frame and suspension

Contents

Degrees of difficulty

Easy, suitable for novice with little experience	**Fairly easy,** suitable for beginner with some experience	**Fairly difficult,** suitable for competent DIY mechanic	**Difficult,** suitable for experienced DIY mechanic	**Very difficult,** suitable for expert DIY or professional

Specifications

Front forks

Fork oil type	Suspension fluid '01' or equivalent
Fork oil capacity (per leg)	467 cc
Fork oil level*	134 mm
Fork spring free length	
Standard.	354 mm
Service limit	347 mm

*Oil level is measured from the top of the inner tube with the fork spring removed and the leg fully compressed.

Torque wrench settings

Brake pedal pinch bolt	8 Nm
Centrestand pivot bolts	73 Nm
Clutch lever bracket clamp bolt	12 Nm
Footrest bracket bolts	30 Nm
Fork clamp bolts	
Bottom yoke.	30 Nm
Top yoke	30 Nm
Fork damper bolt	23 Nm
Fork top bolt	24 Nm
Front brake master cylinder clamp bolts	10 Nm
Handlebar clamp bolts	23 Nm
Handlebar end-weights	26 Nm
Rear brake master cylinder mounting bolts	23 Nm
Rear shock absorber nuts	40 Nm
Sidestand bracket bolts	63 Nm
Sidestand pivot bolt	46 Nm
Steering stem nut	110 Nm
Swingarm pivot bolt nut	120 Nm

1 General information

All models use a twin-spar die-cast aluminium frame, incorporating the engine as a stressed member.

Front suspension is by a pair of conventional telescopic forks with internal coil springs and cartridge damping. The forks are not adjustable.

At the rear, an aluminium alloy swingarm acts directly onto a single shock absorber. The shock absorber is adjustable for spring pre-load only.

2 Frame

1 The frame should not require attention unless accident damage has occurred. In most cases, fitting a new frame is the only satisfactory remedy for such damage. A few frame specialists have the jigs and other equipment necessary for straightening the frame to the required standard of accuracy, but even then there is no simple way of assessing to what extent the frame may have been over-stressed.

2 After the machine has covered a high mileage, the frame should be examined closely for signs of cracking or splitting at the welded joints. Loose engine mount bolts

3.2 Footrest rubbers are secured by screws (arrowed) on the underside

3.4a Footrests are secured by nuts and bolts on S2 models

3.1a Remove the split pin (arrowed) ...

can cause ovaling or fracturing of the mounts themselves. Minor damage can often be repaired by welding, depending on the extent and nature of the damage, but this is a task for an expert.

3 Remember that a frame which is out of alignment will cause handling problems. If misalignment is suspected as the result of an accident, first check the wheel alignment (see Chapter 6). To have the frame checked thoroughly it will be necessary to strip the machine completely.

3 Footrests, gearchange lever and rear brake pedal

Footrests

1 To remove the rider's footrests on all machines except S2 models, remove the split

3.3 Note the location of the sprung ball (arrowed) on the passenger footrest

3.4b Passenger footrest brackets are bolted to the rear sub-frame (arrowed) – S2 models

3.1b ... then withdraw clevis pin (arrowed)

pin from the clevis pin, then pull the clevis pin out (see illustrations). Note the location of the footrest return spring.

2 If required, the footrest rubbers can be removed by undoing the screws on the underside of the footrest (see illustration).

3 Follow the same procedure to remove the passenger's footrests – note that a spring-loaded ball is located between the footrest and its bracket to secure the footrest in the UP position when not in use (see illustration). Take care not to loose the ball, spring and detent plate when the footrest is removed. The brackets for the passenger's footrests are welded to the rear sub-frame.

4 The procedure is similar for S2 models, noting that the footrests are secured by nuts and bolts (see illustration). Both rider and passenger footrests on S2 models are fitted with rubbers. The passenger's footrest brackets are separate items bolted to the rear sub-frame (see illustration).

5 Installation is the reverse of removal. If removed, tighten the passenger footrest bracket bolts to the torque setting specified at the beginning of this Chapter.

Gearchange lever and footrest bracket assembly

6 First follow the procedure in Chapter 2, Section 15, and unscrew the gearchange lever linkage rod. Separate the rod from the lever and the arm and withdraw the rod from the frame – the rod is reverse-threaded on the lever end, so will unscrew from both lever and arm simultaneously when turned in the one direction (see illustration).

3.6 Unscrew the gearchange lever linkage rod

3.7 Unscrew the gearchange lever pivot bolt (A). Note the alignment between the end of the gearchange lever and the lower bracket mounting bolt (B)

3.8a Unscrew the mounting bolts and washers (arrowed) . . .

7 To remove the gearchange lever only, unscrew the gearchange lever pivot bolt and remove the bolt, washers (noting their order) and lever **(see illustration)**.

8 To remove the footrest bracket assembly, unscrew the bolts securing the bracket to the frame and remove the bracket **(see illustrations)**. Note the location of the washers on the mounting bolts. Note the location of the collars and bushes in the bracket.

9 Inspect the bracket assembly for damage, especially around the mounting lugs. If the mounting bushes are loose or perished, renew them. Ensure that the gearchange lever is straight and that the pivot bolt is tightened securely **(see illustration)**.

10 Installation is the reverse of removal. If removed, lubricate the gearchange lever pivot bolt and make sure the washers are correctly fitted. Tighten the footrest bracket bolts to the torque setting specified at the beginning of this Chapter.

11 If required, follow the procedure in Chapter 2, Section 15, to adjust the gearchange lever position – the end of the lever should be

3.8b . . . and lift the assembly off. Note the collars and bushes (arrowed)

approximately in-line with the lower bracket mounting bolt **(see illustration 3.7)**.

Rear brake pedal and footrest bracket assembly

12 To remove the brake pedal only, first note the alignment of the punch marks on the pedal and pedal pivot shaft **(see illustration)**. Unscrew the pinch bolt on the brake pedal and slide the pedal and large washer off the

3.9 Inspect the bracket assembly for damage

shaft. **Note:** *If no marks are visible, make your own before removing the arm so that it can be correctly aligned with the shaft on installation.*

13 To remove the footrest bracket assembly, first remove the fuel tank (see Chapter 4).

14 Trace the wiring from the rear brake light switch on the back of the footrest bracket and disconnect it at the wiring connector **(see illustration)**. Feed the wiring back to the switch, noting the location of any ties.

3.12 Note the alignment of the punch marks on the pedal (A) and the shaft (B). Unscrew the bolt (C)

3.14 Location of the rear brake light switch wiring connector (arrowed)

3.15a Remove the split pin . . .

3.15b . . . and washer . . .

3.15c . . . then push the clevis pin out

3.16 Rear brake master cylinder is secured by two bolts (arrowed)

3.17a Unscrew the mounting bolts (arrowed) . . .

15 Remove the split pin and washer from the clevis pin connecting the brake pedal to the master cylinder pushrod, then push the clevis pin out **(see illustrations)**. Discard the split pin as a new one must be used on reassembly.

16 Unscrew the bolts securing the rear brake master cylinder to the footrest bracket and remove the bolts **(see illustration)**. To prevent straining the hydraulic hose, use a cable-tie to secure the master cylinder to the frame clear of the bracket.

17 Unscrew the bolts securing the footrest bracket to the frame and remove the bracket **(see illustrations)**.

18 Note the location of the rear brake light switch and spring, and the pedal return spring **(see illustration)**.

19 If required, unhook the springs from the arms on the pivot shaft, then follow the procedure in Step 12 and separate the pedal from the pivot shaft.

20 Follow the procedure in Step 9 to inspect the bracket and mounting bushes.

21 Installation is the reverse of removal. If removed, lubricate the pedal pivot shaft and make sure the washer is installed on the shaft behind the brake lever **(see illustration)**. Align the punch marks on the pedal and the shaft and tighten the pinch bolt to the torque setting specified at the beginning of this Chapter.

3.17b . . . noting the large washers . . .

3.17c . . . and lift the assembly off

3.18 Rear brake light switch (A), switch spring (B) and brake pedal return spring (C)

3.21 Note the location of the washer (arrowed) behind the brake pedal

3.23 Note how the ends (arrowed) of the split pin are arranged

4.2 Unhook the plate (A) on the top end of the spring, then hold the nut (B) and undo the pivot bolt (C)

22 Tighten the footrest bracket bolts and the rear brake master cylinder mounting bolts to the specified torque setting.

23 Install the clevis pin from behind the arm on the pivot shaft (see illustration 3.15c). Install the washer and secure the clevis pin with a new split pin – bend both ends of the split pin around the clevis pin for security (see illustration).

24 Ensure that the wiring for the rear brake light switch is correctly routed and secured with any ties noted on removal.

25 If required, follow the procedure in Chapter 1, Section 11, to adjust the rear brake light switch and pedal position.

4 Stands

Sidestand

1 To remove the sidestand, support the motorcycle securely in an upright position using either the centrestand or an auxiliary stand.

2 To remove the stand leg only, first unhook the spring with the stand in the raised position, then counterhold the nut on the pivot bolt and unscrew the bolt (see illustration). Support the stand leg and withdraw the bolt. Note the location of the stand switch plunger.

3 To remove the complete sidestand assembly, first undo the retaining nuts and bolts and displace the stand switch (see illustration). Alternatively, remove the fuel tank (see Chapter 4), then trace the wiring from the switch and disconnect it at the wiring connector (see illustration). Feed the wiring back to the switch, noting the location of any clips or ties.

4 Undo the stand bracket bolts and lift the assembly off (see illustration).

5 Installation is the reverse of removal, noting the following points:
- Apply lithium-based grease to the pivot contact areas.
- Apply a suitable thread locking compound to the bracket bolts before installation
- Tighten the bracket bolts and pivot nut and bolt to the torque settings specified at the beginning of this Chapter.
- Check the spring tension – it must hold the stand up when it is not in use. If the spring has sagged, renew it.
- Check the operation of the sidestand

switch and starter safety circuit (see Chapter 1, Section 15).

Centrestand

6 To remove the centrestand, support the motorcycle securely in an upright position using an auxiliary stand. If the machine is supported on its sidestand, place the transmission in gear to prevent the bike moving forwards and have an assistant on hand to steady the bike.

7 Unhook the spring plate on the right-hand side with the stand in the raised position (see illustration).

4.3a Undo the screws (arrowed) to displace the stand switch . . .

4.3b . . . and disconnect its wiring at the 2-pin connector

4.4 Location of the sidestand bracket bolts (arrowed)

4.7 Unhook the spring plate (arrowed)

8 Counterhold the left and right-hand stand pivot bolts and unscrew the nuts **(see illustrations)**. Support the stand and withdraw the bolts. Note that the centrestand is fitted with two springs.

9 Installation is the reverse of removal, noting the following points:
● Apply lithium-based grease to the pivot contact areas.
● Tighten the pivot bolts to the torque setting specified at the beginning of this Chapter.
● Check the spring tension – they must hold the stand up when it is not in use. If the springs have sagged, renew them.

4.8a Centrestand left (arrowed) . . .

4.8b . . . and right-hand pivot bolts (arrowed)

5 Handlebars and levers

Handlebars

Removal

Note: *The handlebars can be displaced from the forks or top yoke without having to remove the throttle twistgrip, switch assemblies or levers (see Step 11). In all cases, take care to avoid straining the handlebar wiring. Support or tie the handlebar assembly using rags to cushion it and anything it sits against. Also cover the front brake master cylinder with rag in case of leakage.*

1 On machines fitted with a fairing, follow the procedure in Chapter 7 and remove the windshield. If the mirrors are mounted on the handlebars, remove the mirrors (see Chapter 7).

2 Disconnect the battery negative lead (see Chapter 8).

3 Follow the procedure in Chapter 4 to displace the throttle twistgrip housing and combined right-hand switch assembly. There is no need to disconnect the wiring from its connectors, but free it from any ties on the handlebar. Disconnect the brake light switch wiring connectors **(see illustration)**.

4 Unscrew the handlebar end-weight with a suitable Allen key, then slide the twistgrip off the handlebar **(see illustrations)**.

5 Follow the procedure in Chapter 6 and displace the front brake master cylinder. There is no need to disconnect the brake hose. Keep the reservoir upright to prevent fluid spillage and make sure no strain in placed on the hose.

6 Follow the procedure in Chapter 8 to displace the left-hand switch assembly. Unscrew the handlebar end-weight with a suitable Allen key. Pull the left-hand grip off the handlebar. Push a screwdriver between the grip and the bar and use spray lubricant to loosen the grip. If the grip has been bonded in place you may need to cut it free.

Caution: Wear eye protection when using a spray lube for this purpose – it can spray back into your face.

7 Disconnect the clutch switch wiring connector and free the wiring from any ties on the handlebar **(see illustration)**.

8 Follow the procedure in Chapter 2, Section 12, to disconnect the clutch cable from the clutch lever.

9 Loosen the clutch lever bracket pinch bolt and slide the lever off the handlebar **(see illustration)**.

10 Where fitted, prise the plugs off the handlebar clamp bolts **(see illustration)**.

5.3 Front brake light switch wiring connectors (arrowed)

5.4a Unscrew the handlebar end-weight . . .

5.4b . . . and slide the twistgrip off the handlebar

5.7 Disconnect the clutch switch wiring connector

5.9 Clutch lever bracket pinch bolt (arrowed)

5.10 Prise the plugs off the handlebar clamp bolts

5.11a Loosen the clamp bolts (arrowed)

5.11b One-piece handlebar clamp is secured by bolts (arrowed)

5.12 Check the alignment of the register mark (arrowed)

11 Loosen the bolts securing the handlebar clamp(s) **(see illustrations)**. Support the handlebars and remove the clamp(s), then lift the handlebars off.

Installation

12 Position the handlebars, ensuring that the register mark on the bar is aligned with the top edge of the right-hand bracket **(see illustration)**.

13 Install the handlebar clamp(s). Tighten the front clamp bolts first, then tighten the rear clamp bolts, to the torque setting specified at the beginning of this Chapter. Where fitted, install the plugs in the handlebar clamp bolts **(see illustration 5.10)**.

14 Install the remaining components in the reverse order of removal, noting the following.

● Align the slot in the clutch lever bracket with the punch mark on the underside of the handlebar **(see illustration)**. Tighten the clamp bolt to the specified torque.

● Ensure that the peg on the switch housing locates in the hole in the underside of the handlebar.

● After installation, adjust the clutch cable freeplay (see Chapter 1).

● Align the front brake master cylinder clamp mating surfaces with the punch mark on the top of the handlebar, and fit the clamp with the UP mark facing up **(see illustration)**. Tighten the clamp bolts to the specified torque, tightening the top bolt first.

● Lubricate the right-hand bar end before sliding on the throttle twistgrip.

● Ensure that the peg on the throttle twistgrip housing and combined right-hand switch assembly locates in the hole in the underside of the handlebar **(see illustration)**.

● Check and adjust throttle cable freeplay (see Chapter 1).

● Do not forget to reconnect the front brake light switch and clutch switch wiring connectors **(see illustrations 5.3 and 5.7)**.

● Tighten the handlebar end-weights to the specified torque.

● Check the operation of all switches, the front brake and clutch before taking the machine on the road.

Clutch lever

15 Follow the procedure in Chapter 2, Section 12, to disconnect the clutch cable from the clutch lever.

16 Counter-hold the lever pivot bolt and unscrew the locknut, then push the pivot bolt out of the bracket and remove the lever **(see illustrations)**.

17 Installation is the reverse of removal. Apply grease to the pivot bolt shaft and the contact areas between the lever and its bracket, and to the inner clutch cable. Adjust the clutch cable freeplay (see Chapter 1).

Front brake lever

18 Follow the procedure in Chapter 6, Section 5, to remove and install the front brake lever. Note that it is not necessary to remove the master cylinder from the handlebar. Prior to installation, apply grease to the pivot bolt shaft and the contact areas between the lever and its bracket.

5.14a Align the slot in the bracket with the punch mark (arrowed)

5.14b Align the clamp mating surfaces with the punch mark (arrowed)

5.14c Peg (arrowed) locates in hole in the underside of the handlebar

5.16a Counter-hold the pivot bolt (arrowed) . . .

5.16b . . . and unscrew the locknut on the underside of the lever

6 Fork removal and installation

Removal

1 Support the motorcycle upright on level ground so that the front wheel is off the ground. If fitted, remove the fairing (see Chapter 7).

2 Remove the front wheel (see Chapter 6).

3 Remove the front mudguard (see Chapter 7).

4 Work on each fork leg individually. Note the routing of the various cables and hoses around the forks, then release any cable-ties on the fork **(see illustration)**.

5 Note the alignment between the top of the fork inner tube and the top fork yoke, then slacken the fork clamp bolt in the top yoke **(see illustration)**. If the fork leg is to be disassembled, or if the fork oil is being changed, loosen the fork top bolt at this stage, but don't remove it.

6 Support the fork leg, then loosen the fork clamp bolt in the bottom yoke **(see illustration)**. Remove the fork leg by twisting it and pulling it downwards **(see illustration)**. Note which fork leg fits on which side. Note the arrangement of the wiring, cables and hoses around the fork leg.

Installation

7 Remove all traces of corrosion from the fork tubes and the yokes.

6.4 Release the cable-ties on the front fork

6.5 Note the alignment (A). Slacken the clamp bolt (B)

6.6a Slacken the bottom yoke clamp bolt . . .

6.6b . . . and pull the leg downwards

8 Slide the fork leg up through the bottom yoke and into the top yoke, making sure the wiring, cables and hoses are the correct side of the leg as noted on removal. Align the top of the fork tube with the top yoke **(see illustration 6.5)**.

9 Tighten the fork clamp bolt in the bottom yoke to the torque setting specified at the beginning of this Chapter **(see illustration 6.6a)**. If the fork leg has been dismantled or if the oil has been changed, tighten the top bolt to the specified torque setting. Tighten the fork clamp bolt in the top yoke to the specified torque setting **(see illustration 6.5)**.

10 Install the remaining components in the reverse order of removal. Do not forget to fit new cable-ties, where removed.

11 Check the operation of the front forks and brakes before taking the machine on the road.

7.2 Note the O-ring (arrowed) on the fork top bolt

7.3a Withdraw the spacer . . .

7.3b . . . and the washer from the fork leg . . .

7.3c . . . then pull out the spring

7 Fork oil change

Note: *After a high mileage the fork oil will deteriorate and its damping and lubrication qualities will be impaired. Always change the oil in both fork legs.*

1 Remove the fork leg, ensuring that the top bolt is loosened while the leg is still clamped in the bottom yoke (see Section 6).

2 Unscrew the top bolt from the top of the fork inner tube carefully as it is under spring pressure **(see illustration)**. Note the location of the O-ring on the top bolt.

3 Withdraw the spacer and washer from inside the fork tube, then pull out the fork spring, noting which way round it fits **(see illustrations)**.

7.4 Ensure all the old oil is drained from the fork leg

7.6 Pour in the correct amount of fresh oil

7.7 Measure the oil level with the leg fully compressed

7.8 Closer-wound coils (arrowed) should be at the bottom of the spring

7.9 Press the top bolt down against spring pressure

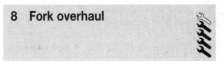

8 Fork overhaul

Special Tools: *Yamaha service tools are available for holding the damper and installing the fork top bush and oil seal, although alternatives are discussed in the procedure.*

Disassembly

Note: *Always dismantle the fork legs separately to avoid interchanging parts and thus causing an accelerated rate of wear. Store all components in separate, clearly marked containers.*

1 Remove the fork leg. Ensure that the top bolt is loosened while the leg is still clamped in the bottom yoke (see Section 6).

2 Remove the stone guard by carefully easing it off its seat on the top of the outer tube, then carefully prise off the dust seal **(see illustrations)**. Discard the dust seal as a new one must be used.

3 If the right-hand fork leg is being disassembled, unscrew the axle pinch bolt **(see illustration)**.

4 Have an assistant hold the fork leg, or clamp the slider in the soft-jaws of a vice to avoid damaging the surface, then slacken the damper bolt in the base of the outer tube **(see**

4 Invert the fork leg over a suitable container and pump the inner tube and outer tube vigorously to expel as much oil as possible **(see illustrations)**.

5 Support the fork upside down and allow it to drain for a few minutes, then pump the fork again. Wipe any excess oil off the spring and spacer. If required, the fork spring free length can be checked (see Section 8). **Note:** *If the fork oil contains metal particles, follow the procedure in Section 8 and inspect the fork bushes and the surface of the tube for wear.*

6 Fully compress the inner tube in the outer tube. Hold the leg upright and slowly pour in the correct quantity of the specified grade of fork oil **(see illustration)**. Pump the inner tube in the outer tube to distribute the oil, then stand the leg upright for ten minutes to allow any air bubbles to disperse.

7 Ensure the inner tube is still fully compressed into the outer tube, then measure the fork oil level from the top of the inner tube **(see illustration)**. Add or subtract fork oil until it is at the level specified at the beginning of this Chapter.

8 Pull the inner tube out of the outer tube to its full extension, then install the spring with its closer-wound coils at the bottom **(see illustration)**. Fit the washer and the spacer **(see illustrations 7.3b and a)**.

9 Lubricate the top bolt O-ring with fork oil, fitting a new one if necessary. Carefully press the top bolt into the tube and screw it into place, making sure it is not cross-threaded **(see illustration)**. **Note:** *The top bolt can be tightened to the specified torque setting when the fork leg has been installed and is securely held in the bottom yoke.*

10 Install the fork leg (see Section 6).

8.2a Remove the stone guard . . .

8.2b . . . and the dust seal from the outer tube

8.3 Remove the axle pinch bolt on the right-hand side

8.4 Use a suitable Allen key to slacken the damper bolt

8.6a Using a small screwdriver . . .

8.6b . . . carefully ease out the seal retaining clip

illustration). If the damper turns inside the fork, turn the leg upside down and compress the fork leg using spring pressure to hold the damper while the bolt is loosened. If the bolt cannot be loosened at this stage, Yamaha produce a service tool (Part No. 90890-01294) and T-bar (Part No. 90890-01326) which can be inserted down inside the inner tube once the spring has been removed; the tool has a tapered head that engages in the top end of the damper to hold it while the bolt is loosened.

5 Follow the procedure in Section 7 to remove the spacer, washer and spring, and drain the oil form the fork.

6 Compress the fork leg to avoid damaging its working surface, then using a small screwdriver, carefully remove the oil seal retaining clip, taking care not to scratch the surface of the inner tube (see illustrations).

7 Unscrew the previously slackened damper bolt and its copper sealing washer from the bottom of the outer tube (see illustration). If necessary, use the Yamaha service tool described in Step 4. Discard the sealing washer as a new one must be used on reassembly.

8 To separate the inner tube from the outer tube it is necessary to displace the oil seal and top bush in the top of the outer tube. The bottom bush on the fork leg will not pass through the top bush, and this can be used to good effect. Gently compress the fork leg until the inner tube stops against the damper. Now pull the inner tube sharply outwards until the bottom bush strikes the top bush. Repeat this operation until the seal and top bush are tapped out of the outer tube and the inner tube can be fully withdrawn (see illustrations).

9 Withdraw the damper and spring from inside the inner tube (see illustration).

10 Slide the oil seal, washer and the top bush off the inner tube, noting which way up they fit (see illustration 8.8b). Discard the oil seal as a new one must be fitted on reassembly.

11 Tip the damper seat out of the outer tube, noting which way up it fits.

Inspection

12 Clean all parts in solvent and blow them dry with compressed air, if available. Check the inner tube for score marks, scratches, flaking or pitted chrome finish and excessive or abnormal wear. Look for dents in the inner tube and replace the inner tubes in both forks with new ones if any are found. Check the fork seal seat for nicks, gouges and scratches. If

8.7 Unscrew the damper bolt and sealing washer

8.8a To separate the inner tube from the outer tube, pull them apart firmly several times . . .

8.8b . . . the slide-hammer effect of the bottom bush (4) will displace the top bush (3), washer (2) and oil seal (1)

8.9 Withdraw the damper and spring

8.13 Check the inner tube for run-out using V-blocks and a dial gauge

8.14 Measure the free length of the fork spring

8.16 Examine damper (A), spring (B) and damper seat (C)

damage is evident, leaks will occur. Also check the oil seal washer for damage or distortion; replace damaged or worn parts with new ones as necessary.

13 Check the fork inner tube for runout (bending) using V-blocks and a dial gauge, or have it done by a Yamaha dealer or suspension specialist **(see illustration)**. Yamaha specify a runout limit of 0.2 mm, so if the inner tube is bent beyond the limit fit new inner tubes.

 Warning: If either inner tube is bent, it should not be straightened (particularly after an accident) – replace both inner tubes with a new pair.

14 Check the spring for cracks and other damage. Measure the spring free length and compare the measurement to the specifications at the beginning of this Chapter **(see illustration)**. If a spring is defective or has sagged below the service limit, replace the springs in both fork legs with new ones. Never replace only one spring.

15 Examine the working surfaces of the two bushes. If there is any evidence of wear or scuff marks they should be replaced with new ones. **Note:** *Yamaha advise that both top and bottom bushes should be renewed when the forks are disassembled.* The bottom bush (on the inner tube) can be removed by carefully opening out its slot with a large flat-bladed screwdriver so that it will slide off the end of the tube; use the same method to install the new bush.

16 Check the damper and short spring for

damage and wear, and renew any components as necessary **(see illustration)**.

17 Examine the damper seat and replace it with a new one if it is worn or distorted.

Reassembly

18 If removed, ensure that a new bottom bush is installed on the fork tube (see Step 15).

19 Fit the damper and spring into the inner tube so that the damper projects fully from the bottom of the tube, then fit the seat onto the bottom of the damper **(see illustration)**.

20 Temporarily insert the fork spring and spacer into the inner tube to ensure that the damper is held in place in the bottom of the tube.

21 Lubricate the inner tube and bottom bush with fork oil, then insert the inner tube/ damper assembly as far as it will go into the outer tube so that the damper seat locates in the bottom of the outer tube **(see illustration)**.

22 Fit a new sealing washer to the damper bolt and apply a few drops of a suitable non-permanent thread-locking compound **(see illustrations)**. Thread the bolt into the bottom of the outer tube **(see illustration)**.

23 Hold the damper with spring pressure, or the Yamaha service tool, to prevent it turning, and tighten the damper bolt to the specified torque setting.

24 Push the inner tube fully into the outer tube. Lubricate the top bush, then slide it down over the inner tube and press it

8.19 Fit the damper seat onto the projecting end of the damper

8.21 Installing the inner tube/damper assembly – note the damper seat (arrowed)

8.22a Fit a new sealing washer . . .

8.22b . . . and apply locking compound to the bolt threads

8.22c Maintain spring pressure on the damper while the bolt is installed

8.24a Install the top bush . . .

8.24b . . . then slide on the washer

8.25 Installing the top bush with a pin punch and hammer

8.26a Fit the new oil seal . . .

8.26b . . . and tap it into place

8.27 Ensure that the clip is located securely in its groove (arrowed)

squarely into its recess in the outer tube **(see illustration)**. Fit the washer on top of the bush **(see illustration)**.

25 If available, slide a suitable piece of tubing down over the inner tube to tap the bush into its recess. Yamaha produce service tools to do this (Part Nos. 90890-01367 and 90890-01374). If necessary, the bush can be tapped into place using a pin punch and hammer – take great care to drive the bush in evenly **(see illustration)**. **Note:** *Excessive force should be unnecessary and will damage the bush. Take care not to scratch the inner tube during reassembly; if the inner tube is pushed fully into the outer tube any accidental scratching is confined to the area above the oil seal.*

26 Lubricate the **new** oil seal with lithium-based grease and slide it down over the inner tube with its markings facing

upwards **(see illustration)**. Press the seal squarely into the outer tube. Tap it lightly into place as described in Step 25, until the retaining clip groove is visible above the seal **(see illustration)**.

27 Fit the retaining clip, making sure it is correctly located in its groove **(see illustration)**.

28 Lubricate the inside of the new dust seal then slide it down the inner tube and press it into position **(see illustration)**.

29 Fit the stone guard, ensuring that the tab locates in the notch in the top of the outer tube **(see illustration)**.

30 Follow the procedure in Section 7 to fill the fork leg with the correct amount of specified fork oil, and install the spring, washer and spacer.

31 Install the fork leg (see Section 6).

9 Steering stem

Removal

1 Support the motorcycle upright on level ground so that the front wheel is off the ground.
2 As applicable, either remove the fairing (see Chapter 7) or the headlight (see Chapter 8).
3 Remove the fuel tank (see Chapter 4).
4 Follow the procedure in Section 5 and displace the handlebars. Make sure they are adequately supported to avoid straining the brake hose, cables and wiring.
5 On machines fitted with a fairing, remove the horn (see Chapter 8), then undo the bolts securing the horn/front brake hose support bracket to the bottom yoke and displace the bracket **(see illustration)**.

8.28 Install the new dust seal

8.29 Ensure the tab (A) on the stone guard locates in the notch (B)

9.5 Undo the bolts (arrowed) and remove the bracket

9.6a Release the brake hose clamp (A), then undo the lower bracket bolt (B)

9.6b Location of the upper left-hand . . .

9.6c . . . and upper right-hand headlight bracket bolts (arrowed)

6 On machines fitted with a separate headlight, first release the front brake hose from the clamp on the headlight bracket, then undo the lower headlight bracket mounting bolt (see illustration). Undo the left and right-hand upper headlight bracket mounting bolts displace the bracket (see illustrations). To remove the bracket from the machine it is first necessary to release the cable-ties securing the wiring to the bracket – note the location of the ties as an aid to reassembly.

7 If you prefer to remove the top yoke completely rather than just displace it, trace the wiring from the ignition switch, and, where fitted, the immobiliser transceiver, and disconnect it at the connector(s) (see illustration). To access the connectors, remove the air filter housing (see Chapter 4). Feed the wiring back to the top yoke. Unscrew the bolt securing the cable guide to the top yoke (see illustration).

8 On machines fitted with a separate headlight, if required, follow the procedure in Chapter 8 and remove the instrument cluster.

9 Remove the front forks (see Section 6).

10 Unscrew the steering stem nut and remove the washer (see illustrations). Lift the top yoke up off the steering stem.

11 Remove the tabbed lockwasher, noting how it fits, then unscrew and remove the locknut using a C-spanner (see illustrations). **Note:** *The locknut shouldn't be tight and will probably undo by hand.* Remove the rubber washer (see illustration).

9.7a Location of the immobiliser transceiver (A) and ignition switch (B)

9.7b Bolt (arrowed) secures cable guide to top yoke

9.10a Undo the steering stem nut . . .

9.10b . . . and remove the washer

9.11a Remove the tabbed lockwasher . . .

9.11b . . . then unscrew the locknut . . .

9.11c . . . and remove the rubber washer

9.12a Unscrew the adjuster nut . . .

9.12b . . . and remove the bearing cover

9.13 Lower the bottom yoke/steering stem out of the frame

12 Supporting the bottom yoke, unscrew the adjuster nut using a C-spanner, then remove the adjuster nut and the bearing cover from the steering stem **(see illustrations)**.

13 Carefully lower the bottom yoke and steering stem out of the frame **(see illustration)**.

14 Remove the inner race and bearing from the top of the steering head **(see illustrations 9.17b)**.

15 Remove the bearing and dust seal from the base of the steering stem **(see illustrations)**. Discard the dust seal as a new one must be fitted on reassembly. Use a suitable solvent to remove all traces of old grease from the bearings and races and check them for wear or damage as described in Section 10. **Note:** *Do not remove the races from the steering head or the steering stem unless they are to be replaced with new ones – do not re-use the races if they have been removed.*

Installation

16 Smear a liberal quantity of lithium-based grease onto the bearing races and work some grease well into both the upper and lower bearings. Fit the new dust seal over the lower bearing inner race on the steering stem, then fit the bearing **(see illustration 9.15b and a)**.

17 Carefully lift the bottom yoke and steering stem up through the steering head **(see illustration 9.13)**. Install the upper bearing and the inner race into the top of the steering head **(see illustrations)**. Fit the bearing cover then thread the adjuster nut onto the steering stem making sure it is tight enough to hold the stem in the head without any play **(see illustrations 9.12b and a)**. Install the forks and wheel, as their leverage and inertia need to be taken into account to properly set the bearings, then refer to the procedure in Chapter 1, Section 14, and adjust the bearings as described. Note

that if new bearings have been fitted, you may need to carry out the procedure several times to allow them to settle.

18 Install the rubber washer and the locknut **(see illustrations 9.11c and b)**. Tighten the locknut finger-tight, then tighten it further until its notches align with those in the adjuster nut. If necessary, counter-hold the adjuster nut to prevent it turning. Install the tabbed lockwasher so that the tabs fit into the notches in both the locknut and adjuster nut **(see illustration)**.

19 Fit the top yoke onto the steering stem, then install the washer and steering stem nut and tighten it to the torque setting specified at the beginning of this Chapter.

20 Install the remaining components in the reverse order of removal. Carry out a check of the steering head bearing freeplay as described in Chapter 1, and if necessary re-adjust.

10 Steering head bearings

Inspection

1 Remove the steering stem (see Section 9). Using a suitable solvent, remove all traces of old grease from the bearings and races.

2 Check for wear or damage – the races should be polished and free from indentations. Inspect the bearing balls for signs of wear, damage or discoloration, and examine the retainer cages for cracks or splits. Spin the

9.15a Remove the lower bearing . . .

9.15b . . . and the dust deal from the steering stem

9.17a Fit the upper bearing . . .

9.17b . . . and the inner race

9.18 Align the notches and fit the tabbed lockwasher

10.3a Locate the end of the drift in the cutout (arrowed) . . .

10.3b . . . and drive the race out

bearing balls by hand. They should spin freely and smoothly. If there are signs of wear on any of the above components, both upper and lower bearing assemblies must be replaced with a new set. **Note:** *Do not remove the races from the steering head or the steering stem unless they are to be replaced with new ones – do not re-use the races if they have been removed.*

1 Long bolt or threaded bar
2 Thick washer
3 Guide for lower outer race

10.5 Drawbolt arrangement for fitting steering head bearing races

Renewal

3 The outer races are an interference fit in the steering head and can be tapped out with a suitable drift located in the cut-outs in the head **(see illustrations)**. Alternate between the left and right-hand cut-outs so that the race is driven out squarely. It may prove advantageous to curve the end of the drift slightly to improve access.
4 Alternatively, the races can be removed using a slide-hammer type bearing extractor – these can often be hired from tool shops.
5 The new outer races can be installed in the head using a drawbolt arrangement **(see illustration)**, or by using a large diameter tubular drift. Ensure that the drawbolt washer or drift (as applicable) bears only on the outer edge of the race and does not contact the bearing surface.
6 To remove the lower bearing race from the steering stem, first thread the steering stem nut onto the top of the stem to protect the threads, they lay the stem over and drive a chisel between the base of the race and the bottom yoke. Work the chisel around the race to ensure it lifts squarely. Once there is clearance beneath the race, use two levers placed on opposite sides of the race to work it free, using blocks of wood to improve leverage and protect the yoke **(see illustration)**. If

the race is firmly in place it will be necessary to use a bearing puller **(see illustration)**. Alternatively, take the steering stem to a Yamaha dealer.
7 Fit the new lower race onto the steering stem. A length of tubing with an internal diameter slightly larger than the steering stem will be needed to tap the new race into position **(see illustration)**. Do not allow the tubing to bear on the working surface of the race.
8 Install the steering stem (see Section 9).

11 Rear shock absorber

⚠️ *Warning: Do not attempt to disassemble the shock absorber. It is nitrogen-charged under high pressure. Improper disassembly could result in serious injury. Take the shock to a Yamaha dealer or suspension specialist for servicing or disposal.*

Removal

1 Support the motorcycle upright on level ground on its centrestand. Ensure that no weight is transmitted through any part of the rear suspension.

10.6a Remove the lower bearing race as described . . .

10.6b . . . or using a puller if necessary

10.7 Install the new race using a suitable driver or length of tubing

11.3a Undo the bolts (arrowed)

11.3b Release the centre of the trim clip (arrowed) . . .

11.3c . . . and pull it out

2 Remove the rear wheel (see Chapter 6). Position a support under the swingarm so that it does not drop when the shock absorber is removed.
3 Undo the bolts on the right-hand side

securing the hugger to the swingarm **(see illustration)**. Note how the brake hose and, where applicable, the ABS sensor wiring, is secured to the swingarm. Push-in the centre of the trim clip securing the hugger and pull

the trim clip out **(see illustrations)**. Undo the bolts on the left-hand side securing the chainguard, then lift the hugger/chainguard unit off **(see illustrations)**.
4 Unscrew the nut on the shock absorber upper mounting bolt and remove the washer **(see illustrations)**.
5 Unscrew the nut on the shock absorber lower mounting bolt and withdraw the bolt, noting the location of the sleeve **(see illustration)**. Ensure that the swingarm is supported, then withdraw the sleeve **(see illustration)**.
6 Support the shock absorber and withdraw the upper mounting bolt, then lift the shock out **(see illustrations)**.

Inspection

7 Inspect the body of the shock absorber for obvious physical damage and the coil spring for looseness, cracks or signs of fatigue.

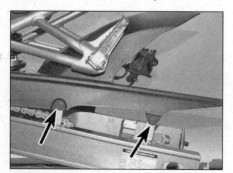

11.3d Undo the bolts (arrowed) . . .

11.3e . . . and lift the hugger/chainguard off

11.4a Undo the nut (arrowed) . . .

11.4b . . . and remove the washer on the upper mounting bolt

11.5a Remove the lower mounting bolt, noting the sleeve (arrowed)

11.5b Withdraw the sleeve

11.6a Withdraw the upper mounting bolt . . .

11.6b . . . and lift the shock out

11.8 Check the damper rod for wear, pitting and signs of leakage (arrowed)

11.9 Pre-load adjusting ring (A). Upper mounting pivot bush (B)

11.12 Inspect the seals and needle bearing (arrowed)

8 Inspect the shock damper rod for signs of bending, pitting and oil leakage **(see illustration)**.

9 Ensure that the spring pre-load adjuster ring is clean and free to rotate; inspect the cam on the inside of the ring for wear and check that it holds the ring firmly in position **(see illustration)**.

10 With the exception of the upper and lower mountings, Yamaha do not supply replacement parts for the shock, although it is worth seeking advice from a suspension specialist on the possibility of repair.

11 Inspect the pivot bush in the upper mounting for wear **(see illustration 11.9)**. If the bush is loose, worn or deteriorated, a new one must be fitted. Follow the procedure in *Tools and Workshop Tips* in the *Reference* section to press the old bush out and install a new one.

12 Inspect the bearing seals, sleeve and needle bearing in the lower mounting **(see illustration)**. If necessary, lever out the seals with a small screwdriver and discard them. If necessary, clean the old grease out of the bearing with a suitable solvent and inspect the needle rollers for pitting and corrosion. Inspect the sleeve for wear and corrosion also – its surface must be perfectly smooth. The bearing can be pressed out with a suitably sized socket if a new one has to be fitted (see *Tools and Workshop Tips* in the *Reference* section).

13 Clean and grease the bearing. Grease the lips of new bearing seals and press them into place with their marked side facing out.

11.14a Pull the centre (A) out to retract the locking tabs (B)

11.14b Push the centre (A) in to extend the locking tabs (B)

Installation

14 Installation is the reverse of removal. Tighten the mounting nuts to the torque setting specified at the beginning of this Chapter. Ensure that the brake hose and, where applicable, the ABS sensor wiring, are correctly secured when the hugger is installed **(see illustration 11.3a)**. Prior to installation, pull the centre of the trim clip out, then fit the clip and press the centre in so that it is level with the head of the clip to lock it in place **(see illustrations)**.

12 Suspension adjustment

Caution: Never attempt to turn the adjuster beyond the minimum or maximum setting.

1 The rear shock absorber is adjustable for spring pre-load.

2 Spring pre-load is adjusted using a suitable C-spanner (one is provided in the bike's toolkit) to turn the adjuster ring on the top of the shock absorber **(see illustration)**.

3 There are seven positions. Position 1 is the softest setting, position 3 is the standard, and position 7 is the hardest. Align the setting required with the adjustment stopper. Turn the spring seat clockwise to increase pre-load and anti-clockwise to decrease it **(see illustration)**.

13 Swingarm removal and installation

Removal

1 Support the motorcycle upright on level ground. Ensure that no weight is transmitted through any part of the rear suspension – tie the front brake lever to the handlebar to ensure the bike can't roll forward.

2 Follow the procedure in Chapter 6 and remove the front sprocket. Displace the chain from the gearbox output shaft.

3 Remove the rear shock absorber (see Section 11).

4 Remove the exhaust silencer and mid-section (see Chapter 4).

5 Before removing the swingarm it is advisable to check for play in the bearings (see section 14). Any problems which were not evident

12.2 A spanner is provided in the toolkit for pre-load adjustment

12.3 Direction (A) increases pre-load. Direction (B) reduces pre-load

13.6a Unscrew the nut (arrowed) . . .

13.6b . . . and remove the washer

13.7 Note how the head of the bolt aligns with the frame recess

with the other suspension components attached may now show up.

6 Unscrew the nut on the right-hand end of the swingarm pivot bolt and remove the washer (see illustrations). Push the pivot bolt in slightly so the head is accessible on the opposite side.

7 Note how the flat edges of the pivot bolt head locate in the recess in the frame (see illustration).

8 Support the swingarm, then withdraw the pivot bolt and remove the swingarm together with the chain (see illustrations). If required, knock the pivot bolt through using a large drift, but be careful not to damage the threaded end.

9 On all machines except S2 models, the chain adjusters are a loose fit in the ends of the swingarm – remove them for safekeeping (see illustration).

10 Thoroughly clean the swingarm, removing all traces of dirt, corrosion and grease. Note the location of the bearing end covers and remove them if they are loose. Clean the covers and check the condition of the seal inside (see illustration). If the seals are in good condition, the covers can be reused, otherwise discard them and fit new ones.

11 If required undo the screw securing the chain slider to the swingarm and remove it, noting how it fits (see illustration). Note the collar on the screw. If the slider is badly worn or damaged, it should be replaced with a new one.

12 Note how the rear brake caliper bracket locates on a lug on the inside of the swingarm – check for wear on the lug and in the slot in the bracket (see illustration).

13 Inspect the rear axle slots for wear.

14 On S2 models, ensure that the chain adjuster plates are a good sliding fit in their slots in the ends of the swingarm (see illustration). Unscrew the chain adjusters and check the condition of the threads in the swingarm; if they are damaged consult a specialist engineer or a Yamaha dealer to have them repaired.

15 On all other models, check the threads on

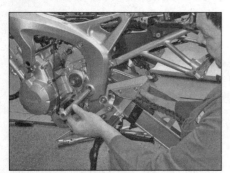

13.8a Withdraw the pivot bolt . . .

13.8b . . . and lift out the swingarm and chain

13.9 Remove the chain adjusters for safekeeping

13.10 Check the seal (arrowed) inside both bearing end covers

13.11 Note the small collar (arrowed) on the chain slider mounting screw

13.12 Check the lug (A) and slot (B) for wear

13.14 Chain adjuster plates (arrowed) should be a good sliding fit

13.15 Check the chain adjusters for wear

the adjusters and adjuster nuts, and ensure that the adjusters are a tight fit in the axle plates (see illustration).

16 Inspect the swingarm bearings for wear and damage as described in Section 14. Prior to installation, ensure that the bearings and inner sleeve have been lubricated with fresh lithium-based grease.

Installation

17 If removed, install the chain slider (see illustration 13.11).
18 Grease the inside of the bearing covers and fit them (see illustration 13.10).
19 Ensure that the swingarm pivot bolt is clean and free from corrosion, then lubricate it with a smear of lithium-based grease.

20 Loop the drive chain over the swingarm, then manoeuvre the swingarm into position (see illustration 13.8b). Slide the pivot bolt all the way through from the left-hand side, locating the flats on its head in the flats in the frame (see illustrations 13.8a and 7). Fit the washer and nut onto the pivot bolt and tighten the nut to the specified torque setting (see illustration 13.6b and a).
21 Check that the swingarm moves up and down freely.
22 Install the remaining components in the reverse order of removal. Check and adjust the drive chain slack (see Chapter 1), and check the operation of the rear suspension before taking the machine on the road.

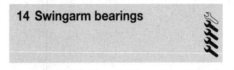

14 Swingarm bearings

Inspection

1 Remove the swingarm (see Section 13).
2 If not already done, remove the bearing cover from each side of the swingarm and withdraw the long inner sleeve (see illustration).
3 Clean all old grease off the sleeve and the bearings at both ends of the pivot tube (see illustration).

4 Inspect the bearings and bearing surfaces for signs of wear such as pitting and heavy scoring. Check the swingarm for cracks or distortion due to accident damage. Any damaged or worn component must be replaced with a new one.
5 Remove any corrosion from the swingarm pivot bolt and the inner sleeve with steel wool. Check they are straight by rolling them on a flat surface such as a piece of plate glass. If available, measure the runout with V-blocks and replace either component with a new one if it is bent (see illustration).

Bearing renewal

6 A needle roller bearing is located in each end of the swingarm pivot tube (see illustration 14.3). Follow the procedure in Tools and Workshop Tips in the Reference section to drive out the old bearings. Note that once removed, the bearings cannot be reused.
7 Inspect the bearing seats and remove any scoring or corrosion carefully with steel wool or a suitable scraper.
8 The new bearings must be pressed or drawn into their bores, rather than driven into position. In the absence of a press, a suitable drawbolt arrangement can be made up as described in Tools and Workshop Tips (Section 5) in the Reference section. Lubricate the bearings with lithium-based grease.

14.2 Withdraw the long inner bearing sleeve

14.3 A needle roller bearing is located at each end of the pivot tube

14.5 Clean the surface of the sleeve (A) and pivot bolt (B) and check that they are straight

Chapter 6
Brakes, wheels and final drive

Contents

Degrees of difficulty

Easy, suitable for novice with little experience	**Fairly easy,** suitable for beginner with some experience	**Fairly difficult,** suitable for competent DIY mechanic	**Difficult,** suitable for experienced DIY mechanic	**Very difficult,** suitable for expert DIY or professional

Specifications

ABS

Sensor-to-rotor clearance	0.9 to 1.5 mm
Speed sensor signal	
High	1.1 to 1.7V
Low	0.5 to 0.9V
Modulator solenoid resistance	2.96 to 3.20 ohms
Modulator relay resistance	50.0 to 150.0 ohms

Brakes

Brake fluid type	DOT 4
Brake pad friction material wear limit	see Chapter 1
Front caliper bore ID	
S2 models	
Upper bore	30.2 mm
Lower bore	27.0 mm
All other models	
Upper bore	30.2 mm
Lower bore	25.4 mm
Front disc thickness	
Standard	5.0 mm
Service limit	4.5 mm
Front disc maximum runout	0.1 mm
Front master cylinder bore ID	16.0 mm
Rear caliper bore ID	38.1 mm
Rear disc thickness	
Standard	5.0 mm
Service limit	4.5 mm
Rear disc maximum runout	0.15 mm
Rear master cylinder bore ID	12.7 mm

Wheels

Rim size
    Front . . . . 17 x MT3.50
    Rear . . . . 17 x MT5.50
Wheel runout (max)
    Axial (side-to-side) . . . . 0.5 mm
    Radial (out-of-round) . . . . 1.0 mm

Tyres

Tyre pressures . . . . see *Pre-ride checks*
Tyre sizes*
    Front 120/70-ZR17 (58W)
    Rear 180/55-ZR17 (73W)
Refer to the owners manual or your Yamaha dealer for approved tyre brands.

Final drive

Chain type . . . . DAIDO 50V4 (118 links)
Chain freeplay . . . . see Chapter 1
Chain stretch service limit
    2004 and 2005 models x 10 links (see text) . . . . 150.1 mm
    2006 and 2007 models x 15 links (see text) . . . . 239.3 mm
Sprocket sizes . . . . Front 16T, Rear 46T

Torque wrench settings

ABS sensor mounting bolt . . . . 7 Nm
ABS modulator mounting bracket and cover bolts . . . . 10 Nm
Brake caliper bleed valves . . . . 6 Nm
Brake hose banjo bolts . . . . 30 Nm
Front brake caliper bracket mounting bolts . . . . 40 Nm
Front brake caliper slider pins . . . . 40 Nm
Front brake caliper mounting bolts (S2 models) . . . . 40 Nm
Front brake disc bolts . . . . 18 Nm
Front brake hose guide . . . . 7 Nm
Front brake master cylinder clamp bolts . . . . 10 Nm
Front sprocket cover bolts . . . . 10 Nm
Front sprocket nut . . . . 85 Nm
Front wheel axle . . . . 72 Nm
Front wheel axle pinch bolt . . . . 23 Nm
Rear ABS rotor bolts . . . . 6 Nm
Rear brake caliper front slider pin . . . . 27 Nm
Rear brake caliper rear mounting bolt/slider pin . . . . 22 Nm
Rear brake pad retaining pin . . . . 17 Nm
Rear brake pad retaining pin plug . . . . 3 Nm
Rear brake disc bolts . . . . 30 Nm
Rear brake master cylinder mounting bolts . . . . 23 Nm
Rear sprocket nuts . . . . 100 Nm
Rear wheel axle nut . . . . 120 Nm

1 General information

All models are fitted with cast alloy wheels designed for tubeless tyres only.

Both front and rear brakes are hydraulically-operated disc brakes.

The front brakes have twin floating discs. On S2 models, the brake calipers have four opposed pistons. All other models are equipped with two-piston sliding calipers at the front.

The rear brake on all models is a single disc with a single-piston sliding caliper.

ABS is available on certain models.

Drive from the gearbox to the rear wheel is by chain and sprockets.

Caution: Disc brake components rarely require disassembly. Do not disassemble components unless absolutely necessary. If an hydraulic brake line is loosened, the entire system must be disassembled, drained, cleaned and then properly filled and bled upon reassembly. Do not use solvents on internal brake components. Solvents will cause the seals to swell and distort. Use only clean DOT 4 brake fluid or denatured alcohol for cleaning. Use care when working with brake fluid as it can injure your eyes and it will damage painted surfaces and plastic parts.

2 Front brake pads

 Warning: The dust created by the brake system may contain asbestos, which is harmful to your health. Never blow it out with compressed air and don't inhale any of it. An approved filtering mask should be worn when working on the brakes.

2.1a Undo the slider pins . . .

2.1b . . . and draw the caliper off

2.2a Lift out the outer . . .

Two-piston sliding caliper

1 Undo the caliper slider pins and draw the caliper off the disc **(see illustrations)**. The pads will remain in the caliper bracket. **Note:** *Do not operate the brake lever while the caliper is off the bracket.*

2 Lift the outer and inner pads off the bracket **(see illustrations)**. Note the location of the anti-chatter shim on the back of the inner pad.

3 Note the location of the pad plates on the bracket and the pad spring inside the caliper **(see illustrations)**.

4 Inspect the surface of each pad for contamination and check that the friction material has not worn down to the service limit (see Chapter 1, Section 11). If either pad is worn down to, or beyond the limit, is fouled with oil or grease, or is heavily scored or damaged, both pads in each caliper must be replaced with new ones. **Note:** *It is not possible to degrease the friction material – if the pads are contaminated in any way they must be replaced with new ones*

5 Check that each pad has worn evenly at each end, and that each has the same amount of wear as the other. If uneven wear is noticed, one of the pistons is probably sticking in the caliper, in which case the caliper must be overhauled (see Section 3).

6 If the pads are in good condition clean them carefully, using a fine wire brush which is completely free of oil and grease, to remove all traces of road dirt and corrosion. Using a

pointed instrument, dig out any embedded particles of foreign matter.

7 Spray the inside of the caliper with brake system cleaner, paying particular attention to the exposed section of both pistons to remove any dirt or debris that could cause the seals to be damaged. If required, remove the pad spring, noting how it fits **(see illustration 2.3b)**. Remove any traces of corrosion which might cause sticking of the caliper/pad operation.

8 Check the condition of the brake disc (see Section 4).

9 If new pads are being fitted, push the pistons all the way back into the caliper to create room for them **(see illustration)**. Push the pistons using finger pressure or a piece of wood as leverage, or place the old

pads back in the caliper and use a large, flat-bladed screwdriver inserted between them (see Step 11 for machines fitted with ABS). Alternatively obtain a piston retracting tool from a good tool supplier **(see illustration)**.

10 As the pistons are pushed into the caliper, brake fluid will be displaced back into the reservoir on the master cylinder. Depending on the initial level, it may be necessary to remove the reservoir cap, plate and diaphragm, and siphon out some fluid (see *Pre-ride checks*).

11 On machines fitted with ABS it will be necessary to open the caliper bleed valve to enable the pistons to be pushed back into the caliper. Remove the bleed valve cap, then attach a length of clear hose to the valve and place the open end in a suitable container. Open the valve and exert pressure on the

2.2b . . . and inner brake pads

2.3a Location of the upper (A) and lower (B) pad plates

2.3b Location of the pad spring

2.9a Push the pistons back into the caliper

2.9b Set-up using a commercially available piston retracting tool

2.11a Attach a length of hose to the bleed valve (arrowed)

2.11b Open the valve and press the pistons into the caliper

2.19 Remove the R-clips (arrowed) . . .

2.20a . . . then pull out the pin . . .

2.20b . . . and lift off the pad spring

2.21 Withdraw the pads, noting the location of the anti-chatter shims (arrowed)

pistons **(see illustrations)**. Take great care not to draw any air into the system. If in doubt, bleed the brake afterwards (see Section 11).

12 If any of the pistons appear to be sticking in the caliper, the caliper must be overhauled (see Section 3).

13 Smear the backs of the pads lightly with copper-based grease, making sure that none gets on the front or sides of the pads. Don't forget the anti-chatter shim that is clipped on the back of the inner pad.

14 Make sure that the pad plates are in position on the caliper bracket **(see illustration 2.3a)**. Install the pads so that the friction material faces the disc **(see illustrations 2.2a and b)**.

15 If removed, install the pad spring **(see illustration 2.3b)**. Slide the caliper onto the disc, taking care not to dislodge the brake pads, and secure it with the slider pins **(see illustrations 2.1b and a)**. Tighten the slider pins to the torque setting specified at the beginning of this Chapter.

16 Operate the brake lever several times to bring the pads into contact with the discs.

17 Check the fluid level in the master cylinder reservoir (see *Pre-ride checks*).

18 Check the operation of the brake before riding the motorcycle.

Opposed-piston caliper

19 Remove the R-clip from each end of the pad retaining pin **(see illustration)**.

20 Withdraw the pin, noting how it fits through the pad spring and remove the pad

spring, noting which way round it fits **(see illustrations)**.

21 Withdraw the pads from the top of the caliper, noting how they fit **(see illustration)**. Note the location of the anti-chatter shim on the back of both pads. **Note:** *Do not operate the brake lever while the pads are out of the caliper.*

22 Follow the procedure in Steps 4 to 6 to inspect and clean the pads **(see illustration)**. Remove all traces of corrosion from the pad retaining pin. If the pin is worn, and if the R-clips are distorted or corroded, discard them and fit new ones on reassembly.

23 Spray the inside of the caliper with brake system cleaner to remove any dust and remove any traces of corrosion which might cause sticking of the caliper/pad operation.

24 Check the condition of the brake disc (see Section 4).

25 If new pads are being fitted, displace the caliper (see Section 3), then clean around the exposed section of each piston to remove any dirt or debris that could cause the seals to be damaged **(see illustration)**. Push the pistons all the way back into the caliper to create room for the new pads (see Steps 9 to 12), then install the caliper.

26 Smear the backs of the pads and the pad pin lightly with copper-based grease, making sure that none gets on the front or sides of the pads. Ensure that the anti-chatter shims are clipped to the back of both pads.

27 Insert the pads into the caliper so that

2.22 Front brake components

1 Brake pads
2 Anti-chatter shim
3 Pad spring
4 Pad pin and R-clips

2.25 Ensure the exposed ends of the caliper pistons (arrowed) are clean the friction material faces the disc **(see illustration)**.

28 Fit the pad spring onto the pads, making sure the arrow points in the direction of normal disc rotation **(see illustration)**.

29 Insert the pad retaining pin through the hole in the outside edge of the caliper and the outer pad, then press down on the pad spring and push the pin through the spring, then through the hole in the inner pad and the inside edge of the caliper **(see illustration 2.20a)**.

30 Install the R-clips, using new ones if necessary **(see illustration 2.19)**.

31 Operate the brake lever several times to bring the pads into contact with the discs.

32 Check the fluid level in the master cylinder reservoir (see *Pre-ride checks*).

33 Check the operation of the brake before riding the motorcycle.

---

3 Front brake calipers

> ⚠ *Warning: If a caliper is in need of an overhaul all old brake fluid should be flushed from the system. Also, the dust created by the brake system may contain asbestos, which is harmful to your health. Never blow it out with compressed air and do not inhale any of it. An approved filtering mask should be worn when working on the brakes. Overhaul must be done in a spotlessly clean work area to avoid contamination*

2.27 Ensure the friction material on both pads faces the brake disc

and possible failure of the brake hydraulic system components. Do not, under any circumstances, use petroleum-based solvents to clean brake parts. Use clean DOT 4 brake fluid, dedicated brake cleaner or denatured alcohol only, as described. To prevent damage from spilled brake fluid, always cover paintwork when working on the braking system.

Note: *If the caliper is being overhauled (usually due to sticking pistons or fluid leaks) read through the entire procedure first and make sure that you have obtained all the new parts required, including some new DOT 4 brake fluid.*

Two-piston sliding caliper

Removal

1 To displace the left-hand caliper (e.g. for wheel removal), first undo the bolt securing the

2.28 Arrow on pad spring should point to the front

brake hose union to the fork **(see illustration)**. Undo the caliper bracket mounting bolts and slide the caliper assembly off the brake disc **(see illustrations)**. Secure the caliper to the motorcycle with a cable-tie to avoid straining the brake hose. **Note:** *Do not operate the brake lever while either caliper is off its disc.*

2 To displace the right-hand caliper (e.g. for wheel removal), first undo the bolt securing the brake hose to the fork **(see illustration)**. On machines fitted with ABS, undo the bolt securing the ABS sensor and draw the sensor out of its mounting plate (see Section 17). Undo the caliper bracket mounting bolts noting, where fitted, the ABS wiring guide, and slide the caliper assembly off the brake disc **(see illustrations)**. Secure the caliper to the motorcycle with a cable-tie to avoid straining the brake hose.

3 If the caliper is being completely removed or overhauled, note the alignment of the

3.1a Unscrew the bolt securing the hose union to the fork leg

3.1b Undo the caliper bracket bolts (arrowed) . . .

3.1c . . . and slide the caliper assembly off the disc

3.2a Unscrew the bolt securing the brake hose to the fork leg

3.2b Caliper bracket mounting bolts (A). Note the ABS wiring guide (B)

3.2c Slide the caliper assembly off the disc

3.3a Note the alignment of the brake hose banjo fitting (arrowed)

3.3b Detach the banjo fitting, catching any residual brake fluid with rag

3.3c Seal the banjo fitting as described – note the sealing washers (arrowed)

brake hose banjo fitting with the caliper, then unscrew the banjo bolt and detach the fitting **(see illustrations)**. Be prepared with a rag to catch any drops of brake fluid. Seal the banjo union with a suitable nut and bolt and two new sealing washers **(see illustration)**. Discard the old sealing washers as new ones must be used on reassembly.

4 Undo the caliper slider pins and draw the caliper off its bracket **(see illustrations 2.1a and b)**. If required, lift off the brake pads **(see illustrations 2.2a and b)**, then undo the caliper bracket mounting bolts and remove the bracket (see Steps 1 and 2 as applicable).

Overhaul

5 Clean the exterior of the caliper with brake system cleaner. Check the pad spring – if it is

worn or corroded, discard it and fit a new one on installation **(see illustration 2.3b)**.

6 Using low pressure compressed air directed into the brake fluid inlet, ease the pistons out of the caliper body. Place a block of wood or a wad of rag between the pistons and the caliper to act as a cushion **(see illustrations)**. Make sure both pistons are displaced at the same time. **Note:** *If the air pressure is too high and the pistons are forced out, the caliper and/or pistons may be damaged.*

7 If one piston sticks, block the other to prevent it coming out of its bore fully while continuing to apply air pressure to dislodge the stuck piston **(see illustration)**.

⚠️ *Warning: Never place your fingers in front of the pistons in an attempt to catch or protect them*

when applying compressed air, as injury could result.

8 The pistons are of two different sizes (see Specifications at the beginning of this Chapter). Mark each piston head and the caliper body with a suitable marker to ensure that the pistons can be matched to their original bores on reassembly **(see illustration)**.

9 If a piston sticks in its bore and cannot be displaced, the caliper will have to be replaced with a new one.

Caution: Do not try to remove the pistons by levering them out, or by using pliers or any other grips.

10 Remove the dust seals and the piston seals from the piston bores using a soft wooden or plastic tool to avoid scratching the bores **(see illustration)**. Discard the seals as new ones must be fitted on reassembly.

11 Clean the pistons and bores with clean DOT 4 brake fluid. Blow compressed air through the fluid passages in the caliper to ensure they are clear (make sure the air is filtered and unlubricated).

Caution: Do not, under any circumstances, use a petroleum-based solvent to clean brake parts.

12 Inspect the caliper bores and pistons for signs of corrosion, nicks and burrs and loss of plating. If surface defects are present, the caliper assembly must be replaced with a new one. If the caliper is in bad shape the master cylinder should also be checked.

13 Compare the new seals and measure them if necessary to ensure that the correct

3.6a Use a block of wood . . .

3.6b . . . or a wad of rag to cushion the pistons against the caliper

3.7 Blocking one piston while the other is forced out under air pressure

3.8 The pistons are different sizes – mark their locations in the caliper

3.10 Remove the seals carefully to avoid damage to the bore and seal groove

3.13 Check the size of the new seals to ensure they are fitted correctly

3.14 Fit the new piston seals and dust seals into the appropriate grooves (arrowed)

seals are fitted in the correct bores **(see illustration)**.

14 Lubricate the new piston seals with the brake grease supplied in the rebuild kit, or with clean DOT 4 brake fluid if preferred, then carefully fit them into the lower grooves in the caliper bores **(see illustration)**.

15 Lubricate the new dust seals and fit them into the upper grooves in the caliper bores.

16 Lubricate the pistons and fit them, closed-end first, into the caliper bores **(see illustration)**. Using your thumbs, push the pistons all the way in, making sure they enter the bores squarely and do not displace the seals **(see illustration)**. Wipe away any excess lubricant as it will attract dirt.

Installation

17 If the caliper assembly was simply displaced, ease the brake pads apart with a large, flat-bladed screwdriver to provide clearance for the disc, then slide the caliper into place **(see illustration 3.1c)**. Make sure the pads sit squarely each side of the disc, then install the bracket mounting bolts and tighten them to the torque setting specified at the beginning of this Chapter. Don't forget to secure the ABS wiring guide and install the sensor, where fitted (see Section 17). Secure the brake hose to the fork slider **(see illustrations 3.1a or 3.2a)**. Operate the brake lever several times to bring the pads into contact with the discs.

18 If the caliper has been overhauled, clean any old grease off the slider pins and check them for wear and pitting. If the pins are damaged, replace them with new ones. Lubricate the pins with a smear of silicone based brake assembly grease.

19 Remove any traces of corrosion from the caliper bracket which might cause sticking of the caliper/pad operation. Ensure that the pad plates are in good condition and are clipped securely in place on the bracket **(see illustration)**.

20 Install the caliper bracket and tighten the

3.16a Install the pistons closed end first

3.16b Push the pistons in squarely using hand pressure

mounting bolts to the torque setting specified at the beginning of this Chapter.

21 Install the brake pads **(see illustrations 2.2a and b)**.

22 Ensure that the pad spring is in place inside the caliper, then slide the caliper onto the disc, taking care not to dislodge the brake pads, and secure it with the slider pins **(see illustrations 2.1b and a)**. Tighten the slider pins to the torque setting specified at the beginning of this Chapter.

23 Connect the brake hose to the caliper, using **new** sealing washers on each side of the banjo fitting. Align the fitting as noted on removal. Tighten the banjo bolt to the torque

setting specified at the beginning of this Chapter.

24 Top-up the brake fluid reservoir with new DOT 4 brake fluid (see *Pre-ride checks*) and bleed the system as described in Section 11.

25 Check that there are no fluid leaks and thoroughly test the operation of the brake before riding the motorcycle.

Opposed-piston caliper

Removal

26 To displace the left-hand caliper (e.g. for wheel removal), first release the brake hoses from the clip on the side of the front mudguard **(see illustration)**. Undo the caliper mounting

3.19 Fit new pad plates if necessary and ensure they are secure

3.26a Release the brake hoses from the clip

3.26b Unscrew the mounting bolts (arrowed) . . .

3.26c . . . and slide the caliper off the disc

3.27 Release the brake hoses from the clip (arrowed)

bolts and slide the caliper off the brake disc **(see illustrations)**. Secure the caliper to the motorcycle with a cable tie to avoid straining the brake hose. **Note:** *Do not operate the brake lever while either caliper is off its disc.*

27 To displace the right-hand caliper (e.g. for wheel removal), first release the brake hose from the clip on the top of the front mudguard **(see illustration)**. On machines fitted with ABS, undo the bolt securing the ABS sensor and draw the sensor out of its mounting plate (see Section 17). Undo the caliper mounting bolts noting, where fitted, the ABS wiring guide, and slide the caliper assembly off the brake disc. Secure the caliper to the motorcycle with a cable tie to avoid straining the brake hose. See **Note** above.

28 If the caliper is being completely removed or overhauled, first follow the procedure in Section 2 and remove the brake pads.

29 Note the alignment of the brake hose banjo fitting(s) with the caliper, then unscrew the banjo bolt and detach the fitting(s) **(see illustration)**. Note that there are two fittings on the left-hand side. Be prepared with a rag to catch any drops of brake fluid. Seal the banjo union with a suitable nut and bolt and two or three new sealing washers as applicable **(see illustration 3.3c)**. Discard the old sealing washers as new ones must be used on reassembly.

30 Undo the caliper mounting bolts and slide the caliper off the brake disc (see Steps 26 or 27 as applicable).

Overhaul

31 Clean the exterior of the caliper with brake system cleaner.

32 Due to their construction, it is easier to overhaul one side of the caliper and refit the

components before working on the other side, rather than remove all the components at once.

33 Push the pistons on one side of the caliper fully into their bores until they are flush with the body **(see illustration)**. Hold these pistons in place using a piece of wood that is between 10 and 14 mm thick, or use a retracting tool and one of the brake pads to provide the extra thickness **(see illustrations)**.

34 Using low pressure compressed air directed into the brake fluid inlet, ease out the pistons on the other side of the caliper. When the pistons are sufficiently displaced, remove the wood or retracting tool and lift the pistons out **(see illustration)**. Make sure both pistons are displaced at the same time. **Note:** *If the air pressure is too high and the pistons are forced out, the caliper and/or pistons may be damaged.*

35 If one piston sticks, block the other to prevent it coming out of its bore fully while continuing to apply air pressure to dislodge the stuck piston.

⚠️ *Warning: Never place your fingers in front of the pistons in an attempt to catch or protect them when applying compressed air, as injury could result.*

36 The pistons are of two different sizes (see Specifications at the beginning of this Chapter). Mark each piston head and the caliper body with a suitable marker to ensure that the pistons can be matched to their original bores on reassembly.

3.29 Note the alignment of the banjo fittings (arrowed)

3.33a Push the pistons on one side of the caliper fully into their bores

3.33b Holding the pistons with a block of wood while applying compressed air to expel the pistons opposite

3.33c Holding the pistons with a retracting tool and brake pad

3.34 Ease the pistons out by hand once they are sufficiently displaced

3.38 Remove the old seals carefully to avoid damage to the bore and seal groove

3.43a Lubricate the pistons . . .

3.43b . . . and push them all the way into their bores

37 If a piston sticks in its bore and cannot be displaced, the caliper will have to be replaced with a new one.

Caution: Do not try to remove the pistons by levering them out, or by using pliers or any other grips. Do not attempt to remove the caliper bore plugs on the outside of the caliper.

38 Remove the dust seals and the piston seals from the piston bores using a soft wooden or plastic tool to avoid scratching the bores **(see illustration)**. Discard the seals as new ones must be fitted on reassembly.

39 Follow the procedure in Steps 11 and 12 to clean and inspect the pistons and bores for wear and damage.

40 Compare the new seals and measure them if necessary to ensure that the correct seals are fitted in the correct bores **(see illustration 3.13)**.

41 Lubricate the new piston seals with the brake grease supplied in the rebuild kit, or with clean DOT 4 brake fluid if preferred, then carefully fit them into the lower grooves in the caliper bores.

42 Lubricate the new dust seals and fit them into the upper grooves in the caliper bores.

43 Lubricate the pistons and fit them, closed-end first, into the caliper bores **(see illustrations)**. Using your thumbs, push the pistons all the way in, making sure they enter the bores squarely and do not displace the seals. Wipe away any excess lubricant as it will attract dirt.

44 Now hold these pistons in place as

described in Step 33 and follow the same procedure to overhaul the other side of the caliper.

Installation

45 If the caliper assembly was simply displaced, ease the brake pads apart with a large, flat-bladed screwdriver to provide clearance for the disc, then slide the caliper into place **(see illustration 3.26c)**. Make sure the pads sit squarely each side of the disc, then install the mounting bolts and tighten them to the torque setting specified at the beginning of this Chapter. Don't forget to secure the ABS wiring guide and install the sensor, where fitted (see Section 17). Secure the brake hose with the appropriate clip **(see illustrations 3.26a or 27)**. Operate the brake lever several times to bring the pads into contact with the discs.

46 If the caliper has been overhauled, ensure all the pistons are pushed back into their bores, then install the caliper and tighten the mounting bolts to the specified torque setting.

47 Install the brake pads (see Section 2).

48 If removed, connect the brake hose(s) to the caliper, using **new** sealing washers on each side of the banjo fitting **(see illustration)**. Note that on the left-hand side, an additional sealing washer should be fitted between the two banjo unions. Align the fitting as noted on removal. Tighten the banjo bolt to the torque setting specified at the beginning of this Chapter.

49 Top-up the hydraulic reservoir with new

DOT 4 brake fluid (see *Pre-ride checks*) and bleed the system as described in Section 11.

50 Check that there are no fluid leaks and thoroughly test the operation of the brake before riding the motorcycle.

4 Front brake discs

Inspection

1 Inspect the surface of each disc for score marks and other damage. Light scratches are normal after use and will not affect brake operation, but deep grooves and heavy score marks will reduce braking efficiency and accelerate pad wear. If a disc is badly grooved it must be replaced with a new one.

2 The disc must not be allowed to wear down to a thickness less than the service limit listed in this Chapter's Specifications. The thickness of the disc can be checked with a micrometer **(see illustration)**. If the thickness of the disc is less than the service limit, a new one must be fitted.

3 To check disc runout, support the bike upright so that the front wheel is raised off the ground. Mount a dial gauge to a fork leg, with the plunger on the gauge touching the surface of the disc about 10 mm (1/2 in) from the outer edge **(see illustration)**. Rotate the wheel and watch the gauge needle, comparing the reading with the limit listed in the Specifications at the beginning of this

3.48 Always fit new sealing washers on both sides of the banjo union

4.2 Measuring brake disc thickness

4.3 Set-up for checking brake disc runout

4.5 Undo the bolts (arrowed) and remove the disc

5.2 Disconnect the brake light switch wiring connectors (arrowed)

5.3 Loosen the banjo bolt (A). Note the alignment of the banjo fitting with the master cylinder (B)

Chapter. If the runout is greater than the service limit, check the wheel bearings for play (see Chapter 1). If the bearings are worn, install new ones (see Section 16) and repeat this check. If disc runout is still excessive, a new pair of discs will have to be fitted.

Removal

4 Remove the front wheel (see Section 14). *Caution: Don't lay the wheel down and allow it to rest on either disc – they could become warped. Set the wheel on wood blocks so the wheel rim supports the weight of the wheel.*
5 If you are not replacing the disc with a new one, mark the relationship of the disc to the wheel so that it can be installed in the same position. Unscrew the disc retaining bolts, loosening them evenly and a little at a time in a criss-cross pattern to avoid distorting the disc, then remove the disc from the wheel **(see illustration)**.

Installation

6 Before installing the disc, make sure there is no dirt or corrosion where the disc seats on the hub, particularly right in the angle of the seat. If the disc does not sit flat when it is bolted down, it will appear to be warped when checked or when the front brake is used.
7 Install the disc on the wheel; align the previously applied register marks if you are reinstalling the original disc.
8 Clean the threads of the disc mounting bolts, then apply a suitable non-permanent thread locking compound. Install the bolts

and tighten them evenly and a little at a time in a criss-cross pattern to the torque setting specified at the beginning of this Chapter. Clean the brake disc using acetone or brake system cleaner. If a new brake disc has been installed, remove any protective coating from its working surfaces. **Note:** *If new discs have been fitted, also fit new brake pads.*
9 Install the front wheel (see Section 14).
10 Operate the brake lever several times to bring the pads into contact with the disc. Check the operation of the brake carefully before riding the motorcycle.

5 Front brake master cylinder

⚠ *Warning: If the brake master cylinder is in need of an overhaul all old brake fluid should be flushed from the system. Overhaul must be done in a spotlessly clean work area to avoid contamination and possible failure of the brake hydraulic system components. Do not, under any circumstances, use petroleum-based solvents to clean brake parts. Use clean DOT 4 brake fluid, dedicated brake cleaner or denatured alcohol only, as described. To prevent damage from spilled brake fluid, always cover paintwork when working on the braking system.*
Note: *If the master cylinder is being overhauled (usually due to sticking or poor action, or fluid*

leaks) read through the entire procedure first and make sure that you have obtained all the new parts required, including some new DOT 4 brake fluid.

Removal

1 If the right-hand mirror is mounted on the master cylinder, remove the mirror (see Chapter 7).
2 Disconnect the brake light switch wiring connectors **(see illustration)**.
3 If the master cylinder is being completely removed or overhauled, loosen, then temporarily re-tighten, the brake hose banjo bolt – note the alignment of the brake hose banjo fitting with the master cylinder **(see illustration)**.
4 Note the alignment of the handlebar clamp with the register mark on the handlebar, then unscrew the clamp bolts and remove the clamp, noting how it fits **(see illustrations)**. If the master cylinder is just being displaced, secure it with a cable-tie to avoid straining the brake hose. Keep the reservoir upright to prevent air entering the system.
5 To remove the master cylinder, unscrew the banjo bolt and detach the banjo fitting **(see illustration)**. Be prepared with a rag to catch any drops of brake fluid. Wrap a plastic bag tightly around the end of the hose to stop dirt entering the system and secure the hose in an upright position to prevent fluid spills. Discard the old sealing washers as new ones must be used on reassembly.
6 Undo the reservoir top screws and

5.4a Note the alignment of the clamp with the register mark (arrowed)

5.4b Unscrew the clamp bolts and remove clamp

5.5 Note the sealing washers (arrowed) both sides of the banjo fitting

5.7 Screw (A) secures brake light switch.
Undo the locknut (B) . . .

5.8a . . . then pull out the pivot bolt . . .

5.8b . . . and remove the brake lever

5.9 Withdraw the pushrod and boot

5.10a Note the location of the circlip
(arrowed)

5.10b Remove the circlip . . .

remove the top, the diaphragm plate and the diaphragm (see *Pre-ride checks*). Drain the brake fluid into a suitable container. Wipe any remaining fluid out of the reservoir with a clean rag.

7 If required, undo the screw securing the brake light switch and remove the switch **(see illustration)**.

8 Undo the lever pivot bolt locknut, then draw out the pivot bolt and separate the lever from the master cylinder **(see illustrations)**.

Overhaul

9 Remove the pushrod and boot **(see illustration)**.

10 The piston assembly is secured by a circlip **(see illustration)**. Using circlip pliers, remove the circlip, then draw out the piston and spring **(see illustrations)**.

11 Lay the parts out in order as they are removed to prevent confusion during reassembly **(see illustration)**.

12 Clean inside the master cylinder with fresh DOT 4 brake fluid. If compressed air is available, blow it through the fluid passages to ensure they are clear (make sure the air is filtered and unlubricated).

Caution: Do not, under any circumstances, use a petroleum-based solvent to clean brake parts.

13 Check the master cylinder bore for corrosion, scratches, nicks and score marks. If damage or wear is evident, the master

5.10c . . . and draw out the piston and spring

5.11 Front brake master cylinder components

1 Circlip
2 Pushrod and boot
3 Piston and spring
4 Brake lever
5 Pivot bolt and locknut
6 Banjo bolt and sealing washers

5.15 Fit the narrow end of the spring onto the piston

5.17 Ensure the boot is pressed into the recess (arrowed) in the master cylinder

5.22 Note the UP mark (arrowed) on the clamp

cylinder must be replaced with a new one. If the master cylinder is in poor condition, then the calipers should be checked as well.

14 The pushrod and boot, circlip, piston (with seals) and spring are included in the master cylinder rebuild kit. Use all of the new parts, regardless of the apparent condition of the old ones. Fit them in the reverse order of disassembly.

15 Fit the narrow end of the spring over the inner end of the piston (see illustration). Lubricate the piston and seals with clean brake fluid and fit the assembly into the master cylinder, wide end of the spring first (see illustration 5.10c).

16 Depress the piston and install the new circlip, making sure it is properly located in the groove (see illustrations 5.10b and a).

17 If not already assembled, fit the boot onto the pushrod so that it locates in the

groove on the pushrod (see illustration 5.9). Locate the pushrod against the outer end of the piston and press the boot into place (see illustration).

18 Inspect the fluid reservoir top, diaphragm plate and diaphragm and replace them with new ones if they are damaged or deteriorated.

Installation

19 If the master cylinder was simply displaced, follow the procedure in Step 22 to install it on the handlebar. Connect the brake light switch wiring connectors (see illustration 5.2) and, if removed, install the mirror (see Chapter 7).

20 If the master cylinder has been overhauled, lubricate the brake lever pivot bolt and the contact areas between the lever and its bracket with a smear of grease. Install the brake lever and secure it with the pivot bolt

(see illustration 5.8a). Tighten the pivot bolt locknut securely.

21 If removed, fit the brake light switch onto the bottom of the master cylinder, making sure the pin locates in the hole, and tighten the screw (see illustration 5.7).

22 Install the master cylinder on the handlebar, aligning the clamp joint with the register mark on the top of the handlebar (see illustration 5.4a). Fit the back of the clamp with its UP mark facing up, then install the clamp bolts – tighten the bolts to the torque setting specified at the beginning of this Chapter, tightening the top bolt first (see illustration).

23 Align the brake hose banjo fitting with the master cylinder, then install the banjo bolt using a new sealing washer on each side of the fitting (see illustration 5.3). Tighten the banjo bolt to the torque setting specified at the beginning of this Chapter.

24 Connect the brake light switch wiring connectors (see illustration 5.2) and, if removed, install the mirror (see Chapter 7).

25 Fill the master cylinder reservoir with new DOT 4 brake fluid (see Pre-ride checks). Refer to Section 11 and bleed the air from the system.

26 Check the operation of the brake carefully before riding the motorcycle.

---

6 Rear brake pads

⚠ Warning: The dust created by the brake system may contain asbestos, which is harmful to your health. Never blow it out with compressed air and don't inhale any of it. An approved filtering mask should be worn when working on the brakes.

1 Unscrew the pad retaining pin plug, then slacken, but do not remove, the pad pin (see illustrations).

2 Unscrew the caliper slider pins, noting how they fit (see illustration).

3 On machines fitted with ABS, release the clips securing the rear ABS sensor wiring to the rear brake hose (see illustration).

4 Lift the caliper off the disc, then undo the pad pin and remove the pads, noting how they

6.1a Unscrew the plug . . .

6.1b . . . then slacken the pad pin

6.2 Unscrew the front and rear slider pins

6.3 Release the ABS sensor wiring clips (arrowed)

fit **(see illustrations)**. **Note:** *Do not operate the brake pedal while the caliper is off the disc.*

5 Note the location of the pad spring inside the caliper and the pad plate on the caliper bracket **(see illustrations)**.

6 Both pads have two-piece anti-chatter shim sets clipped to the back – if required for cleaning, ease the shims off **(see illustration)**. **Note:** *New pads should come with new shim sets fitted. Make sure they do, especially if fitting after-market pads.*

7 Inspect the surface of each pad for contamination and check that the friction material has not worn down to the service limit (see Chapter 1, Section 11). If either pad is worn down to, or beyond the limit, is fouled with oil or grease, or is heavily scored or damaged, fit a new set of pads. **Note:** *It is not possible to degrease the friction material – if the pads are contaminated in any way they must be replaced with new ones.*

8 If the pads are in good condition clean them carefully, using a fine wire brush which is completely free of oil and grease, to remove all traces of road dirt and corrosion. Using a pointed instrument, dig out any embedded particles of foreign matter.

9 Spray the inside of the caliper with brake system cleaner, paying particular attention to the exposed section of the piston to remove any dirt or debris that could cause the seals to be damaged. If required, remove the pad spring, noting how it fits **(see illustration 6.5a)**.

10 Check the condition of the brake disc (see Section 8).

11 Remove all traces of corrosion from the pad pin and check it for wear and damage.

12 If new pads are being fitted, push the piston all the way back into the caliper to create room for them. Push the piston using finger pressure or a piece of wood as leverage, or place the old pads back in the caliper and use a large, flat-bladed screwdriver inserted between them (see Step 14 for machines fitted with ABS). Alternatively obtain a piston retracting tool from a good tool supplier **(see illustration 2.9b)**.

6.4a Lift the rear caliper off . . .

6.4b . . . then undo the pad pin and remove the pads

6.5a Location of the pad spring (arrowed)

6.5b Location of the pad plate (arrowed)

13 As the piston is pushed into the caliper, brake fluid will be displaced back into the reservoir. Depending on the initial level, it may be necessary to remove the reservoir cap, plate and diaphragm, and siphon out some fluid (see *Pre-ride checks*).

14 On machines fitted with ABS it will be necessary to open the caliper bleed valve to enable the piston to be pushed back into the caliper. Remove the bleed valve cap, then attach a length of clear hose to the valve and place the open end in a suitable container. Open the valve and exert pressure on the piston **(see illustrations 2.11a and b)**. Take great care not to draw any air into the system. If in doubt, bleed the brake afterwards (see Section 11).

15 If the piston appears to be sticking in the caliper, the caliper must be overhauled (see Section 7).

16 Smear the backs of the pads lightly with copper-based grease, making sure that none gets on the front or sides of the pads. If removed, clip the anti-chatter shim sets in place and smear grease on the back of the shims also.

17 Make sure that the pad plate is in position on the caliper bracket and that the pad spring is correctly located inside the caliper **(see illustrations 6.5b and a)**.

18 Apply a smear of copper-based grease to the pad pin. Assemble the pads in the caliper so that the friction material will face the disc when the caliper is installed, and secure them with the pad pin **(see illustration)**.

6.6 Brake pads (A) and anti-chatter shim sets (B)

6.18 Secure the pads with the pad pin

6.19a Ensure the leading edge of the outer (arrowed) . . .

6.19b . . . and inner pad locates against the pad plate (arrowed)

6.19c Hold the caliper down and install the rear slider pin . . .

6.19d . . . then install the front slider pin

19 Slide the caliper onto the disc, making sure the pads are located each side of the disc. Ensure that the leading edges of both pads locate correctly against the pad plate **(see illustrations)**. Press the caliper down against the pressure of the pad spring and install the rear slider pin, then install the front slider pin **(see illustrations)**.
20 Tighten the slider pins to the torque setting specified at the beginning of this Chapter. Tighten the pad pin to the specified torque, then fit the pin plug **(see illustrations 6.1b and a)**.
21 On machines fitted with ABS, secure the rear ABS sensor wiring to the rear brake hose with the clips **(see illustration 6.3)**.
22 Operate the brake pedal several times to bring the pads into contact with the disc.
23 Check the fluid level in the master cylinder reservoir (see *Pre-ride checks*).
24 Check the operation of the brake carefully before riding the motorcycle.

7 Rear brake caliper

⚠️ *Warning: If the caliper is in need of an overhaul all old brake fluid should be flushed from the system. Also, the dust created by the brake system may contain asbestos, which is harmful to your health. Never blow it out with compressed air and do not inhale any of it. An approved filtering mask should be worn when working on the brakes. Overhaul must be done in a spotlessly clean work area to avoid contamination and possible failure of the brake hydraulic system components. Do not, under any circumstances, use petroleum-based solvents to clean brake parts. Use clean DOT 4 brake fluid, dedicated brake cleaner*

or denatured alcohol only, as described. To prevent damage from spilled brake fluid, always cover paintwork when working on the braking system.
Note: *If the caliper is being overhauled (usually due to a sticking piston or fluid leaks) read through the entire procedure first and make sure that you have obtained all the new parts required, including some new DOT 4 brake fluid.*

Removal

1 To displace the caliper (e.g. for wheel removal), unscrew the front and rear slider pins and lift the caliper off the disc **(see illustrations 6.2 and 6.4b)**. Secure the caliper to the motorcycle with a cable-tie to avoid straining the brake hose. **Note:** *Do not operate the brake pedal while the caliper is off its disc.*
2 On machines fitted with ABS, either release the clips securing the rear ABS sensor wiring to the rear brake hose **(see illustration 6.3)**, or displace the ABS sensor together with the brake caliper (see Section 17). If the caliper is being completely removed, release the clips securing the rear ABS sensor wiring to the rear brake hose.
3 If the caliper is being completely removed or overhauled, note the alignment of the brake hose banjo fitting with the caliper, then unscrew the banjo bolt and detach the fitting **(see illustration)**. Be prepared with a rag to catch any drops of brake fluid. Seal the banjo union with a suitable nut and bolt and two new sealing washers **(see illustration 3.3c)**. Discard the old sealing washers as new ones must be used on reassembly.
4 Follow the procedure in Section 6, Steps 1 to 4, to remove the caliper and the brake pads.

Overhaul

5 Clean the exterior of the caliper with brake system cleaner. Check the pad spring – if it is worn or corroded, discard it and fit a new one on installation **(see illustration)**.
6 Using low pressure compressed air directed into the brake fluid inlet, ease the piston out of the caliper body. Place a block of wood or a wad of rag between the piston and the caliper to act as a cushion, then lift the piston out **(see illustrations)**. **Note:** *If the air pressure*

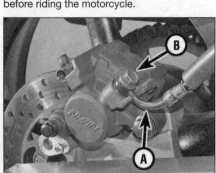

7.3 Note the alignment of the fitting (A) then undo the banjo bolt (B)

7.5 Location of the pad spring (arrowed)

7.6a Ease the piston out with compressed air . . .

7.6b ... until it is displaced from the caliper bore

7.8 Remove the old seals carefully to avoid damage to the bore and seal groove

7.11 Rear brake caliper components

1 Pad spring	3 Dust seal
2 Piston	4 Piston seal

is too high and the piston is forced out, the caliper and/or piston may be damaged.

⚠️ **Warning: Never place your fingers in front of the piston in an attempt to catch or protect it when applying compressed air, as injury could result.**

7 If the piston sticks in its bore and cannot be displaced, the caliper will have to be replaced with a new one.

Caution: Do not try to remove the piston by levering it out, or by using pliers or any other grips.

8 Remove the dust seal and the piston seal from the piston bore using a soft wooden or plastic tool to avoid scratching the bore **(see illustration)**. Discard the seals as new ones must be fitted on reassembly.

9 Clean the piston and bore with clean DOT 4 brake fluid. Blow compressed air through

the fluid passages in the caliper to ensure they are clear (make sure the air is filtered and unlubricated).

Caution: Do not, under any circumstances, use a petroleum-based solvent to clean brake parts.

10 Inspect the caliper bore and piston for signs of corrosion, nicks and burrs and loss of plating. If surface defects are present, the caliper assembly must be replaced with a new one. If the caliper is in poor condition, the master cylinder should also be checked.

11 Compare the new seals to ensure that they are fitted correctly – the outer dust seal is thinner than the inner piston seal **(see illustration)**.

12 Lubricate the new piston seal with the brake grease supplied in the rebuild kit, or clean DOT 4 brake fluid if preferred, then carefully fit it into the lower groove in the caliper bore **(see illustration)**.

13 Lubricate the new dust seal and fit it into the upper groove in the caliper bore.

14 Lubricate the piston and fit it, closed-end first, into the caliper bore **(see illustration)**. Using your thumbs, push the piston all the way in, making sure it enters the bore squarely and does not displace the seals. Wipe away any excess lubricant as it will attract dirt.

Installation

15 If the caliper was simply displaced, follow the procedure in Section 6, Steps 19 to 24, and install the caliper.

16 If the caliper has been overhauled, clean any old grease off the slider pins and check them for wear and pitting. If the pins are damaged, replace them with new ones. Lubricate the pins with a smear of silicone based brake assembly grease.

17 Clean off all traces of corrosion and hardened grease from the slider pin sleeve in the caliper **(see illustration)**. If the sleeve or its bushing is damaged, press them out and fit new ones.

18 Clean the slider pin boot on the caliper bracket **(see illustration)**. If the boot is damaged, press it out and fit a new one. Check that the pad plate on the bracket is not worn and is clipped securely in place.

19 Ensure that the pad spring is in place inside the caliper **(see illustration 7.5)**.

20 Follow the procedure in Section 6, Steps 18 to 20, and install the pads and caliper.

21 Connect the brake hose to the caliper, using **new** sealing washers on each side of the banjo fitting. Align the fitting as noted on removal **(see illustration 7.3)**. Tighten the banjo bolt to the torque setting specified at the beginning of this Chapter.

22 On machines fitted with ABS, secure the rear ABS sensor wiring to the rear brake hose with the clips **(see illustration 6.3)**.

23 Top-up the brake fluid reservoir with new DOT 4 brake fluid (see *Pre-ride checks*) and bleed the system as described in Section 11.

24 Check that there are no fluid leaks and thoroughly test the operation of the brake before riding the motorcycle.

7.12 Fit the new piston seal and dust seal into the appropriate grooves (arrowed)

7.14 Install the piston squarely, closed end first

7.17 Location of the slider pin sleeve (arrowed) in the caliper

7.18 Slider pin boot (A) on the caliper bracket. Location of the pad plate (B)

8.4 The brake disc is secured by five bolts

9.1 Location of the rear brake fluid reservoir (arrowed) – early, non-ABS equipped machines

9.2 Location of the rear brake hose banjo bolt

8 Rear brake disc

Inspection

1 Refer to Section 4 of this Chapter. To check the disc runout, support the bike upright so that the rear wheel is raised off the ground. Mount the dial gauge to the swingarm.

Removal

2 Remove the rear wheel (see Section 15). **Caution: Don't lay the wheel down and allow it to rest on the disc or the sprocket – they could become warped. Set the wheel on wood blocks so the wheel rim supports the weight of the wheel.**
3 On machines fitted with ABS, first undo the bolts securing the ABS rotor (see Section 17).
4 If you are not replacing the disc with a new one, mark the relationship of the disc to the wheel so that it can be installed in the same position. Unscrew the disc retaining bolts, loosening them evenly and a little at a time in a criss-cross pattern to avoid distorting the disc, then remove the disc from the wheel **(see illustration)**.

Installation

5 Before installing the disc, make sure there is no dirt or corrosion where the disc seats on the hub, particularly right in the angle of the seat. If the disc does not sit flat when it is bolted down, it will appear to be warped when checked or when the rear brake is used.
6 Install the disc on the wheel; align the

previously applied register marks if you are reinstalling the original disc.
7 Clean the threads of the disc mounting bolts, then apply a suitable non-permanent thread locking compound. Install the bolts and tighten them evenly and a little at a time in a criss-cross pattern to the torque setting specified at the beginning of this Chapter **(see illustration 8.4)**. Clean the brake disc using acetone or brake system cleaner. If a new brake disc has been installed, remove any protective coating from its working surfaces. **Note:** *If a new disc is fitted, also fit new brake pads.*
8 On machines fitted with ABS, install the ABS rotor (see Section 17).
9 Install the rear wheel (see Section 15).
10 Operate the brake pedal several times to bring the pads into contact with the disc. Check the operation of the brake carefully before riding the motorcycle.

9 Rear brake master cylinder

⚠️ *Warning: If the brake master cylinder is in need of an overhaul all old brake fluid should be flushed from the system. Overhaul must be done in a spotlessly clean work area to avoid contamination and possible failure of the brake hydraulic system components. Do not, under any circumstances, use petroleum-based solvents to clean brake parts. Use clean DOT 4 brake fluid, dedicated brake cleaner or denatured alcohol only, as*

described. To prevent damage from spilled brake fluid, always cover paintwork when working on the braking system.
Note: *If the master cylinder is being overhauled (usually due to sticking or poor action, or fluid leaks) read through the entire procedure first and make sure that you have obtained all the new parts required, including some new DOT 4 brake fluid.*

Removal

1 On early machines, not fitted with ABS, the rear brake fluid reservoir is located inside the frame below the rear of the fuel tank on the right-hand side **(see illustration)**. To gain access, remove the fuel tank (see Chapter 4), then follow the procedure in Chapter 8 and displace the regulator/rectifier. On all other machines, the reservoir is located on the outside of the frame.
2 If the master cylinder is being completely removed or overhauled, loosen, then temporarily re-tighten, the brake hose banjo bolt **(see illustration)**.
3 Follow the procedure in Chapter 5, Section 3, and remove the rear brake pedal and footrest bracket assembly.
4 Undo the screw securing the fluid reservoir **(see illustration)**. If the master cylinder is just being displaced, secure the reservoir and master cylinder with cable-ties to avoid straining the hoses. Keep the reservoir upright to prevent air entering the system.
5 To remove the master cylinder, unscrew the banjo bolt and detach the banjo fitting **(see illustrations)**. Be prepared with a rag to catch any drops of brake fluid. Seal the banjo

9.4 Undo the screw securing the brake fluid reservoir

9.5a Unscrew the banjo bolt . . .

9.5b . . . and detach the brake hose banjo fitting

9.7 Disconnect the reservoir hose from the union on the master cylinder

9.8 Location of the reservoir hose union (A). Note the clevis and nut (B) and locknut (C)

9.10a Pull back the boot (A) to access the circlip (B)

9.10b Draw out the pushrod . . .

9.10c . . . the piston and the spring

union with a suitable nut and bolt and two new sealing washers **(see illustration 3.3c)**. Discard the old sealing washers as new ones must be used on reassembly.

6 Remove the reservoir cap, diaphragm plate and diaphragm (see *Pre-ride checks*). Drain the brake fluid into a suitable container.

7 Release the clip securing the reservoir hose to the union on the master cylinder and detach the hose **(see illustration)**. Wipe any remaining fluid out of the reservoir with a clean rag.

Overhaul

8 The reservoir hose union is a firm press fit in the master cylinder – unless there are signs

that the seal is leaking, do not remove the hose union **(see illustration)**. If necessary, prise out the hose union, taking care not to damage the sealing surface of the master cylinder. If the union breaks in the process, both the seal and union are available as separate items.

9 Measure the position of the clevis on the pushrod, then slacken the locknut and thread the clevis and nut off the pushrod **(see illustration 9.8)**.

10 Pull back the boot from the end of the master cylinder to reveal the retaining circlip **(see illustration)**. Depress the pushrod and use circlip pliers to remove the circlip, then draw out the pushrod, the piston and spring

(see illustrations). Note how the spring is clipped to the inner end of the piston.

11 Lay the parts out in order as they are removed to prevent confusion during reassembly **(see illustration)**.

12 Clean inside the master cylinder with fresh DOT 4 brake fluid. If compressed air is available, blow it through the fluid passages to ensure they are clear (make sure the air is filtered and unlubricated).

Caution: Do not, under any circumstances, use a petroleum-based solvent to clean brake parts.

13 Check the master cylinder bore for corrosion, scratches, nicks and score marks. If damage or wear is evident, the master cylinder must be replaced with a new one. If the master cylinder is in poor condition, then the caliper should be checked as well.

14 The pushrod and boot, circlip, piston (with seals) and spring are included in the master cylinder rebuild kit. Use all of the new parts, regardless of the apparent condition of the old ones. Fit them in the reverse order of disassembly.

15 Fit one end of the spring over the inner end of the piston, ensuring it clips into place over the metal tabs **(see illustration)**. Lubricate the piston and seals with clean brake fluid and fit the assembly into the master cylinder **(see illustration 9.10c)**.

9.11 Rear brake master cylinder components

1 Circlip   2 Pushrod and boot   3 Piston   4 Spring

9.15 Push the end of the spring over the tabs (arrowed)

9.17 Push the boot down into the end of the master cylinder

9.20 Rear brake master cylinder and reservoir assembly

16 Thread the locknut, clevis and nut onto the end of the pushrod. Press the pushrod into the master cylinder so that it depresses the piston, then install the new circlip, making sure it is properly located in its groove **(see illustrations 9.10a)**.

17 Push the boot into place with its wider end located inside the groove in the master cylinder **(see illustration)**.

18 Position the clevis as noted on removal (see Step 9), then tighten the locknut securely. Note that the clevis position sets brake pedal position and final adjustments can be made after installation (see Chapter 1, Section 11).

19 If removed, lubricate a new reservoir hose union seal with clean brake fluid, then press the seal into the master cylinder. Make sure the union is facing towards the top of the master cylinder, then press it firmly into place **(see illustration 9.8)**.

20 Inspect the fluid reservoir, cap, diaphragm plate and diaphragm and renew any parts if they are damaged or deteriorated. Inspect the reservoir hose for cracks or splits and replace

it with a new one if necessary. Check the hose clips and replace them if they are strained or corroded. Push the reservoir hose fully onto its union and secure it with the clip **(see illustration)**.

Installation

21 If the master cylinder was simply displaced, secure the fluid reservoir to the frame **(see illustration 9.4)**, then follow the procedure in Chapter 5, Section 3, and install the rear brake pedal and footrest bracket assembly.

22 If the master cylinder has been removed, align the brake hose banjo fitting with the master cylinder – the fitting should be in front of the rear facing tab on the top of the master cylinder – then install the banjo bolt using a new sealing washer on each side of the fitting **(see illustration)**. It is not possible to tighten the banjo bolt with a torque wrench once the master cylinder is in position. Thread a suitable long bolt or length of studding into the upper master cylinder mounting, then hold

this firmly while tightening the banjo bolt to the torque setting specified at the beginning of this Chapter **(see illustration)**.

23 Secure the fluid reservoir to the frame **(see illustration 9.4)**, then follow the procedure in Chapter 5, Section 3, and install the rear brake pedal and footrest bracket assembly.

24 Fill the fluid reservoir with new DOT 4 brake fluid (see *Pre-ride checks*). Refer to Section 11 and bleed the air from the system.

25 Install the remaining components in the reverse order of removal.

26 Check the operation of the rear brake carefully before riding the motorcycle.

10 Brake hoses and fittings

Inspection

1 Brake hose condition should be checked

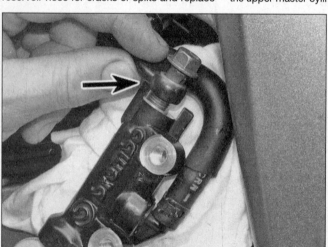

9.22a Banjo fitting locates in front of the tab (arrowed)

9.22b Tightening the banjo bolt with a torque wrench as described

10.4a Brake hose/pipe union located on the left-hand side above the radiator

10.4b Brake hose/pipe union located on the left-hand side above the gearchange mechanism cover

10.4c Brake hose/pipe union located on the swingarm

regularly and the hoses replaced with new ones at the specified interval (see Chapter 1).

2 Twist and flex the hoses while looking for cracks, bulges and seeping hydraulic fluid. Check extra carefully around the areas where the hoses connect with the banjo fittings and unions, as these are common areas for hose failure.

3 Check the banjo fittings and unions connected to the brake hoses. If the fittings are rusted, scratched or cracked, fit new hoses.

Renewal

4 On machines not fitted with ABS, the brake hoses have banjo fittings on each end (see illustrations 3.3a and 5.3 or 7.3 and 9.22a). On machines fitted with ABS, the brake hoses have screw-in unions where they are joined to sections of brake pipe between the master cylinder, ABS unit and brake caliper (see illustrations). Also note that the link hose between the two front brake calipers is a one-piece unit – only the banjo union on the hose to the ABS unit can be unscrewed (see illustration). For full details on the ABS system see Section 17.

5 Cover the surrounding area with plenty of rags to catch any drops of brake fluid and unscrew the banjo bolt or union at each end of the hose. On machines fitted with ABS, hold the connector block with an adjustable spanner to prevent it twisting and damaging the mounting bracket and brake pipes. Note

the alignment of the banjo fitting with the master cylinder or brake caliper.

6 Free the hose from any clips or guides and remove it, noting its routing. Discard the banjo sealing washers.

7 Position the new hose, making sure it is not twisted or otherwise strained, and ensure that it is correctly routed through any clips or guides and is clear of all moving components.

8 On machines fitted with ABS, screw the union into the connector block first (see illustrations 10.4a, b and c).

9 Check that the banjo fittings align correctly, then install the banjo bolts, using new sealing washers on both sides of the fittings (see illustrations 3.3a and 5.3 or 7.3 and 9.22a). On machines with opposed-piston calipers, an additional sealing washer should be fitted between the two banjo unions on the left-hand side (see Section 3).

10 Tighten the banjo bolts to the torque setting specified at the beginning of this Chapter.

11 Flush the old brake fluid from the system (see Section 11).

12 Check the operation of the brakes carefully before riding the motorcycle.

11 Brake system bleeding and fluid change

Special Tool: *In its simplest form, the brake bleeding equipment described in Step 2 will*

be required. A quicker alternative would be a 'one-man' brake bleeding kit consisting of a non-return valve in the pipe which prevents air being drawn back into the caliper.

Bleeding air from the system

1 Bleeding the brakes is simply the process of removing air from the brake fluid reservoirs, the hoses and the brake calipers. Bleeding is necessary whenever a brake system connection is loosened, after a component or hose is removed, or when the master cylinder or caliper is overhauled. Leaks in the system may also allow air to enter, but leaking brake fluid will reveal their presence and warn you of the need for repair.

2 To bleed the brakes, you will need some new DOT 4 brake fluid, a length of clear vinyl or plastic hose, a small container partially filled with clean brake fluid, some rags and a spanner to fit the brake caliper bleed valve (see illustrations).

3 Support the bike upright on level ground and cover the fuel tank and other painted components to prevent damage in the event that brake fluid is spilled.

4 Refer to *Pre-ride checks* at the start of this manual and remove the reservoir top (front brake) or cap (rear brake), diaphragm plate and diaphragm.

5 Slowly pump the brake lever or pedal a few times, until no air bubbles can be seen floating up from the holes in the bottom of the

10.4d Front caliper link hose (A) and ABS hose banjo union (B)

11.2a Set-up for bleeding the front ...

11.2b ... and rear brakes

11.5 Check for air bubbles (arrowed) in the brake fluid

11.6 Pull the cap off the bleed valve – rear caliper shown

11.11a Location of the ABS test connector (arrowed)

11.11b Pull out the blanking plug . . .

11.11c . . . and join the light blue and black wire terminals

reservoir **(see illustration)**. This bleeds the air from the master cylinder end of the line.

6 Pull the dust cap off the bleed valve **(see illustration)**. If available, use a ring spanner to loosen, and then temporarily tighten the bleed valve, then attach one end of the clear vinyl or plastic hose to the valve with the spanner still in place. Submerge the other end of the hose in the clean brake fluid in the container **(see illustrations 11.2a or b)**. Alternatively, the valve can be opened and closed with an open-ended spanner.

7 Check the fluid level in the reservoir – do not allow it to drop below the lower mark during the procedure.

8 Carefully pump the brake lever or pedal three or four times, then hold it in (front) or down (rear) while opening the bleed valve. When the valve is opened, brake fluid will flow out into the clear tubing, and the lever will move toward the handlebar, or the pedal will

move down. If there is air in the system you will see air bubbles in the brake fluid coming out.

9 Retighten the bleed valve, then release the brake lever or pedal gradually. Top-up the reservoir as required and repeat the process until no air bubbles are visible in the brake fluid, and the lever or pedal is firm when applied. **Note:** *When bleeding the front brake system, bleed the left-hand caliper first, then the right-hand caliper.*

10 At this point, the procedure for machines not fitted with ABS is complete. Go to Step 15.

11 On machines fitted with ABS, ensure that the battery is fully charged (see Chapter 8). Where fitted, remove the left-hand cockpit trim panel (see Chapter 7) or remove the fuel tank (see Chapter 4). Locate the ABS test connector in the main wiring loom on the left-hand side of the machine, either in front of,

or underneath, the fuel tank **(see illustration)**. Ensure that the ignition switch is OFF, then remove the blanking plug and use an insulated jumper wire to connect the light blue and black wire terminals inside the connector **(see illustrations)**. **Note:** *If the front and rear brake systems are being bled, they should be tested together – ensure that both fluid reservoirs are topped-up.*

12 Turn the engine stop switch OFF, then turn the ignition switch ON **(see illustrations)**. Wait until the ABS indicator in the instrument cluster goes OFF, then push the start button for at least 4 seconds.

13 Next, release the start button and pull the brake lever in and press the brake pedal down, both at the SAME TIME. Continue to hold the lever in and the pedal down – the lever will pulse for approximately 1 second, then the pedal will pulse for approximately 1 second, then the lever will pulse again for approximately 1 second. It is vital to hold the lever in and the pedal down throughout the procedure.

14 Turn the ignition switch OFF, then repeat Steps 7 to 9.

15 Disconnect the hose, tighten the bleed valve to the torque setting specified at the beginning of this Chapter and fit the dust cap.

16 Check the fluid level in the reservoir, install the diaphragm, diaphragm plate and top or cap, and wipe up any spilled brake fluid. Check the entire system for fluid leaks.

17 Install any remaining components in the reverse order of removal.

18 Check the operation of the brakes carefully before riding the motorcycle.

Changing the fluid

19 Changing the brake fluid is a similar process to bleeding the brakes and requires the same materials plus a suitable tool for siphoning the old fluid out of the reservoir. Also ensure that the container is large enough to take all the old fluid when it is flushed out of the system.

20 Follow Steps 3, 4 and 6, then siphon the old fluid out of the reservoir. Fill the reservoir with new brake fluid, then follow Step 8.

21 Retighten the bleed valve, then release the brake lever or pedal gradually. Keep the reservoir topped-up with new fluid to above the LOWER level at all times or air may enter

11.12a Turn the stop switch OFF (arrowed) . . .

11.12b . . . then turn the ignition switch ON

12.2 Check the wheel for radial (out-of-round) runout (A) and axial (side-to-side) runout (B)

the system and greatly increase the length of the task. Repeat the process until new fluid can be seen emerging from the bleed valve.

22 Follow Steps 15 to 18. Note that on machines fitted with ABS, the operation of the ABS should be checked before riding the motorcycle (see Section 17).

12 Wheel inspection and repair

1 In order to carry out a proper inspection of the wheels, it is necessary to support the bike securely in an upright position so that the wheel being inspected is raised off the ground. Clean the wheels thoroughly to remove mud and dirt that may interfere with the inspection procedure or mask defects. Make a general check of the wheels (see Chapter 1) and tyres (see *Pre-ride checks*).

2 Attach a dial gauge to the fork or the swingarm and position its tip against the side of the wheel rim **(see illustration)**. Spin the wheel slowly and check the axial (side-to-side) runout at the rim.

3 In order to accurately check radial (out of round) runout with the dial gauge, remove the wheel from the machine, and the tyre from the wheel. With the axle clamped in a vice and the dial gauge positioned on the top of the rim, the wheel can be rotated to check the runout.

4 An easier, though slightly less accurate, method is to attach a stiff wire pointer to the fork or the swingarm and position the end a fraction of an inch from the edge of the wheel rim where the wheel and tyre join. If the wheel is true, the distance from the pointer to the rim will be constant as the wheel is rotated. **Note:** *If wheel runout is excessive, check the wheel bearings very carefully before renewing the wheel.*

5 The wheels should also be inspected for cracks, flat spots on the rim and other damage. Look very closely for dents in the area where the tyre bead contacts the rim. Dents in this

area may prevent complete sealing of the tyre against the rim, which leads to deflation of the tyre over a period of time.

6 If damage is evident, or if runout in either direction is excessive, the wheel will have to be replaced with a new one. Never attempt to repair a damaged cast alloy wheel.

13 Wheel alignment check

1 Misalignment of the wheels due to a bent frame or forks can cause strange and possibly serious handling problems. If the frame or forks are at fault, repair by a frame specialist or replacement with new parts are the only options.

2 To check wheel alignment you will need an assistant, a length of string or a perfectly straight piece of wood and a ruler. A plumb bob or spirit level for checking that the wheels are vertical will also be required.

3 In order to make a proper check of the wheels it is necessary to support the bike in an upright position on its centrestand. First ensure that the chain adjuster markings coincide on each side of the swingarm (see Chapter 1, Section 1). Next, measure the width of both tyres at their widest points. Subtract the smaller measurement from the larger measurement, then divide the difference by two. The result is the amount of offset that should exist between the front and rear tyres on both sides of the machine.

4 If a string is used, have your assistant hold one end of it about halfway between the floor and the rear axle, with the string touching the back edge of the rear tyre sidewall.

5 Run the other end of the string forward and pull it tight so that it is roughly parallel to the floor **(see illustration)**. Slowly bring the string into contact with the front edge of the rear tyre sidewall, then turn the front wheel until it is parallel with the string. Measure the distance from the front tyre sidewall to the string.

6 Repeat the procedure on the other side of the motorcycle. The distance from the front tyre sidewall to the string should be equal on both sides.

7 As previously mentioned, a perfectly

13.5 Wheel alignment check using string

straight length of wood or metal bar may be substituted for the string **(see illustration)**.

8 If the distance between the string and tyre is greater on one side, or if the rear wheel appears to be out of alignment, have your machine checked by a Yamaha dealer.

9 If the front-to-back alignment is correct, the wheels still may be out of alignment vertically.

10 Using a plumb bob or spirit level, check the rear wheel to make sure it is vertical. To do

13.7 Wheel alignment check using a straight-edge

14.2 Displace the front ABS sensor

14.3a Slacken the pinch bolt (arrowed) . . .

14.3b . . . then use a suitable tool . . .

this, hold the string of the plumb bob against the tyre upper sidewall and allow the weight to settle just off the floor. If the string touches both the upper and lower tyre sidewalls and is perfectly straight, the wheel is vertical. If it is not, adjust the stand until it is.

11 Once the rear wheel is vertical, check that the front wheel is vertical also. If both wheels are not perfectly vertical, the frame and/or major suspension components are bent.

14 Front wheel

Removal

1 Support the motorcycle securely in an upright position with the front wheel off the ground.

14.3c . . . to slacken the axle

14.4b Remove the wheel

2 Displace the front brake calipers (see Section 3). On machines fitted with ABS, follow the procedure in Section 17 and displace the front sensor **(see illustration)**.
3 Slacken the axle pinch bolt on the bottom of the right-hand fork leg, then slacken the axle using an automotive sump plug tool or a bolt with two locknuts as shown **(see illustrations)**.
4 Support the wheel to avoid damaging the axle threads, then unscrew and withdraw the axle **(see illustration)**. Remove the wheel from between the forks **(see illustration)**.
5 Remove the shouldered spacers from both sides of the wheel, noting how they fit inside the bearing seals **(see illustration)**. On machines fitted with ABS, the right-hand spacer is integral with the mounting plate for the ABS sensor **(see illustration)**.

14.4a Unscrew and withdraw the axle

14.5a Remove the shouldered spacers

Caution: Don't lay the wheel down and allow it to rest on either brake disc – they could become warped. Set the wheel on wood blocks so the wheel rim supports the weight of the wheel, or keep the wheel upright. Don't operate the brake lever with the wheel removed.
6 Clean the axle and remove any corrosion using steel wool. Check the axle for straightness by rolling it on a flat surface such as a piece of plate glass. If available, place the axle in V-blocks and check for runout using a dial gauge. If the axle is bent, replace it with a new one.
7 Wipe any old grease off the bearing seals and check the condition of the seals and the wheel bearings (see Section 16).
8 Clean the axle spacers and remove any corrosion with steel wool. The spacers should be perfectly smooth where they locate in the seals.

Installation

9 Apply lithium-based grease to the insides of the bearing seals, then fit the spacers into the seals so that the shouldered end of the spacers faces out **(see illustration 14.5a)**.
10 Apply a thin coat of lithium-based grease to the axle, then lift the wheel into position between the forks, making sure the spacers remain in place. Make sure that the wheel is fitted the correct way round. On machines fitted with ABS, ensure the peg on the inside of the right-hand fork leg locates in

14.5b Remove the mounting plate for the ABS sensor

14.10 Ensure the peg (A) locates inside the slot (B)

14.11a Install the axle from the right-hand side . . .

14.11b . . . making sure it passes through the spacer (A) and screws into the fork leg (B)

the slot on the sensor mounting plate **(see illustration)**.

11 Support the wheel and slide the axle in from the right-hand side, making sure it passes through the left-hand spacer, then screw the axle into the bottom of the left hand fork **(see illustrations)**.

12 Check that the axle is correctly located then tighten it to the torque setting specified at the beginning of the Chapter.

13 Install the brake calipers, making sure the pads sit squarely on each side of the discs (see Section 3). Apply the front brake to bring the pads back into contact with the discs. Take the bike off its stand and compress the forks by applying the brake and pressing down on the handlebars to align the wheel and the suspension.

14 Tighten the pinch bolt on the bottom of the right-hand fork leg to the specified torque setting **(see illustration 14.3a)**.

15 On machines fitted with ABS, install the front sensor **(see illustration 14.2)**.

16 Check the operation of the front brake carefully before riding the motorcycle.

15 Rear wheel and sprocket coupling

Removal

1 Support the motorcycle securely in an upright position with the rear wheel off the ground.

2 Displace the rear brake caliper (see Section 7). On machines fitted with ABS, displace the ABS sensor together with the brake caliper (see Section 17).

3 Loosen the chain adjuster locknuts and turn

the adjusters to provide some slack in the chain (see Chapter 1).

4 Unscrew the axle nut and remove the nut and washer **(see illustration)**. On S2 models, remove the left-hand chain adjuster plate **(see illustration)**.

5 Support the wheel, then withdraw the axle and washer, and lower the wheel to the ground **(see illustration)**. On S2 models, the right-hand chain adjuster plate will come off with the axle – note how it fits **(see illustration)**. **Note:** *On S2 models, the left and right-hand adjuster plates are different and must not be swapped around on reassembly.*

6 Disengage the chain from the rear wheel sprocket and lay it along the swingarm **(see illustration)**.

7 Draw the wheel out from the swingarm – note how the brake caliper bracket locates between the wheel and the swingarm and remove the bracket **(see illustration)**.

15.4a Remove the axle nut and washer

15.4b On S2 models, remove the axle nut, washer and chain adjuster plate (arrowed)

15.5a Support the wheel and withdraw the axle

15.5b On S2 models, note how the axle (arrowed) locates inside the right-hand axle plate

15.6 Disengage the chain from the sprocket

15.7 Note the location of the caliper bracket

15.8a Remove the spacer from the seal on the left . . .

15.8b . . . and right-hand side of the rear wheel

15.9 Lift out the sprocket coupling

15.10 Check the dampers for wear and deterioration

15.15 Locate the slot (arrowed) over the peg on the swingarm

15.17 Ensure that the chain adjusters are correctly aligned

8 Remove the shouldered spacers from both sides of the wheel, noting how they fit inside the bearing seals **(see illustrations)**.
Caution: Don't lay the wheel down and allow it to rest on the disc or the sprocket – they could become warped. Set the wheel on wood blocks so the wheel rim supports the weight of the wheel, or keep the wheel upright. Don't operate the brake pedal with the wheel removed.
9 Lift the sprocket coupling out of the hub, leaving the rubber dampers in position **(see illustration)**. Check the coupling for cracks or any obvious signs of damage. Also check the sprocket studs for looseness, wear or damage.
10 Note the location of the damper segments – lift the segments from the hub and check them for cracks, hardening, wear and general deterioration **(see illustration)**. Renew the dampers as a set, if necessary.
11 Clean the axle and remove any corrosion using steel wool. Check the axle for straightness by rolling it on a flat surface such as a piece of plate glass. If available, place the axle in V-blocks and check for runout using a dial gauge. If the axle is bent, replace it with a new one.
12 Wipe any old grease off the bearing seals and check the condition of the seals and the wheel bearings (see Section 16). Don't forget to check the bearing in the sprocket coupling.
13 Clean the spacers and remove any corrosion with steel wool. The spacers should be perfectly smooth where they locate in the seals.

Installation

14 Ensure that the sprocket coupling is pressed firmly into the hub. Apply lithium-based grease to the insides of the bearing seals, then fit the spacers **(see illustrations 15.8a and b)**. Lubricate the axle with a smear of grease.
15 Manoeuvre the wheel and the caliper bracket into place, ensuring that the slot in the bracket engages with the peg on the inside of the swingarm **(see illustration)**.
16 Lift the drive chain onto the sprocket **(see illustration 15.6)**.
17 On all machines except S2 models, the chain adjusters are a loose fit in the ends of the swingarm – ensure that the adjusters are correctly aligned with the axle slots in the swingarm **(see illustration)**.
18 On S2 models, slide the right-hand chain adjuster plate onto the axle and align the raised sections of the plate with the flats on the axle head. On all other models, slide the washer onto the axle.
19 Lift the wheel into position, making sure the spacers and caliper bracket remain in place, and slide the axle through from the right-hand side **(see illustration 15.5a)**.
20 On S2 models, locate the right-hand chain adjuster plate in the slot in the swingarm with the raised sections vertical **(see illustration 15.5b)**. Fit the left-hand chain adjuster plate **(see illustrations 15.4b)**.
21 Fit the washer and the axle nut, then follow the procedure in Chapter 1 and adjust the chain tension.
22 Install the brake caliper (see Section 7). If

applicable, install the ABS sensor (see Section 17).
23 Apply the rear brake to bring the pads into contact with the disc. Check the operation of the rear brake carefully before riding the motorcycle.

16 Wheel and sprocket coupling bearings

Front wheel bearings
Note: *Always fit the wheel bearings in sets, never individually.*
1 Remove the wheel (see Section 14).
2 Lever out the bearing seals from both sides of the hub using a seal hook or a large, flat-bladed screwdriver and a piece of wood, taking care not to damage the hub **(see illustration)**. Discard the seals as new ones must be fitted on reassembly.

16.2 Lever out the bearing seals – front wheel

16.4 Using an expanding puller and slide-hammer

16.7 Using a socket to drive the bearing in

3 Inspect the bearings (see *Tools and Workshop Tips (Section 5)* in the Reference Section) – a caged ball bearing is fitted in each side of the hub. **Note:** *Do not remove the bearings unless they are going to be replaced with new ones.*

4 If the bearings are worn, remove them using an internal expanding puller with slide-hammer attachment, which can be obtained commercially (see *Tools and Workshop Tips*) **(see illustration and 16.15a)**. Remove the spacer which fits between the bearings.

5 Turn the wheel over and remove the remaining bearing using the same procedure.

6 Thoroughly clean the hub area of the wheel with a suitable solvent and inspect the bearing seats for scoring and wear. If the seats are damaged, consult a Yamaha dealer before reassembling the wheel.

7 The new bearings can be installed in the hub using a drawbolt arrangement or by using a bearing driver or suitable socket (see *Tools and Workshop Tips*) **(see illustration)**. Ensure that the drawbolt washer or driver (as applicable) bears only on the outer edge of the race and does not contact the bearing seat.

8 Install the bearings with the marked or sealed side facing outwards. Ensure the bearing is fitted squarely and all the way into its seat. Turn the wheel over then install the bearing spacer and the other new bearing.

9 Apply a smear of grease to the new

16.9 Press the bearing seal into place

16.12 Lever out the bearing seal – rear wheel

seals, then press them into the hub **(see illustration)**. Level the seals with the rim of the hub using a hammer and a small block of wood if necessary.

10 Clean the brake discs using acetone or brake system cleaner, then install the wheel (see Section 14).

Rear wheel bearings

11 Remove the rear wheel (see Section 15) and lift the sprocket coupling out of the hub **(see illustration 15.9)**.

12 Set the wheel on wooden blocks with the disc (right-hand side) facing up, then lever out the bearing seal using a seal hook or a large flat-bladed screwdriver and a piece of

wood, taking care not to damage the hub **(see illustration)**. Discard the seal as a new one must be fitted on reassembly.

13 Inspect the bearings (see *Tools and Workshop Tips (Section 5)* in the Reference Section) – a caged ball bearing is fitted in the right-hand side of the hub and a needle roller bearing is fitted in the left-hand side. To inspect the roller bearing, pull out the sleeve and wipe any old grease off the rollers **(see illustrations)**. **Note:** *Do not remove the bearings unless they are going to be replaced with new ones.*

14 If the bearings are worn, remove the circlip securing the caged ball bearing **(see illustration)**. Turn the wheel over and rest it on the wooden blocks, then withdraw the bearing

16.13a Remove the bearing sleeve . . .

16.13b . . . to inspect the bearing needle rollers (arrowed)

16.14a Remove the circlip from the right-hand side

16.14b Withdraw the bearing spacer from the left-hand side

16.14c Using a metal rod to drive the bearing out

16.15a Lock the lower end of the puller underneath the bearing . . .

spacer **(see illustration)**. Using a metal rod (preferably a brass punch) inserted through the centre of the needle bearing, tap evenly around the outer race of the caged ball bearing to drive it from the hub **(see illustration)**.
15 Turn the wheel over and drive the needle bearing out of the hub using the same procedure. Alternatively use an internal expanding puller with slide-hammer attachment **(see illustrations)**.
16 Thoroughly clean the hub area of the wheel with a suitable solvent and inspect the bearing seats for scoring and wear. If the seats are damaged, consult a Yamaha dealer before reassembling the wheel.
17 First install the caged ball bearing into its recess in the right-hand side of the hub,

with its marked side facing outwards. Using an old bearing, a bearing driver or a socket large enough to contact the outer race of the bearing, drive it in squarely until it is completely seated **(see illustration)**. Fit the circlip, making sure it locates correctly in its groove **(see illustration 16.14a)**.
18 Lubricate the right-hand bearing seal with lithium-based grease and press it into the hub. A hammer and small block of wood can be used to level the seal with the edge of its housing if necessary **(see illustration)**.
19 Turn the wheel over and install the bearing spacer **(see illustration 16.14b)**. Fit the new needle bearing, which must be pressed or drawn (not driven) into position. In the absence of a press, a suitable drawbolt arrangement

can be made up as described in *Tools and Workshop Tips (Section 5)* in the Reference section. Fit the sleeve into the needle bearing **(see illustration 16.13a)**.
20 Clean the brake disc using acetone or brake system cleaner,
21 Check the sprocket coupling bearing, then install the wheel (see Section 15).

Sprocket coupling bearing

22 Lever out the bearing seal using a seal hook or a large flat-bladed screwdriver and a piece of wood, taking care not to damage the rim of the coupling **(see illustration)**. Discard the seal as a new one must be fitted on reassembly.
23 Inspect the bearing (see *Tools and Workshop Tips (Section 5)* in the Reference Section). **Note:** *Do not remove the bearing unless it is going to be replaced with a new one.*
24 Support the coupling on blocks of wood and drive the bearing out from the inside using a bearing driver or socket **(see illustration)**.
25 Thoroughly clean the bearing seat with a suitable solvent and inspect the seat for scoring and wear. If the seat is damaged, consult a Yamaha dealer before reassembling the wheel.
26 Fit the new bearing into the coupling with its marked side facing out. Using the old bearing, a bearing driver or a socket large enough to contact the outer race of the

16.15b . . . then use the slide-hammer to pull the bearing out

16.17 Using a suitable socket to drive the caged ball bearing in

16.18 Level the bearing seal with a block of wood

16.22 Lever the bearing seal out of the coupling

16.24 Drive the coupling bearing out from the inside

16.26 A socket can be used to drive in the new bearing

16.27 Lubricate the new seal and press it into the coupling

17.3 ABS 10A fuse (A) and ABS modulator 30A fuse (B)

bearing, drive it in until it is completely seated **(see illustration)**.
27 Lubricate the new seal with lithium-based grease and press it into the coupling, using a bearing driver or a suitable socket to tap it in if necessary **(see illustration)**.
28 Check the sprocket coupling dampers, then install the coupling in the hub and install the wheel (see Section 15).

17 Anti-lock brake system (ABS)

General information

 Warning: The ABS control unit compares the relative speed of the wheels, and is thus programmed using the wheel and tyre sizes fitted as standard. If different sized wheels or tyres are fitted the control unit may not function correctly.

1 The ABS prevents the wheels from locking under heavy braking or on rough road surfaces. A sensor on each wheel transmits wheel rotation speed to the control unit. If the unit senses a difference between the speed of the front and rear wheels, it momentarily releases brake pressure to the relevant wheel. Brake pressure is governed by the ABS modulator.
2 The ABS is self checking, and is always switched on, though is inactive at speeds below 6 mph (10 kmh). The start-up self-diagnosis assesses the electrical control system as well as the function of the modulator. In the event of a problem, the fault can be located via a fault code.
3 When the ignition is switched on, the ABS indicator in the instrument cluster should come on for approximately 2 seconds, and then go off. If the indicator does not come on, remove the fuel tank (see Chapter 4) to access the ABS fusebox on the left-hand side of the battery. Open the fusebox and check the ABS fuses **(see illustration)**. If the fuses are good, check that the ABS control unit wiring connector is secure, and check the wiring between the control unit and the instrument cluster (see *Wiring Diagrams* in Chapter 8).

4 If a problem is detected at start-up, the ABS indicator flashes in one of the following sequences:
5 ON for 0.25 seconds and OFF for 0.75 seconds – check the engine stop switch or one of the causes in Step 9.
6 ON for 0.75 seconds and OFF for 0.25 seconds – check the ABS modulator fuse, relay and wiring (see *Wiring Diagrams* in Chapter 8), or one of the causes in Step 9.
7 ON for 1.0 seconds and OFF for 1.0 seconds – same as for fault code 28 (see details below).
8 ON for 0.5 seconds and OFF for 0.5 seconds – check for a malfunction code number displayed alongside the ABS indicator in the instrument cluster. A previous ABS fault may not have been deleted from the control unit memory.
9 Under certain conditions, a fault can be simulated in the ABS system and the ABS indicator will flash:
● If the rear wheel is rotated while the machine is supported on a stand with the rear wheel off the ground.
● If the rear tyre loses traction and the wheel spins.
● If the machine is ridden with the front wheel off the ground.
● If the machine is ridden continuously on very bumpy roads.

● If the brake light switch is damaged or incorrectly adjusted (see Chapter 1, Section 11).
● Low battery voltage (see Chapter 8).
If one of the above is the likely cause, carry out an ABS operation check, then delete the fault codes (see Steps 91 to 105).
10 In the event of a problem being detected while the machine is being ridden, the indicator will come ON. Depending upon the nature of the problem, the control unit may disable the ABS, in which case the brakes will work at reduced efficiency. DO NOT ignore the ABS indicator. Have the machine checked by a Yamaha dealer or follow the fault code retrieval procedure to determine the cause of the problem.

Fault codes

11 In the event of a problem, the fault code must be retrieved from the control unit using an analogue voltmeter. The fault code is represented by a series of timed electrical pulses in 10 digit/1 digit groups. Each group represents a number, with a 3 second break between each group **(see illustration)**.
12 If more than one fault code is displayed, they appear in ascending order. Write the fault code(s) down to avoid having to repeat the retrieval procedure.

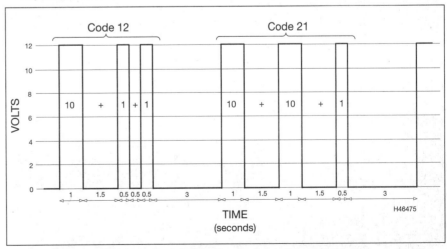

17.11 Fault codes are represented in timed pulses – the example shows code 12, followed by a three second gap, then code 21

17.15 Set-up for retrieving a fault code via the ABS test connector

1 *Light green wire terminal*
2 *White/red wire terminal*
3 *Light blue wire terminal*
4 *Black wire terminal*

13 Once the problems have been corrected, carry-out an ABS operation check, then delete the fault codes (see Steps 91 to 105).

Retrieval

14 Ensure that the battery is fully charged (see Chapter 8). Where fitted, remove the left-hand cockpit trim panel (see Chapter 7). Locate the ABS test connector in the main wiring loom on the left-hand side of the machine, either in front of, or underneath, the fuel tank **(see illustration 11.11a)**. Ensure that the ignition switch is OFF, then remove the blanking plug and use an insulated jumper wire to connect the light blue and black wire terminals inside the connector **(see illustrations 11.11b and c)**.

15 Using an analogue voltmeter, connect the negative (-) meter probe to the light green wire terminal in the connector and the positive (+) meter probe to the positive (+) terminal of the bike's battery **(see illustration)**. Note the sequence of pulses shown on the voltmeter scale.

16 Compare the fault code(s) with those in the table to identify the faulty component and test action required.

17 Before checking the individual components according to the fault code table, first check the wiring for damage and ensure that all connectors between the components are secure (see *Wiring Diagrams* at the end of Chapter 8). A continuity test of all wires will locate a break or short in any circuit. Inspect the terminals inside the wiring connectors and ensure they are not broken, loose or corroded. Spray the inside of the connectors with an electrical terminal cleaner before reconnection. Repair or renew the wiring and/or connectors as necessary.

18 If, after checking the components identified by the fault code, no problems can be found, carry out an ABS operation check, then delete the fault codes (see Steps 91 to 105).

Fault codes 11, 13 and 26

19 Check that the front wheel sensor mounting bolt is tight.

20 Check that the peg on the inside of the

ABS fault codes

Fault code	Faulty component	Test action
11	No front wheel sensor signal	Front ABS sensor Front ABS rotor Wiring and wiring connector
12	No rear wheel sensor signal	Rear ABS sensor Rear ABS rotor Wiring and wiring connector
13 and 26	Incorrect front wheel sensor signal	Front ABS sensor Front ABS rotor
14 and 27	Incorrect rear wheel sensor signal	Rear ABS sensor Rear ABS rotor
15	No continuity in front wheel sensor circuit	Wiring and wiring connector Sensor signal
16	No continuity in rear wheel sensor circuit	Wiring and wiring connector Sensor signal
18	Rear ABS rotor	Inspect and renew rotor
21	ABS modulator solenoids	Wiring and wiring connector Modulator solenoid resistance Battery terminal connections
22	ABS control unit	Wiring and wiring connector ABS control unit
24	Brake light	Wiring and wiring connectors Brake light adjustment Brake light switch Brake light
25	No front wheel sensor signal	Rear wheel rotated with machine on stand Rear wheel spin Machine ridden with the front wheel off the ground Front ABS sensor
28	ABS control unit	ABS control unit
31	No power at ABS control unit	30A circuit fuse Wiring and wiring connectors Control unit wiring connector
32	ABS control unit wiring	10A circuit fuse Wiring and wiring connectors ABS control unit
33	ABS modulator	30A circuit fuse Wiring and wiring connectors ABS modulator wiring connector ABS modulator relay
34	ABS modulator	Wiring and wiring connectors ABS modulator wiring connector ABS modulator relay ABS modulator
35	Wiring between ABS control unit and relay	Wiring and wiring connectors Relay connector Battery terminal connections
41	Front brake	Front brake dragging/locking Brake hoses Brake fluid
42	Rear brake	Rear brake dragging/locking Brake hoses Brake fluid
51	Front brake	Front brake dragging/locking Brake hoses Battery
52	Rear brake	Rear brake dragging/locking Brake hoses Battery
61	Front brake sensor power supply	Battery terminal connections Battery
62	Rear brake sensor power supply	Battery terminal connections Battery
63	Front brake sensor power supply	Wiring and wiring connector Battery terminal connections ABS control unit
64	Rear brake sensor power supply	Wiring and wiring connector Battery terminal connections ABS control unit
Constant signal	ABS control unit	Wiring and wiring connectors ABS control unit

right-hand fork leg is correctly located in the slot on the sensor mounting plate.

21 Check that the front wheel is correctly installed (see Section 14).

22 Check the front wheel bearings (see Chapter 1).

23 Undo the mounting bolt and draw the sensor out of the mounting plate **(see illustrations)**. Inspect the sensor for damage and accumulations of dirt or corrosion. If necessary, clean the sensor carefully with a soft cloth and metal polish. If it is damaged, replace the sensor with a new one. Trace the wiring from the sensor to the wiring connector and disconnect it. Release the wiring from any clips or ties **(see illustrations 3.2a and b)**. Ensure that the terminals in the connector are clean and connect the new sensor securely. Secure the wiring as noted on removal.

24 Remove the front wheel (see Section 14) and clean out any dirt trapped behind the sensor mounting plate **(see illustration 14.5b)**.

25 Inspect the ABS rotor for damage **(see illustration)**. The rotor is a press-fit in the wheel hub – if it is loose or damaged, a new wheel will have to be fitted.

26 On installation, tighten the sensor mounting bolt to the torque setting specified at the beginning of this Chapter. Ensure that sensor wiring is not pinched or twisted and secure it with the clips on the right-hand fork **(see illustrations 3.2a and b)**.

Fault codes 12, 14 and 27

27 Using a feeler gauge, check that the air gap between the tip of the rear wheel sensor and the castellations on the rotor is as specified at the beginning of this Chapter **(see illustration)**. Check the gap at several points by turning the wheel.

28 The gap is not adjustable – if it is incorrect, check that the sensor and rotor mounting bolts are tight.

29 Check that the rear brake caliper bracket is held firmly between the axle and the swingarm.

30 Check the rear wheel bearings (see Chapter 1).

31 Undo the mounting bolt and draw the sensor out of the caliper bracket **(see illustrations)**. Inspect the sensor for damage and accumulations of dirt or corrosion. If necessary, clean the sensor carefully with a

17.23a Undo the mounting bolt . . .

17.23b . . . and draw the sensor out of the mounting plate

17.25 Check the rotor (arrowed) for damage

17.27 Checking the air gap (arrowed) with a feeler gauge

soft cloth and metal polish. If it is damaged, replace the sensor with a new one. Trace the wiring from the sensor to the wiring connector and disconnect it. Release the wiring from any clips or ties **(see illustration 6.3)**. Ensure that the terminals in the connector are clean and connect the new sensor securely. Secure the wiring as noted on removal.

32 If the rotor is loose, warped or damaged, remove the rear wheel (see Section 15). Undo the rotor mounting bolts and lift the rotor off **(see illustration)**.

33 Before installing the rotor, make sure there is no dirt or corrosion where it seats on the hub, particularly right in the angle of the seat. If the rotor does not sit flat when it is bolted down, it will appear to be warped when the sensor-to-rotor air gap is checked.

34 Clean the threads of the rotor mounting bolts, then apply a suitable non-permanent

thread locking compound. Install the bolts and tighten them evenly and a little at a time in a criss-cross pattern to the torque setting specified at the beginning of this Chapter.

35 On installation, tighten the sensor mounting bolt to the torque setting specified at the beginning of this Chapter. Ensure that sensor wiring is not pinched or twisted and secure it with the clips to the rear brake hose **(see illustration 6.3)**. Check the air gap (see Step 27).

Fault codes 15 and 16

Note: *If the machine is ridden after fault codes 15 or 16 are displayed, the codes will be over-written from 15 to 11 or from 16 to 12.*

36 To check the sensor signal, support the bike upright with either the front or rear wheel off the ground as appropriate. Trace the wiring from the sensor to be checked to the wiring connector, but do not disconnect it.

17.31a Undo the mounting bolt . . .

17.31b . . . and draw the sensor out of the caliper bracket

17.32 Rear ABS rotor is secured by five bolts (arrowed)

n

17.43a Location of the ABS modulator solenoids (arrowed)

17.43b Location of the solenoid wiring connector (arrowed)

37 Using a multimeter set to the volts (DC) scale, backprobe the connector on the loom side, connecting the meter positive (+) probe to the black wire terminal and the negative (-) probe either to the blue wire terminal (front wheel), or the yellow/white wire terminal (rear wheel) .

38 Turn the ignition switch ON and slowly turn the wheel in the normal direction of rotation. The signal voltage should rise and fall between the high and low limits specified at the beginning of this Chapter, once every complete rotation of the wheel.

39 If the signal voltage is outside the specified limits, a new sensor must be fitted – see Steps 23 and 26 (front) or 31 and 35 (rear).

40 If fitting a new sensor does not clear the problem, have the ABS control unit checked by a Yamaha dealer.

Fault code 18

41 Inspect the ABS rotor on the rear wheel for trapped dirt or damage to the castellations.

42 To renew the rotor, follow the procedure in Steps 32 to 34. After installing the wheel and ABS sensor, check the air gap (see Step 27).

Fault code 21

43 The ABS modulator solenoids are located on the lower, left-hand side of the modulator **(see illustration)**. To check the solenoid resistance, first trace the wiring from the solenoids and disconnect it at the four-pin connector on the inside of the frame on the left-hand side **(see illustration)**.

44 Using a multimeter set to the ohms x 1

scale, connect the meter probes across the two blue wire terminals in the solenoid side of the connector to check the front brake solenoid, then connect the probes across the two green wire terminals to check the rear brake solenoid (see *Wiring Diagrams* at the end of Chapter 8). Compare the results with the specification at the beginning of this Chapter.

45 If the resistance of either solenoid is outside the specified range, a new modulator will have to be fitted (see Steps 112 to 122) – individual components are not available.

Fault code 22

46 Referring to the appropriate wiring diagram at the end of Chapter 8, check the wiring between the ABS control unit and the starter relay (blue/white wire).

Fault code 24

47 Check the operation of the front and rear brake light switches and adjust the rear switch if required (see Chapter 1, Section 11). Check the operation of the brake light (see Chapter 8).

Fault code 25

48 Refer to the conditions listed in Step 9.

49 Check the installation of the front wheel sensor (see Steps 19 to 26).

Fault code 28

50 Indicates an ABS control unit internal memory failure. Have the unit checked by a Yamaha dealer.

Fault code 31

50 Check the ABS 30A fuse (see Step 3), then check for continuity in the wiring between the fuse and the ABS control unit.

51 If the fuse and wiring are good, have the control unit checked by a Yamaha dealer.

Fault code 32

52 Check the ABS 10A fuse (see Step 3), then check for continuity in the wiring between the fuse and the ABS control unit.

53 Check the operation of the ignition switch, then check for continuity in the wiring between the switch and the fuse.

54 If the fuse and wiring are good, have the control unit checked by a Yamaha dealer.

Fault code 33

55 Check the ABS 30A fuse (see Step 3), then check for continuity in the wiring between the fuse, the ABS relay and the modulator **(see illustration)**.

56 To check the ABS modulator relay, first unclip the relay from the battery clamp, then disconnect the wiring connector **(see illustration)**.

57 Using a multimeter set to the ohms x 1 scale, connect the meter negative (-) probe to the No. 1 terminal on the relay and the positive (+) probe to the No. 2 terminal **(see illustration)**. Compare the result with the specification at the beginning of this Chapter.

58 Next connect the meter positive (+) probe to the No. 3 terminal on the relay and the negative (-) probe to the No. 4 terminal. There should be infinite resistance. Using insulated jumper wires and a fully charged 12V battery, connect the battery negative terminal to the No. 1 terminal on the relay and the battery positive terminal to the No. 2 relay terminal. The relay should be heard to click and the meter should show 0 ohms (no resistance).

59 If the meter indicates high resistance in either of these tests the relay is faulty and must be renewed.

Fault code 34

60 Check the ABS modulator relay (see Steps 56 to 59).

H46467

17.57 ABS modulator relay – wiring connector terminal identification

1 *Red wire terminal*
2 *Black/white wire terminal*
3 *Red/white wire terminal*
4 *Brown wire terminal*

17.55 Location of the ABS relay (arrowed)

17.56 Release the catch (arrowed) to disconnect the relay wiring connector

17.107a Release the holding strap . . .

17.107b . . . and displace the ABS control unit (arrowed)

17.108a Peel back the cover . . .

17.108b . . . to access the wiring connectors

102 Turn the ignition switch OFF, then turn it ON again.
103 The ABS indicator in the instrument cluster will come ON for 2 seconds and then go OFF for 3 seconds, then the indicator will start to flash.
104 Turn the ignition switch OFF. Disconnect the jumper wire from the ABS test connector and install the blanking plug. The ABS indicator should now function as normal (see Step 3).
105 Install the remaining components in the reverse order of removal.

ABS control unit

Removal and installation

106 Remove the fuel tank (see Chapter 4). Disconnect the battery negative (-) lead (see Chapter 8).
107 The ABS control unit is located on top of the ABS modulator cover plate. Release the holding strap and displace the unit **(see illustrations)**.
108 Peel back the cover to access the multi-pin wiring connectors **(see illustrations)**.
109 To disconnect the connectors, press down on the catch and pull the connector out **(see illustration)**.
110 Prior to installation, ensure that the terminals inside the connectors are clean and free from corrosion. If necessary, spray the terminals with electrical systems cleaner.
111 Install the connectors carefully and ensure that the locking tab clicks into place. Cover the unit and ensure that it is strapped securely into place. If the strap is damaged or deteriorated, fit a new one.

ABS modulator

112 Remove the ABS control unit (see Steps 106 to 109), then follow the procedure in Chapter 4, Section 18, to displace the ECU.
113 Remove the rear shock absorber (see Chapter 5).
114 Undo the screw securing the fluid reservoir to the modulator mounting bracket **(see illustration 9.4)**. Secure the reservoir in an upright position to prevent air entering the system.
115 Undo the bolts securing the modulator top cover and lift the cover off **(see illustrations)**.

92 Ensure that the battery is fully charged (see Chapter 8). Where fitted, remove the left-hand cockpit trim panel (see Chapter 7) or remove the fuel tank (see Chapter 4). Locate the ABS test connector in the main wiring loom on the left-hand side of the machine, either in front of, or underneath, the fuel tank **(see illustration 11.11a)**. Ensure that the ignition switch is OFF, then remove the blanking plug and use an insulated jumper wire to connect the light blue and black wire terminals inside the connector **(see illustration 11.11b and c)**.
93 Pull the brake lever in and press the brake pedal down. Continue to hold the lever in and the pedal down, the turn the ignition switch ON.
94 The ABS indicator in the instrument cluster will come ON for 2 seconds and then go OFF for 3 seconds, then the indicator will start to flash.
95 When the indicator starts flashing, hydraulic pressure from the ABS modulator will push the brake lever out to its rest position, then it will push the pedal up to its

rest position, then it will push the brake lever out to its rest position again. Continue to hold the lever and pedal against the pressure from the modulator throughout this procedure.
96 Turn the ignition switch OFF.
97 If the ABS operates as described, the system is working correctly.
98 If required, disconnect the jumper wire from the ABS test connector and install the blanking plug. Otherwise, delete the ABS fault code(s) as follows.

Deleting ABS fault code(s)

99 Ensure that the ignition switch is OFF. Install the jumper wire in the ABS test connector (see Step 92).
100 Turn the ignition switch ON. The ABS indicator in the instrument cluster will display the previously recorded fault code(s).
101 Turn the engine stop switch OFF, then press the starter button repeatedly (more than 10 times in 4 seconds) to delete the fault code(s).

17.109 Press the catch down to release the connector

17.115a Remove the bolts securing the modulator cover (arrowed) . . .

17.115b . . . and lift the cover off

116 Disconnect the wiring connectors for the modulator motor and solenoids **(see illustrations 17.61 and 17.43b)**.
117 Cover the area around the modulator with clean rag to catch any drops of brake fluid
118 Note the location of the hose fittings on the top of the modulator **(see illustration 17.68)**. If required, as an aid to reassembly, mark the fittings with dabs of paint.
119 Unscrew the bolts securing the brake hose banjo fittings to the modulator and detach the fittings. Plug the fittings or wrap a plastic bag tightly around each one to minimise fluid loss and prevent dirt entering the system. Discard the sealing washers as new ones must be used on installation. Plug each hole in the modulator with a rubber bung or a suitable 10 mm bolt.
120 Unscrew the modulator bracket mounting bolts and remove the modulator with its bracket. Unscrew the modulator mounting bolts and separate the modulator from its bracket.
121 Installation is the reverse of removal, noting the following:
● Tighten the mounting bracket bolts to the torque setting specified at the beginning of this Chapter.
● Use a new sealing washer on each side of the brake hose banjo fittings.

● Ensure that the hoses are connected to the correct locations on the modulator.
● Tighten the banjo bolts to the specified torque setting.
● Ensure that the wiring connectors are secure.
122 Bleed the hydraulic system following the procedure in Section 11. Check the operation of both front and rear brakes carefully before riding the motorcycle. If required, carry out an ABS operation check (see Steps 91 to 97).

18 Tyres

General information

1 The wheels fitted on all models are designed to take tubeless tyres only. Tyre sizes are given in the Specifications at the beginning of this chapter.
2 Refer to *Pre-ride checks* at the beginning of this manual for tyre maintenance and pressures.

Fitting new tyres

3 When selecting new tyres, refer to the tyre information in the Owner's Manual. Ensure that front and rear tyre types are compatible,

and of the correct size and speed rating; if necessary, seek advice from a Yamaha dealer or motorcycle tyre specialist **(see illustration)**.
4 It is recommended that tyres are fitted by a motorcycle tyre specialist and that this is not attempted in the home workshop. This is particularly relevant in the case of tubeless tyres because the force required to break the seal between the wheel rim and tyre bead is substantial, and is usually beyond the capabilities of an individual working with normal tyre levers. Additionally, the specialist will be able to balance the wheels after tyre fitting.
5 Note that punctured tubeless tyres can in some cases be repaired. Seek the advice of a Yamaha dealer or a motorcycle tyre specialist concerning tyre repairs.

19 Drive chain and sprockets

Drive chain

Removal

1 All models were fitted with an endless drive chain as original equipment. This type of

18.3 Common tyre sidewall markings

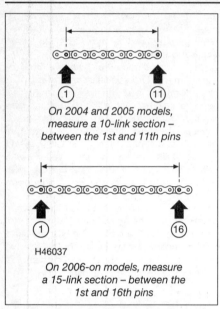

On 2004 and 2005 models, measure a 10-link section – between the 1st and 11th pins

On 2006-on models, measure a 15-link section – between the 1st and 16th pins

H46037

19.5 Measure chain link sections as shown to determine chain stretch

chain can only be removed if the swingarm is removed. Follow the procedure in Steps 10 to 13 to remove the front sprocket, then refer to Chapter 5, Section 13, and remove the swingarm.

2 If a chain with a riveted soft (joining) link has been fitted subsequently, it can be removed by splitting the soft link with a chain cutter. Such chains can be recognised by the soft link side plate's identification marks (and usually its different colour), as well as by the riveted ends of the link's two pins which look as if they have been deeply centre-punched, instead of peened over as with all the other pins (see Section 8 in *Tools and Workshop Tips* in the *Reference* section).

3 If the chain is going to be split, support the bike on its centrestand with the rear wheel off the ground. Remove the front sprocket cover (see Steps 10 and 11), then slacken the chain as described in Chapter 1. Follow the procedure in *Tools and Workshop Tips* to split the soft link and draw the chain off.

⚠ *Warning: Use ONLY the correct service tools to disassemble and assemble the riveted-type*

19.11a Remove the sprocket cover bolts (arrowed) . . .

of soft link – if you do not have access to such tools or do not have the skill to operate them correctly, have the old chain removed and a new one fitted by a Yamaha dealer.

Chain stretch check

4 Chain condition can be determined by the amount it has stretched between a specified number of links. To assess the chain accurately, first it must be removed from the bike (see above), then follow the procedure in Chapter 1 to clean it. The chain must be free of any kinks and binding links must be loosened-up before the check is made.

5 Stretch a section of the chain across a flat surface and measure the distance between the pins as shown **(see illustration)**. Note that Yamaha specify two different service limit measurements, depending upon the year of manufacture of the machine. Ensure that the chain is stretched taut when taking the measurement.

6 Measure the chain in several places to compensate for uneven wear along its length, then calculate the average and compare it to the limit specified at the beginning of the Chapter. If the chain stretch exceeds the service limit, the chain must be replaced with a new one.

Caution: Never install a new chain on old sprockets, and never use the old chain if you install new sprockets – replace the chain and sprockets as a set.

19.11b . . . and lift the cover off

Installation

⚠ *Warning: NEVER install a drive chain which uses a clip-type master (split) link.*

7 If an endless drive chain is being fitted, follow the procedure in Chapter 5 and install the chain with the swingarm. Install the front sprocket (see Steps 14 to 18), then refer to Chapter 1 and lubricate and adjust the chain.

8 If a chain with a riveted soft (joining) link is being fitted, route it over the swingarm and around the front and rear sprockets, leaving the two ends in a convenient position to work on. Follow the procedure in *Tools and Workshop Tips* to fit a new soft link. NEVER re-use old soft link components.

9 Once the chain is installed, fit the sprocket cover, then refer to Chapter 1 and lubricate and adjust the chain.

Front sprocket

10 Make sure the transmission is in neutral. Loosen the gearchange linkage rod locknuts, then unscrew the rod and separate it from the lever and the arm (see Chapter 2, Section 15). Withdraw the rod from the frame.

11 Unscrew the bolts securing the front sprocket cover and remove it **(see illustrations)**.

12 Bend back the tab on the sprocket nut lockwasher **(see illustration)**. Have an assistant apply the rear brake hard, then unscrew the nut and remove the washer **(see illustrations)**. Discard the washer, as a new one must be used on reassembly. Adjust the

19.12a Bend the locking tab back with a hammer and chisel

19.12b Undo the sprocket nut . . .

19.12c . . . and remove the old lockwasher

19.13a Draw the sprocket and chain off the shaft . . .

19.13b . . . then lift the sprocket out of the chain

19.14 Install the nut with the shouldered side facing in

chain so that it is fully slack (see Chapter 1, Section 1).

13 Draw the sprocket and chain off the transmission output shaft and slip the sprocket out of the chain **(see illustrations)**. If there is not enough slack in the chain to disengage the front sprocket, slip the chain off the rear wheel sprocket. **Note:** *If the sprocket is not being replaced with a new one, mark its outside face with a dab of paint, so that it can be installed the same way round.*

14 To install the front sprocket, first engage it with the chain, then slide it onto the transmission shaft. If removed, install the chain on the rear sprocket. Install the **new** lockwasher, then fit the nut with the shouldered side facing in and tighten it finger-tight **(see illustration)**.

15 Adjust the drive chain (see Chapter 1).

16 Tighten the sprocket nut to the torque setting specified at the beginning of this Chapter, applying the rear brake to prevent the sprocket from turning. Bend the tab of the lockwasher up against the flats of the nut **(see illustration)**.

17 Install the front sprocket cover **(see illustrations 19.11b and a)**.

18 Install the remaining components in the reverse order of removal.

Rear sprocket

19 Remove the rear wheel (see Section 15). *Caution: Don't lay the wheel down and allow it to rest on the disc or the sprocket – they could become warped. Set the wheel on wood blocks so the wheel rim supports the weight of the wheel. Don't operate the brake pedal with the wheel removed.*

20 Unscrew the nuts securing the sprocket to

19.16 Lock the nut by bending the lockwasher against it

the hub assembly **(see illustration)**. Remove the nuts and washers, then lift off the sprocket, noting which way round it fits. **Note:** *The size of the sprocket (i.e. its number of teeth) is stamped on the outside face of the sprocket.*

21 Install the sprocket onto the hub with the stamped mark facing out. Tighten the nuts and washers evenly and in a criss-cross sequence to the torque setting specified at the beginning of this Chapter.

22 Install the rear wheel (see Section 15).

19.20 Rear sprocket is secured by six nuts

Chapter 7
Bodywork

Contents

Degrees of difficulty

| Easy, suitable for novice with little experience | Fairly easy, suitable for beginner with some experience | Fairly difficult, suitable for competent DIY mechanic | Difficult, suitable for experienced DIY mechanic | Very difficult, suitable for expert DIY or professional |

Specifications

Torque wrench settings

Fairing stay-to-frame bolts .... 33 Nm
Passenger grab handle bolts .... 23 Nm
Side panel bolts .... 10 Nm

1 General information

1 This Chapter covers the procedures necessary to remove and install the body parts. Since many service and repair operations on these motorcycles require the removal of the body parts, the procedures are grouped here and referred to from other Chapters.

2 In the case of damage to the body parts, it is usually necessary to remove the broken component and replace it with a new (or used) one. The material from which the body panels are made does not lend itself to conventional repair techniques. There are, however, some shops that specialise in 'plastic welding', so it may be worthwhile seeking the advice of one of these specialists before consigning an expensive component to the bin. There are also bodywork repair kits available for DIY use.

3 When attempting to remove any body panel, first study it closely, noting any fasteners and associated fittings, to be sure of returning everything to its correct place on installation. Once the evident fasteners have been removed, try to withdraw the panel as described but DO NOT FORCE IT – if it will not release, check that all fasteners have been removed and try again.

4 Where a panel engages another by means of tabs, be careful not to break the tab or its mating slot or to damage the paintwork. Remember that a few moments of patience at this stage will save you a lot of money in replacing broken panels!

5 To remove trim clips, unscrew the centre, then draw the clip out of the panel (see illustration).

6 When installing a body panel, first study it closely, noting any fasteners and associated fittings removed with it, to be sure of returning everything to its correct place. Check that all fasteners are in good condition, including all trim clips and rubber mounts; any of these that are faulty must be replaced with new ones before the panel is reassembled.

7 Check also that all mounting brackets are straight, and repair or renew them if necessary before attempting to install the panel.

8 To install trim clips, fit the clip into its hole, then push the centre in so that it is flush with the top of the clip.

9 Tighten the fasteners securely, but be careful not to overtighten any of them or the panel may break (not always immediately) due to the uneven stress.

1.5 Unscrew the centre, then pull the trim clip out of the panel

2.1a Turn key anti-clockwise and lift the back of the seat

2.1b Note how tab (A) locates under bracket (B) and seat latch (C) locates in lock (D)

2 Seat

1 To remove the seat, insert the ignition key into the seat lock located on the left-hand side of the bike, and turn it anti-clockwise to unlock the seat. Lift up the back of the seat and draw it rearwards, noting how the tab at the front locates under the fuel tank mounting bracket **(see illustrations)**.

2 Installation is the reverse of removal. Push down on the seat to engage the latch.

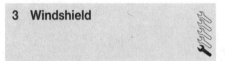

3 Windshield

S2 models

1 The windshield is secured by three screws on both sides **(see illustration)**.

2 Undo the screws and lift the windshield off **(see illustrations)**.
3 Note that the screws thread into rubber-bodied wellnuts set in the fairing **(see illustration)**. On installation, take care not to over-tighten the screws and loosen the wellnuts in the fairing.

All other models

4 Undo the screw on the lower front edge of the windshield **(see illustration)**.
5 Peel back the boot on the mirror stem. Undo the two screws on both sides securing

3.1 The windshield is secured by three screws on both sides – S2 models

3.2a Undo the screws . . .

3.2b . . . and lift the windshield off

3.3 Note the location of the wellnuts (arrowed)

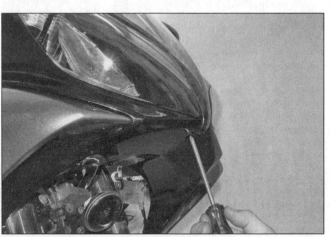

3.4 Undo the screw at the front . . .

3.5a . . . and the two screws on both sides (arrowed) . . .

3.5b . . . then lift the windshield off

the windshield to the fairing, then lift the windshield off **(see illustrations)**.
6 Installation is the reverse of removal. Do not overtighten the screws.

4 Mirrors

1 If the mirror is mounted on the handlebars, support the mirror and loosen the stem locknut, then unscrew the mirror from the handlebar bracket **(see illustrations)**. Note that the right-hand mirror has a left-hand thread – loosen clockwise, tighten anti-clockwise.
2 On installation, take care not to cross-thread the mirror stem **(see illustration)**. Tighten the locknut securely
3 Final adjustment can be made using the threaded joints on the mirror stem **(see illustration)**.
4 If the mirror is mounted on the fairing, first follow the procedure in the following section and remove either the right or left-hand cockpit trim panel.
5 Undo the nuts securing the mirror assembly and lift it off **(see illustrations)**.
6 On S2 models, note the rubber pad with collars for the mirror bolts fixed between the fairing and fairing stay **(see illustration)**.
7 Installation is the reverse of removal.

4.1a Loosen the locknut . . .

4.1b . . . then unscrew the mirror

4.2 Take care when installing the mirror stem threads

4.3 Final adjustments can be made at the joints (arrowed)

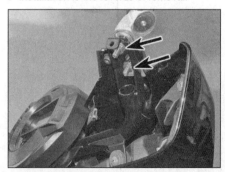

4.5a Undo the nuts (arrowed) . . .

4.5b . . . and lift the mirror off

4.6 Note the location of the pad and collars (arrowed) – S2 models

5.1a Undo the screws, noting the location of the large washers

5.1b Ease the panel rearwards . . .

5.1c . . . to release the tabs on the front edge . . .

5 Fairing panels

Cockpit trim panels

S2 models

1 Undo the two screws securing the rear half of the trim panel to the fairing side panel, noting the location of the washers (see illustration). Ease the panel rearwards to release the tabs on the front edge, then lift the panel off (see illustrations).

2 To remove the front half of the trim panel, undo the screw on the inside rear edge, and the two screws on the upper edge (see illustrations). Manoeuvre the panel off (see illustration).

3 Installation is the reverse of removal. Make sure the rear half panel locates correctly with

5.1d . . . then lift the panel off

the front half and the inside edge of the fairing side panel (see illustration 5.1c). Don't forget to install the large washers on the outside of the fairing side panel (see illustration 5.1a).

All other models

4 Undo the two screws securing the trim

5.2a Undo the inside screw (arrowed) . . .

panel to the fairing side panel, noting the location of the washers (see illustrations).

5 Lift the boot on the mirror stem to access the trim clip (see illustrations). Follow the procedure in Section 1 to remove the trim clip.

5.2b . . . and the screws (arrowed) on the upper edge . . .

5.2c . . . then manoeuvre the panel off

5.4a Undo the large screws . . .

5.4b . . . noting the location of the large washers (arrowed)

5.5a Lift the boot on the mirror stem . . .

5.5b . . . to access the trim clip (arrowed)

5.6a Undo the screw (arrowed) . . .

5.6b . . . then lift the trim panel off

5.7 Note the location of the U-clip (arrowed)

6 Undo the screw securing the trim panel to the bracket on the inside of the fairing, then lift the trim panel off **(see illustrations)**.

7 Installation is the reverse of removal. Make sure the U-clip is in place on the bracket inside of the fairing **(see illustration)**. Ensure that the trim panel locates correctly with the inside edge of the fairing side panel **(see illustration 5.6b)**. Don't forget to install the large washers on the outside of the fairing side panel **(see illustration 5.4b)**. Follow the procedure in Section 1 to install the trim clip.

Fairing

S2 models

8 Remove the cockpit trim panels (see Steps 1 and 2).

9 Remove the windshield (see Section 3) and the mirrors (see Section 4).

10 Using a flat-bladed screwdriver, release the catch securing the fairing assembly wiring connector, then undo the screw securing the earth (ground) wire to the fairing bracket **(see illustrations)**.

11 Ease the fairing off the mirror brackets **(see illustration 4.6)**, then draw it forwards to release the pegs on the back of the headlight assembly from the grommets on the fairing bracket **(see illustration)**. If required, remove the headlight unit (see Chapter 8).

12 If required, remove the instrument cluster (see Chapter 8), then unclip the wiring from the fairing bracket. Undo the bolts securing the fairing bracket and lift it off **(see illustration)**.

13 Installation is the reverse of removal.

Ensure that the grommets on the fairing bracket are not deformed or deteriorated and renew them if necessary. Don't forget to connect the fairing assembly wiring connector securely and to tighten the earth wire screw.

14 Check the operation of the headlight and turn signals before riding the motorcycle.

All other models

15 Remove the cockpit trim panels (see Steps 4 to 6).

16 Remove the windshield (see Section 3) and the mirrors (see Section 4).

17 Follow the procedure in Section 1 to remove the trim clips located in the middle of the mirror mountings **(see illustration)**.

5.10a Release the catch (arrowed) . . .

5.10b . . . and disconnect the multi-pin wiring connector

5.10c Release the earth wire from the bracket

5.11 Draw the fairing off its support bracket

5.12 Location of the fairing bracket mounting bolts (arrowed)

5.17 Remove the trim clips

5.18 Remove the two screws (arrowed)

5.19a Release the wiring from the clip

5.19b Release the catches . . .

5.19c . . . and disconnect both wiring connectors

5.20a Undo the screws on the lower (arrowed) . . .

5.20b . . . and upper mounting points, noting the location of the washers (arrowed)

5.21a Instrument cluster wiring connectors (arrowed)

18 Remove the screws located below the top edge of the instrument cluster (see illustration).
19 Release the fairing assembly wiring from the clip on the left-hand bracket (see illustration). Release the catches securing the fairing assembly wiring connectors and disconnect the connectors (see illustrations).
20 Undo the two screws on each side, on the lower and upper sections of the fairing bracket, noting the location of the large washers (see illustrations).
21 Ease the fairing forwards off the mounting bracket and disconnect the instrument cluster wiring connectors (see illustration). Note

how the pegs on the back of the headlight assembly locate in the grommets on the fairing bracket (see illustrations). If required, remove the headlight unit (see Chapter 8).
22 If required, remove the instrument cluster (see Chapter 8), then unclip the wiring from the fairing bracket. Undo the bolts securing the fairing bracket and lift it off (see illustration 5.12).
23 Installation is the reverse of removal. Ensure that the grommets on the fairing bracket are not deformed or deteriorated and renew them if necessary. Don't forget to connect the instrument cluster and fairing assembly wiring connectors securely. Follow the procedure

5.21b Note how the pegs (arrowed) . . .

5.21c . . . locate in the grommets (arrowed)

5.23a Location of the left (arrowed) . . .

5.23b . . . and right-hand support brackets (arrowed)

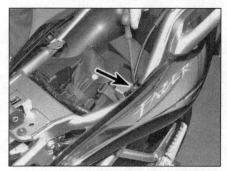

6.2 Location of panel fixing screw (arrowed)

in Section 1 to install the trim clips. Note the location of the left and right-hand fairing support brackets **(see illustrations)**. Ensure that the brackets align correctly with the holes for the lower cockpit trim panel screws.

24 Check the operation of the headlight and turn signals before riding the motorcycle.

6 Side panels, seat and exhaust cowlings

Side panels

1 Remove the seat (see Section 2).
2 Undo the screw securing the panel to the rear sub-frame **(see illustration)**.
3 Ease the panel off, noting how the pegs on the back of the panel are located in grommets on the sub-frame **(see illustration)**.
4 Installation is the reverse of removal. Lubricate the grommets with dry film lubricant to aid installation.

Seat cowling

5 Remove the seat (see Section 2). Remove the side panels (see above).
6 Undo the two top mounting bolts, noting the location of the spacers **(see illustration)**.
7 Undo the left and right-hand side mounting bolts, noting the location of the spacers **(see illustration)**.
8 Undo the screws securing the underside of the cowling, noting the location of the spacers **(see illustrations)**.
9 Ease the cowling up and disconnect the tail

light wiring connector on the left-hand side **(see illustration)**.
10 Draw the cowling and tail light assembly back and off the bike **(see illustration)**. If required, remove the tail light (see Chapter 8).

11 Installation is the reverse of removal. Ensure that the tail light wiring connector is secure.
12 Check the operation of the tail light and brake light before riding the motorcycle.

6.3 Note how the pegs (arrowed) locate in grommets

6.6 Location of the top mounting bolts (arrowed)

6.7 Note how the spacers (arrowed) fit on the side mounting bolts

6.8a Undo the lower fixing screws . . .

6.8b . . . noting the location of the spacers (arrowed)

6.9 Disconnect the tail light wiring connector

6.10 Lift the cowling assembly off carefully

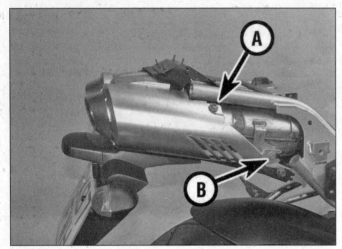

6.14 Undo the mounting screws (A) on both sides. Note how the cowling fits on the pegs (B)

6.15a Draw the cowling off . . .

6.15b . . . noting how the pegs (A) locate in the grommets (B)

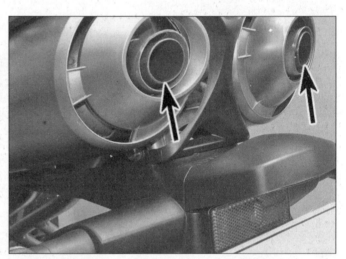

6.16 Don't allow the cowling to rest on the tail pipes (arrowed)

Exhaust cowling

13 Remove the seat cowling (see above).
14 Undo the left and right-hand mounting screws (see illustration). Note how the sides of the cowling locate over the pegs on the silencer assembly.
15 Draw the cowling back and off the bike (see illustration). Note how the pegs inside the cowling locate in the grommets on the silencer assembly brackets (see illustration).
16 Installation is the reverse of removal. Ensure that the pegs inside the cowing are correctly located in the grommets and that the inner edges of the cowling are not resting on the exhaust tail pipes (see illustration).

7 Mudguards

Front mudguard

S2 models

1 Release the clips securing the brake hoses to the mudguard (see illustration).
2 Undo the screws securing the mudguard to the forks (see illustration). Note that there is a nut on the inside of the rear screw and that the brake hose bracket is retained by the rear screw on the left-hand side.
3 Draw the mudguard forwards from between the forks and remove it.
4 Note the collars and bushes in the mudguard mounting holes and remove them if they are loose. The bushes should be a tight fit in the mudguard – replace them with new ones if they are worn or perished.
5 Installation is the reverse of removal. Don't

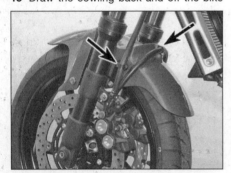

7.1 Release the brake hoses from the clips (arrowed)

7.2 Front mudguard screws (arrowed)

7.5 Install the brake hose bracket on the left-hand side (arrowed)

7.6 Release the brake hose from the clip

7.8a Front mudguard screws (arrowed)

7.8b Rear screws (arrowed) are installed from the inside

7.9 Draw the mudguard forwards to remove it

7.10 Collar (A) and bush (B) should be a secure fit

forget to install the brake hose bracket **(see illustration)**.

All other models

6 Release the clip securing the brake hose to the mudguard **(see illustration)**.
7 Follow the procedure in Chapter 6 and remove the front wheel.
8 Undo the screws securing the mudguard to the forks – note that the rear screws are accessible from inside the mudguard **(see illustration)**.
9 Draw the mudguard forwards from between the forks and remove it **(see illustration)**.
10 Note the collars and bushes in the mudguard mounting holes and remove them if they are loose **(see illustration)**. The bushes should be a tight fit in the mudguard – replace

them with new ones if they are worn or perished.
11 Installation is the reverse of removal.

Rear mudguard

12 Remove the side panels, seat and exhaust cowlings (see Section 6).
13 Disconnect the wiring connectors for the rear turn signals and for the licence plate light **(see illustrations)**. Release the wiring from any cable-ties.
14 Loosen the bolts securing the rear mudguard assembly on both sides, then support the mudguard and remove the bolts **(see illustrations)**.
15 Installation is the reverse of removal. Ensure that the turn signal and licence plate light wiring connectors are secure.

7.13a Rear turn signal wiring connectors (arrowed)

16 Check the operation of the lights before riding the motorcycle.

7.13b Licence plate light wiring connectors – note the cable-ties (arrowed)

7.14a Undo the bolts (arrowed) on both sides . . .

7.14b . . . and lift the mudguard assembly off

Chapter 8
Electrical system

Contents

Degrees of difficulty

| **Easy,** suitable for novice with little experience | **Fairly easy,** suitable for beginner with some experience | **Fairly difficult,** suitable for competent DIY mechanic | **Difficult,** suitable for experienced DIY mechanic | **Very difficult,** suitable for expert DIY or professional |

Specifications

Battery

Capacity	12V, 10Ah
Type	GT12B-4
Charge condition	
Fully charged	12.8V
Half-charged..	12.4V
Discharged	12V or less
Charging time..	Until fully charged (12.8V) (see Section 4)

Charging system

Alternator nominal output	14V, 310W @ 5000 rpm
Alternator stator coil resistance	0.22 to 0.34 ohms @ 20°C
Current leakage	1mA (max)
Regulated voltage output (no load)	14.1 to 14.9V @ 5000 rpm

Oil level sensor

Resistance
Upright (minimum level)	484 to 536 ohms @ 20°C
Upside down (maximum level)	114 to 126 ohms @ 20°C

Speed sensor

Output voltage	0.6 to 4.8V recycling

Starter relay

Resistance	4.18 to 4.62 ohms @ 20°C

Starter safety cut-off relay

Resistance	162 to 198 ohms @ 20°C

Starter motor

Brush length
Standard	10 mm
Service limit (min)	3.5 mm

Commutator diameter
Standard	28 mm
Service limit (min)	27 mm
Mica undercut	0.7 mm
Commutator resistance	0.012 to 0.022 ohms

Fuses

Main	30A
Ignition	10A
Fuel injection system	10A
Headlight	20A
Brake light, horn	10A
Turn signals, side light, tail light and licence plate light	10A
Cooling fan	20A
Back-up	10A
ABS control unit fuse	10A
ABS modulator fuse	30A

Bulbs

Headlight
N models	60/55W halogen (H4)

S models
Left-hand	60/55W halogen (H4)
Right-hand	55W halogen (H7)
Sidelight	5W
Brake/tail light	21/5W

Turn signal lights
UK models	10W

US models
Front with running light	21/5W
Rear	21W
Licence plate light	5W
Instrument cluster illumination lights	LED
Instrument warning lights	LED

Torque wrench settings

Alternator cover bolts	12 Nm
Alternator rotor bolt	75 Nm
Alternator stator bolts	10 Nm
Neutral switch	20 Nm
Oil level sensor bolts	10 Nm
Starter motor long bolts	3.4 Nm
Starter motor mounting bolts	10 Nm

2.4a A digital multimeter can be used for all electrical tests

2.4b A battery powered continuity tester

2.4c A simple test light can be used for voltage checks

1 General information

All models have a 12 volt electrical system charged by a three-phase alternator with a separate regulator/rectifier.

The regulator maintains the charging system output within the specified range to prevent overcharging, and the rectifier converts the ac (alternating current) output of the alternator to dc (direct current) to power the lights and other components and to charge the battery. The alternator rotor is mounted on the left-hand end of the crankshaft.

The starting system includes the starter motor, the battery, the relay and the various wires and switches. If the engine stop switch is in the RUN position and the ignition switch is ON, the starter relay allows the starter motor to operate only if the transmission is in neutral (neutral switch on) or, if the transmission is in gear, if the clutch lever is pulled into the handlebar and the sidestand is up. The starter motor is mounted on the top of the crankcase.
Note: *Keep in mind that electrical parts, once purchased, cannot be returned. To avoid unnecessary expense, make very sure the faulty component has been positively identified before buying a replacement part.*

2 Electrical system fault finding

⚠️ *Warning: To prevent the risk of short circuits, the battery negative (-ve) terminal should be disconnected before any of the bike's other electrical components are disturbed. Don't forget to reconnect the terminal securely once work is finished or if battery power is needed for circuit testing.*

1 A typical electrical circuit consists of an electrical component, the switches, relays, etc, related to that component and the wiring and connectors that link the component to the battery and the frame.
2 Before tackling any troublesome electrical circuit, first study the wiring diagram thoroughly to get a complete picture of what makes up that individual circuit. Trouble spots, for instance, can often be narrowed down by noting if other components related to that circuit are operating properly or not. If several components or circuits fail at one time, chances are the fault lies either in the fuse or in the common earth (ground) connection, as several circuits are often routed through the same fuse and earth (ground) connections.
3 Electrical problems often stem from simple causes, such as loose or corroded connections or a blown fuse. Prior to any electrical fault finding, always visually check the condition of the fuse, wires and connections in the problem circuit. Intermittent failures can be especially frustrating, since you can't always duplicate the failure when it's convenient to test. In such situations, a good practice is to clean all connections in the affected circuit, whether or not they appear to be good. All of the connections and wires should also be wiggled to check for looseness which can cause intermittent failure.
4 If you don't have a multimeter it is highly advisable to obtain one – they are not expensive and will enable a full range of electrical tests to be made. Go for a modern digital one with LCD display as they are easier to use. A continuity tester and/or test light are useful for certain electrical checks as an alternative, though are limited in their usefulness compared to a multimeter **(see illustrations)**.

Continuity checks

5 The term continuity describes the uninterrupted flow of electricity through an electrical circuit. Continuity can be checked with a multimeter set either to its continuity function (a beep is emitted when continuity is found), or to the resistance (ohms/Ω) function, or with a dedicated continuity tester. Both instruments are powered by an internal battery, therefore the checks are made with the ignition OFF. As a safety precaution, always disconnect the battery negative (-) lead before making continuity checks, particularly if ignition system checks are being made.
6 If using a multimeter, select the continuity function if it has one, or the resistance (ohms) function. Touch the meter probes together and check that a beep is emitted or the meter reads zero, which indicates continuity. If there is no continuity there will be no beep or the meter will show infinite resistance. After using the meter, always switch it OFF to conserve its battery.
7 A continuity tester can be used in the same way – its light should come on or it should beep to indicate continuity in the switch ON position, but should be off or silent in the OFF position.
8 Note that the polarity of the test probes doesn't matter for continuity checks, although care should be taken to follow specific test procedures if a diode or solid-state component is being checked.

Switch continuity checks

9 If a switch is at fault, trace its wiring to the wiring connectors. Separate the connectors and inspect them for security and condition. A build-up of dirt or corrosion here will most likely be the cause of the problem – clean up and apply a water dispersant such as WD40, or alternatively use a dedicated contact cleaner and protection spray.
10 If using a multimeter, select the continuity function if it has one, or the resistance (ohms) function, and connect its probes to the terminals in the connector **(see illustration)**. Simple ON/OFF type switches, such as brake light switches, only have two wires whereas combination switches, like the handlebar switches, have many wires. Study the wiring diagram to ensure that you are connecting to the correct pair of wires. Continuity should be indicated with the switch ON and no continuity with it OFF.

2.10 Testing a brake light switch for continuity

2.12 Testing for continuity in a wiring loom

Wiring continuity checks

11 Many electrical faults are caused by damaged wiring, often due to incorrect routing or chaffing on frame components. Loose, wet or corroded wire connectors can also be the cause of electrical problems.

12 A continuity check can be made on a single length of wire by disconnecting it at each end and connecting the meter or continuity tester probes to each end of the wire (see illustration). Continuity should be indicated if the wire is good. If no continuity is shown, suspect a broken wire.

13 To check for continuity to earth in any earth wire connect one probe of your meter or tester to the earth wire terminal in the connector and the other to the frame, engine, or battery earth (-) terminal. Continuity should be indicated if the wire is good. If no continuity is shown, suspect a broken wire or corroded or loose earth point (see below).

Voltage checks

14 A voltage check can determine whether power is reaching a component. Use a multimeter set to the dc (direct current) voltage scale to check for power from the battery or regulator/rectifier, or set to the ac (alternating current) voltage scale to check for power from the alternator. A test light can be used to check for dc voltage. The test light is the cheaper component, but the meter has the advantage of being able to give a voltage reading.

15 Connect the meter or test light in parallel, i.e. across the load (see illustration).

16 First identify the relevant wiring circuit by referring to the wiring diagram at the end of this manual. If other electrical components share the same power supply (i.e. are fed from

2.15 Connect the multimeter in parallel, or across the load, as shown

the same fuse), take note whether they are working correctly – this is useful information in deciding where to start checking the circuit.

17 If using a meter, check first that the meter leads are plugged into the correct terminals on the meter (red to positive (+), black to negative (-)). Set the meter to the appropriate volts function (dc or ac), where necessary at a range suitable for the battery voltage – 0 to 20 vdc. Connect the meter red probe (+) to the power supply wire and the black probe to a good metal earth (ground) on the motorcycle's frame or directly to the battery negative terminal. Battery voltage, or the specified voltage, should be shown on the meter with the ignition switch, and if necessary any other relevant switch, ON.

18 If using a test light (see illustration 2.4c), connect its positive (+) probe to the power supply terminal and its negative (-) probe to a good earth (ground) on the motorcycle's frame. With the switch, and if necessary any other relevant switch, ON, the test light should illuminate.

19 If no voltage is indicated, work back towards the power source continuing to check for voltage. When you reach a point where there is voltage, you know the problem lies between that point and your last check point.

Earth (ground) checks

20 Earth connections are made either directly to the engine or frame (such as the starter motor or ignition coil which only have a positive feed) or by a separate wire into the earth circuit of the wiring harness. Alternatively a short earth wire is sometimes run from the component directly to the motorcycle's frame.

21 Corrosion is a common cause of a poor earth connection, as is a loose earth terminal fastener.

22 If total or multiple component failure is

experienced, check the security of the main earth lead from the negative (-) terminal of the battery, the earth lead bolted to the engine, and the main earth point(s) on the frame. If corroded, dismantle the connection and clean all surfaces back to bare metal. Remake the connection and prevent further corrosion from forming by smearing battery terminal grease over the connection.

23 To check the earthing of a component, use an insulated jumper wire to temporarily bypass its earth connection (see illustration) – connect one end of the jumper wire to the earth terminal or metal body of the component and the other end to the motorcycle's frame. If the circuit works with the jumper wire installed, the earth circuit is faulty.

24 To check an earth wire first check for corroded or loose connections, then check the wiring for continuity (Step 13) between each connector in the circuit in turn, and then to its earth point, to locate the break.

> **HAYNES HINT** *Remember that all electrical circuits are designed to conduct electricity from the battery, through the wires, switches, relays, etc. to the electrical component (light bulb, starter motor, etc). From there it is directed to the frame (earth) where it is passed back to the battery. Electrical problems are basically an interruption in the flow of electricity from the battery or back to it.*

3 Battery

Caution: Be extremely careful when handling or working around the battery. The electrolyte is very caustic and an explosive gas (hydrogen) is given off when the battery is charging.

Removal and installation

1 Remove the fuel tank (see Chapter 4).

2 Unscrew the negative (-) terminal bolt first and disconnect the lead from the battery (see illustration). Lift up the insulating cover to access the positive (+) terminal, then unscrew the bolt and disconnect the lead (see illustration).

2.23 A selection of jumper wires for making earth (ground) checks

3.2a Disconnect the negative lead first . . .

3.2b . . . then lift the cover and disconnect the positive lead

3.4 Displace the starter relay

3.5a Undo the left-hand . . .

3.5b . . . and the right-hand fixing bolts (arrowed) . . .

3 On machines fitted with ABS, unclip the ABS motor relay from the battery clamp (see Chapter 6, Section 17).

4 Unclip the starter relay from the battery clamp **(see illustration)**.

5 Undo the two bolts securing the battery clamp and lift the clamp off **(see illustrations)**.

6 Lift the battery out of its housing **(see illustration)**.

7 Installation is the reverse of removal. Ensure the battery terminals and lead ends are clean, then reconnect the leads, connecting the positive (+) terminal first.

Inspection and maintenance

8 The battery is of the maintenance-free (sealed) gel type, therefore requiring no specific maintenance. Do not attempt to open the battery as resulting damage will mean it will be unfit for further use. However, the following checks should still be regularly performed.

9 Check the battery terminals and leads for tightness and corrosion. If corrosion is evident, unscrew the terminal bolts and disconnect the leads from the battery, disconnecting the negative (-) terminal first. Clean the terminals and lead ends with a wire brush or penknife and steel wool. Reconnect the leads, connecting the positive (+) terminal first, and apply a thin coat of petroleum jelly or battery terminal grease to the connections to slow further corrosion.

10 The battery case should be kept clean to

3.5c . . . and lift off the battery clamp

prevent current leakage, which can discharge the battery over a period of time (especially when it sits unused). Remove the battery from the motorcycle and wash the outside of the case with a solution of baking soda and water. Rinse the battery thoroughly, then dry it.

11 Look for cracks in the case and replace the battery with a new one if any are found.

12 If the motorcycle sits unused for long periods of time, disconnect the leads from the battery terminals, negative (-) terminal first. Refer to Section 4 and charge the battery once every month to six weeks.

13 The condition of the battery can be assessed by checking the open-circuit voltage between the battery terminals, and comparing

3.6 Lift the battery out of its housing

the figure against the chart **(see illustrations)**. Disconnect the battery leads, then connect the voltmeter positive (+) probe to the battery positive (+) terminal, and the negative (-) probe to the battery negative (-) terminal. When fully charged, there should be 12.8 volts (or more) present. If the voltage has fallen below 12.4 volts, the battery is half-charged. If the voltage has fallen below 12 volts, the battery is fully discharged. Recharge as described in Section 4.

Battery housing

14 To remove the battery housing, first remove the battery (see Steps 1 to 6).

15 Remove the air filter housing (see Chapter 4).

16 Undo the two bolts securing the battery housing and displace the housing.

17 Follow the procedure in Chapter 4, Section 17, and undo the bolts and trim clips securing the ignition coils to the front of the battery housing, then lift the housing out.

18 Installation is the reverse of removal.

---

4 Battery charging

Caution: Be extremely careful when handling or working around the battery. The electrolyte is very caustic and an explosive gas (hydrogen) is given off when the battery is charging.

1 Ensure the charger is suitable for charging a 12V battery.

3.13a Check the battery open-circuit voltage . . .

3.13b . . . and assess the battery condition using the chart

Voltage
(volts)

13.0

12.5

12.0

11.5

6.5

5.0   10.0

Charge time (hours)

H45525

4.2 Open circuit voltage will determine the charging time required

2 Remove the battery from the motorcycle (see Section 3). If not already done, refer to Section 3, Step 13, and check the open circuit voltage of the battery. Refer to the chart **(see illustration)** and read off the charging time required according to the voltage reading taken.

3 Connect the charger to the battery BEFORE switching the charger ON. Make sure that the positive (+) lead on the charger is connected to the positive (+) terminal on the battery, and the negative (-) lead is connected to the negative (-) terminal. The battery should be charged for the specified time, or until the open circuit voltage reaches 12.8V (allow the battery to stabilise for 30 minutes after charging, before taking a voltage reading). Note that exceeding this

CHARGER

AMMETER

4.4 If the charger doesn't have a built-in ammeter, connect one in series as shown. DO NOT connect the ammeter between the battery terminals or it will be ruined

charging time can cause the battery to overheat, buckling the plates and rendering it useless.

4 Charge the battery at the rate marked on its casing, e.g. 0.8A for 5 to 10 hours. Few owners will have access to an expensive current controlled charger, so if a normal domestic charger is used check that after a possible initial peak, the charge rate falls to a safe level **(see illustration)**. If the battery becomes hot during charging **STOP**. Further charging will cause damage. **Note:** *In emergencies the battery can be charged at a higher rate of around 3.0 amps for a period of 1 hour. However, this is not recommended and the low amp charge is by far the safer method of charging the battery.*

5 If the recharged battery discharges rapidly when left disconnected it is likely that an internal short caused by physical damage or

sulphation has occurred. A new battery will be required. A sound battery will tend to lose its charge at about 1% per day.

6 Install the battery (see Section 3).

7 If the motorcycle sits unused for long periods of time, charge the battery once every month to six weeks and leave it disconnected. Alternatively purchase a trickle charger which allows the battery to remain connected.

5 Fuses

1 The electrical system is protected by fuses of different ratings (see *Specifications* at the beginning of this Chapter).

● The main fuse is integral with the starter relay, which is located on the battery clamp under the fuel tank **(see illustration)**.

● The headlight, brake light and horn, ignition, cooling fan, back-up and fuel injection system fuses are housed in the fusebox on the rear, right-hand side of the bike **(see illustration)**.

● The turn signal fuse is housed in a separate box (marked PARK) next to the main fusebox **(see illustration)**.

● The ABS control unit and modulator fuses are located in a fusebox underneath the fuel tank on the left-hand side **(see illustration)**.

2 To access the main fuse, first remove the fuel tank (see Chapter 4). Unclip the fuse holder lid and pull out the fuse **(see illustrations)**. Note the location of the spare fuse.

3 To access the main fusebox and the turn signal fuse, first remove the right-hand side panel (see

5.1a Location of the main fuse (arrowed) on the starter relay

5.1b Location of the fusebox behind the right-hand side panel

5.1c Location of the turn signal fuse (arrowed)

5.1d Fusebox (arrowed) houses the ABS control unit and modulator fuses

5.2a Remove the fuse holder lid . . .

5.2b . . . and pull out the main fuse

5.3 Release the catch on the fusebox lid carefully

5.4 The ABS system is protected by two fuses

5.5 A blown fuse can be identified by a break in its element

Headlight and relays

Chapter 7). Unclip the fusebox lid to access the fuses **(see illustration)**. Note the location of the spare fuses **(see illustration 5.1b)**.

4 To access the ABS fuses, first remove the fuel tank (see Chapter 4). Unclip the fuse holder lid and pull out the relevant fuse **(see illustration)**. Note the location of the spare fuse.

5 The fuses can be removed and checked visually. If you can't pull the fuse out with your fingertips, use a suitable pair of pliers. A blown fuse is easily identified by a break in the element **(see illustration)**, or the fuse can be tested for continuity using an ohmmeter or continuity tester – if there is no continuity, it has blown. Each fuse is clearly marked with its rating and must only be replaced by a fuse of the same rating. Spare fuses are housed in the fusebox and next to the starter relay. If a spare fuse is used, always replace it with a new one so that a spare of each rating is carried on the bike at all times.

⚠️ *Warning: Never put in a fuse of a higher rating or bridge the terminals with any other substitute, however temporary it may be. Serious damage may be done to the circuit, or a fire may start.*

6 If a fuse blows, be sure to check the wiring circuit very carefully for evidence of a short-circuit. Look for bare wires and chafed, melted or burned insulation. If the fuse is renewed before the cause is located, the new fuse will blow immediately.

7 Occasionally a fuse will blow or cause an

open-circuit for no obvious reason. Corrosion of the fuse ends and fusebox terminals may occur and cause poor fuse contact. If this happens, remove the corrosion with a penknife or steel wool, then spray the fuse end and terminals with electrical contact cleaner.

6 Lighting system check

Note: If the ignition is switched ON for any checks, remember to switch it OFF again before proceeding further or removing any electrical component from the system.

1 The battery provides power for operation of the headlight, tail light, brake light, turn signals and instrument cluster lights. If none of the lights operate, always check battery condition before proceeding. Low battery voltage indicates either a faulty battery or a defective charging system. Refer to Section 3 for battery checks and Section 30 for charging system tests. Also, check the condition of the fuses (see Section 5). When checking for a blown filament in a bulb, it is advisable to back up a visual check with a continuity test of the filament as it is not always apparent that a bulb has blown. When testing for continuity, remember that on tail light and turn signal bulbs it is often the metal body of the bulb that is the ground or earth.

2 If the headlight fails to work, check the bulb first (see Section 7), and then the main fuse and headlight fuse. Next disconnect the headlight wiring connector **(see illustrations 7.12 and 8.2b)**. Check for battery voltage on the loom side of the connector with a test light or multimeter – connect the negative probe of the multimeter to earth (black wire) terminal and the positive probe to first the high beam terminal and then the low beam terminal with the ignition switch ON (see *Wiring Diagrams* at the end of this Chapter). Don't forget to select either high or low beam as appropriate at the handlebar switch while conducting this test.

3 If no voltage is indicated at either terminal, check the wiring between the headlight connector, headlight relay, dimmer switch and the ignition switch, referring to *Wiring Diagrams* at the end of the chapter, then check the switches themselves. On models fitted with a fairing, don't forget to check the fairing assembly wiring connector(s) (see Chapter 7, Section 5).

4 If voltage is indicated, check for continuity between the black wire connector terminal and earth (ground). If there is no continuity, check the earth (ground) circuit for an open or poor connection.

5 To check the headlight relay, first remove the left-hand side panel (see Chapter 7); all the relays are mounted on a bracket **(see illustration)**. Displace the headlight relay and disconnect the wiring connector **(see illustration)**.

6.5a Relay identification. Turn signal (A), radiator fan (B), headlight (C) and starter circuit cut-off (D)

6.5b Release the catch to disconnect the relay wiring connector

6.6 Headlight relay – wiring connector terminal identification

1 *Red/yellow wire terminal*
2 *Green wire terminal*
3 *Yellow/black wire terminal*
4 *Red/yellow wire terminal*

6 Using a continuity tester or a multimeter set to the resistance (ohms) range, test for continuity between the red/yellow (positive meter probe) and green (negative meter probe) wire terminals on the relay **(see illustration)**. There should be no continuity (infinite resistance). Now, using insulated jumper wires and a fully charged 12V battery, connect the battery positive (+) terminal to the red/yellow wire terminal on the relay and the battery negative (-) terminal to the yellow/black wire terminal. Continuity (0 ohms) should now be shown on the meter. Note that it is important to differentiate between the two red/yellow wires.
7 If the relay does not operate as described, replace it with a new one.

Sidelight (European models)

8 If the sidelight fails to work with the ignition switch either in the ON position or the P position, check the bulb first (see Section 7), and then the main fuse and turn signal fuse. Check the terminals in the bulbholder and the wiring connector (see Section 7).
9 Next check for battery voltage at the blue/red wire terminal on the loom side of the sidelight wiring connector, with the ignition switch first in the ON position, then in the P position.
10 If no voltage is indicated in either position, check the wiring between the sidelight,

fusebox and the ignition switch, then check the switch (Section 18).
11 If voltage is indicated, check for continuity between the wiring connector terminals on the bulb side of the wiring connector and the corresponding terminals in the bulbholder; no continuity indicates a break in the circuit. If continuity is present, check for continuity between the black wire terminal and earth (ground). If there is no continuity, check the earth (ground) circuit for a broken or poor connection.
12 If the sidelight bulbs work with the ignition switch in one position (ON or P) but not the other, the switch is faulty.

Tail light

13 If the tail light fails to work, check the bulb first (see Section 9), and then the main fuse and circuit fuse. Next, remove the left-hand side panel (see Chapter 7) and disconnect the brake/tail light wiring connector. Check for battery voltage at the blue wire terminal on the loom side of the connector, with the ignition switch ON.
14 If no voltage is indicated, check the wiring between the tail light, fusebox and the ignition (main) switch, then check the switch itself.
15 If voltage is indicated, check for continuity between the black wire terminal and earth (ground). If there is no continuity, check the earth (ground) circuit for a broken or poor connection.

Brake light

16 If the brake light fails to work, check the bulb first (see Section 9), and then the main fuse and circuit fuse. Next, remove the left-hand side panel (see Chapter 7) and disconnect the wiring connector. Check for battery voltage at the yellow wire terminal on the loom side of the connector, with the ignition switch ON and the brake lever or pedal applied.
17 If no voltage is indicated, check the brake light switches (see Section 14), then the wiring between the brake/tail light and the switches.
18 If voltage is indicated, check for continuity between the black wire terminal and earth (ground). If there is no continuity, check the earth (ground) circuit for a broken or poor connection.

Licence plate light

19 If the licence plate light fails to work, check the bulb first (see Section 9), and then the main fuse and circuit fuse. Next, remove the left-hand side panel (see Chapter 7) and disconnect the light wiring connectors **(see illustration 10.5)**. Check for battery voltage at the blue wire terminal on the loom side of the connector, with the ignition switch ON.
20 If no voltage is indicated, check the wiring between the tail light, fusebox and the ignition switch, then check the switch itself.
21 If voltage is indicated, check for continuity between the black wire terminal and earth (ground). If there is no continuity, check the earth (ground) circuit for a broken or poor connection.

Turn signal lights

22 If one light fails to work, check the bulb and the bulb terminals (see Section 12), then the wiring connector. If none of the turn signals work, first check the battery, main fuse and turn signal fuse.
23 If the fuse is good, check the turn signal relay (see Section 11).

Instrument cluster lights

24 See Section 17.

---

7 Headlight bulbs and sidelight bulbs

Caution: The headlight bulb is of the quartz-halogen type. Do not touch the bulb glass as skin acids will shorten the bulb's service life. If the bulb is accidentally touched, it should be wiped carefully when cold with a rag soaked in methylated spirit and dried before fitting.

N models

Headlight bulb

1 Remove the headlight assembly (see Section 8).
2 Remove the cover from the back of the headlight, noting how it fits **(see illustration)**.
3 Release the bulb retaining clip, noting how it fits, then remove the bulb from the back of the headlight **(see illustrations)**.

7.2 Note how the cover fits over the back of the headlight reflector

7.3a Release the clip . . .

7.3b . . . and lift out the bulb

7.8 Pull the sidelight bulb out of its holder

7.12 Disconnect the wiring connector

7.13 Note how the cover fits over the back of the headlight unit

4 Fit the new bulb, bearing in mind the information in the **Note** above. Make sure the tabs on the bulb flange are aligned with the slots in the back of the headlight, and secure the bulb in position with the retaining clip.
5 Install the cover.
6 Install the headlight assembly (see Section 8). Check the operation of the headlight and the turn signals.

Sidelight bulb (European models)

7 Remove the headlight assembly (see Section 8).
8 The bulb is of the capless type – carefully pull it out of its holder **(see illustration)**.
9 Align the new bulb with its holder and press it into place. Check the operation of the light.
10 Install the headlight assembly (see Section 8). Check the operation of the headlight and the turn signals.

S models

Note: *An H4 60/55W bulb is fitted on the right-hand side (high beam) and an H7 55W bulb is fitted on the left side (low beam). They are wired independently for most markets (as shown in the wiring diagrams at the end of this chapter), and thus comply with lighting regulations.*

Headlight bulb

11 Remove the left or right-hand cockpit trim panel (see Chapter 7).
12 Disconnect the wiring connector from the back of the headlight bulb **(see illustration)**.
13 Remove the cover from the back of the

headlight, noting how it fits **(see illustration)**.
14 Release the bulb retaining clip, noting how it fits, then remove the bulb assembly from the back of the headlight unit **(see illustrations)**. Carefully pull the bulb out of the bulbholder **(see illustration)**.
15 Fit the new bulb, bearing in mind the information in the **Note** above. Make sure the bulb is pressed securely into its holder, then align the holder with the back of the headlight unit and secure the assembly with the retaining clip.
16 Fit the cover and install the wiring connector.
17 Check the operation of the headlight, then install the cockpit trim panel.

Sidelight (European models)

18 Remove the left or right-hand cockpit trim panel (see Chapter 7).
19 Pull the bulbholder out of the back of

7.14a Release the clip . . .

the headlight unit. The bulb is of the capless type – carefully pull it out of the holder **(see illustrations)**.
20 Align the new bulb with its holder and press it into place. Check the operation of the light, then fit the bulbholder into the back of the headlight unit.
21 Install the cockpit trim panel (see Chapter 7).

8 Headlight

N models

Removal and installation

1 Undo the bolts securing the headlight assembly on both sides, then support

7.14b . . . and draw out the bulb assembly

7.14c Pull the headlight bulb out of its holder

7.19a Draw the bulbholder out . . .

7.19b . . . then pull the bulb out of the holder

8.1 Headlight assembly is secured by two bolts (arrowed) on each side

8.2a Note the location of the headlight assembly bracket (arrowed)

8.2b Disconnect the headlight connector . . .

the assembly and remove the bolts **(see illustration)**.

2 Draw the assembly forwards, noting the location of the mounting bracket, then disconnect the headlight connector and pull the sidelight bulbholder out of the headlight **(see illustrations)**.

3 Disconnect the turn signals wiring connector and remove the headlight assembly **(see illustration)**.

4 If required, undo the bolts securing the left and right-hand headlight brackets and remove the brackets, noting how the support plates locate in the back of the headlight **(see illustration)**.

5 Note the location of the grommets in the headlight brackets and the support plates

and renew them if they are damaged or deteriorated.

6 To remove the headlight assembly mounting bracket, first remove the instrument cluster (see Section 15).

7 Release the clip securing the front brake hose to the mounting bracket, then undo the lower bracket bolt **(see illustration)**.

8 Undo the left and right-hand upper mounting bracket bolts **(see illustrations)**. Release the clips securing the wiring to the mounting bracket and lift the bracket off.

9 Installation is the reverse of removal. Make sure all the wiring is correctly connected and secured. Check the operation of the headlight and sidelight. Check the headlight aim. Check the operation of the turn signals.

Headlight aim

Note: *An improperly adjusted headlight may cause problems for oncoming traffic or provide poor, unsafe illumination of the road ahead. Before adjusting the headlight aim, be sure to consult with local traffic laws and regulations – for UK models refer to MOT Test Checks in the Reference section.*

10 The headlight beam can adjusted both horizontally and vertically. Before making any adjustment, check that the tyre pressures are correct. Make any adjustments to the headlight aim with the machine on level ground, with the fuel tank half full and with an assistant sitting on the seat. If the bike is usually ridden with a passenger on the back, have a second assistant to do this.

8.2c . . . and pull the sidelight bulbholder out

8.3 Disconnect the turn signals wiring connector

8.4 Undo the bracket bolt (A), noting the location of the plate (B) – left side shown

8.7 Brake hose clip (A) and lower mounting bracket bolt (B)

8.8a Undo the left . . .

8.8b . . . and right-hand upper mounting bracket bolts (arrowed)

8.11 Location of the left-hand side headlight adjuster (arrowed)

8.12 Vertical adjuster screw (A) and horizontal adjuster screw (B)

8.16 Undo the screws (arrowed) to remove the headlight unit

8.17 Headlight sub-loom wiring is secured by clip (arrowed)

8.20 Location of the left-hand side upper (A) and lower (B) headlight adjusters

8.21 Horizontal adjuster screws (A) and vertical adjuster screws (B)

11 The headlight adjusters are located on the back of the headlight, on the lower left-hand side and the upper right-hand side (see illustration).

12 Vertical adjustment is made by turning the left-hand adjuster screw (see illustration). Turn it clockwise to move the beam down, and anti-clockwise to move it up.

13 Horizontal adjustment is made by turning the right-hand adjuster screw (see illustration 8.12). Turn it clockwise to move the beam to the right, and anti-clockwise to move it to the left.

S models

Removal and installation

14 Remove the fairing (see Chapter 7).

15 Disconnect the headlight bulb wiring connectors and pull the sidelight bulbholders out of the back of the headlight unit (see Section 7).

16 Undo the screws securing the headlight unit and lift it out of the fairing (see illustration).

17 If required, undo the screw securing the sub-loom wiring clip and remove the sub-loom (see illustration).

18 Installation is the reverse of removal. Make sure all the wiring is correctly connected and secured. Check the operation of the headlight and sidelight. Check the headlight aim. Check the operation of the turn signals.

Headlight aim

Note: *An improperly adjusted headlight may cause problems for oncoming traffic or provide poor, unsafe illumination of the road ahead. Before adjusting the headlight aim, be sure to consult with local traffic laws and regulations – for UK models refer to MOT Test Checks in the Reference section.*

19 The headlight beams can adjusted both horizontally and vertically. Before making any adjustment, check that the tyre pressures are correct. Make any adjustments to the headlight aim with the machine on level ground, with the fuel tank half full and with an assistant sitting on the seat. If the bike is usually ridden with a passenger on the back, have a second assistant to do this.

20 Remove the cockpit trim panels to access the headlight adjusters (see Chapter 7). The adjusters are located on the back of each headlight – there are two upper (inner) adjusters and two lower (outer) adjusters (see illustration).

21 Horizontal adjustment is made by turning the upper adjuster screws (see illustration). To adjust the left-hand headlight, turn the screw clockwise to move the beam to the right, and anti-clockwise to move it to the left. To adjust the right-hand headlight, turn the screw anti-clockwise to move the beam to the right, and clockwise to move it to the left.

22 Vertical adjustment is made by turning the lower adjuster screws (see illustration 8.21).

On both headlights, turn the screw clockwise to move the beam down, and anti-clockwise to move it up.

9 Brake/tail light bulb and licence plate bulb

Brake/tail light bulb

Note: *It is a good idea to use a paper towel or dry cloth when handling a new bulb to prevent injury if it breaks, and to increase bulb life.*

1 Remove the seat (see Chapter 7). The brake/tail light bulbholder is accessible inside the seat cowling (see illustration).

9.1 Location of the brake/tail light bulbholder (arrowed)

9.2 Twist the bulbholder anti-clockwise to remove it

9.3 Push the bulb and twist it anti-clockwise to remove it

9.6 Undo the screws securing the licence plate light unit

2 Twist the bulbholder anti-clockwise and withdraw it from the back of the light unit **(see illustration)**.
3 Push the bulb into the holder, then turn it anti-clockwise to remove it **(see illustration)**.
4 Ensure that the terminals inside the bulbholder are clean and free from corrosion.
5 Line up the pins of the new bulb with the slots in the holder, then push the bulb in and turn it clockwise until it locks into place. Install the remaining components in the reverse order of removal. Check the operation of the brake/tail light.

Licence plate light bulb

6 Undo the screws securing the licence plate light unit in its holder and pull the unit out **(see illustrations)**.
7 Pull the bulbholder out of the unit. The bulb is of the capless type – carefully pull it out of its holder **(see illustrations)**.
8 Align the new bulb with its holder and press it into place. Check the operation of the light.
9 Installation is the reverse of removal.

9.7a Pull the bulbholder out . . .

9.7b . . . then pull the bulb out of the holder

3 Undo the screws securing the tail light unit and remove it **(see illustration)**.
4 Installation is the reverse of removal. Ensure that the wiring is properly secured inside the seat cowling. Check the operation of the tail light and brake light prior to installing the seat.
5 To remove the licence plate light unit, first disconnect the single bullet wiring connectors and release the wiring from any ties **(see illustration)**. Feed the wiring back to the light unit. Note that the turn signal wiring is secured by the same ties.
6 Follow the procedure in Section 9 to displace the light unit, then pull the wiring through the back of the holder. Note that it is easier to remove the licence plate light unit once the rear mudguard assembly has been removed (see Chapter 7).

7 Installation is the reverse of removal. Ensure that the wiring is properly secured and connected. Check the operation of the light before installing the seat cowling.

---

10 Tail light and licence plate light units

1 Remove the seat cowling (see Chapter 7).
2 The tail light unit is installed in the seat cowling. Remove the brake/tail light bulbholder (see Section 9). If required, release the wiring sub-loom from the clips securing it to the inside of the seat cowling **(see illustration)**.

---

11 Turn signal circuit check

1 Most turn signal problems are the result of a burned-out bulb or corroded socket. This is especially true when the turn signals function properly in one direction, but fail to flash in the other direction. Check the bulbs and the sockets (see Section 12) and the wiring connectors. Also, check the main fuse and turn signal fuse (see Section 5) and the switch (see Section 19).

10.2 Note how the wiring sub-loom is secured inside the seat cowling (arrowed)

10.3 Tail light unit is secured by two screws (arrowed)

10.5 Licence plate light wiring connectors. Note the cable-ties securing the wiring

11.4a Displace the relay from the bracket . . .

11.4b . . . then disconnect the wiring connector

12.1 Undo the screw and remove the lens

2 The battery provides power for operation of the turn signals, so if they do not operate, check the battery voltage. Low battery voltage indicates either a faulty battery or a defective charging system. Refer to Section 3 for battery checks and Section 30 for charging system tests.
3 If the bulbs, sockets, connectors, fuses, switch and battery are good, remove the left-hand side panel (see Chapter 7) and check the turn signal relay as follows **(see illustration 6.5a)**.
4 Pull the relay off the mounting bracket and disconnect the wiring connector**(see illustrations)**.
5 Using a voltmeter, check for battery voltage between the brown/green wire terminal in the connector and earth (ground) with the ignition ON. If no voltage is indicated, refer to the appropriate wiring diagram at the end of this Chapter and check the wiring between the relay, fusebox and the ignition switch for continuity.
6 If voltage is indicated, reconnect the relay connector. Backprobe the brown/white wire terminal in the connector and check for voltage with the ignition ON, and with the signal switch turned to either LEFT or RIGHT.
7 If no voltage is indicated, replace the relay with a new one.
8 If voltage is indicated, check the wiring between the relay, turn signal switch and turn signal lights for continuity.

12.4 Pins on the bulb must align with slots in the bulbholder

12.5 Ensure the lens is correctly located

running lights, use dual filament bulbs which have offset pins and can only be fitted one way in their holders.
5 Fit the lens onto the holder, making sure the tab locates correctly **(see illustration)**. Do not overtighten the screw as the lens or threads could be damaged.

13 Turn signal assemblies

Front

N models

1 Remove the headlight assembly (see Section 8).

13.3 Unclip the mounting plate (arrowed)

2 Disconnect the wiring connectors for the left and right-hand turn signals.
3 Unclip the mounting plate from the inner end if the turn signal stem, then draw the signal assembly out from the headlight bracket **(see illustration)**.
4 Installation is the reverse of removal. Make sure the mounting plate is a secure fit. Check the operation of the turn signals.

S models

5 Remove the fairing (see Chapter 7).
6 Trace the wiring from either the left or right-hand turn signal and disconnect it at the connector. Release the wiring from any clips, noting its routing **(see illustration)**.
7 Unclip the mounting plate from the inner end if the turn signal stem, then draw the

12 Turn signal bulbs

1 Remove the screw securing the turn signal lens and remove the lens, noting how it fits **(see illustration)**.
2 Push the bulb into the holder and twist it anti-clockwise to remove it.
3 Ensure that the terminals inside the bulbholder are clean and free from corrosion.
4 Line up the pins of the new bulb with the slots in the holder, then push the bulb in and turn it clockwise until it locks into place **(see illustration)**. Note: *US models fitted with front*

13.6 Release the wiring from any clips (arrowed) – S2 model shown

13.7a Unclip the mounting plate . . .

13.7b . . . then remove the turn signal assembly

13.10 Turn signal wiring connectors (arrowed)

13.11 Unclip the mounting plate (arrowed) to release the turn signal assembly

With the brake lever applied, there should be continuity. If the switch does not behave as described, replace it with a new one (the switch is not adjustable).

4 The rear brake light switch is mounted on the inside of the rider's right-hand footrest bracket **(see illustration)**. To access the switch wiring connector, first remove the fuel tank (see Chapter 4). Trace the wiring from the switch and disconnect it at the brown, two-pin connector **(see illustration)**.

5 Using a continuity tester, connect the probes to the two terminals on the switch side of the wiring connector. With the brake pedal at rest, there should be no continuity. With the brake pedal applied, there should be continuity. If the switch does not behave as described, replace it with a new one.

6 If the switches are good, check for voltage at the brown wire terminal on the supply side of the switch wiring connector with the ignition switch ON. If no voltage is indicated, check the wiring between the switch, fusebox and the ignition switch (see *Wiring Diagrams* at the end of this Chapter).

signal assembly out from the fairing **(see illustrations)**.

8 Installation is the reverse of removal. Make sure the mounting plate is a secure fit. Check the operation of the turn signals.

Rear

9 Remove the seat cowling (see Chapter 7).
10 Disconnect the turn signal wiring connectors **(see illustration)**. Release the wiring from any ties, then feed it back to the individual signal assemblies. Note that the licence plate light wiring is secured by the same ties.
11 Unclip the mounting plate from the inner end if the turn signal stem, then draw the signal assembly out from the rear mudguard **(see illustration)**.
12 Installation is the reverse of removal. Make sure the mounting plate is a secure fit. Ensure that the wiring is properly secured and connected. Check the operation of the turn signals before installing the seat cowling.

Disconnect the wiring connectors from the switch **(see illustration)**.
3 Using a continuity tester, connect its probes to the terminals of the switch. With the brake lever at rest, there should be no continuity.

Removal and installation

Front brake light switch

7 Disconnect the wiring connectors from the switch **(see illustration 14.2)**.
8 Undo the single screw securing the switch to the bottom of the master cylinder and remove the switch **(see illustration)**.
9 Installation is the reverse of removal. Check the operation of the switch.

14.2 Front brake light switch wiring connectors (arrowed)

14.4a Location of the rear brake light switch (arrowed)

14 Brake light switches

Check

1 Before checking the switches, check the brake light circuit (see Section 6).
2 The front brake light switch is mounted on the underside of the brake master cylinder.

14.4b Rear brake light switch wiring connector (arrowed)

14.8 Brake light switch is secured by screw (arrowed)

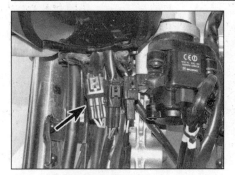

15.2 Instrument cluster wiring connectors (arrowed) – N models

15.3a Undo the instrument cluster cover screws (arrowed) . . .

15.3b . . . noting the fine-pitched thread

Rear brake light switch

10 Disconnect the switch wiring connector **(see illustration 14.4b).**

11 Follow the procedure in Chapter 5, Section 3, to remove the right-hand footrest bracket assembly.

12 Detach the lower end of the switch spring from the brake pedal arm, then thread the switch out of its bracket, noting the location of the adjuster nut.

13 Installation is the reverse of removal. Check the operation of the switch and adjust as necessary (see Chapter 1, Section 11).

15.3c Undo the instrument cluster bracket screws (arrowed) . . .

15.3d . . . noting the coarse-pitched thread

15 Instrument cluster removal and installation

N models

1 Remove the headlight assembly (see Section 8).

2 Disconnect the instrument cluster wiring connectors **(see illustration).**

3 On FZ6-N models, undo the two screws securing the instrument cluster cover – note that these screws have a fine-pitched thread **(see illustrations)**. Undo the two screws securing the instrument cluster to its bracket – note that these screws have a coarse-pitched thread **(see illustrations)**. Lift the instrument cluster off, feeding the wiring through the cover **(see illustration)**. If required, release the trim clips securing the cover to the mounting bracket and lift the cover off **(see illustration)**.

4 On S2 models, undo the screws securing the instrument cluster and remove the cluster with its shield.

5 Check the mounting bushes in the bracket – if they are worn or perished, replace them with new ones.

6 Installation is the reverse of removal. Ensure that the wiring connectors are secure and check the operation of the instruments before riding the motorcycle.

S models

7 Remove the fairing (see Chapter 7).

8 Undo the screws securing the instrument

15.3e Remove the instrument cluster

cluster to the fairing bracket **(see illustrations)**.

9 Check the mounting bushes in the bracket – if they are worn or perished, replace them with new ones.

15.8a Instrument cluster on S2 models is secured by three screws (arrowed)

15.3f Cover is secured by trim clips (A). Note the mounting bushes (B)

10 Installation is the reverse of removal. Ensure that the wiring connectors are secure. Following the instructions in the Owners Manual, turn the ignition switch ON and press the 'SELECT' button to find the appropriate

15.8b Instrument cluster on all other S models is secured by two screws (arrowed)

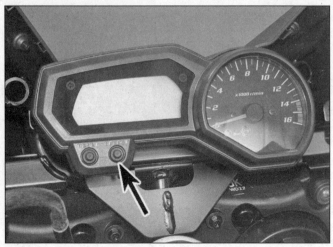

15.10a SELECT button (arrowed) – S2 models

15.10b SELECT button (arrowed) – all other S models

tripmeter display **(see illustrations)**. Check the operation of the instruments before riding the motorcycle.

16 Instrument cluster check

1 If all instrument and display functions fail at the same time, check the ignition fuse and the wiring and connectors, referring to Section 15 and the *Wiring Diagrams* at the end of this Chapter.
2 The warning and indicator functions (oil level, fuel level and engine warning, neutral, high beam and turn signals) are all illuminated by LEDs (see Section 17).
3 The oil level, fuel level, coolant temperature and speedometer displays are controlled by the appropriate sensor/sender. If a display fails or is thought to be faulty, refer to the test details for the sensor/sender as follows:
● Oil level sender – refer to Section 26 for test details. If the sensor is good, check the LED (see Section 17).
● Coolant temperature sensor – refer to Chapter 3 for test details.
● Fuel level sensor – refer to Chapter 4 for

18.2 Location of the ignition switch wiring connectors (arrowed)

test details. Note that on some market models, a low fuel level warning LED is mounted on the instrument cluster.
● Speed sensor – refer to Chapter 4 for test details.
4 If a display is proved to be faulty, a new instrument cluster will have to be fitted (see Section 15).
5 No test details are available for the tachometer.

17 Warning and indicator lights

1 The warning and indicator functions (oil level, fuel level and engine management warning, neutral, high beam and turn signals) are all illuminated by LEDs.
2 With the exception of the engine management warning indicator, the LEDs will only illuminate when the functions are selected by the appropriate switch or sender. If an indicator does not illuminate, first check the switch, then test the LED as described below.
3 The oil level warning indicator should come on for a few seconds when the ignition is switched ON as a check of the LED, and then go off. If the indicator does not come on, does not go off, or starts flashing, first check the oil level (see *Pre-ride checks*). If the level is good, check the sensor (see Section 26). **Note:** *If there is a fault in the wiring circuit it will be detected by a self diagnosis function and the warning indicator will flash ten times, then go out for 2.5 seconds, and this will be repeated until the fault is repaired.*
4 The engine warning indicator should come on for a few seconds when the ignition is switched ON as a check of the LED, and then go off. If the indicator does not come on, does not go off, or starts flashing, have the machine checked by a Yamaha dealer.

LED check

5 Refer to the appropriate *Wiring Diagram* at the end of this Chapter. If both a power supply and earth (ground) terminal for the LED to be checked can be identified, proceed as follows. **Note:** *The oil level and fuel level warning indicators cannot be checked using this test. If the LEDs are thought to be faulty (after checking the appropriate sender/sensor and wiring) have the instrument cluster checked by a Yamaha dealer.*
6 Remove the instrument cluster (see Section 15). Using a fully charged 12V battery and two suitable jumper wires, connect the positive (+) battery terminal to the relevant power supply terminal on the instrument cluster and the negative (-) battery terminal to the relevant earth (ground) terminal.
7 If the LED comes on, the fault lies elsewhere in the electrical circuit for the LED in question. Check the fuse, wiring and the operation of the component linked to the LED.
8 If the LED has failed a new instrument cluster will have to be fitted.

18 Ignition switch

 Warning: To prevent the risk of short circuits, disconnect the battery negative (–) lead before making any ignition (main) switch checks.

Check

1 To check the switch, first remove the fuel tank (see Chapter 4) to access its wiring connector.
2 Trace the ignition switch wiring back from the switch and disconnect it at the white connectors **(see illustration)**. **Note:** *It may be necessary to displace the battery housing to access the wiring connectors (see Section 3).*
3 Using a multimeter or a continuity tester, make the following checks on the switch side

18.7 Location of the immobiliser transceiver (A) and ignition switch (B)

18.10 Remove the shear-head bolts (arrowed)

of the connector. Check the continuity of the connector terminal pairs (see *Wiring Diagrams* at the end of this Chapter). Continuity should exist between the terminals connected by a solid line on the diagram when the switch key is turned to the indicated position.

4 If the switch fails any of the tests, replace it with a new one.

Removal

5 Disconnect the battery negative (–) lead.

6 Trace the ignition switch wiring back from the switch and disconnect it at the connectors (see Step 2). Release the wiring from any cable-ties and feed it back to the switch, noting the correct routing.

7 If an immobiliser is fitted, disconnect the transceiver wiring at the connector and feed the wiring back to the transceiver, noting the correct routing **(see illustration)**.

8 Follow the procedure in Chapter 5, Section 9, and remove the top yoke. Note that it is not necessary to remove the front forks if only the top yoke is being removed.

9 If applicable, undo the Torx screws and remove the immobiliser transceiver, noting how it fits **(see illustration 18.7)**.

10 Two shear-head security bolts mount the ignition switch to the underside of the top yoke **(see illustration)**. The heads of the bolts must be tapped around using a suitable punch or drift, or drilled off, before the switch can be removed. To do this, mount the yoke in a vice equipped with soft jaws to avoid damaging the yoke.

11 Remove the bolts and discard them as new ones must be used on reassembly, then withdraw the switch from the top yoke.

Installation

12 Installation is the reverse of removal, noting the following:
● Obtain the correct type shear-head bolts from a Yamaha dealer – do not use another type of bolt. Tighten the bolts until their heads shear off.

● Ensure the wiring is securely connected and correctly routed.
● Ensure all top yoke and handlebar nuts and bolts are tightened to the torque settings specified in Chapter 5.

19 Handlebar switch check

1 Generally speaking, the handlebar switch units are reliable and trouble-free. Most problems are caused by dirty or corroded contacts, but wear and breakage of internal parts is a possibility that should not be overlooked. If breakage does occur, the entire switch unit and related wiring harness will have to be replaced with a new one, as individual parts are not available.

2 The switches can be checked for continuity using a multimeter or a continuity tester.

3 Trace the wiring harness of the switch in question back to its connector and disconnect it **(see illustration)**. Follow the procedure in Section 3 to displace the battery housing in order to access the wiring connectors.

4 Check for continuity between the terminals of the switch harness with the switch in the various positions (i.e. switch OFF – no

19.3 Location of the handlebar switch wiring connectors (arrowed)

continuity, switch ON – continuity) – see *Wiring Diagrams* at the end of this Chapter.

5 If the continuity check indicates a problem exists, refer to Section 20 and displace the switch from the handlebar. Spray the inside of the switch with electrical contact cleaner.

6 If they are accessible, the contacts can be scraped clean with a penknife or polished with steel wool **(see illustration)**. If switch components or wiring connections are damaged or broken, it should be obvious when the switch is disassembled.

20 Handlebar switch removal and installation

Removal

1 If the switch unit is to be removed from the motorcycle, rather than just displaced from the handlebar, follow the procedure in Section 19 and disconnect the appropriate wiring connector **(see illustration 19.3)**. Feed the wiring back to the switch, freeing it from any clips and ties and noting its correct routing.

2 Disconnect the wiring connectors from the brake light switch (if removing the right-hand switch unit) or the clutch switch (if removing

19.6 Keep the switch terminals clean and free from corrosion

20.3 Removing the right-hand switch unit.
Note the throttle twistgrip (arrowed)

20.4a Undo the front (arrowed) . . .

20.4b . . . and rear (arrowed) left-hand
switch unit screws

20.4c The front screw is longer than the
rear one

20.5a Separate the halves of the switch
unit

the left-hand switch unit) **(see illustration 14.2 or 23.2).**

3 Note that the right-hand switch unit incorporates the throttle twistgrip housing. Follow the procedure in Chapter 4, Section 12, to detach the throttle cables from the lower half of the switch housing, then lift the switch unit off **(see illustration).**

4 To remove the left-hand switch unit, undo the front and rear screws, noting where they fit **(see illustrations).**

5 Separate the two halves of the switch unit and lift it off, noting how the pin on the wiring clamp locates in the hole in the underside of the handlebar **(see illustrations).**

Installation

6 Installation is the reverse of removal. Refer to Chapter 4 for installation of the throttle cables. Make sure the locating pin on the wiring clamp locates in the hole in the handlebar **(see**

illustrations 20.5b and c). Ensure the screws are fitted the correct way round. Make sure the wiring is securely connected and correctly routed. Check the operation of all switches before riding the motorcycle.

21 Neutral switch

Check

1 Before checking the electrical circuit, check the ignition fuse (see Section 5).

2 The switch is located on the back of the engine unit **(see illustration).** Remove the fuel tank (see Chapter 4), then disconnect the wiring connector from the switch. Make sure the transmission is in neutral.

3 With the connector disconnected and the ignition switch ON, the neutral light should be

out. If not, the wire between the connector and instrument cluster must be earthed (grounded) at some point.

4 Check for continuity between the terminal on the switch and the crankcase – with the transmission in neutral, there should be continuity; with the transmission in gear, there should be no continuity. If there is continuity when in gear or no continuity when in neutral, remove the switch (see below), and check that the contact plunger is not damaged or seized in the switch body.

5 If the switch is good, check the wire between the connector, the starter circuit cut-off relay and the instrument cluster for continuity (see *Wiring Diagrams* at the end of this Chapter). Refer to Section 24 for details of checking the diode in the cut-off relay.

6 Check for battery voltage at the light green wire terminal on the cut-off relay side of the instrument cluster wiring connector with the ignition ON. If no voltage is indicated, check for continuity between the connector and the ignition fuse.

7 If voltage is indicated, check the LED in the instrument cluster (see Section 17), then check the starter circuit cut-off relay (Section 24) and other components in the starter circuit as described in the relevant Sections of this Chapter. If all components are good, check the wiring between the various components (see *Wiring Diagrams* at the end of this Chapter).

Removal and installation

8 The switch is located on the back of the engine unit **(see illustration 21.2).** Pull the

20.5b Note how the pin (arrowed) . . .

20.5c . . . locates in the hole (arrowed) in
the handlebar

21.2 Location of the neutral switch
(arrowed)

22.2 Location of the sidestand switch wiring connector

23.2 Disconnect the clutch switch wiring connector

23.4 Clutch switch is secured by single screw (arrowed)

wire connector off the switch terminal, then unscrew the switch and withdraw it from the casing. Discard the sealing washer as a new one must be used on reassembly.

9 Install the switch using a new sealing washer and tighten it to the torque setting specified at the beginning of this Chapter.

10 Connect the wire to the switch terminal and check the operation of the neutral light.

22 Sidestand switch

Check

1 The sidestand switch is mounted on the back of the sidestand bracket (see Chapter 5, Section 4). The switch is part of the safety circuit which prevents or stops the engine running if the transmission is in gear whilst the sidestand is down, and prevents the engine from starting if the transmission is in gear unless the sidestand is up and the clutch lever is pulled in. Before checking the electrical circuit, check the main and ignition fuses (see Section 5).

2 To access the switch wiring connector, first remove the fuel tank (see Chapter 4). Trace the wiring from the switch and disconnect it at the 2-pin connector **(see illustration)**.

3 Check the operation of the switch using a multimeter or continuity tester. Connect the meter probes to the terminals on the switch side of the connector. With the sidestand up there should be continuity (zero resistance) between the terminals, and with the stand down there should be no continuity (infinite resistance).

4 If the switch does not perform as expected, check the plunger is not seized in the switch body. If the plunger is free, replace the switch with a new one.

5 If the switch is good, check the starter circuit cut-off relay (Section 24) and other components in the starter circuit as described in the relevant Sections of this Chapter. If all components are good, check the wiring between the various components (see *Wiring Diagrams* at the end of this Chapter).

Renewal

6 The sidestand switch is mounted on the back of the sidestand bracket. Follow the procedure in Chapter 5, Section 4, to remove and install the switch, then check operation of the sidestand switch and starter safety circuit (see Chapter 1, Section 15).

23 Clutch switch

Check

1 The clutch switch is mounted on the underside of the clutch lever bracket. The switch is part of the safety circuit which prevents or stops the engine running if the transmission is in gear whilst the sidestand is down, and prevents the engine from starting if the transmission is in gear unless the sidestand is up and the clutch lever is pulled in. The switch is not adjustable.

2 Disconnect the switch wiring connector **(see illustration)** and check the operation of the switch using a multimeter or continuity tester. Connect the meter probes to the terminals on the switch. With the lever pulled in there should be continuity (zero resistance) between the terminals, and with the lever out there should be no continuity (infinite resistance).

3 If the switch is good, check the starter circuit cut-off relay (Section 24) and other components in the starter circuit as described in the relevant Sections of this Chapter. If

all components are good, check the wiring between the various components (see *Wiring Diagrams* at the end of this Chapter).

Renewal

4 Disconnect the wiring connector **(see illustration 23.2)**. Undo the screw securing the switch and remove it **(see illustration)**.

5 Installation is the reverse of removal.

24 Starter circuit cut-off relay

1 The starter circuit cut-off relay and its associated diodes are contained within the relay assembly. They are part of the safety circuit which prevents or stops the engine running if the transmission is in gear whilst the sidestand is down, and prevents the engine from starting if the transmission is in gear unless the sidestand is up and the clutch lever is pulled in.

2 To check the operation of the relay, first remove the left-hand side panel (see Chapter 7); all the relays are mounted on a bracket **(see illustration 6.5a)**.

3 Disconnect the battery negative (–) lead, then displace the relay and disconnect the wiring connector **(see illustrations)**. Move the relay to the bench and test the operation of the relay and the relay diodes as follows.

4 Using a continuity tester or a multimeter set to the resistance (ohms) range, test for continuity between the white/blue (positive meter probe) and blue/white (negative meter

24.3a Remove the starter circuit cut-off relay . . .

24.3b . . . then release the catch (arrowed) and disconnect the wiring connector

24.4 Starter circuit cut-off relay – wiring connector terminal identification

1 Blue/white wire terminal
2 White/blue wire terminal
3 Red/black wire terminal
4 Black/yellow wire terminal

24.6 Starter circuit cut-off relay diode check – wiring connector terminal identification

1 Light blue wire terminal
2 Black/yellow wire terminal
3 Black/red wire terminal
4 Light green wire terminal
5 Blue/green wire terminal

probe) wire terminals on the relay (see illustration). There should be no continuity (infinite resistance). Now, using insulated jumper wires and a fully charged 12V battery, connect the battery positive (+) terminal to the red/black wire terminal on the relay and the battery negative (-) terminal to the black/yellow wire terminal. Continuity (0 ohms) should now be shown on the meter.

5 If the relay does not operate as described, replace it with a new one.

6 The diodes contained within the relay assembly can be checked by performing a continuity test – diodes should show continuity in one direction and no continuity when the meter or tester probes are reversed. Connect the multimeter (set to ohms) or continuity tester across the wire terminals for the diode being tested (see illustration). Refer to the appropriate wiring diagram at the end of this Chapter if necessary, and perform the following tests. If any diode shows continuity in both directions it is faulty, and the relay assembly must be replaced with a new one.

Positive probe (+)	Negative probe (-)	Result
Light blue	Black/yellow	No continuity
Black/yellow	Light blue	Continuity
Light blue	Black/red	No continuity
Black/red	Light blue	Continuity
Light blue	Light green	No continuity
Light green	Light blue	Continuity
Blue/green	Black/red	No continuity
Black/red	Blue/green	Continuity

7 If the cut-out relay and diodes are good, but the starting system fault still exists, check all other components in the starting circuit (i.e. the neutral switch, sidestand switch, clutch switch, starter switch and starter relay) as described in the relevant Sections of this Chapter. If all components are good, check the wiring between the various components (see *Wiring Diagrams* at the end of this Chapter).

8 Installation is the reverse of removal.

Fuel pump relay

9 The fuel pump relay is integral with the starter circuit cut-off relay. Refer to Chapter 4, Section 8, for details

25 Horn

Check

1 If the horn doesn't work, first check the horn fuse (see Section 5) and the battery (see Section 3).

2 On N models, the horn is mounted on the right-hand side of the frame below the fuel tank and on S models it is mounted on the bottom yoke (see illustrations). On S models, remove the fairing for access (see Chapter 7).

3 Pull the wiring connectors off the horn terminals (see illustration). Using two jumper wires and a fully charged 12V battery, apply voltage directly to the terminals on the horn. If the horn sounds, check the switch (see Section 19) and the wiring between the switch and the horn (see *Wiring Diagrams* at the end of this Chapter).

4 If the horn sounds weak or distorted, the tone can be adjusted by turning the screw on the back of the horn cover (see illustration).

5 If the horn doesn't sound, replace it with a new one.

25.2a Location of the horn – N models

25.2b Location of the horn – S models

25.3 Pull the connectors off the horn terminals (arrowed)

25.4 Screw (arrowed) for adjusting the tone of the horn

Removal and installation

6 Pull the wiring connectors off the horn terminals.

7 Unscrew the nut securing the horn and remove it from the bike.

8 Install the horn and tighten the nut securely. Connect the wiring connectors and check the operation of the horn. If removed, install the fairing.

26 Oil level sensor

Check

1 The oil level warning light will come on for a few seconds when the ignition is switched ON as a check of the LED. It should then go out and the motorcycle can be started. If the warning indicator does not go off or starts flashing, check the engine oil level as described in *Pre-ride checks*. If the oil level is correct, check the sensor as described below. Equally, if the warning light comes on (and/or flashes) whilst the motorcycle is being ridden, stop the engine and check the engine oil level immediately.

2 If the warning light does not come on when the ignition is switched ON, check the LED as described in Section 17.

3 To check the sensor, remove it from the sump (see Steps 4 to 6). Connect one probe of a multimeter set to the ohms x 100 scale to the sensor wire and the other probe to the base of the sensor. With the sensor upright (i.e. in its normal installed position with the wiring at the bottom), the resistance should be as specified (minimum level) at the beginning of this Chapter. Turn the sensor upside down and check the resistance again – it should be as specified (maximum level). If either result is not as specified, replace the sensor with a new one.

Removal

4 Drain the engine oil (see Chapter 1).

5 Remove the fuel tank (see Chapter 4), then trace the wire back from the sensor and disconnect it at the connector **(see illustration)**.

6 Release the wire from any cable-ties and the clamp secured by one sump bolt **(see illustration)**. Feed the wire back to the sensor, noting the correct routing.

7 Unscrew the two bolts securing the sensor to the bottom of the sump and withdraw it from the sump, being prepared to catch any residual oil **(see illustration 26.6)**. Check the condition of the O-ring and replace it with a new one if it is damaged or deteriorated.

Installation

8 Smear the sensor O-ring with lithium-based grease, then fit the sensor into the sump. Tighten its bolts to the torque setting specified at the beginning of this Chapter.

9 Feed the wiring to the connector **(see illustration 26.5)** and secure it with the cable-ties. Don't forget to install the clamp and sump bolt **(see illustration 26.6)**.

10 Fill the engine with the specified amount of oil (see Chapter 1) and check the operation of the sensor.

27 Starter relay

Check

1 If the starter circuit appears to be faulty, first check the main fuse and ignition fuse (see Section 5).

2 Remove the fuel tank (see Chapter 4). The starter relay is located on the battery clamp **(see illustration)**.

3 Displace the relay, then lift the cover and unscrew the bolt securing the black starter motor lead **(see illustration 27.2)**. Position the lead away from the relay terminal.

4 With the ignition switch ON, the engine

26.5 Oil level sensor wiring connector

kill switch in the RUN position and the transmission in neutral, press the starter switch. The relay should be heard to click.

5 If the relay doesn't click, switch the ignition OFF, remove the relay (see Steps 10 to 12) and test it as follows.

6 Using a continuity tester or a multimeter set to the resistance (ohms) range, test for continuity between the relay's starter motor (black) and battery (red) lead terminals. There should be no continuity (infinite resistance). Now, using insulated jumper wires and a fully charged 12V battery, connect the battery positive (+) terminal to the red/white wire terminal on the relay and the battery negative (-) terminal to the blue/white wire terminal. With voltage applied, the relay should be heard to click and continuity (0 ohms) should now be shown on the meter.

7 If the relay does not click when battery voltage is applied and indicates no continuity (infinite resistance) across its terminals, it is faulty and must be replaced with a new one.

8 The starter relay coil resistance can be checked by connecting a multimeter set to the ohms x 1 range across the red/white and blue/white terminals of the relay wire connector; the value should be as specified at the beginning of this Chapter.

9 If the relay is good, check for battery voltage at the red/white wire terminal on the loom side of the relay wiring connector when the starter

26.6 Bolt (A) secures oil level sensor wiring clamp. Bolts (B) secure sensor

27.2 Location of the starter relay (A). Note the battery lead (B) and starter motor lead (C)

28.2 Location of the starter motor (arrowed)

28.3 Detach the lead from the starter motor terminal (arrowed)

28.4a Unscrew the two bolts . . .

28.4b . . . and draw the starter motor out

28.6 Ensure the new O-ring is correctly seated

28.7 Manoeuvre the starter motor into position

button is pressed with the ignition switched ON. If voltage is present, check the other components in the starter circuit as described in the relevant Sections of this Chapter. If no voltage is present, check the wiring between the various components (see *Wiring Diagrams* at the end of this Chapter).

Renewal

10 Remove the fuel tank (see Chapter 4). Disconnect the battery negative (–) lead.
11 Disconnect the relay wiring connector.
12 Displace the relay and remove the terminal cover. Unscrew the two bolts securing the starter motor and battery leads to the relay and detach the leads, noting which fits where **(see illustration 27.2)**.
13 Installation is the reverse of removal. Ensure the terminal bolts are tightened securely and fit the terminal cover. Clip the starter relay into place on the battery clamp.

28 Starter motor removal and installation

Removal

1 Remove the fuel tank (see Chapter 4). Disconnect the battery negative (–) lead (see Section 3).
2 The starter motor is mounted on the crankcase, behind the cylinder block **(see illustration)**. To gain access, follow the procedure in Chapter 6, Section 19, to remove the front sprocket cover.
3 Peel back the terminal boot and unscrew

the nut securing the lead to the starter motor terminal and detach the lead **(see illustration)**.
4 Unscrew the two bolts securing the starter motor and draw the starter motor out of the crankcase and remove it from the machine **(see illustrations)**.
5 Remove the O-ring on the end of the starter motor and discard it, as a new one must be used.

Installation

6 Fit a new O-ring onto the end of the starter motor, making sure it is seated in its groove, and smear it with grease **(see illustration)**.
7 Manoeuvre the motor into position and slide it into the crankcase **(see illustration)**. Ensure that the starter motor teeth mesh correctly with those of the starter idler gear.
8 Install the mounting bolts and tighten them to the torque setting specified at the beginning of this Chapter.

29.2 Note the alignment marks (A) then unscrew the two bolts, noting the O-rings

9 Connect the lead to the starter motor terminal and secure it with the nut **(see illustration 28.3)**. Make sure the boot is correctly seated over the terminal.
10 Install the front sprocket cover.
11 Connect the battery negative (–) lead and install the fuel tank (see Chapter 4).

29 Starter motor overhaul

Disassembly

1 Remove the starter motor (see Section 28).
2 Note the alignment marks between the main housing and the front and rear covers, or make your own if they are unclear, then unscrew and remove the two long bolts **(see illustration)**.
3 Remove the front cover from the motor **(see illustration)**.

29.3 Remove the front cover and sealing ring (arrowed)

29.4a Remove the tabbed washer . . .

**29.4b . . . and the insulating washer (A)
and shim(s) (B)**

**29.5 Carefully draw the main housing off
the armature**

4 Remove the tabbed washer from inside the cover and slide the insulating washer and shim(s) from the front end of the armature, noting the order in which they are fitted **(see illustrations)**.

5 Holding the armature in place, draw the main housing off, noting that the attraction of the magnets will have to be overcome. Remove the sealing rings and discard them as new ones must be fitted on reassembly **(see illustration)**.

6 Remove the rear cover and brushplate assembly from the armature commutator **(see illustration)**. Remove the shim(s) from the rear end of the armature shaft **(see illustration)**.

7 Noting the order in which they are fitted, unscrew the terminal nut and remove it along with its washer and insulating washers **(see illustration)**.

8 Withdraw the terminal and brushplate assembly from the rear cover and remove the O-ring and square insulating washer from the terminal **(see illustrations)**.

9 Lift the brush springs and slide the brushes out from their holders, noting that one brush is attached to the terminal and the other is attached to the brushplate **(see illustration)**.

Inspection

10 Check the general condition of all the starter motor components. The parts that are most likely to require attention are the brushes. Measure the length of the brushes and compare the results to the brush length listed in this Chapter's Specifications **(see illustration)**. If either of the brushes are worn beyond the service limit, renew the brushplate

**29.6a Draw the rear cover and brushplate
off . . .**

**29.6b . . . and remove the shims from the
end of the shaft**

assembly. If the brushes are not worn excessively, cracked, chipped, or otherwise damaged, they may be re-used.

11 Inspect the commutator bars on the armature for scoring, scratches and

discoloration. The commutator can be cleaned and polished with steel wool, but do not use sandpaper or emery paper. After cleaning, wipe away any residue with a cloth soaked in electrical system cleaner or denatured alcohol.

**29.7 Unscrew the nut (A) and remove the
plain washer (B) and the large and small
insulating washers (C)**

**29.8a Remove the brushplate from the
cover . . .**

**29.8b . . . then remove the O-ring (A) and
insulating washer (B) from the terminal**

**29.9 Move the brush springs aside and
slide the brushes out**

29.10 Measure the length of each brush

29.12 Continuity should exist between the commutator bars

29.13 There should be no continuity between the bars and the armature shaft

29.14 Mica (1) must be the specified depth below the commutator bars (2)

12 Using a multimeter or a continuity tester, check for continuity between the commutator bars **(see illustration)**. Continuity should exist (Yamaha specify 0.0012 to 0.0022 ohms) between each bar and all of the others.

13 Check for continuity between the commutator bars and the armature shaft **(see illustration)**. There should be no continuity (infinite resistance – Yamaha specify a resistance of over 1 M-ohm); if the checks indicate otherwise, the armature is defective.

14 Check the depth of the insulating mica undercut between the commutator bars **(see illustration)** – if it is less than the amount specified at the beginning of this Chapter, scrape the mica away using a suitably shaped hacksaw blade until it is correct.

15 Measure the diameter of the commutator and replace the starter motor with a new one if it has worn below the minimum diameter specified.

16 Check the starter pinion gear for worn, cracked, chipped and broken teeth. If the gear is damaged or worn, replace the starter motor with a new one.

17 Inspect the end covers for signs of cracks or wear. Check the oil seal and needle bearing in the front cover and the bush in the rear cover for wear and damage. Inspect the magnets in the main housing and the housing itself for cracks.

18 Inspect the terminal insulating washers, the O-ring and square insulating washer for signs of damage, and renew them if necessary.

Reassembly

19 Slide the brushes back into their holders

29.23 Fit new O-rings onto the main housing

and place the brush spring ends onto the brushes **(see illustration 29.9)**.

20 Fit the square insulating washer and O-ring onto the terminal and fit the terminal and brushplate assembly into the rear cover **(see illustrations 29.8b and a)**.

21 Fit the insulating washers onto the terminal, followed by the plain washer and nut, and tighten the nut **(see illustration 29.7)**.

22 Slide the shims onto the rear end of the armature shaft **(see illustration 29.6b)**. Lubricate the shaft with a smear of grease, then insert the shaft into the rear cover, locating the brushes on the commutator as you do, taking care not to damage the brushes **(see illustration 29.6a)**. Check that each brush is securely pressed against the commutator by its spring and is free to move easily in its holder.

23 Fit new O-rings onto the main housing, then fit the housing over the armature and onto the rear cover, aligning the marks made on removal – hold the armature to prevent it being drawn out of the rear cover by the attraction of the magnets, and make sure you do not get your fingers caught between the housing and the rear cover as the housing is drawn on **(see illustration and 29.5 and 29.2)**.

24 Slide the shims and then the insulating washer onto the front end of the armature shaft and lubricate the shaft with a smear of grease **(see illustration 29.4b)**. Apply a smear of grease to the inside of the front cover oil seal. Fit the tabbed washer into the cover,

30.5 Checking the electrical system leakage rate – connect the meter as shown

making sure the tabs locate correctly **(see illustrations 29.4a)**. Fit the cover onto the main housing, aligning the marks made on removal **(see illustration 29.3)**.

25 Check that the marks on the rear cover, main housing and front cover are correctly aligned, then install the bolts and tighten them to the specified torque setting **(see illustration 29.2)**.

26 Install the starter motor (see Section 28).

30 Charging system testing

1 If the performance of the charging system is suspect, the system as a whole should be checked first, followed by testing of the individual components. **Note:** *Before beginning the checks, make sure the battery is fully charged and that all system connections are clean and tight.*

2 Checking the output of the charging system and the performance of the various components within the charging system requires the use of a multimeter (with voltage, current and resistance checking facilities). If a multimeter is not available, the job of checking the charging system should be left to a Yamaha dealer or automotive electrician.

3 When making the checks, follow the procedures carefully to prevent incorrect connections or short circuits, as irreparable damage to electrical system components may result if short circuits occur.

Leakage test

Caution: Always connect an ammeter in series, never in parallel with the battery, otherwise it will be damaged. Do not turn the ignition ON or operate the starter motor when the ammeter is connected – a sudden surge in current will blow the meter's fuse.

4 Turn the ignition switch OFF. Remove the fuel tank (see Chapter 4). Disconnect the lead from the battery negative (–) terminal (see Section 3).

5 Set the multimeter to the Amps function and connect its negative (–) probe to the battery negative (–) terminal, and positive (+) probe to the disconnected negative (–) lead **(see illustration)**. Always set the meter to

30.9 Checking the regulated voltage output – connect the meter as shown

31.2 Alternator wiring connector

31.6 Note the location of the wiring guide (arrowed)

a high amps range initially and then bring it down to the mA (milli Amps) range; if there is a high current flow in the circuit it may blow the meter's fuse.

6 No current flow should be indicated. If current leakage is indicated (generally greater than 1mA, but may be more if an alarm is fitted), there is a short circuit in the wiring. Using the wiring diagrams at the end of this Chapter, systematically disconnect individual electrical components, checking the meter each time until the source is identified.

7 If no leakage is indicated, disconnect the meter and connect the negative (–) lead to the battery, tightening it securely.

Output test

8 Start the engine and warm it up to normal operating temperature. Raise the fuel tank and support it temporarily to allow access to the battery terminals (see Chapter 4).

9 To check the regulated voltage output, allow the engine to idle and connect a multimeter set to the 0 to 20 volts DC scale (voltmeter) across the terminals of the battery, positive (+) lead to battery positive (+) terminal, negative (–) lead to battery negative (–) terminal **(see illustration)**. Slowly increase the engine speed to 5000 rpm and note the reading obtained.

10 The regulated voltage should be as specified at the beginning of this Chapter. If the voltage is outside these limits, check the alternator, then the regulator/rectifier (see Sections 31 and 32).

31.7 Note the rotor bolt washer (arrowed) – a new one must be fitted on installation

11 Stop the engine and disconnect the test meter.

31 Alternator rotor and stator

Check

1 Remove the fuel tank (see Chapter 4).

2 Trace the wiring from the top of the alternator cover on the left-hand side of the engine and disconnect it at the white connector containing the three white wires **(see illustration)**.

3 Using a multimeter set to the ohms x 1 (ohmmeter) scale, measure the resistance between the centre wire and each of the other two on the alternator side of the connector, then between the outer two wires, taking a total of three readings, then check for continuity between each terminal and ground (earth). If the stator coil windings are in good condition the resistance readings should be within the range shown in *Specifications* at the beginning of this Chapter and there should be no continuity (infinite resistance) between the terminals and ground (earth). If not, check the fault is not due to damaged wiring between the connector and coils. If the wiring is good, the alternator stator coil assembly is at fault and should be replaced with a new one.

Removal

Special Tool: *A centre-bolt type puller is*

31.8 Removing the rotor using a commercially available puller

essential for removal of the alternator rotor from the crankshaft.

4 Remove the fuel tank (see Chapter 4). Remove the front sprocket cover (see Chapter 6).

5 Trace the wiring from the top of the alternator cover on the left-hand side of the engine and disconnect it at the white connector containing the three white wires **(see illustration 31.2)**. Free the wiring from any clips or guides and feed it through to the alternator cover.

6 Place a drain tray under the alternator cover. Working in a criss-cross pattern, unscrew the bolts securing the alternator cover and the wiring guide **(see illustration)**. Remove the cover, being prepared to catch any residual oil. If the cover will not lift away easily, break the gasket seal by tapping gently around the edge with a soft-faced hammer or block of wood. Note the dowels in the cover or the crankcase, and remove them if they are loose. Discard the gasket, as a new one must be used on reassembly.

7 To remove the rotor bolt it is necessary to stop the rotor from turning. This is best achieved using a rotor holding tool (Yamaha Part No. 90890-01701 or YS-01880-A). Alternatively there are several commercially available types **(see illustration 31.13)**. Keep the tool strap away from any raised projections on the rotor. If a rotor holding tool is not available and the engine is still in the frame, place the transmission in gear and have an assistant apply the rear brake. Unscrew the rotor bolt and remove the washer **(see illustration)**. Discard the washer as a new one should be used.

8 To remove the rotor from the shaft it is necessary to use a rotor puller. Yamaha provide a special tool (Part Nos. 90890-01362 and 90890-04089 or YU-33270 and YM-33282). Alternatively a similar tool can be obtained commercially **(see illustration)**. **Note:** *The rotor has three threaded holes designed to accept the bolts of the puller.*

9 To remove the stator, undo the screw securing the wiring clamp and the three screws securing the stator to the inside of the cover, then remove the assembly, noting how

31.9 Alternator stator bolts (A), wiring clamp bolt (B) and wiring grommet (C)

31.12 Slide the rotor onto the crankshaft

the wiring grommet locates in the edge of the cover **(see illustration)**.

Installation

10 Install the stator, aligning the wiring grommet with the recess in the alternator cover **(see illustration 31.9)**. Apply a suitable non-permanent thread locking compound to the stator screw threads, then install the

31.13 Tighten the rotor bolt to the specified torque

screws and tighten them to the torque setting specified at the beginning of this Chapter.
11 Apply a suitable sealant to the wiring grommet, then press it into the recess in the cover and secure the wiring with the clamp.
12 Clean the tapered end of the crankshaft and the corresponding mating surface on the inside of the rotor with a suitable solvent. Make sure that no metal objects have attached themselves to the magnet on the inside of the rotor, then slide the rotor onto the shaft **(see illustration)**.
13 Apply some clean engine oil to the rotor bolt threads and fit a new washer onto the bolt. Use the method employed on removal to prevent the rotor from turning and tighten the bolt to the torque setting specified at the beginning of this Chapter **(see illustration)**.
14 If removed, install the dowels in the crankcase, then fit the new gasket, making sure it locates onto the dowels **(see illustration)**.
15 Install the alternator cover, making sure the starter idle gear shaft locates in its bore

(see illustration). Tighten the cover bolts evenly in a criss-cross pattern to the specified torque setting, not forgetting the wiring guide **(see illustration 31.6)**.
16 Feed the wiring to the connector, making sure it is correctly routed and secured by any cable-ties **(see illustration 31.2)**.
17 Install the front sprocket cover (see Chapter 6) and the fuel tank (see Chapter 4). Top-up the engine with oil to the correct level (see *Pre-ride checks*).

32 Regulator/rectifier

Check

1 Yamaha provide no test specifications for the regulator/rectifier other than the charging system output test (see Section 30). If the regulator/rectifier is suspected of being faulty, first check all other components and the wiring and connectors in the charging

31.14 Ensure the cover gasket locates on the dowels (arrowed)

31.15 Ensure idle gear shaft (A) locates in bore (B)

32.4a Undo the mounting screws (arrowed) . . .

32.4b . . . and lift the regulator/rectifier out

32.5a Release the wiring clip (A) and wiring connector catch (B) . . .

32.5b . . . then disconnect the wiring connector

32.8a Locate the tab over the pin (arrowed) . . .

32.8b . . . then install the mounting screws. Note the mounting bush (arrowed)

circuit, referring to the relevant Sections in this Chapter and to the *Wiring Diagrams* at the end.

2 If all other components and the wiring are good, remove the unit (see below) and take it to a Yamaha dealer for testing. Alternatively, substitute the suspect unit with a known good one and see if the fault is cured.

Renewal

3 The regulator/rectifier is mounted to the frame underneath the rear mounting for the fuel tank – remove the tank for access (see Chapter 4).

4 Undo the regulator/rectifier mounting screws and draw the assembly out, noting how it fits **(see illustrations)**.

5 Release the wiring from the clip on the mounting bracket, then release the catch and disconnect the wiring connector **(see illustrations)**.

6 Unscrew the two bolts securing the regulator/rectifier to its bracket.

7 Prior to installation, check the mounting bushes in the frame – if they are worn or perished, replace them with new ones **(see illustration 32.8b)**.

8 Installation is the reverse of removal. Ensure that the tab on the regulator/rectifier bracket locates on the pin on the frame, then tighten the mounting screws securely **(see illustrations)**.

Instruments FZ6-S2

Ignition switch

Oil level switch

Engine stop switch

Start switch

Front brake switch

ON OFF PARK

OFF RUN

FREE PUSH

Alarm (optional equipment)

Instruments FZ6-N

Immobiliser

(FZ6-N) Blue/yellow

(2004-06) Yellow

S2 only

Headlight relay

Right hand turn signal

Headlight

Sidelight

Left hand turn signal

Horn

Fan relay

Horn switch	Turn signal switch	Hazard switch	Dimmer switch	Clutch switch	Passing switch	Fan motor	Coolant temperature sensor	Intake air temperature sensor	Intake air pressure sensor	Throttle position sensor	Injectors
OFF ON	LEFT OFF RIGHT	OFF ON	HI LO		OFF ON	M					1 2 3 4

Europe FZ6-N and FZ6 S2

DS
H33689

Ignition HT coils
Cyl 1 & 4   Cyl 2 & 3

Spark plugs

Rear brake switch

Fuel level sensor   Fuel pump

Tip-over sensor   Oxygen sensor

Fuse and relay key
A	Headlight	20A
B	Horn, brake lights	10A
C	Ignition	10A
D	Cooling fan	20A
E	Backup	10A
F	Fuel injection	10A
G	Turn signals	10A
H	Main	30A
J	Fuel pump relay	
K	Starter circuit cut-off relay	

2007 on

Relays and diodes

2007 on

(FZ6-N models)
Blue/yellow

Engine control unit

Right hand turn signal

Brake / tail light

Left hand turn signal

Licence plate light

Starter relay

Fusebox
A B C   D   E   F   G

Turn signal relay

Air cut-off valve

Crankshaft position sensor

Speed sensor

Neutral switch

Sidestand switch

Regulator/ rectifier

Alternator

Starter motor

Battery

Europe FZ6-N and FZ6 S2

H33689

Instruments - FZ6-SA2

Ignition switch

ON	
OFF	
PARK	

Oil level switch

Engine stop switch

| OFF | |
| RUN | |

Start switch

| FREE | |
| PUSH | |

Front brake switch

Instruments - FZ6-NA

Immobiliser

Alarm (optional equipment)

Yellow (fuel)

Right hand turn signal

Headlight

Sidelight

Left hand turn signal

Horn

Headlight relay

Fan relay

| OFF | |
| ON | |

Horn switch

LEFT	
OFF	
RIGT	

Turn signal switch

| OFF | |
| ON | |

Hazard switch

| HI | |
| LO | |

Dimmer switch

Clutch switch

| OFF | |
| ON | |

Passing switch

Fan motor

Coolant temperature sensor

Intake air temperature sensor

Intake air pressure sensor

Throttle position sensor

1 2 3 4

Injectors

Europe FZ6 NA and FZ6 SA2

DS
H8

Europe FZ6 NA and FZ6 SA2

Instruments FZ Fazer S

Ignition switch

Diesel switch

Engine stop switch

Start switch

Front brake switch

Alarm (optional equipment)

Immobiliser

Instruments FZ

S only

Right hand turn signal

Sidelight

Headlight low beam

(06 model) Yellow

Headlight high beam

Sidelight

Left hand turn signal

Horn

Headlight relay

Fan relay

OFF	ON		
Horn switch	Turn signal switch	Hazard switch	Dimmer switch	Clutch switch	Passing switch

Fan motor

Coolant temperature sensor

Intake air temperature sensor

Intake air pressure sensor

Throttle position sensor

Injectors 1 2 3 4

Europe FZ6-S and FZ6 Fazer S2

Europe FZ6-S and FZ6 Fazer S2

H33691

Europe FZ6-SA and FZ6 Fazer SA2

Europe FZ6-SA and FZ6 Fazer SA2

H33692

Instruments FZ6-S2

Ignition switch

Diesel switch

Engine stop switch

Start switch

Front brake switch

OFF / ON

OFF / RUN

FREE / PUSH

Instruments FZ6-S

(2007 on) Black/red

2008 only

(2008 on) Black/yellow

Right hand turn signal

Headlight relay

Headlight low beam

Headlight high beam

Left hand turn signal

Fan relay

Horn

Horn switch	Turn signal switch	Hazard switch	Dimmer switch	Clutch switch	Fan motor	Coolant temperature sensor	Intake air temperature sensor	Intake air pressure sensor	Throttle position sensor	Injectors
OFF / ON	LEFT / OFF / RIGHT	OFF / ON	HI / LO		M					1 2 3 4

US models FZ6-S

US models FZ6-S

H33693

Reference

Buying tools

A toolkit is a fundamental requirement for servicing and repairing a motorcycle. Although there will be an initial expense in building up enough tools for servicing, this will soon be offset by the savings made by doing the job yourself. As experience and confidence grow, additional tools can be added to enable the repair and overhaul of the motorcycle. Many of the specialist tools are expensive and not often used so it may be preferable to hire them, or for a group of friends or motorcycle club to join in the purchase.

As a rule, it is better to buy more expensive, good quality tools. Cheaper tools are likely to wear out faster and need to be renewed more often, nullifying the original saving.

> ⚠ **Warning: To avoid the risk of a poor quality tool breaking in use, causing injury or damage to the component being worked on, always aim to purchase tools which meet the relevant national safety standards.**

The following lists of tools do not represent the manufacturer's service tools, but serve as a guide to help the owner decide which tools are needed for this level of work. In addition, items such as an electric drill, hacksaw, files, soldering iron and a workbench equipped with a vice, may be needed. Although not classed as tools, a selection of bolts, screws, nuts, washers and pieces of tubing always come in useful.

For more information about tools, refer to the Haynes *Motorcycle Workshop Practice Techbook* (Bk. No. 3470).

Manufacturer's service tools

Inevitably certain tasks require the use of a service tool. Where possible an alternative tool or method of approach is recommended, but sometimes there is no option if personal injury or damage to the component is to be avoided. Where required, service tools are referred to in the relevant procedure.

Service tools can usually only be purchased from a motorcycle dealer and are identified by a part number. Some of the commonly-used tools, such as rotor pullers, are available in aftermarket form from mail-order motorcycle tool and accessory suppliers.

Maintenance and minor repair tools

1 Set of flat-bladed screwdrivers
2 Set of Phillips head screwdrivers
3 Combination open-end and ring spanners
4 Socket set (3/8 inch or 1/2 inch drive)
5 Set of Allen keys or bits

6 Set of Torx keys or bits
7 Pliers, cutters and self-locking grips (Mole grips)
8 Adjustable spanners
9 C-spanners
10 Tread depth gauge and tyre pressure gauge

11 Cable oiler clamp
12 Feeler gauges
13 Spark plug gap measuring tool
14 Spark plug spanner or deep plug sockets
15 Wire brush and emery paper

16 Calibrated syringe, measuring vessel and funnel
17 Oil filter adapters
18 Oil drainer can or tray
19 Pump type oil can
20 Grease gun

21 Straight-edge and steel rule
22 Continuity tester
23 Battery charger
24 Hydrometer (for battery specific gravity check)
25 Anti-freeze tester (for liquid-cooled engines)

Repair and overhaul tools

1 Torque wrench
  (small and mid-ranges)
2 Conventional, plastic or
  soft-faced hammers
3 Impact driver set

4 Vernier gauge
5 Circlip pliers (internal and
  external, or combination)
6 Set of cold chisels
  and punches

7 Selection of pullers
8 Breaker bars
9 Chain breaking/
  riveting tool set

10 Wire stripper and
   crimper tool
11 Multimeter (measures
   amps, volts and ohms)
12 Stroboscope (for
   dynamic timing checks)

13 Hose clamp
   (wingnut type shown)
14 Clutch holding tool
15 One-man brake/clutch
   bleeder kit

Specialist tools

1 Micrometers
  (external type)
2 Telescoping gauges
3 Dial gauge

4 Cylinder
  compression gauge
5 Vacuum gauges (left) or
  manometer (right)
6 Oil pressure gauge

7 Plastigauge kit
8 Valve spring compressor
  (4-stroke engines)
9 Piston pin drawbolt tool

10 Piston ring removal and
   installation tool
11 Piston ring clamp
12 Cylinder bore hone
   (stone type shown)

13 Stud extractor
14 Screw extractor set
15 Bearing driver set

1 Workshop equipment and facilities

The workbench

● Work is made much easier by raising the bike up on a ramp - components are much more accessible if raised to waist level. The hydraulic or pneumatic types seen in the dealer's workshop are a sound investment if you undertake a lot of repairs or overhauls (see illustration 1.1).

1.1 Hydraulic motorcycle ramp

● If raised off ground level, the bike must be supported on the ramp to avoid it falling. Most ramps incorporate a front wheel locating clamp which can be adjusted to suit different diameter wheels. When tightening the clamp, take care not to mark the wheel rim or damage the tyre - use wood blocks on each side to prevent this.
● Secure the bike to the ramp using tie-downs (see illustration 1.2). If the bike has only a sidestand, and hence leans at a dangerous angle when raised, support the bike on an auxiliary stand.

1.2 Tie-downs are used around the passenger footrests to secure the bike

● Auxiliary (paddock) stands are widely available from mail order companies or motorcycle dealers and attach either to the wheel axle or swingarm pivot (see illustration 1.3). If the motorcycle has a centrestand, you can support it under the crankcase to prevent it toppling whilst either wheel is removed (see illustration 1.4).

1.3 This auxiliary stand attaches to the swingarm pivot

1.4 Always use a block of wood between the engine and jack head when supporting the engine in this way

Fumes and fire

● Refer to the Safety first! page at the beginning of the manual for full details. Make sure your workshop is equipped with a fire extinguisher suitable for fuel-related fires (Class B fire - flammable liquids) - it is not sufficient to have a water-filled extinguisher.
● Always ensure adequate ventilation is available. Unless an exhaust gas extraction system is available for use, ensure that the engine is run outside of the workshop.
● If working on the fuel system, make sure the workshop is ventilated to avoid a build-up of fumes. This applies equally to fume build-up when charging a battery. Do not smoke or allow anyone else to smoke in the workshop.

Fluids

● If you need to drain fuel from the tank, store it in an approved container marked as suitable for the storage of petrol (gasoline) (see illustration 1.5). Do not store fuel in glass jars or bottles.

1.5 Use an approved can only for storing petrol (gasoline)

● Use proprietary engine degreasers or solvents which have a high flash-point, such as paraffin (kerosene), for cleaning off oil, grease and dirt - never use petrol (gasoline) for cleaning. Wear rubber gloves when handling solvent and engine degreaser. The fumes from certain solvents can be dangerous - always work in a well-ventilated area.

Dust, eye and hand protection

● Protect your lungs from inhalation of dust particles by wearing a filtering mask over the nose and mouth. Many frictional materials still contain asbestos which is dangerous to your health. Protect your eyes from spouts of liquid and sprung components by wearing a pair of protective goggles (see illustration 1.6).

1.6 A fire extinguisher, goggles, mask and protective gloves should be at hand in the workshop

● Protect your hands from contact with solvents, fuel and oils by wearing rubber gloves. Alternatively apply a barrier cream to your hands before starting work. If handling hot components or fluids, wear suitable gloves to protect your hands from scalding and burns.

What to do with old fluids

● Old cleaning solvent, fuel, coolant and oils should not be poured down domestic drains or onto the ground. Package the fluid up in old oil containers, label it accordingly, and take it to a garage or disposal facility. Contact your local authority for location of such sites or ring the oil care hotline.

OIL CARE

OIL BANK LINE
0800 66 33 66
www.oilbankline.org.uk

Note: It is antisocial and illegal to dump oil down the drain. To find the location of your local oil recycling bank, call this number free.

In the USA, note that any oil supplier must accept used oil for recycling.

2 Fasteners -
screws, bolts and nuts

Fastener types and applications

Bolts and screws

● Fastener head types are either of hexagonal, Torx or splined design, with internal and external versions of each type **(see illustrations 2.1 and 2.2)**; splined head fasteners are not in common use on motorcycles. The conventional slotted or Phillips head design is used for certain screws. Bolt or screw length is always measured from the underside of the head to the end of the item **(see illustration 2.11)**.

2.1 Internal hexagon/Allen (A), Torx (B) and splined (C) fasteners, with corresponding bits

2.2 External Torx (A), splined (B) and hexagon (C) fasteners, with corresponding sockets

● Certain fasteners on the motorcycle have a tensile marking on their heads, the higher the marking the stronger the fastener. High tensile fasteners generally carry a 10 or higher marking. Never replace a high tensile fastener with one of a lower tensile strength.

Washers (see illustration 2.3)

● Plain washers are used between a fastener head and a component to prevent damage to the component or to spread the load when torque is applied. Plain washers can also be used as spacers or shims in certain assemblies. Copper or aluminium plain washers are often used as sealing washers on drain plugs.

2.3 Plain washer (A), penny washer (B), spring washer (C) and serrated washer (D)

● The split-ring spring washer works by applying axial tension between the fastener head and component. If flattened, it is fatigued and must be renewed. If a plain (flat) washer is used on the fastener, position the spring washer between the fastener and the plain washer.

● Serrated star type washers dig into the fastener and component faces, preventing loosening. They are often used on electrical earth (ground) connections to the frame.

● Cone type washers (sometimes called Belleville) are conical and when tightened apply axial tension between the fastener head and component. They must be installed with the dished side against the component and often carry an OUTSIDE marking on their outer face. If flattened, they are fatigued and must be renewed.

● Tab washers are used to lock plain nuts or bolts on a shaft. A portion of the tab washer is bent up hard against one flat of the nut or bolt to prevent it loosening. Due to the tab washer being deformed in use, a new tab washer should be used every time it is disturbed.

● Wave washers are used to take up endfloat on a shaft. They provide light springing and prevent excessive side-to-side play of a component. Can be found on rocker arm shafts.

Nuts and split pins

● Conventional plain nuts are usually six-sided **(see illustration 2.4)**. They are sized by thread diameter and pitch. High tensile nuts carry a number on one end to denote their tensile strength.

2.4 Plain nut (A), shouldered locknut (B), nylon insert nut (C) and castellated nut (D)

● Self-locking nuts either have a nylon insert, or two spring metal tabs, or a shoulder which is staked into a groove in the shaft - their advantage over conventional plain nuts is a resistance to loosening due to vibration. The nylon insert type can be used a number of times, but must be renewed when the friction of the nylon insert is reduced, ie when the nut spins freely on the shaft. The spring tab type can be reused unless the tabs are damaged. The shouldered type must be renewed every time it is disturbed.

● Split pins (cotter pins) are used to lock a castellated nut to a shaft or to prevent slackening of a plain nut. Common applications are wheel axles and brake torque arms. Because the split pin arms are deformed to lock around the nut a new split pin must always be used on installation - always fit the correct size split pin which will fit snugly in the shaft hole. Make sure the split pin arms are correctly located around the nut **(see illustrations 2.5 and 2.6)**.

2.5 Bend split pin (cotter pin) arms as shown (arrows) to secure a castellated nut

2.6 Bend split pin (cotter pin) arms as shown to secure a plain nut

Caution: If the castellated nut slots do not align with the shaft hole after tightening to the torque setting, tighten the nut until the next slot aligns with the hole - never slacken the nut to align its slot.

● R-pins (shaped like the letter R), or slip pins as they are sometimes called, are sprung and can be reused if they are otherwise in good condition. Always install R-pins with their closed end facing forwards **(see illustration 2.7)**.

2.7 Correct fitting of R-pin. Arrow indicates forward direction

Circlips (see illustration 2.8)

● Circlips (sometimes called snap-rings) are used to retain components on a shaft or in a housing and have corresponding external or internal ears to permit removal. Parallel-sided (machined) circlips can be installed either way round in their groove, whereas stamped circlips (which have a chamfered edge on one face) must be installed with the chamfer facing away from the direction of thrust load **(see illustration 2.9)**.

2.8 External stamped circlip (A), internal stamped circlip (B), machined circlip (C) and wire circlip (D)

● Always use circlip pliers to remove and install circlips; expand or compress them just enough to remove them. After installation, rotate the circlip in its groove to ensure it is securely seated. If installing a circlip on a splined shaft, always align its opening with a shaft channel to ensure the circlip ends are well supported and unlikely to catch **(see illustration 2.10)**.

2.9 Correct fitting of a stamped circlip

THRUST LOAD

THRUST WASHER

SHARP EDGE

CHAMFERED EDGE

0650H

2.10 Align circlip opening with shaft channel

● Circlips can wear due to the thrust of components and become loose in their grooves, with the subsequent danger of becoming dislodged in operation. For this reason, renewal is advised every time a circlip is disturbed.
● Wire circlips are commonly used as piston pin retaining clips. If a removal tang is provided, long-nosed pliers can be used to dislodge them, otherwise careful use of a small flat-bladed screwdriver is necessary. Wire circlips should be renewed every time they are disturbed.

Thread diameter and pitch

● Diameter of a male thread (screw, bolt or stud) is the outside diameter of the threaded portion **(see illustration 2.11)**. Most motorcycle manufacturers use the ISO (International Standards Organisation) metric system expressed in millimetres, eg M6 refers to a 6 mm diameter thread. Sizing is the same for nuts, except that the thread diameter is measured across the valleys of the nut.
● Pitch is the distance between the peaks of the thread **(see illustration 2.11)**. It is expressed in millimetres, thus a common bolt size may be expressed as 6.0 x 1.0 mm (6 mm thread diameter and 1 mm pitch). Generally pitch increases in proportion to thread diameter, although there are always exceptions.
● Thread diameter and pitch are related for conventional fastener applications and the accompanying table can be used as a guide. Additionally, the AF (Across Flats), spanner or socket size dimension of the bolt or nut **(see illustration 2.11)** is linked to thread and pitch specification. Thread pitch can be measured with a thread gauge **(see illustration 2.12)**.

2.11 Fastener length (L), thread diameter (D), thread pitch (P) and head size (AF)

AF

L

D

P

2.12 Using a thread gauge to measure pitch

AF size	Thread diameter x pitch (mm)
8 mm	M5 x 0.8
8 mm	M6 x 1.0
10 mm	M6 x 1.0
12 mm	M8 x 1.25
14 mm	M10 x 1.25
17 mm	M12 x 1.25

● The threads of most fasteners are of the right-hand type, ie they are turned clockwise to tighten and anti-clockwise to loosen. The reverse situation applies to left-hand thread fasteners, which are turned anti-clockwise to tighten and clockwise to loosen. Left-hand threads are used where rotation of a component might loosen a conventional right-hand thread fastener.

Seized fasteners

● Corrosion of external fasteners due to water or reaction between two dissimilar metals can occur over a period of time. It will build up sooner in wet conditions or in countries where salt is used on the roads during the winter. If a fastener is severely corroded it is likely that normal methods of removal will fail and result in its head being ruined. When you attempt removal, the fastener thread should be heard to crack free and unscrew easily - if it doesn't, stop there before damaging something.
● A smart tap on the head of the fastener will often succeed in breaking free corrosion which has occurred in the threads **(see illustration 2.13)**.
● An aerosol penetrating fluid (such as WD-40) applied the night beforehand may work its way down into the thread and ease removal. Depending on the location, you may be able to make up a Plasticine well around the fastener head and fill it with penetrating fluid.

2.13 A sharp tap on the head of a fastener will often break free a corroded thread

● If you are working on an engine internal component, corrosion will most likely not be a problem due to the well lubricated environment. However, components can be very tight and an impact driver is a useful tool in freeing them **(see illustration 2.14)**.

2.14 Using an impact driver to free a fastener

● Where corrosion has occurred between dissimilar metals (eg steel and aluminium alloy), the application of heat to the fastener head will create a disproportionate expansion rate between the two metals and break the seizure caused by the corrosion. Whether heat can be applied depends on the location of the fastener - any surrounding components likely to be damaged must first be removed **(see illustration 2.15)**. Heat can be applied using a paint stripper heat gun or clothes iron, or by immersing the component in boiling water - wear protective gloves to prevent scalding or burns to the hands.

2.15 Using heat to free a seized fastener

● As a last resort, it is possible to use a hammer and cold chisel to work the fastener head unscrewed **(see illustration 2.16)**. This will damage the fastener, but more importantly extreme care must be taken not to damage the surrounding component.

Caution: Remember that the component being secured is generally of more value than the bolt, nut or screw - when the fastener is freed, do not unscrew it with force, instead work the fastener back and forth when resistance is felt to prevent thread damage.

2.16 Using a hammer and chisel to free a seized fastener

Broken fasteners and damaged heads

● If the shank of a broken bolt or screw is accessible you can grip it with self-locking grips. The knurled wheel type stud extractor tool or self-gripping stud puller tool is particularly useful for removing the long studs which screw into the cylinder mouth surface of the crankcase or bolts and screws from which the head has broken off **(see illustration 2.17)**. Studs can also be removed by locking two nuts together on the threaded end of the stud and using a spanner on the lower nut **(see illustration 2.18)**.

2.17 Using a stud extractor tool to remove a broken crankcase stud

2.18 Two nuts can be locked together to unscrew a stud from a component

● A bolt or screw which has broken off below or level with the casing must be extracted using a screw extractor set. Centre punch the fastener to centralise the drill bit, then drill a hole in the fastener **(see illustration 2.19)**. Select a drill bit which is approximately half to three-quarters the

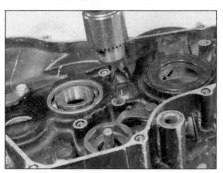

2.19 When using a screw extractor, first drill a hole in the fastener . . .

diameter of the fastener and drill to a depth which will accommodate the extractor. Use the largest size extractor possible, but avoid leaving too small a wall thickness otherwise the extractor will merely force the fastener walls outwards wedging it in the casing thread.

● If a spiral type extractor is used, thread it anti-clockwise into the fastener. As it is screwed in, it will grip the fastener and unscrew it from the casing **(see illustration 2.20)**.

2.20 . . . then thread the extractor anti-clockwise into the fastener

● If a taper type extractor is used, tap it into the fastener so that it is firmly wedged in place. Unscrew the extractor (anti-clockwise) to draw the fastener out.

> *Warning: Stud extractors are very hard and may break off in the fastener if care is not taken - ask an engineer about spark erosion if this happens.*

● Alternatively, the broken bolt/screw can be drilled out and the hole retapped for an oversize bolt/screw or a diamond-section thread insert. It is essential that the drilling is carried out squarely and to the correct depth, otherwise the casing may be ruined - if in doubt, entrust the work to an engineer.

● Bolts and nuts with rounded corners cause the correct size spanner or socket to slip when force is applied. Of the types of spanner/socket available always use a six-point type rather than an eight or twelve-point type - better grip

2.21 Comparison of surface drive ring spanner (left) with 12-point type (right)

is obtained. Surface drive spanners grip the middle of the hex flats, rather than the corners, and are thus good in cases of damaged heads **(see illustration 2.21)**.

● Slotted-head or Phillips-head screws are often damaged by the use of the wrong size screwdriver. Allen-head and Torx-head screws are much less likely to sustain damage. If enough of the screw head is exposed you can use a hacksaw to cut a slot in its head and then use a conventional flat-bladed screwdriver to remove it. Alternatively use a hammer and cold chisel to tap the head of the fastener around to slacken it. Always replace damaged fasteners with new ones, preferably Torx or Allen-head type.

A dab of valve grinding compound between the screw head and screw-driver tip will often give a good grip.

Thread repair

● Threads (particularly those in aluminium alloy components) can be damaged by overtightening, being assembled with dirt in the threads, or from a component working loose and vibrating. Eventually the thread will fail completely, and it will be impossible to tighten the fastener.

● If a thread is damaged or clogged with old locking compound it can be renovated with a thread repair tool (thread chaser) **(see illustrations 2.22 and 2.23)**; special thread

2.22 A thread repair tool being used to correct an internal thread

2.23 A thread repair tool being used to correct an external thread

chasers are available for spark plug hole threads. The tool will not cut a new thread, but clean and true the original thread. Make sure that you use the correct diameter and pitch tool. Similarly, external threads can be cleaned up with a die or a thread restorer file **(see illustration 2.24)**.

2.24 Using a thread restorer file

● It is possible to drill out the old thread and retap the component to the next thread size. This will work where there is enough surrounding material and a new bolt or screw can be obtained. Sometimes, however, this is not possible - such as where the bolt/screw passes through another component which must also be suitably modified, also in cases where a spark plug or oil drain plug cannot be obtained in a larger diameter thread size.

● The diamond-section thread insert (often known by its popular trade name of Heli-Coil) is a simple and effective method of renewing the thread and retaining the original size. A kit can be purchased which contains the tap, insert and installing tool **(see illustration 2.25)**. Drill out the damaged thread with the size drill specified **(see illustration 2.26)**. Carefully retap the thread **(see illustration 2.27)**. Install the

2.25 Obtain a thread insert kit to suit the thread diameter and pitch required

2.26 To install a thread insert, first drill out the original thread . . .

2.27 . . . tap a new thread . . .

2.28 . . . fit insert on the installing tool . . .

2.29 . . . and thread into the component . . .

2.30 . . . break off the tang when complete

insert on the installing tool and thread it slowly into place using a light downward pressure **(see illustrations 2.28 and 2.29)**. When positioned between a 1/4 and 1/2 turn below the surface withdraw the installing tool and use the break-off tool to press down on the tang, breaking it off **(see illustration 2.30)**.

● There are epoxy thread repair kits on the market which can rebuild stripped internal threads, although this repair should not be used on high load-bearing components.

Thread locking and sealing compounds

● Locking compounds are used in locations where the fastener is prone to loosening due to vibration or on important safety-related items which might cause loss of control of the motorcycle if they fail. It is also used where important fasteners cannot be secured by other means such as lockwashers or split pins.

● Before applying locking compound, make sure that the threads (internal and external) are clean and dry with all old compound removed. Select a compound to suit the component being secured - a non-permanent general locking and sealing type is suitable for most applications, but a high strength type is needed for permanent fixing of studs in castings. Apply a drop or two of the compound to the first few threads of the fastener, then thread it into place and tighten to the specified torque. Do not apply excessive thread locking compound otherwise the thread may be damaged on subsequent removal.

● Certain fasteners are impregnated with a dry film type coating of locking compound on their threads. Always renew this type of fastener if disturbed.

● Anti-seize compounds, such as copper-based greases, can be applied to protect threads from seizure due to extreme heat and corrosion. A common instance is spark plug threads and exhaust system fasteners.

3 Measuring tools and gauges

Feeler gauges

● Feeler gauges (or blades) are used for measuring small gaps and clearances (see illustration 3.1). They can also be used to measure endfloat (sideplay) of a component on a shaft where access is not possible with a dial gauge.

● Feeler gauge sets should be treated with care and not bent or damaged. They are etched with their size on one face. Keep them clean and very lightly oiled to prevent corrosion build-up.

3.1 Feeler gauges are used for measuring small gaps and clearances - thickness is marked on one face of gauge

● When measuring a clearance, select a gauge which is a light sliding fit between the two components. You may need to use two gauges together to measure the clearance accurately.

Micrometers

● A micrometer is a precision tool capable of measuring to 0.01 or 0.001 of a millimetre. It should always be stored in its case and not in the general toolbox. It must be kept clean and never dropped, otherwise its frame or measuring anvils could be distorted resulting in inaccurate readings.

● External micrometers are used for measuring outside diameters of components and have many more applications than internal micrometers. Micrometers are available in different size ranges, eg 0 to 25 mm, 25 to 50 mm, and upwards in 25 mm steps; some large micrometers have interchangeable anvils to allow a range of measurements to be taken. Generally the largest precision measurement you are likely to take on a motorcycle is the piston diameter.

● Internal micrometers (or bore micrometers) are used for measuring inside diameters, such as valve guides and cylinder bores. Telescoping gauges and small hole gauges are used in conjunction with an external micrometer, whereas the more expensive internal micrometers have their own measuring device.

External micrometer

Note: *The conventional analogue type instrument is described. Although much easier to read, digital micrometers are considerably more expensive.*

● Always check the calibration of the micrometer before use. With the anvils closed (0 to 25 mm type) or set over a test gauge (for

3.2 Check micrometer calibration before use

the larger types) the scale should read zero (see illustration 3.2); make sure that the anvils (and test piece) are clean first. Any discrepancy can be adjusted by referring to the instructions supplied with the tool. Remember that the micrometer is a precision measuring tool - don't force the anvils closed, use the ratchet (4) on the end of the micrometer to close it. In this way, a measured force is always applied.

● To use, first make sure that the item being measured is clean. Place the anvil of the micrometer (1) against the item and use the thimble (2) to bring the spindle (3) lightly into contact with the other side of the item (see illustration 3.3). Don't tighten the thimble down because this will damage the micrometer - instead use the ratchet (4) on the end of the micrometer. The ratchet mechanism applies a measured force preventing damage to the instrument.

● The micrometer is read by referring to the linear scale on the sleeve and the annular scale on the thimble. Read off the sleeve first to obtain the base measurement, then add the fine measurement from the thimble to obtain the overall reading. The linear scale on the sleeve represents the measuring range of the micrometer (eg 0 to 25 mm). The annular scale

3.3 Micrometer component parts

1 Anvil	3 Spindle	5 Frame
2 Thimble	4 Ratchet	6 Locking lever

on the thimble will be in graduations of 0.01 mm (or as marked on the frame) - one full revolution of the thimble will move 0.5 mm on the linear scale. Take the reading where the datum line on the sleeve intersects the thimble's scale. Always position the eye directly above the scale otherwise an inaccurate reading will result.

In the example shown the item measures 2.95 mm **(see illustration 3.4)**:

Linear scale	2.00 mm
Linear scale	0.50 mm
Annular scale	0.45 mm
Total figure	**2.95 mm**

3.5 Micrometer reading of 46.99 mm on linear and annular scales . . .

3.7 Expand the telescoping gauge in the bore, lock its position . . .

3.4 Micrometer reading of 2.95 mm

3.6 . . . and 0.004 mm on vernier scale

3.8 . . . then measure the gauge with a micrometer

Most micrometers have a locking lever (6) on the frame to hold the setting in place, allowing the item to be removed from the micrometer.

● Some micrometers have a vernier scale on their sleeve, providing an even finer measurement to be taken, in 0.001 increments of a millimetre. Take the sleeve and thimble measurement as described above, then check which graduation on the vernier scale aligns with that of the annular scale on the thimble **Note**: *The eye must be perpendicular to the scale when taking the vernier reading - if necessary rotate the body of the micrometer to ensure this.* Multiply the vernier scale figure by 0.001 and add it to the base and fine measurement figures.

In the example shown the item measures 46.994 mm **(see illustrations 3.5 and 3.6)**:

Linear scale (base)	46.000 mm
Linear scale (base)	00.500 mm
Annular scale (fine)	00.490 mm
Vernier scale	00.004 mm
Total figure	**46.994 mm**

Internal micrometer

● Internal micrometers are available for measuring bore diameters, but are expensive and unlikely to be available for home use. It is suggested that a set of telescoping gauges and small hole gauges, both of which must be used with an external micrometer, will suffice for taking internal measurements on a motorcycle.

● Telescoping gauges can be used to

measure internal diameters of components. Select a gauge with the correct size range, make sure its ends are clean and insert it into the bore. Expand the gauge, then lock its position and withdraw it from the bore **(see illustration 3.7)**. Measure across the gauge ends with a micrometer **(see illustration 3.8)**.

● Very small diameter bores (such as valve guides) are measured with a small hole gauge. Once adjusted to a slip-fit inside the component, its position is locked and the gauge withdrawn for measurement with a micrometer **(see illustrations 3.9 and 3.10)**.

Vernier caliper

Note: *The conventional linear and dial gauge type instruments are described. Digital types are easier to read, but are far more expensive.*

● The vernier caliper does not provide the precision of a micrometer, but is versatile in being able to measure internal and external diameters. Some types also incorporate a depth gauge. It is ideal for measuring clutch plate friction material and spring free lengths.

● To use the conventional linear scale vernier, slacken off the vernier clamp screws (1) and set its jaws over (2), or inside (3), the item to be measured **(see illustration 3.11)**. Slide the jaw into contact, using the thumb-wheel (4) for fine movement of the sliding scale (5) then tighten the clamp screws (1). Read off the main scale (6) where the zero on the sliding scale (5) intersects it, taking the whole number to the left of the zero; this provides the base measurement. View along the sliding scale and select the division which

3.9 Expand the small hole gauge in the bore, lock its position . . .

3.10 . . . then measure the gauge with a micrometer

lines up exactly with any of the divisions on the main scale, noting that the divisions usually represents 0.02 of a millimetre. Add this fine measurement to the base measurement to obtain the total reading.

3.11 Vernier component parts (linear gauge)

1 Clamp screws	3 Internal jaws	5 Sliding scale	7 Depth gauge
2 External jaws	4 Thumbwheel	6 Main scale	

In the example shown the item measures 55.92 mm **(see illustration 3.12)**:

Base measurement	55.00 mm
Fine measurement	00.92 mm
Total figure	**55.92 mm**

3.12 Vernier gauge reading of 55.92 mm

3.13 Vernier component parts (dial gauge)

1 Clamp screw	5 Main scale
2 External jaws	6 Sliding scale
3 Internal jaws	7 Dial gauge
4 Thumbwheel	

● Some vernier calipers are equipped with a dial gauge for fine measurement. Before use, check that the jaws are clean, then close them fully and check that the dial gauge reads zero. If necessary adjust the gauge ring accordingly. Slacken the vernier clamp screw (1) and set its jaws over (2), or inside (3), the item to be measured **(see illustration 3.13)**. Slide the jaws into contact, using the thumbwheel (4) for fine movement. Read off the main scale (5) where the edge of the sliding scale (6) intersects it, taking the whole number to the left of the zero; this provides the base measurement. Read off the needle position on the dial gauge (7) scale to provide the fine measurement; each division represents 0.05 of a millimetre. Add this fine measurement to the base measurement to obtain the total reading.

In the example shown the item measures 55.95 mm **(see illustration 3.14)**:

Base measurement	55.00 mm
Fine measurement	00.95 mm
Total figure	**55.95 mm**

3.14 Vernier gauge reading of 55.95 mm

Plastigauge

● Plastigauge is a plastic material which can be compressed between two surfaces to measure the oil clearance between them. The width of the compressed Plastigauge is measured against a calibrated scale to determine the clearance.

● Common uses of Plastigauge are for measuring the clearance between crankshaft journal and main bearing inserts, between crankshaft journal and big-end bearing inserts, and between camshaft and bearing surfaces. The following example describes big-end oil clearance measurement.

● Handle the Plastigauge material carefully to prevent distortion. Using a sharp knife, cut a length which corresponds with the width of the bearing being measured and place it carefully across the journal so that it is parallel with the shaft **(see illustration 3.15)**. Carefully install both bearing shells and the connecting rod. Without rotating the rod on the journal tighten its bolts or nuts (as applicable) to the specified torque. The connecting rod and bearings are then disassembled and the crushed Plastigauge examined.

3.15 Plastigauge placed across shaft journal

● Using the scale provided in the Plastigauge kit, measure the width of the material to determine the oil clearance **(see illustration 3.16)**. Always remove all traces of Plastigauge after use using your fingernails.

Caution: Arriving at the correct clearance demands that the assembly is torqued correctly, according to the settings and sequence (where applicable) provided by the motorcycle manufacturer.

3.16 Measuring the width of the crushed Plastigauge

Dial gauge or DTI (Dial Test Indicator)

● A dial gauge can be used to accurately measure small amounts of movement. Typical uses are measuring shaft runout or shaft endfloat (sideplay) and setting piston position for ignition timing on two-strokes. A dial gauge set usually comes with a range of different probes and adapters and mounting equipment.

● The gauge needle must point to zero when at rest. Rotate the ring around its periphery to zero the gauge.

● Check that the gauge is capable of reading the extent of movement in the work. Most gauges have a small dial set in the face which records whole millimetres of movement as well as the fine scale around the face periphery which is calibrated in 0.01 mm divisions. Read off the small dial first to obtain the base measurement, then add the measurement from the fine scale to obtain the total reading.

In the example shown the gauge reads 1.48 mm (see illustration 3.17):

Base measurement	1.00 mm
Fine measurement	0.48 mm
Total figure	**1.48 mm**

3.17 Dial gauge reading of 1.48 mm

● If measuring shaft runout, the shaft must be supported in vee-blocks and the gauge mounted on a stand perpendicular to the shaft. Rest the tip of the gauge against the centre of the shaft and rotate the shaft slowly whilst watching the gauge reading (see illustration 3.18). Take several measurements along the length of the shaft and record the

3.18 Using a dial gauge to measure shaft runout

maximum gauge reading as the amount of runout in the shaft. **Note:** *The reading obtained will be total runout at that point - some manufacturers specify that the runout figure is halved to compare with their specified runout limit.*

● Endfloat (sideplay) measurement requires that the gauge is mounted securely to the surrounding component with its probe touching the end of the shaft. Using hand pressure, push and pull on the shaft noting the maximum endfloat recorded on the gauge (see illustration 3.19).

3.19 Using a dial gauge to measure shaft endfloat

● A dial gauge with suitable adapters can be used to determine piston position BTDC on two-stroke engines for the purposes of ignition timing. The gauge, adapter and suitable length probe are installed in the place of the spark plug and the gauge zeroed at TDC. If the piston position is specified as 1.14 mm BTDC, rotate the engine back to 2.00 mm BTDC, then slowly forwards to 1.14 mm BTDC.

Cylinder compression gauges

● A compression gauge is used for measuring cylinder compression. Either the rubber-cone type or the threaded adapter type can be used. The latter is preferred to ensure a perfect seal against the cylinder head. A 0 to 300 psi (0 to 20 Bar) type gauge (for petrol/gasoline engines) will be suitable for motorcycles.

● The spark plug is removed and the gauge either held hard against the cylinder head (cone type) or the gauge adapter screwed into the cylinder head (threaded type) (see illustration 3.20). Cylinder compression is measured with the engine turning over, but not running - carry out the compression test as described in

3.20 Using a rubber-cone type cylinder compression gauge

Fault Finding Equipment. The gauge will hold the reading until manually released.

Oil pressure gauge

● An oil pressure gauge is used for measuring engine oil pressure. Most gauges come with a set of adapters to fit the thread of the take-off point (see illustration 3.21). If the take-off point specified by the motorcycle manufacturer is an external oil pipe union, make sure that the specified replacement union is used to prevent oil starvation.

3.21 Oil pressure gauge and take-off point adapter (arrow)

● Oil pressure is measured with the engine running (at a specific rpm) and often the manufacturer will specify pressure limits for a cold and hot engine.

Straight-edge and surface plate

● If checking the gasket face of a component for warpage, place a steel rule or precision straight-edge across the gasket face and measure any gap between the straight-edge and component with feeler gauges (see illustration 3.22). Check diagonally across the component and between mounting holes (see illustration 3.23).

3.22 Use a straight-edge and feeler gauges to check for warpage

3.23 Check for warpage in these directions

● Checking individual components for warpage, such as clutch plain (metal) plates, requires a perfectly flat plate or piece or plate glass and feeler gauges.

4 Torque and leverage

What is torque?

● Torque describes the twisting force about a shaft. The amount of torque applied is determined by the distance from the centre of the shaft to the end of the lever and the amount of force being applied to the end of the lever; distance multiplied by force equals torque.

● The manufacturer applies a measured torque to a bolt or nut to ensure that it will not slacken in use and to hold two components securely together without movement in the joint. The actual torque setting depends on the thread size, bolt or nut material and the composition of the components being held.

● Too little torque may cause the fastener to loosen due to vibration, whereas too much torque will distort the joint faces of the component or cause the fastener to shear off. Always stick to the specified torque setting.

Using a torque wrench

● Check the calibration of the torque wrench and make sure it has a suitable range for the job. Torque wrenches are available in Nm (Newton-metres), kgf m (kilograms-force metre), lbf ft (pounds-feet), lbf in (inch-pounds). Do not confuse lbf ft with lbf in.

● Adjust the tool to the desired torque on the scale (see illustration 4.1). If your torque wrench is not calibrated in the units specified, carefully convert the figure (see *Conversion Factors*). A manufacturer sometimes gives a torque setting as a range (8 to 10 Nm) rather than a single figure - in this case set the tool midway between the two settings. The same torque may be expressed as 9 Nm ± 1 Nm. Some torque wrenches have a method of locking the setting so that it isn't inadvertently altered during use.

4.1 Set the torque wrench index mark to the setting required, in this case 12 Nm

● Install the bolts/nuts in their correct location and secure them lightly. Their threads must be clean and free of any old locking compound. Unless specified the threads and flange should be dry - oiled threads are necessary in certain circumstances and the manufacturer will take this into account in the specified torque figure. Similarly, the manufacturer may also specify the application of thread-locking compound.

● Tighten the fasteners in the specified sequence until the torque wrench clicks, indicating that the torque setting has been reached. Apply the torque again to double-check the setting. Where different thread diameter fasteners secure the component, as a rule tighten the larger diameter ones first.

● When the torque wrench has been finished with, release the lock (where applicable) and fully back off its setting to zero - do not leave the torque wrench tensioned. Also, do not use a torque wrench for slackening a fastener.

Angle-tightening

● Manufacturers often specify a figure in degrees for final tightening of a fastener. This usually follows tightening to a specific torque setting.

● A degree disc can be set and attached to the socket (see illustration 4.2) or a protractor can be used to mark the angle of movement on the bolt/nut head and the surrounding casting (see illustration 4.3).

4.2 Angle tightening can be accomplished with a torque-angle gauge . . .

4.3 . . . or by marking the angle on the surrounding component

Loosening sequences

● Where more than one bolt/nut secures a component, loosen each fastener evenly a little at a time. In this way, not all the stress of the joint is held by one fastener and the components are not likely to distort.

● If a tightening sequence is provided, work in the REVERSE of this, but if not, work from the outside in, in a criss-cross sequence (see illustration 4.4).

4.4 When slackening, work from the outside inwards

Tightening sequences

● If a component is held by more than one fastener it is important that the retaining bolts/nuts are tightened evenly to prevent uneven stress build-up and distortion of sealing faces. This is especially important on high-compression joints such as the cylinder head.

● A sequence is usually provided by the manufacturer, either in a diagram or actually marked in the casting. If not, always start in the centre and work outwards in a criss-cross pattern (see illustration 4.5). Start off by securing all bolts/nuts finger-tight, then set the torque wrench and tighten each fastener by a small amount in sequence until the final torque is reached. By following this practice,

4.5 When tightening, work from the inside outwards

the joint will be held evenly and will not be distorted. Important joints, such as the cylinder head and big-end fasteners often have two- or three-stage torque settings.

Applying leverage

● Use tools at the correct angle. Position a socket wrench or spanner on the bolt/nut so that you pull it towards you when loosening. If this can't be done, push the spanner without curling your fingers around it **(see illustration 4.6)** - the spanner may slip or the fastener loosen suddenly, resulting in your fingers being crushed against a component.

4.6 If you can't pull on the spanner to loosen a fastener, push with your hand open

● Additional leverage is gained by extending the length of the lever. The best way to do this is to use a breaker bar instead of the regular length tool, or to slip a length of tubing over the end of the spanner or socket wrench.
● If additional leverage will not work, the fastener head is either damaged or firmly corroded in place (see *Fasteners*).

5 Bearings

Bearing removal and installation

Drivers and sockets

● Before removing a bearing, always inspect the casing to see which way it must be driven out - some casings will have retaining plates or a cast step. Also check for any identifying markings on the bearing and if installed to a certain depth, measure this at this stage. Some roller bearings are sealed on one side - take note of the original fitted position.
● Bearings can be driven out of a casing using a bearing driver tool (with the correct size head) or a socket of the correct diameter. Select the driver head or socket so that it contacts the outer race of the bearing, not the balls/rollers or inner race. Always support the casing around the bearing housing with wood blocks, otherwise there is a risk of fracture. The bearing is driven out with a few blows on the driver or socket from a heavy mallet. Unless access is severely restricted (as with wheel bearings), a pin-punch is not recommended unless it is moved around the bearing to keep it square in its housing.

● The same equipment can be used to install bearings. Make sure the bearing housing is supported on wood blocks and line up the bearing in its housing. Fit the bearing as noted on removal - generally they are installed with their marked side facing outwards. Tap the bearing squarely into its housing using a driver or socket which bears only on the bearing's outer race - contact with the bearing balls/rollers or inner race will destroy it **(see illustrations 5.1 and 5.2)**.
● Check that the bearing inner race and balls/rollers rotate freely.

5.1 Using a bearing driver against the bearing's outer race

5.2 Using a large socket against the bearing's outer race

Pullers and slide-hammers

● Where a bearing is pressed on a shaft a puller will be required to extract it **(see illustration 5.3)**. Make sure that the puller clamp or legs fit securely behind the bearing and are unlikely to slip out. If pulling a bearing

5.3 This bearing puller clamps behind the bearing and pressure is applied to the shaft end to draw the bearing off

off a gear shaft for example, you may have to locate the puller behind a gear pinion if there is no access to the race and draw the gear pinion off the shaft as well **(see illustration 5.4)**.

Caution: Ensure that the puller's centre bolt locates securely against the end of the shaft and will not slip when pressure is applied. Also ensure that puller does not damage the shaft end.

5.4 Where no access is available to the rear of the bearing, it is sometimes possible to draw off the adjacent component

● Operate the puller so that its centre bolt exerts pressure on the shaft end and draws the bearing off the shaft.
● When installing the bearing on the shaft, tap only on the bearing's inner race - contact with the balls/rollers or outer race with destroy the bearing. Use a socket or length of tubing as a drift which fits over the shaft end **(see illustration 5.5)**.

5.5 When installing a bearing on a shaft use a piece of tubing which bears only on the bearing's inner race

● Where a bearing locates in a blind hole in a casing, it cannot be driven or pulled out as described above. A slide-hammer with a knife-edged bearing puller attachment will be required. The puller attachment passes through the bearing and when tightened expands to fit firmly behind the bearing **(see illustration 5.6)**. By operating the slide-hammer part of the tool the bearing is jarred out of its housing **(see illustration 5.7)**.
● It is possible, if the bearing is of reasonable weight, for it to drop out of its housing if the casing is heated as described opposite. If this

5.6 Expand the bearing puller so that it locks behind the bearing . . .

5.7 . . . attach the slide hammer to the bearing puller

method is attempted, first prepare a work surface which will enable the casing to be tapped face down to help dislodge the bearing - a wood surface is ideal since it will not damage the casing's gasket surface. Wearing protective gloves, tap the heated casing several times against the work surface to dislodge the bearing under its own weight **(see illustration 5.8)**.

5.8 Tapping a casing face down on wood blocks can often dislodge a bearing

● Bearings can be installed in blind holes using the driver or socket method described above.

Drawbolts

● Where a bearing or bush is set in the eye of a component, such as a suspension linkage arm or connecting rod small-end, removal by drift may damage the component. Furthermore, a rubber bushing in a shock absorber eye cannot successfully be driven out of position. If access is available to a engineering press, the task is straightforward. If not, a drawbolt can be fabricated to extract the bearing or bush.

5.9 Drawbolt component parts assembled on a suspension arm

1 Bolt or length of threaded bar
2 Nuts
3 Washer (external diameter greater than tubing internal diameter)
4 Tubing (internal diameter sufficient to accommodate bearing)
5 Suspension arm with bearing
6 Tubing (external diameter slightly smaller than bearing)
7 Washer (external diameter slightly smaller than bearing)

5.10 Drawing the bearing out of the suspension arm

● To extract the bearing/bush you will need a long bolt with nut (or piece of threaded bar with two nuts), a piece of tubing which has an internal diameter larger than the bearing/bush, another piece of tubing which has an external diameter slightly smaller than the bearing/ bush, and a selection of washers **(see illustrations 5.9 and 5.10)**. Note that the pieces of tubing must be of the same length, or longer, than the bearing/bush.
● The same kit (without the pieces of tubing) can be used to draw the new bearing/bush back into place **(see illustration 5.11)**.

5.11 Installing a new bearing (1) in the suspension arm

Temperature change

● If the bearing's outer race is a tight fit in the casing, the aluminium casing can be heated to release its grip on the bearing. Aluminium will expand at a greater rate than the steel bearing outer race. There are several ways to do this, but avoid any localised extreme heat (such as a blow torch) - aluminium alloy has a low melting point.
● Approved methods of heating a casing are using a domestic oven (heated to 100°C) or immersing the casing in boiling water **(see illustration 5.12)**. Low temperature range localised heat sources such as a paint stripper heat gun or clothes iron can also be used **(see illustration 5.13)**. Alternatively, soak a rag in boiling water, wring it out and wrap it around the bearing housing.

> ⚠️ **Warning: All of these methods require care in use to prevent scalding and burns to the hands. Wear protective gloves when handling hot components.**

5.12 A casing can be immersed in a sink of boiling water to aid bearing removal

5.13 Using a localised heat source to aid bearing removal

● If heating the whole casing note that plastic components, such as the neutral switch, may suffer - remove them beforehand.
● After heating, remove the bearing as described above. You may find that the expansion is sufficient for the bearing to fall out of the casing under its own weight or with a light tap on the driver or socket.
● If necessary, the casing can be heated to aid bearing installation, and this is sometimes the recommended procedure if the motorcycle manufacturer has designed the housing and bearing fit with this intention.

● Installation of bearings can be eased by placing them in a freezer the night before installation. The steel bearing will contract slightly, allowing easy insertion in its housing. This is often useful when installing steering head outer races in the frame.

Bearing types and markings

● Plain shell bearings, ball bearings, needle roller bearings and tapered roller bearings will all be found on motorcycles (see illustrations 5.14 and 5.15). The ball and roller types are usually caged between an inner and outer race, but uncaged variations may be found.

5.14 Shell bearings are either plain or grooved. They are usually identified by colour code (arrow)

5.15 Tapered roller bearing (A), needle roller bearing (B) and ball journal bearing (C)

● Shell bearings (often called inserts) are usually found at the crankshaft main and connecting rod big-end where they are good at coping with high loads. They are made of a phosphor-bronze material and are impregnated with self-lubricating properties.

● Ball bearings and needle roller bearings consist of a steel inner and outer race with the balls or rollers between the races. They require constant lubrication by oil or grease and are good at coping with axial loads. Taper roller bearings consist of rollers set in a tapered cage set on the inner race; the outer race is separate. They are good at coping with axial loads and prevent movement along the shaft - a typical application is in the steering head.

● Bearing manufacturers produce bearings to ISO size standards and stamp one face of the bearing to indicate its internal and external diameter, load capacity and type (see illustration 5.16).

● Metal bushes are usually of phosphor-bronze material. Rubber bushes are used in suspension mounting eyes. Fibre bushes have also been used in suspension pivots.

5.16 Typical bearing marking

Bearing fault finding

● If a bearing outer race has spun in its housing, the housing material will be damaged. You can use a bearing locking compound to bond the outer race in place if damage is not too severe.

● Shell bearings will fail due to damage of their working surface, as a result of lack of lubrication, corrosion or abrasive particles in the oil (see illustration 5.17). Small particles of dirt in the oil may embed in the bearing material whereas larger particles will score the bearing and shaft journal. If a number of short journeys are made, insufficient heat will be generated to drive off condensation which has built up on the bearings.

5.17 Typical bearing failures

● Ball and roller bearings will fail due to lack of lubrication or damage to the balls or rollers. Tapered-roller bearings can be damaged by overloading them. Unless the bearing is sealed on both sides, wash it in paraffin (kerosene) to remove all old grease then allow it to dry. Make a visual inspection looking to dented balls or rollers, damaged cages and worn or pitted races (see illustration 5.18).

● A ball bearing can be checked for wear by listening to it when spun. Apply a film of light oil to the bearing and hold it close to the ear - hold the outer race with one hand and spin the inner

5.18 Example of ball journal bearing with damaged balls and cages

5.19 Hold outer race and listen to inner race when spun

race with the other hand (see illustration 5.19). The bearing should be almost silent when spun; if it grates or rattles it is worn.

6 Oil seals

Oil seal removal and installation

● Oil seals should be renewed every time a component is dismantled. This is because the seal lips will become set to the sealing surface and will not necessarily reseal.

● Oil seals can be prised out of position using a large flat-bladed screwdriver (see illustration 6.1). In the case of crankcase seals, check first that the seal is not lipped on the inside, preventing its removal with the crankcases joined.

6.1 Prise out oil seals with a large flat-bladed screwdriver

● New seals are usually installed with their marked face (containing the seal reference code) outwards and the spring side towards the fluid being retained. In certain cases, such as a two-stroke engine crankshaft seal, a double lipped seal may be used due to there being fluid or gas on each side of the joint.

● Use a bearing driver or socket which bears only on the outer hard edge of the seal to install it in the casing - tapping on the inner edge will damage the sealing lip.

Oil seal types and markings

● Oil seals are usually of the single-lipped type. Double-lipped seals are found where a liquid or gas is on both sides of the joint.
● Oil seals can harden and lose their sealing ability if the motorcycle has been in storage for a long period - renewal is the only solution.
● Oil seal manufacturers also conform to the ISO markings for seal size - these are moulded into the outer face of the seal (see illustration 6.2).

6.2 These oil seal markings indicate inside diameter, outside diameter and seal thickness

7 Gaskets and sealants

Types of gasket and sealant

● Gaskets are used to seal the mating surfaces between components and keep lubricants, fluids, vacuum or pressure contained within the assembly. Aluminium gaskets are sometimes found at the cylinder joints, but most gaskets are paper-based. If the mating surfaces of the components being joined are undamaged the gasket can be installed dry, although a dab of sealant or grease will be useful to hold it in place during assembly.
● RTV (Room Temperature Vulcanising) silicone rubber sealants cure when exposed to moisture in the atmosphere. These sealants are good at filling pits or irregular gasket faces, but will tend to be forced out of the joint under very high torque. They can be used to replace a paper gasket, but first make sure that the width of the paper gasket is not essential to the shimming of internal components. RTV sealants should not be used on components containing petrol (gasoline).
● Non-hardening, semi-hardening and hard setting liquid gasket compounds can be used with a gasket or between a metal-to-metal joint. Select the sealant to suit the application: universal non-hardening sealant can be used on virtually all joints; semi-hardening on joint faces which are rough or damaged; hard setting sealant on joints which require a permanent bond and are subjected to high temperature and pressure. **Note:** *Check first if the paper gasket has a bead of sealant*

impregnated in its surface before applying additional sealant.
● When choosing a sealant, make sure it is suitable for the application, particularly if being applied in a high-temperature area or in the vicinity of fuel. Certain manufacturers produce sealants in either clear, silver or black colours to match the finish of the engine. This has a particular application on motorcycles where much of the engine is exposed.
● Do not over-apply sealant. That which is squeezed out on the outside of the joint can be wiped off, whereas an excess of sealant on the inside can break off and clog oilways.

Breaking a sealed joint

● Age, heat, pressure and the use of hard setting sealant can cause two components to stick together so tightly that they are difficult to separate using finger pressure alone. Do not resort to using levers unless there is a pry point provided for this purpose (see illustration 7.1) or else the gasket surfaces will be damaged.
● Use a soft-faced hammer (see illustration 7.2) or a wood block and conventional hammer to strike the component near the mating surface. Avoid hammering against cast extremities since they may break off. If this method fails, try using a wood wedge between the two components.

Caution: If the joint will not separate, double-check that you have removed all the fasteners.

7.1 If a pry point is provided, apply gently pressure with a flat-bladed screwdriver

7.2 Tap around the joint with a soft-faced mallet if necessary - don't strike cooling fins

Removal of old gasket and sealant

● Paper gaskets will most likely come away complete, leaving only a few traces stuck on

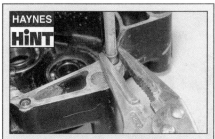

Most components have one or two hollow locating dowels between the two gasket faces. If a dowel cannot be removed, do not resort to gripping it with pliers - it will almost certainly be distorted. Install a close-fitting socket or Phillips screwdriver into the dowel and then grip the outer edge of the dowel to free it.

the sealing faces of the components. It is imperative that all traces are removed to ensure correct sealing of the new gasket.
● Very carefully scrape all traces of gasket away making sure that the sealing surfaces are not gouged or scored by the scraper (see illustrations 7.3, 7.4 and 7.5). Stubborn deposits can be removed by spraying with an aerosol gasket remover. Final preparation of

7.3 Paper gaskets can be scraped off with a gasket scraper tool . . .

7.4 . . . a knife blade . . .

7.5 . . . or a household scraper

7.6 Fine abrasive paper is wrapped around a flat file to clean up the gasket face

7.7 A kitchen scourer can be used on stubborn deposits

the gasket surface can be made with very fine abrasive paper or a plastic kitchen scourer **(see illustrations 7.6 and 7.7)**.
● Old sealant can be scraped or peeled off components, depending on the type originally used. Note that gasket removal compounds are available to avoid scraping the components clean; make sure the gasket remover suits the type of sealant used.

8 Chains

Breaking and joining final drive chains

● Drive chains for all but small bikes are continuous and do not have a clip-type connecting link. The chain must be broken using a chain breaker tool and the new chain securely riveted together using a new soft rivet-type link. Never use a clip-type connecting link instead of a rivet-type link, except in an emergency. Various chain breaking and riveting tools are available, either as separate tools or combined as illustrated in the accompanying photographs - read the instructions supplied with the tool carefully.

> ⚠ **Warning: The need to rivet the new link pins correctly cannot be overstressed - loss of control of the motorcycle is very likely to result if the chain breaks in use.**

● Rotate the chain and look for the soft link. The soft link pins look like they have been

8.1 Tighten the chain breaker to push the pin out of the link . . .

8.2 . . . withdraw the pin, remove the tool . . .

8.3 . . . and separate the chain link

deeply centre-punched instead of peened over like all the other pins **(see illustration 8.9)** and its sideplate may be a different colour. Position the soft link midway between the sprockets and assemble the chain breaker tool over one of the soft link pins **(see illustration 8.1)**. Operate the tool to push the pin out through the chain **(see illustration 8.2)**. On an O-ring chain, remove the O-rings **(see illustration 8.3)**. Carry out the same procedure on the other soft link pin.

> *Caution: Certain soft link pins (particularly on the larger chains) may require their ends to be filed or ground off before they can be pressed out using the tool.*

● Check that you have the correct size and strength (standard or heavy duty) new soft link - do not reuse the old link. Look for the size marking on the chain sideplates **(see illustration 8.10)**.
● Position the chain ends so that they are engaged over the rear sprocket. On an O-ring

8.4 Insert the new soft link, with O-rings, through the chain ends . . .

8.5 . . . install the O-rings over the pin ends . . .

8.6 . . . followed by the sideplate

chain, install a new O-ring over each pin of the link and insert the link through the two chain ends **(see illustration 8.4)**. Install a new O-ring over the end of each pin, followed by the sideplate (with the chain manufacturer's marking facing outwards) **(see illustrations 8.5 and 8.6)**. On an unsealed chain, insert the link through the two chain ends, then install the sideplate with the chain manufacturer's marking facing outwards.
● Note that it may not be possible to install the sideplate using finger pressure alone. If using a joining tool, assemble it so that the plates of the tool clamp the link and press the sideplate over the pins **(see illustration 8.7)**. Otherwise, use two small sockets placed over

8.7 Push the sideplate into position using a clamp

8.8 Assemble the chain riveting tool over one pin at a time and tighten it fully

8.9 Pin end correctly riveted (A), pin end unriveted (B)

the rivet ends and two pieces of the wood between a G-clamp. Operate the clamp to press the sideplate over the pins.

● Assemble the joining tool over one pin (following the maker's instructions) and tighten the tool down to spread the pin end securely **(see illustrations 8.8 and 8.9)**. Do the same on the other pin.

> **Warning: Check that the pin ends are secure and that there is no danger of the sideplate coming loose. If the pin ends are cracked the soft link must be renewed.**

Final drive chain sizing

● Chains are sized using a three digit number, followed by a suffix to denote the chain type **(see illustration 8.10)**. Chain type is either standard or heavy duty (thicker sideplates), and also unsealed or O-ring/X-ring type.

● The first digit of the number relates to the pitch of the chain, ie the distance from the centre of one pin to the centre of the next pin **(see illustration 8.11)**. Pitch is expressed in eighths of an inch, as follows:

8.10 Typical chain size and type marking

8.11 Chain dimensions

Sizes commencing with a 4 (eg 428) have a pitch of 1/2 inch (12.7 mm)

Sizes commencing with a 5 (eg 520) have a pitch of 5/8 inch (15.9 mm)

Sizes commencing with a 6 (eg 630) have a pitch of 3/4 inch (19.1 mm)

● The second and third digits of the chain size relate to the width of the rollers, again in imperial units, eg the 525 shown has 5/16 inch (7.94 mm) rollers **(see illustration 8.11)**.

9 Hoses

Clamping to prevent flow

● Small-bore flexible hoses can be clamped to prevent fluid flow whilst a component is worked on. Whichever method is used, ensure that the hose material is not permanently distorted or damaged by the clamp.

a) A brake hose clamp available from auto accessory shops **(see illustration 9.1)**.
b) A wingnut type hose clamp **(see illustration 9.2)**.

9.1 Hoses can be clamped with an automotive brake hose clamp . . .

9.2 . . . a wingnut type hose clamp . . .

c) Two sockets placed each side of the hose and held with straight-jawed self-locking grips **(see illustration 9.3)**.
d) Thick card each side of the hose held between straight-jawed self-locking grips **(see illustration 9.4)**.

9.3 . . . two sockets and a pair of self-locking grips . . .

9.4 . . . or thick card and self-locking grips

Freeing and fitting hoses

● Always make sure the hose clamp is moved well clear of the hose end. Grip the hose with your hand and rotate it whilst pulling it off the union. If the hose has hardened due to age and will not move, slit it with a sharp knife and peel its ends off the union **(see illustration 9.5)**.

● Resist the temptation to use grease or soap on the unions to aid installation; although it helps the hose slip over the union it will equally aid the escape of fluid from the joint. It is preferable to soften the hose ends in hot water and wet the inside surface of the hose with water or a fluid which will evaporate.

9.5 Cutting a coolant hose free with a sharp knife

Introduction

In less time than it takes to read this introduction, a thief could steal your motorcycle. Returning only to find your bike has gone is one of the worst feelings in the world. Even if the motorcycle is insured against theft, once you've got over the initial shock, you will have the inconvenience of dealing with the police and your insurance company.

The motorcycle is an easy target for the professional thief and the joyrider alike and

the official figures on motorcycle theft make for depressing reading; on average a motorcycle is stolen every 16 minutes in the UK!

Motorcycle thefts fall into two categories, those stolen 'to order' and those taken by opportunists. The thief stealing to order will be on the look out for a specific make and model and will go to extraordinary lengths to obtain that motorcycle. The opportunist thief on the other hand will look for easy targets which can be stolen with the minimum of effort and risk.

Whilst it is never going to be possible to make your machine 100% secure, it is estimated that around half of all stolen motorcycles are taken by opportunist thieves. Remember that the opportunist thief is always on the look out for the easy option: if there are two similar motorcycles parked side-by-side, they will target the one with the lowest level of security. By taking a few precautions, you can reduce the chances of your motorcycle being stolen.

Security equipment

There are many specialised motorcycle security devices available and the following text summarises their applications and their good and bad points.

Once you have decided on the type of security equipment which best suits your needs, we recommended that you read one of the many equipment tests regularly carried

Ensure the lock and chain you buy is of good quality and long enough to shackle your bike to a solid object

out by the motorcycle press. These tests compare the products from all the major manufacturers and give impartial ratings on their effectiveness, value-for-money and ease of use.

No one item of security equipment can provide complete protection. It is highly recommended that two or more of the items described below are combined to increase the security of your motorcycle (a lock and chain plus an alarm system is just about ideal). The more security measures fitted to the bike, the less likely it is to be stolen.

Lock and chain

Pros: *Very flexible to use; can be used to secure the motorcycle to almost any immovable object. On some locks and chains, the lock can be used on its own as a disc lock (see below).*

Cons: *Can be very heavy and awkward to carry on the motorcycle, although some types*

will be supplied with a carry bag which can be strapped to the pillion seat.

● Heavy-duty chains and locks are an excellent security measure **(see illustration 1)**. Whenever the motorcycle is parked, use the lock and chain to secure the machine to a solid, immovable object such as a post or railings. This will prevent the machine from being ridden away or being lifted into the back of a van.

● When fitting the chain, always ensure the chain is routed around the motorcycle frame or swingarm **(see illustrations 2 and 3)**. Never merely pass the chain around one of the wheel rims; a thief may unbolt the wheel and lift the rest of the machine into a van, leaving you with just the wheel! Try to avoid having excess chain free, thus making it difficult to use cutting tools, and keep the chain and lock off the ground to prevent thieves attacking it with a cold chisel. Position the lock so that its lock barrel is facing downwards; this will make it harder for the thief to attack the lock mechanism.

Pass the chain through the bike's frame, rather than just through a wheel . . .

. . . and loop it around a solid object

U-locks

Pros: *Highly effective deterrent which can be used to secure the bike to a post or railings. Most U-locks come with a carrier which allows the lock to be easily carried on the bike.*

Cons: *Not as flexible to use as a lock and chain.*

● These are solid locks which are similar in use to a lock and chain. U-locks are lighter than a lock and chain but not so flexible to use. The length and shape of the lock shackle limit the objects to which the bike can be secured **(see illustration 4)**.

U-locks can be used to secure the bike to a solid object – ensure you purchase one which is long enough

Disc locks

Pros: *Small, light and very easy to carry; most can be stored underneath the seat.*

Cons: *Does not prevent the motorcycle being lifted into a van. Can be very embarrassing if you*

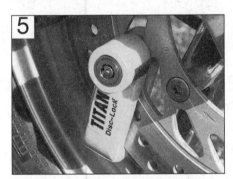

A typical disc lock attached through one of the holes in the disc

forget to remove the lock before attempting to ride off!

● Disc locks are designed to be attached to the front brake disc. The lock passes through one of the holes in the disc and prevents the wheel rotating by jamming against the fork/brake caliper **(see illustration 5)**. Some are equipped with an alarm siren which sounds if the disc lock is moved; this not only acts as a theft deterrent but also as a handy reminder if you try to move the bike with the lock still fitted.

● Combining the disc lock with a length of cable which can be looped around a post or railings provides an additional measure of security **(see illustration 6)**.

Alarms and immobilisers

Pros: *Once installed it is completely hassle-free to use. If the system is 'Thatcham' or 'Sold Secure-approved', insurance companies may give you a discount.*

Cons: *Can be expensive to buy and complex to install. No system will prevent the motorcycle from being lifted into a van and taken away.*

● Electronic alarms and immobilisers are available to suit a variety of budgets. There are three different types of system available: pure alarms, pure immobilisers, and the more expensive systems which are combined alarm/immobilisers **(see illustration 7)**.
● An alarm system is designed to emit an audible warning if the motorcycle is being tampered with.
● An immobiliser prevents the motorcycle being started and ridden away by disabling its electrical systems.
● When purchasing an alarm/immobiliser system, check the cost of installing the system unless you are able to do it yourself. If the motorcycle is not used regularly, another consideration is the current drain of the system. All alarm/immobiliser systems are powered by the motorcycle's battery; purchasing a system with a very low current drain could prevent the battery losing its charge whilst the motorcycle is not being used.

A disc lock combined with a security cable provides additional protection

A typical alarm/immobiliser system

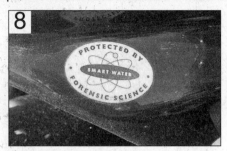

Indelible markings can be applied to most areas of the bike – always apply the manufacturer's sticker to warn off thieves

Chemically-etched code numbers can be applied to main body panels . . .

. . . again, always ensure that the kit manufacturer's sticker is applied in a prominent position

Security marking kits

Pros: *Very cheap and effective deterrent. Many insurance companies will give you a discount on your insurance premium if a recognised security marking kit is used on your motorcycle.*

Cons: *Does not prevent the motorcycle being stolen by joyriders.*

● There are many different types of security marking kits available. The idea is to mark as many parts of the motorcycle as possible with a unique security number **(see illustrations 8, 9 and 10)**. A form will be included with the kit to register your personal details and those of the motorcycle with the kit manufacturer. This register is made available to the police to help them trace the rightful owner of any motorcycle or components which they recover should all other forms of identification have been removed. Always apply the warning stickers provided with the kit to deter thieves.

Ground anchors, wheel clamps and security posts

Pros: *An excellent form of security which will deter all but the most determined of thieves.*

Cons: *Awkward to install and can be expensive.*

● Whilst the motorcycle is at home, it is a good idea to attach it securely to the floor or a solid wall, even if it is kept in a securely locked garage. Various types of ground anchors, security posts and wheel clamps are available for this purpose **(see illustration 11)**. These security devices are either bolted to a solid concrete or brick structure or can be cemented into the ground.

Permanent ground anchors provide an excellent level of security when the bike is at home

Security at home

A high percentage of motorcycle thefts are from the owner's home. Here are some things to consider whenever your motorcycle is at home:

✔ Where possible, always keep the motorcycle in a securely locked garage. Never rely solely on the standard lock on the garage door, these are usual hopelessly inadequate. Fit an additional locking mechanism to the door and consider having the garage alarmed. A security light, activated by a movement sensor, is also a good investment.

✔ Always secure the motorcycle to the ground or a wall, even if it is inside a securely locked garage.
✔ Do not regularly leave the motorcycle outside your home, try to keep it out of sight wherever possible. If a garage is not available, fit a motorcycle cover over the bike to disguise its true identity.
✔ It is not uncommon for thieves to follow a motorcyclist home to find out where the bike is kept. They will then return at a later date. Be aware of this whenever you are returning

home on your motorcycle. If you suspect you are being followed, do not return home, instead ride to a garage or shop and stop as a precaution.
✔ When selling a motorcycle, do not provide your home address or the location where the bike is normally kept. Arrange to meet the buyer at a location away from your home. Thieves have been known to pose as potential buyers to find out where motorcycles are kept and then return later to steal them.

Security away from the home

As well as fitting security equipment to your motorcycle here are a few general rules to follow whenever you park your motorcycle.
✔ Park in a busy, public place.
✔ Use car parks which incorporate security features, such as CCTV.

✔ At night, park in a well-lit area, preferably directly underneath a street light.
✔ Engage the steering lock.
✔ Secure the motorcycle to a solid, immovable object such as a post or railings with an additional lock. If this is not possible,

secure the bike to a friend's motorcycle. Some public parking places provide security loops for motorcycles.
✔ Never leave your helmet or luggage attached to the motorcycle. Take them with you at all times.

Lubricants and fluids

A wide range of lubricants, fluids and cleaning agents is available for motor-cycles. This is a guide as to what is available, its applications and properties.

Four-stroke engine oil

● Engine oil is without doubt the most important component of any four-stroke engine. Modern motorcycle engines place a lot of demands on their oil and choosing the right type is essential. Using an unsuitable oil will lead to an increased rate of engine wear and could result in serious engine damage. Before purchasing oil, always check the recommended oil specification given by the manufacturer. The manufacturer will state a recommended 'type or classification' and also a specific 'viscosity' range for engine oil.

● The oil 'type or classification' is identified by its API (American Petroleum Institute) rating. The API rating will be in the form of two letters, e.g. SG. The S identifies the oil as being suitable for use in a petrol (gasoline) engine (S stands for spark ignition) and the second letter, ranging from A to J, identifies the oil's performance rating. The later this letter, the higher the specification of the oil; for example API SG oil exceeds the requirements of API SF oil. **Note:** *On some oils there may also be a second rating consisting of another two letters, the first letter being C, e.g. API SF/CD. This rating indicates the oil is also suitable for use in a diesel engines (the C stands for compression ignition) and is thus of no relevance for motorcycle use.*

● The 'viscosity' of the oil is identified by its SAE (Society of Automotive Engineers) rating. All modern engines require multigrade oils and the SAE rating will consist of two numbers, the first followed by a W, e.g.

10W/40. The first number indicates the viscosity rating of the oil at low temperatures (W stands for winter – tested at –20°C) and the second number represents the viscosity of the oil at high temperatures (tested at 100°C). The lower the number, the thinner the oil. For example an oil with an SAE 10W/40 rating will give better cold starting and running than an SAE 15W/40 oil.

● As well as ensuring the 'type' and 'viscosity' of the oil match the recommendations, another consideration to make when buying engine oil is whether to purchase a standard mineral-based oil, a semi-synthetic oil (also known as a synthetic blend or synthetic-based oil) or a fully-synthetic oil. Although all oils will have a similar rating and viscosity, their cost will vary considerably; mineral-based oils are the cheapest, the fully-synthetic oils the most expensive with the semi-synthetic oils falling somewhere in-between. This decision is very much up to the owner, but it should be noted that modern synthetic oils have far better lubricating and cleaning qualities than traditional mineral-based oils and tend to retain these properties for far longer. Bearing in mind the operating conditions inside a modern, high-revving motorcycle engine it is highly recommended that a fully synthetic oil is used. The extra expense at each service could save you money in the long term by preventing premature engine wear.

● As a final note always ensure that the oil is specifically designed for use in motorcycle engines. Engine oils designed primarily for use in car engines sometimes contain additives or friction modifiers which could cause clutch slip on a motorcycle fitted with a wet-clutch.

Two-stroke engine oil

● Modern two-stroke engines, with their high power outputs, place high demands on their oil. If engine seizure is to be avoided it is essential that a high-quality oil is used. Two-stroke oils differ hugely from four-stroke oils. The oil lubricates only the crankshaft and piston(s) (the transmission has its own lubricating oil) and is used on a total-loss basis where it is burnt completely during the combustion process.

● The Japanese have recently introduced a classification system for two-stroke oils, the JASO rating. This rating is in the form of two letters, either FA, FB or FC – FA is the lowest classification and FC the highest. Ensure the oil being used meets or exceeds the recommended rating specified by the manufacturer.

● As well as ensuring the oil rating matches the recommendation, another consideration to make when buying engine oil is whether to purchase a standard mineral-based oil, a semi-synthetic oil (also known as a synthetic blend or synthetic-based oil) or a fully-synthetic oil. The cost of each type of oil varies considerably; mineral-based oils are the cheapest, the fully-synthetic oils the most expensive with the semi-synthetic oils falling somewhere in-between. This decision is very much up to the owner, but it should be noted that modern synthetic oils have far better lubricating properties and burn cleaner than traditional mineral-based oils. It is therefore recommended that a fully synthetic oil is used. The extra expense could save you money in the long term by preventing premature engine wear, engine performance will be improved, carbon deposits and exhaust smoke will be reduced.

● Always ensure that the oil is specifically designed for use in an injector system. Many high quality two-stroke oils are designed for competition use and need to be pre-mixed with fuel. These oils are of a much higher viscosity and are not designed to flow through the injector pumps used on road-going two-stroke motorcycles.

Transmission (gear) oil

● On a two-stroke engine, the transmission and clutch are lubricated by their own separate oil bath which must be changed in accordance with the Maintenance Schedule.
● Although the engine and transmission units of most four-strokes use a common lubrication supply, there are some exceptions where the engine and gearbox have separate oil reservoirs and a dry clutch is used.
● Motorcycle manufacturers will either recommend a monograde transmission oil or a four-stroke multigrade engine oil to lubricate the transmission.
● Transmission oils, or gear oils as they are often called, are designed specifically for use in transmission systems. The viscosity of these oils is represented by an SAE number, but the scale of measurement applied is different to that used to grade engine oils. As a rough guide a SAE90 gear oil will be of the same viscosity as an SAE50 engine oil.

Shaft drive oil

● On models equipped with shaft final drive, the shaft drive gears are will have their own oil supply. The manufacturer will state a recommended 'type or classification' and also a specific 'viscosity' range in the same manner as for four-stroke engine oil.
● Gear oil classification is given by the number which follows the API GL (GL standing for gear lubricant) rating, the higher the number, the higher the specification of the oil, e.g. API GL5 oil is a higher specification than API GL4 oil. Ensure the oil meets or

exceeds the classification specified and is of the correct viscosity. The viscosity of gear oils is also represented by an SAE number but the scale of measurement used is different to that used to grade engine oils. As a rough guide an SAE90 gear oil will be of the same viscosity as an SAE50 engine oil.
● If the use of an EP (Extreme Pressure) gear oil is specified, ensure the oil purchased is suitable.

Fork oil and suspension fluid

● Conventional telescopic front forks are hydraulic and require fork oil to work. To ensure the forks function correctly, the fork oil must be changed in accordance with the Maintenance Schedule.
● Fork oil is available in a variety of viscosities, identified by their SAE rating; fork oil ratings vary from light (SAE 5) to heavy (SAE 30). When purchasing fork oil, ensure the viscosity rating matches that specified by the manufacturer.
● Some lubricant manufacturers also produce a range of high-quality suspension fluids which are very similar to fork oil but are designed mainly for competition use. These fluids may have a different viscosity rating system which is not to be confused with the SAE rating of normal fork oil. Refer to the manufacturer's instructions if in any doubt.

Brake and clutch fluid

● All disc brake systems and some clutch systems are hydraulically operated. To ensure correct operation, the hydraulic fluid must be changed in accordance with the Maintenance Schedule.
● Brake and clutch fluid is classified by its DOT rating with most motorcycle manufacturers specifying DOT 3 or 4 fluid. Both fluid types are glycol-based and can be mixed together without adverse effect; DOT 4 fluid exceeds the requirements of DOT 3

fluid. Although it is safe to use DOT 4 fluid in a system designed for use with DOT 3 fluid, never use DOT 3 fluid in a system which specifies the use of DOT 4 as this will adversely affect the system's performance. The type required for the system will be marked on the fluid reservoir cap.
● Some manufacturers also produce a DOT 5 hydraulic fluid. DOT 5 hydraulic fluid is silicone-based and is not compatible with the glycol-based DOT 3 and 4 fluids. Never mix DOT 5 fluid with DOT 3 or 4 fluid as this will seriously affect the performance of the hydraulic system.

Coolant/antifreeze

● When purchasing coolant/antifreeze, always ensure it is suitable for use in an aluminium engine and contains corrosion inhibitors to prevent possible blockages of the internal coolant passages of the system. As a general rule, most coolants are designed to be used neat and should not be diluted whereas antifreeze can be mixed with distilled water to provide a coolant solution of the required strength. Refer to the manufacturer's instructions on the bottle.
● Ensure the coolant is changed in accordance with the Maintenance Schedule.

Chain lube

● Chain lube is an aerosol-type spray lubricant specifically designed for use on motorcycle final drive chains. Chain lube has two functions, to minimise friction between the final drive chain and sprockets and to prevent corrosion of the chain. Regular use of a good-quality chain lube will extend the life of the drive chain and sprockets and thus maximise the power being transmitted from the transmission to the rear wheel.
● When using chain lube, always allow some time for the solvents in the lube to evaporate before riding the motorcycle. This will minimise the amount of lube which will

'fling' off from the chain when the motorcycle is used. If the motorcycle is equipped with an 'O-ring' chain, ensure the chain lube is labelled as being suitable for use on 'O-ring' chains.

Degreasers and solvents

● There are many different types of solvents and degreasers available to remove the grime and grease which accumulate around the motorcycle during normal use. Degreasers and solvents are usually available as an aerosol-type spray or as a liquid which you apply with a brush. Always closely follow the manufacturer's instructions and wear eye protection during use. Be aware that many solvents are flammable and may give off noxious fumes; take adequate precautions when using them (see Safety First!).

● For general cleaning, use one of the many solvents or degreasers available from most motorcycle accessory shops. These solvents are usually applied then left for a certain time before being washed off with water.

Brake cleaner is a solvent specifically designed to remove all traces of oil, grease and dust from braking system components. Brake cleaner is designed to evaporate quickly and leaves behind no residue.

Carburettor cleaner is an aerosol-type solvent specifically designed to clear carburettor blockages and break down the hard deposits and gum often found inside carburettors during overhaul.

Contact cleaner is an aerosol-type solvent designed for cleaning electrical components. The cleaner will remove all traces of oil and dirt from components such as switch contacts or fouled spark plugs and then dry, leaving behind no residue.

Gasket remover is an aerosol-type solvent designed for removing stubborn gaskets from engine components during overhaul. Gasket remover will minimise the amount of scraping required to remove the gasket and therefore reduce the risk of damage to the mating surface.

Spray lubricants

● Aerosol-based spray lubricants are widely available and are excellent for lubricating lever pivots and exposed cables and switches. Try to use a lubricant which is of the dry-film type as the fluid evaporates, leaving behind a dry-film of lubricant. Lubricants which leave behind an oily residue will attract dust and dirt which will increase the rate of wear of the cable/lever.

● Most lubricants also act as a moisture dispersant and a penetrating fluid. This means they can also be used to 'dry out' electrical components such as wiring connectors or switches as well as helping to free seized fasteners.

Greases

● Grease is used to lubricate many of the pivot-points. A good-quality multi-purpose grease is suitable for most applications but some manufacturers will specify the use of specialist greases for use on components such as swingarm and suspension linkage bushes. These specialist greases can be purchased from most motorcycle (or car) accessory shops; commonly specified types include molybdenum disulphide grease, lithium-based grease, graphite-based grease, silicone-based grease and high-temperature copper-based grease.

Gasket sealing compounds

● Gasket sealing compounds can be used in conjunction with gaskets, to improve their sealing capabilities, or on their own to seal metal-to-metal joints. Depending on their type, sealing compounds either set hard or stay relatively soft and pliable.

● When purchasing a gasket sealing compound, ensure that it is designed specifically for use on an internal combustion engine. General multi-purpose sealants available from DIY stores may appear visibly similar but they are not designed to withstand the extreme heat or contact with fuel and oil encountered when used on an engine (see 'Tools and Workshop Tips' for further information).

Thread locking compound

● Thread locking compounds are used to secure certain threaded fasteners in position to prevent them from loosening due to vibration. Thread locking compounds can be purchased from most motorcycle (and car) accessory shops. Ensure the threads of the both components are completely clean and dry before sparingly applying the locking compound (see 'Tools and Workshop Tips' for further information).

Fuel additives

● Fuel additives which protect and clean the fuel system components are widely available. These additives are designed to remove all traces of deposits that build up on the carburettors/injectors and prevent wear, helping the fuel system to operate more efficiently. If a fuel additive is being used, check that it is suitable for use with your motorcycle, especially if your motorcycle is equipped with a catalytic converter.

● Octane boosters are also available. These additives are designed to improve the performance of highly-tuned engines being run on normal pump-fuel and are of no real use on standard motorcycles.

Length (distance)

Inches (in)	x 25.4	= Millimetres (mm)	x 0.0394	= Inches (in)
Feet (ft)	x 0.305	= Metres (m)	x 3.281	= Feet (ft)
Miles	x 1.609	= Kilometres (km)	x 0.621	= Miles

Volume (capacity)

Cubic inches (cu in; in³)	x 16.387	= Cubic centimetres (cc; cm³)	x 0.061	= Cubic inches (cu in; in³)
Imperial pints (Imp pt)	x 0.568	= Litres (l)	x 1.76	= Imperial pints (Imp pt)
Imperial quarts (Imp qt)	x 1.137	= Litres (l)	x 0.88	= Imperial quarts (Imp qt)
Imperial quarts (Imp qt)	x 1.201	= US quarts (US qt)	x 0.833	= Imperial quarts (Imp qt)
US quarts (US qt)	x 0.946	= Litres (l)	x 1.057	= US quarts (US qt)
Imperial gallons (Imp gal)	x 4.546	= Litres (l)	x 0.22	= Imperial gallons (Imp gal)
Imperial gallons (Imp gal)	x 1.201	= US gallons (US gal)	x 0.833	= Imperial gallons (Imp gal)
US gallons (US gal)	x 3.785	= Litres (l)	x 0.264	= US gallons (US gal)

Mass (weight)

Ounces (oz)	x 28.35	= Grams (g)	x 0.035	= Ounces (oz)
Pounds (lb)	x 0.454	= Kilograms (kg)	x 2.205	= Pounds (lb)

Force

Ounces-force (ozf; oz)	x 0.278	= Newtons (N)	x 3.6	= Ounces-force (ozf; oz)
Pounds-force (lbf; lb)	x 4.448	= Newtons (N)	x 0.225	= Pounds-force (lbf; lb)
Newtons (N)	x 0.1	= Kilograms-force (kgf; kg)	x 9.81	= Newtons (N)

Pressure

Pounds-force per square inch (psi; lbf/in²; lb/in²)	x 0.070	= Kilograms-force per square centimetre (kgf/cm²; kg/cm²)	x 14.223	= Pounds-force per square inch (psi; lbf/in²; lb/in²)
Pounds-force per square inch (psi; lbf/in²; lb/in²)	x 0.068	= Atmospheres (atm)	x 14.696	= Pounds-force per square inch (psi; lbf/in²; lb/in²)
Pounds-force per square inch (psi; lbf/in²; lb/in²)	x 0.069	= Bars	x 14.5	= Pounds-force per square inch (psi; lbf/in²; lb/in²)
Pounds-force per square inch (psi; lbf/in²; lb/in²)	x 6.895	= Kilopascals (kPa)	x 0.145	= Pounds-force per square inch (psi; lbf/in²; lb/in²)
Kilopascals (kPa)	x 0.01	= Kilograms-force per square centimetre (kgf/cm²; kg/cm²)	x 98.1	= Kilopascals (kPa)
Millibar (mbar)	x 100	= Pascals (Pa)	x 0.01	= Millibar (mbar)
Millibar (mbar)	x 0.0145	= Pounds-force per square inch (psi; lbf/in²; lb/in²)	x 68.947	= Millibar (mbar)
Millibar (mbar)	x 0.75	= Millimetres of mercury (mmHg)	x 1.333	= Millibar (mbar)
Millibar (mbar)	x 0.401	= Inches of water (inH₂O)	x 2.491	= Millibar (mbar)
Millimetres of mercury (mmHg)	x 0.535	= Inches of water (inH₂O)	x 1.868	= Millimetres of mercury (mmHg)
Inches of water (inH₂O)	x 0.036	= Pounds-force per square inch (psi; lbf/in²; lb/in²)	x 27.68	= Inches of water (inH₂O)

Torque (moment of force)

Pounds-force inches (lbf in; lb in)	x 1.152	= Kilograms-force centimetre (kgf cm; kg cm)	x 0.868	= Pounds-force inches (lbf in; lb in)
Pounds-force inches (lbf in; lb in)	x 0.113	= Newton metres (Nm)	x 8.85	= Pounds-force inches (lbf in; lb in)
Pounds-force inches (lbf in; lb in)	x 0.083	= Pounds-force feet (lbf ft; lb ft)	x 12	= Pounds-force inches (lbf in; lb in)
Pounds-force feet (lbf ft; lb ft)	x 0.138	= Kilograms-force metres (kgf m; kg m)	x 7.233	= Pounds-force feet (lbf ft; lb ft)
Pounds-force feet (lbf ft; lb ft)	x 1.356	= Newton metres (Nm)	x 0.738	= Pounds-force feet (lbf ft; lb ft)
Newton metres (Nm)	x 0.102	= Kilograms-force metres (kgf m; kg m)	x 9.804	= Newton metres (Nm)

Power

Horsepower (hp)	x 745.7	= Watts (W)	x 0.0013	= Horsepower (hp)

Velocity (speed)

Miles per hour (miles/hr; mph)	x 1.609	= Kilometres per hour (km/hr; kph)	x 0.621	= Miles per hour (miles/hr; mph)

Fuel consumption*

Miles per gallon (mpg)	x 0.354	= Kilometres per litre (km/l)	x 2.825	= Miles per gallon (mpg)

Temperature

Degrees Fahrenheit = (°C x 1.8) + 32   Degrees Celsius (Degrees Centigrade; °C) = (°F - 32) x 0.56

It is common practice to convert from miles per gallon (mpg) to litres/100 kilometres (l/100km), where mpg x l/100 km = 282

About the MOT Test

In the UK, all vehicles more than three years old are subject to an annual test to ensure that they meet minimum safety requirements. A current test certificate must be issued before a machine can be used on public roads, and is required before a road fund licence can be issued. Riding without a current test certificate will also invalidate your insurance.

For most owners, the MOT test is an annual cause for anxiety, and this is largely due to owners not being sure what needs to be checked prior to submitting the motorcycle for testing. The simple answer is that a fully roadworthy motorcycle will have no difficulty in passing the test.

This is a guide to getting your motorcycle through the MOT test. Obviously it will not be possible to examine the motorcycle to the same standard as the professional MOT tester, particularly in view of the equipment required for some of the checks. However, working through the following procedures will enable you to identify any problem areas before submitting the motorcycle for the test.

It has only been possible to summarise the test requirements here, based on the regulations in force at the time of printing. Test standards are becoming increasingly stringent, although there are some exemptions for older vehicles. More information about the MOT test can be obtained from the TSO publications, *How Safe is your Motorcycle* and *The MOT Inspection Manual for Motorcycle Testing*.

Many of the checks require that one of the wheels is raised off the ground. If the motorcycle doesn't have a centre stand, note that an auxiliary stand will be required. Additionally, the help of an assistant may prove useful.

Certain exceptions apply to machines under 50 cc, machines without a lighting system, and Classic bikes - if in doubt about any of the requirements listed below seek confirmation from an MOT tester prior to submitting the motorcycle for the test.

Check that the frame number is clearly visible.

Electrical System

Lights, turn signals, horn and reflector

✔ With the ignition on, check the operation of the following electrical components. **Note:** *The electrical components on certain small-capacity machines are powered by the generator, requiring that the engine is run for this check.*

a) *Headlight and tail light. Check that both illuminate in the low and high beam switch positions.*

b) *Position lights. Check that the front position (or sidelight) and tail light illuminate in this switch position.*

c) *Turn signals. Check that all flash at the correct rate, and that the warning light(s) function correctly. Check that the turn signal switch works correctly.*

d) *Hazard warning system (where fitted). Check that all four turn signals flash in this switch position.*

e) *Brake stop light. Check that the light comes on when the front and rear brakes are independently applied. Models first used on or after 1st April 1986 must have a brake light switch on each brake.*

f) *Horn. Check that the sound is continuous and of reasonable volume.*

✔ Check that there is a red reflector on the rear of the machine, either mounted separately or as part of the tail light lens.

✔ Check the condition of the headlight, tail light and turn signal lenses.

Headlight beam height

✔ The MOT tester will perform a headlight beam height check using specialised beam setting equipment **(see illustration 1)**. This equipment will not be available to the home mechanic, but if you suspect that the headlight is incorrectly set or may have been maladjusted in the past, you can perform a rough test as follows.

✔ Position the bike in a straight line facing a brick wall. The bike must be off its stand, upright and with a rider seated. Measure the height from the ground to the centre of the headlight and mark a horizontal line on the wall at this height. Position the motorcycle 3.8 metres from the wall and draw a vertical

Headlight beam height checking equipment

line up the wall central to the centreline of the motorcycle. Switch to dipped beam and check that the beam pattern falls slightly lower than the horizontal line and to the left of the vertical line **(see illustration 2)**.

Home workshop beam alignment check

Exhaust System and Final Drive

Exhaust

✔ Check that the exhaust mountings are secure and that the system does not foul any of the rear suspension components.
✔ Start the motorcycle. When the revs are increased, check that the exhaust is neither holed nor leaking from any of its joints. On a linked system, check that the collector box is not leaking due to corrosion.

✔ Note that the exhaust decibel level ("loudness" of the exhaust) is assessed at the discretion of the tester. If the motorcycle was first used on or after 1st January 1985 the silencer must carry the BSAU 193 stamp, or a marking relating to its make and model, or be of OE (original equipment) manufacture. If the silencer is marked NOT FOR ROAD USE, RACING USE ONLY or similar, it will fail the MOT.

Final drive

✔ On chain or belt drive machines, check that the chain/belt is in good condition and does not have excessive slack. Also check that the sprocket is securely mounted on the rear wheel hub. Check that the chain/belt guard is in place.
✔ On shaft drive bikes, check for oil leaking from the drive unit and fouling the rear tyre.

Steering and Suspension

Steering

✔ With the front wheel raised off the ground, rotate the steering from lock to lock. The handlebar or switches must not contact the fuel tank or be close enough to trap the rider's hand. Problems can be caused by damaged lock stops on the lower yoke and frame, or by the fitting of non-standard handlebars.
✔ When performing the lock to lock check, also ensure that the steering moves freely without drag or notchiness. Steering movement can be impaired by poorly routed cables, or by overtight head bearings or worn bearings. The tester will perform a check of the steering head bearing lower race by mounting the front wheel on a surface plate, then performing a lock to

lock check with the weight of the machine on the lower bearing (see illustration 3).
✔ Grasp the fork sliders (lower legs) and attempt to push and pull on the forks (see

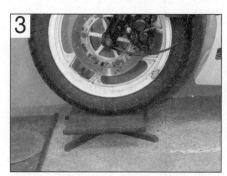

Front wheel mounted on a surface plate for steering head bearing lower race check

illustration 4). Any play in the steering head bearings will be felt. Note that in extreme cases, wear of the front fork bushes can be misinterpreted for head bearing play.
✔ Check that the handlebars are securely mounted.
✔ Check that the handlebar grip rubbers are secure. They should by bonded to the bar left end and to the throttle cable pulley on the right end.

Front suspension

✔ With the motorcycle off the stand, hold the front brake on and pump the front forks up and down (see illustration 5). Check that they are adequately damped.

Checking the steering head bearings for freeplay

Hold the front brake on and pump the front forks up and down to check operation

Inspect the area around the fork dust seal for oil leakage (arrow)

Bounce the rear of the motorcycle to check rear suspension operation

Checking for rear suspension linkage play

✔ Inspect the area above and around the front fork oil seals **(see illustration 6)**. There should be no sign of oil on the fork tube (stanchion) nor leaking down the slider (lower leg). On models so equipped, check that there is no oil leaking from the anti-dive units.

✔ On models with swingarm front suspension, check that there is no freeplay in the linkage when moved from side to side.

Rear suspension

✔ With the motorcycle off the stand and an assistant supporting the motorcycle by its handlebars, bounce the rear suspension **(see illustration 7)**. Check that the suspension components do not foul on any of the cycle parts and check that the shock absorber(s) provide adequate damping.

✔ Visually inspect the shock absorber(s) and check that there is no sign of oil leakage from its damper. This is somewhat restricted on certain single shock models due to the location of the shock absorber.

✔ With the rear wheel raised off the ground, grasp the wheel at the highest point and attempt to pull it up **(see illustration 8)**. Any play in the swingarm pivot or suspension linkage bearings will be felt as movement. **Note:** *Do not confuse play with actual suspension movement. Failure to lubricate suspension linkage bearings can lead to bearing failure* **(see illustration 9)**.

✔ With the rear wheel raised off the ground, grasp the swingarm ends and attempt to move the swingarm from side to side and forwards and backwards - any play indicates wear of the swingarm pivot bearings **(see illustration 10)**.

Worn suspension linkage pivots (arrows) are usually the cause of play in the rear suspension

Grasp the swingarm at the ends to check for play in its pivot bearings

Brake pad wear can usually be viewed without removing the caliper. Most pads have wear indicator grooves (1) and some also have indicator tangs (2)

On drum brakes, check the angle of the operating lever with the brake fully applied. Most drum brakes have a wear indicator pointer and scale.

Brakes, Wheels and Tyres

Brakes

✔ With the wheel raised off the ground, apply the brake then free it off, and check that the wheel is about to revolve freely without brake drag.

✔ On disc brakes, examine the disc itself. Check that it is securely mounted and not cracked.

✔ On disc brakes, view the pad material through the caliper mouth and check that the pads are not worn down beyond the limit **(see illustration 11)**.

✔ On drum brakes, check that when the brake is applied the angle between the operating lever and cable or rod is not too great **(see illustration 12)**. Check also that the operating lever doesn't foul any other components.

✔ On disc brakes, examine the flexible hoses from top to bottom. Have an assistant hold the brake on so that the fluid in the hose is under pressure, and check that there is no sign of fluid leakage, bulges or cracking. If there are any metal brake pipes or unions, check that these are free from corrosion and damage. Where a brake-linked anti-dive system is fitted, check the hoses to the anti-dive in a similar manner.

✔ Check that the rear brake torque arm is secure and that its fasteners are secured by self-locking nuts or castellated nuts with split-pins or R-pins **(see illustration 13)**.

✔ On models with ABS, check that the self-check warning light in the instrument panel works.

✔ The MOT tester will perform a test of the motorcycle's braking efficiency based on a calculation of rider and motorcycle weight. Although this cannot be carried out at home, you can at least ensure that the braking systems are properly maintained. For hydraulic disc brakes, check the fluid level, lever/pedal feel (bleed of air if its spongy) and pad material. For drum brakes, check adjustment, cable or rod operation and shoe lining thickness.

Wheels and tyres

✔ Check the wheel condition. Cast wheels should be free from cracks and if of the built-up design, all fasteners should be secure. Spoked wheels should be checked for broken, corroded, loose or bent spokes.

✔ With the wheel raised off the ground, spin the wheel and visually check that the tyre and wheel run true. Check that the tyre does not foul the suspension or mudguards.

✔ With the wheel raised off the ground, grasp the wheel and attempt to move it about the axle (spindle) **(see illustration 14)**. Any play felt here indicates wheel bearing failure.

Brake torque arm must be properly secured at both ends

Check for wheel bearing play by trying to move the wheel about the axle (spindle)

Checking the tyre tread depth

Tyre direction of rotation arrow can be found on tyre sidewall

Castellated type wheel axle (spindle) nut must be secured by a split pin or R-pin

Two straightedges are used to check wheel alignment

✔ Check the tyre tread depth, tread condition and sidewall condition (see illustration 15).
✔ Check the tyre type. Front and rear tyre types must be compatible and be suitable for road use. Tyres marked NOT FOR ROAD USE, COMPETITION USE ONLY or similar, will fail the MOT.

✔ If the tyre sidewall carries a direction of rotation arrow, this must be pointing in the direction of normal wheel rotation (see illustration 16).
✔ Check that the wheel axle (spindle) nuts (where applicable) are properly secured. A self-locking nut or castellated nut with a split-pin or R-pin can be used (see illustration 17).
✔ Wheel alignment is checked with the motorcycle off the stand and a rider seated. With the front wheel pointing straight ahead, two perfectly straight lengths of metal or wood and placed against the sidewalls of both tyres (see illustration 18). The gap each side of the front tyre must be equidistant on both sides. Incorrect wheel alignment may be due to a cocked rear wheel (often as the result of poor chain adjustment) or in extreme cases, a bent frame.

General checks and condition

✔ Check the security of all major fasteners, bodypanels, seat, fairings (where fitted) and mudguards.

✔ Check that the rider and pillion footrests, handlebar levers and brake pedal are securely mounted.

✔ Check for corrosion on the frame or any load-bearing components. If severe, this may affect the structure, particularly under stress.

Sidecars

A motorcycle fitted with a sidecar requires additional checks relating to the stability of the machine and security of attachment and swivel joints, plus specific wheel alignment (toe-in) requirements. Additionally, tyre and lighting requirements differ from conventional motorcycle use. Owners are advised to check MOT test requirements with an official test centre.

Preparing for storage

Before you start

If repairs or an overhaul is needed, see that this is carried out now rather than left until you want to ride the bike again.

Give the bike a good wash and scrub all dirt from its underside. Make sure the bike dries completely before preparing for storage.

Engine

● Remove the spark plug(s) and lubricate the cylinder bores with approximately a teaspoon of motor oil using a spout-type oil can **(see illustration 1)**. Reinstall the spark plug(s). Crank the engine over a couple of times to coat the piston rings and bores with oil. If the bike has a kickstart, use this to turn the engine over. If not, flick the kill switch to the OFF position and crank the engine over on the starter **(see illustration 2)**. If the nature on the ignition system prevents the starter operating with the kill switch in the OFF position,

remove the spark plugs and fit them back in their caps; ensure that the plugs are earthed (grounded) against the cylinder head when the starter is operated **(see illustration 3)**.

⚠️ **Warning: It is important that the plugs are earthed (grounded) away from the spark plug holes otherwise there is a risk of atomised fuel from the cylinders igniting.**

HAYNES HINT *On a single cylinder four-stroke engine, you can seal the combustion chamber completely by positioning the piston at TDC on the compression stroke.*

● Drain the carburettor(s) otherwise there is a risk of jets becoming blocked by gum deposits from the fuel **(see illustration 4)**.

● If the bike is going into long-term storage, consider adding a fuel stabiliser to the fuel in the tank. If the tank is drained completely, corrosion of its internal surfaces may occur if left unprotected for a long period. The tank can be treated with a rust preventative especially for this purpose. Alternatively, remove the tank and pour half a litre of motor oil into it, install the filler cap and shake the tank to coat its internals with oil before draining off the excess. The same effect can also be achieved by spraying WD40 or a similar water-dispersant around the inside of the tank via its flexible nozzle.

● Make sure the cooling system contains the correct mix of antifreeze. Antifreeze also contains important corrosion inhibitors.

● The air intakes and exhaust can be sealed off by covering or plugging the openings. Ensure that you do not seal in any condensation; run the engine until it is hot,

Squirt a drop of motor oil into each cylinder

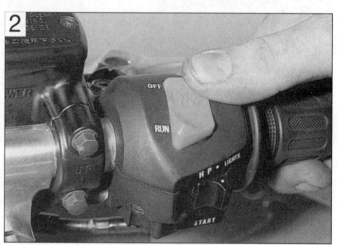

Flick the kill switch to OFF . . .

. . . and ensure that the metal bodies of the plugs (arrows) are earthed against the cylinder head

Connect a hose to the carburettor float chamber drain stub (arrow) and unscrew the drain screw

Exhausts can be sealed off with a plastic bag

Disconnect the negative lead (A) first, followed by the positive lead (B)

Use a suitable battery charger - this kit also assess battery condition

then switch off and allow to cool. Tape a piece of thick plastic over the silencer end(s) **(see illustration 5)**. Note that some advocate pouring a tablespoon of motor oil into the silencer(s) before sealing them off.

Battery

● Remove it from the bike - in extreme cases of cold the battery may freeze and crack its case **(see illustration 6)**.

● Check the electrolyte level and top up if necessary (conventional refillable batteries). Clean the terminals.
● Store the battery off the motorcycle and away from any sources of fire. Position a wooden block under the battery if it is to sit on the ground.
● Give the battery a trickle charge for a few hours every month **(see illustration 7)**.

Tyres

● Place the bike on its centrestand or an auxiliary stand which will support the motorcycle in an upright position. Position wood blocks under the tyres to keep them off the ground and to provide insulation from damp. If the bike is being put into long-term storage, ideally both tyres should be off the ground; not only will this protect the tyres, but will also ensure that no load is placed on the steering head or wheel bearings.
● Deflate each tyre by 5 to 10 psi, no more or the beads may unseat from the rim, making subsequent inflation difficult on tubeless tyres.

Pivots and controls

● Lubricate all lever, pedal, stand and footrest pivot points. If grease nipples are fitted to the rear suspension components, apply lubricant to the pivots.
● Lubricate all control cables.

Cycle components

● Apply a wax protectant to all painted and plastic components. Wipe off any excess, but don't polish to a shine. Where fitted, clean the screen with soap and water.
● Coat metal parts with Vaseline (petroleum jelly). When applying this to the fork tubes, do not compress the forks otherwise the seals will rot from contact with the Vaseline.
● Apply a vinyl cleaner to the seat.

Storage conditions

● Aim to store the bike in a shed or garage which does not leak and is free from damp.
● Drape an old blanket or bedspread over the bike to protect it from dust and direct contact with sunlight (which will fade paint). This also hides the bike from prying eyes. Beware of tight-fitting plastic covers which may allow condensation to form and settle on the bike.

Getting back on the road

Engine and transmission

● Change the oil and replace the oil filter. If this was done prior to storage, check that the oil hasn't emulsified - a thick whitish substance which occurs through condensation.
● Remove the spark plugs. Using a spout-type oil can, squirt a few drops of oil into the cylinder(s). This will provide initial lubrication as the piston rings and bores comes back into contact. Service the spark plugs, or fit new ones, and install them in the engine.

● Check that the clutch isn't stuck on. The plates can stick together if left standing for some time, preventing clutch operation. Engage a gear and try rocking the bike back and forth with the clutch lever held against the handlebar. If this doesn't work on cable-operated clutches, hold the clutch lever back against the handlebar with a strong elastic band or cable tie for a couple of hours **(see illustration 8)**.
● If the air intakes or silencer end(s) were blocked off, remove the bung or cover used.
● If the fuel tank was coated with a rust

Hold clutch lever back against the handlebar with elastic bands or a cable tie preventative, oil or a stabiliser added to the fuel, drain and flush the tank and dispose of the fuel sensibly. If no action was taken with the fuel tank prior to storage, it is advised that the old fuel is disposed of since it will go off over a period of time. Refill the fuel tank with fresh fuel.

Frame and running gear

● Oil all pivot points and cables.
● Check the tyre pressures. They will definitely need inflating if pressures were reduced for storage.
● Lubricate the final drive chain (where applicable).
● Remove any protective coating applied to the fork tubes (stanchions) since this may well destroy the fork seals. If the fork tubes weren't protected and have picked up rust spots, remove them with very fine abrasive paper and refinish with metal polish.
● Check that both brakes operate correctly. Apply each brake hard and check that it's not possible to move the motorcycle forwards, then check that the brake frees off again once released. Brake caliper pistons can stick due to corrosion around the piston head, or on the sliding caliper types, due to corrosion of the slider pins. If the brake doesn't free after repeated operation, take the caliper off for examination. Similarly drum brakes can stick due to a seized operating cam, cable or rod linkage.
● If the motorcycle has been in long-term storage, renew the brake fluid and clutch fluid (where applicable).
● Depending on where the bike has been stored, the wiring, cables and hoses may have been nibbled by rodents. Make a visual check and investigate disturbed wiring loom tape.

Battery

● If the battery has been previously removal and given top up charges it can simply be reconnected. Remember to connect the positive cable first and the negative cable last.
● On conventional refillable batteries, if the battery has not received any attention, remove it from the motorcycle and check its electrolyte level. Top up if necessary then charge the battery. If the battery fails to hold a charge and a visual checks show heavy white sulphation of the plates, the battery is probably defective and must be renewed. This is particularly likely if the battery is old. Confirm battery condition with a specific gravity check.
● On sealed (MF) batteries, if the battery has not received any attention, remove it from the motorcycle and charge it according to the information on the battery case - if the battery fails to hold a charge it must be renewed.

Starting procedure

● If a kickstart is fitted, turn the engine over a couple of times with the ignition OFF to distribute oil around the engine. If no kickstart is fitted, flick the engine kill switch OFF and the ignition ON and crank the engine over a couple of times to work oil around the upper cylinder components. If the nature of the ignition system is such that the starter won't work with the kill switch OFF, remove the spark plugs, fit them back into their caps and earth (ground) their bodies on the cylinder head. Reinstall the spark plugs afterwards.
● Switch the kill switch to RUN, operate the choke and start the engine. If the engine won't start don't continue cranking the engine - not only will this flatten the battery, but the starter motor will overheat. Switch the ignition off and try again later. If the engine refuses to start, go through the fault finding procedures in this manual. **Note:** *If the bike has been in storage for a long time, old fuel or a carburettor blockage may be the problem. Gum deposits in carburettors can block jets - if a carburettor cleaner doesn't prove successful the carburettors must be dismantled for cleaning.*
● Once the engine has started, check that the lights, turn signals and horn work properly.
● Treat the bike gently for the first ride and check all fluid levels on completion. Settle the bike back into the maintenance schedule.

This Section provides an easy reference-guide to the more common faults that are likely to afflict your machine. Obviously, the opportunities are almost limitless for faults to occur as a result of obscure failures, and to try and cover all eventualities would require a book. Indeed, a number have been written on the subject.

Successful troubleshooting is not a mysterious 'black art' but the application of a bit of knowledge combined with a systematic and logical approach to the problem. Approach any troubleshooting by first accurately identifying the symptom and then checking through the list of possible causes, starting with the simplest or most obvious and progressing in stages to the most complex.

Take nothing for granted, but above all apply liberal quantities of common sense.

The main symptom of a fault is given in the text as a major heading below which are listed the various systems or areas which may contain the fault. Details of each possible cause for a fault and the remedial action to be taken are given, in brief, in the paragraphs below each heading. Further information should be sought in the relevant Chapter.

1 Engine doesn't start or is difficult to start
- [ ] Starter motor doesn't rotate
- [ ] Starter motor rotates but engine does not turn over
- [ ] Starter works but engine won't turn over (seized)
- [ ] No fuel flow
- [ ] Engine flooded
- [ ] No spark or weak spark
- [ ] Compression low
- [ ] Stalls after starting
- [ ] Rough idle

2 Poor running at low speed
- [ ] Spark weak
- [ ] Fuel/air mixture incorrect
- [ ] Compression low
- [ ] Poor acceleration

3 Poor running or no power at high speed
- [ ] Firing incorrect
- [ ] Fuel/air mixture incorrect
- [ ] Compression low
- [ ] Knocking or pinking
- [ ] Miscellaneous causes

4 Overheating
- [ ] Engine overheats
- [ ] Firing incorrect
- [ ] Fuel/air mixture incorrect
- [ ] Compression too high
- [ ] Engine load excessive
- [ ] Lubrication inadequate
- [ ] Miscellaneous causes

5 Clutch problems
- [ ] Clutch slipping
- [ ] Clutch not disengaging completely

6 Gearchanging problems
- [ ] Doesn't go into gear, or lever doesn't return
- [ ] Jumps out of gear
- [ ] Overselects

7 Abnormal engine noise
- [ ] Knocking or pinking
- [ ] Piston slap or rattling
- [ ] Valve noise
- [ ] Other noise

8 Abnormal driveline noise
- [ ] Clutch noise
- [ ] Transmission noise
- [ ] Final drive noise

9 Abnormal frame and suspension noise
- [ ] Front end noise
- [ ] Shock absorber noise
- [ ] Brake noise

10 Oil level warning light comes on
- [ ] Engine lubrication system
- [ ] Electrical system

11 Excessive exhaust smoke
- [ ] White smoke
- [ ] Black smoke
- [ ] Brown smoke

12 Poor handling or stability
- [ ] Handlebar hard to turn
- [ ] Handlebar shakes or vibrates excessively
- [ ] Handlebar pulls to one side
- [ ] Poor shock absorbing qualities

13 Braking problems
- [ ] Brakes are spongy, don't hold
- [ ] Brake lever or pedal pulsates
- [ ] Brakes drag

14 Electrical problems
- [ ] Battery dead or weak
- [ ] Battery overcharged

1 Engine doesn't start or is difficult to start

Starter motor doesn't rotate

☐ Engine kill switch OFF.
☐ Main fuse blown (Chapter 8).
☐ Battery voltage low. Check and recharge battery (Chapter 8).
☐ Starter motor defective. Make sure the wiring to the starter is secure. Make sure the starter relay clicks when the start button is pushed. If the relay clicks, then the fault is in the wiring or motor (see Chapter 8).
☐ Starter switch not contacting. The contacts could be wet, corroded or dirty. Disassemble and clean the switch (Chapter 8).
☐ Wiring open or shorted. Check all wiring connections and harnesses to make sure that they are dry, tight and not corroded. Also check for broken or frayed wires that can cause a short to ground (earth) (see Wiring diagrams, Chapter 8).
☐ Ignition switch defective. Check the switch and replace with a new one if it is defective (see Chapter 8).
☐ Engine kill switch defective. Check for wet, dirty or corroded contacts. Clean or replace the switch with a new one as necessary (see Chapter 8).
☐ Faulty neutral switch, sidestand switch or clutch switch. Check the wiring to each switch and the switch itself (see Chapter 8).
☐ Faulty starter circuit cut-off relay or diode (Chapter 8).
☐ Fuel injection system shutdown due to system fault (Chapter 4).

Starter motor rotates but engine does not turn over

☐ Starter clutch defective. Inspect and repair or replace with a new one (see Chapter 2).
☐ Damaged idler or starter gears. Inspect and replace the damaged parts (see Chapter 2).

Starter works but engine won't turn over (seized)

☐ Seized engine caused by one or more internally damaged components. Failure due to wear, abuse or lack of lubrication. Damage can include seized valves, followers, camshafts, pistons, crankshaft, connecting rod bearings, or transmission gears or bearings. Refer to Chapter 2 for engine disassembly.

No fuel flow

☐ No fuel in tank.
☐ Fuel tank breather hose obstructed.
☐ Faulty fuel pump relay. Check the relay (see Chapter 4).
☐ Fuel pump or pressure regulator faulty, or the fuel filter is blocked (see Chapter 4).
☐ Fuel hose clogged. Remove the fuel hose and carefully blow through it. Check the fuel filter for damage.
☐ Fuel rail or injector clogged. For all of the injectors to be clogged, either a very bad batch of fuel with an unusual additive has been used, or some other foreign material has entered the tank. Check the fuel pump. In some cases, if a machine has been unused for several months, the fuel turns to a varnish-like liquid which can cause an injector needle to stick to its seat. Drain the tank and fuel system (Chapter 4).

Engine flooded

☐ Injector needle valve worn or stuck open. A piece of dirt, rust or other debris can cause the needle to seat improperly, causing excess fuel to be admitted to the throttle body. In this case, the injector should be cleaned and the needle and seat inspected (see Chapter 4). If the needle and seat are worn, then the leaking will persist and the parts should be renewed.
☐ Starting technique incorrect. Under normal circumstances (i.e. if all the components of the fuel injection system are good) the machine should start with the throttle closed.

No spark or weak spark

☐ Ignition switch OFF.
☐ Engine kill switch turned to the OFF position.
☐ Ignition or kill switch shorted. This is usually caused by water, corrosion, damage or excessive wear. The switches can be disassembled and cleaned with electrical contact cleaner. If cleaning does not help, replace the switches (see Chapter 8).
☐ Battery voltage low. Check and recharge the battery as necessary (Chapter 8).
☐ Spark plug cap not making good contact. Make sure that the caps fit snugly over the plug ends.
☐ Spark plugs dirty, defective or worn out. Locate reason for fouled plugs using spark plug condition chart on the inside back cover and follow the plug maintenance procedures (see Chapter 1).
☐ Incorrect spark plugs. Wrong type or heat range. Check and install correct plugs (see Chapter 1).
☐ Ignition coil defective. Test and renew if necessary (Chapter 4).
☐ Fuel injection system shutdown due to system fault (Chapter 4).
☐ Crankshaft position (CKP) sensor defective (see Chapter 4).
☐ Engine control unit (ECU) defective (see Chapter 4).
☐ Wiring shorted or broken between:
   a) Ignition switch and engine kill switch (or blown fuse)
   b) ECU and engine kill switch
   c) ECU and ignition coils
   d) ECU and CKP sensor
☐ Make sure that all wiring connections are clean, dry and tight. Look for chafed and broken wires (see Chapters 4 and 8).

Compression low

☐ Spark plugs loose. Remove the plugs and inspect their threads. Reinstall and tighten securely (see Chapter 1).
☐ Cylinder head not sufficiently tightened down. If a cylinder head is suspected of being loose, then there's a chance that the gasket or head is damaged if the problem has persisted for any length of time. The head bolts should be tightened to the proper torque and in the correct sequence (Chapter 2).
☐ Improper valve clearance. This means that the valve is not closing completely and compression pressure is leaking past the valve. Check and adjust the valve clearances (Chapter 1).
☐ Cylinder and/or piston worn. Excessive wear will cause compression pressure to leak past the rings. This is usually accompanied by worn rings as well. A top-end overhaul is necessary (Chapter 2).
☐ Piston rings worn, weak, broken, or sticking. Broken or sticking piston rings usually indicate a lubrication or fuelling problem that causes excess carbon deposits to form on the pistons and rings. Top-end overhaul is necessary (Chapter 2).
☐ Piston ring-to-groove clearance excessive. This is caused by excessive wear of the piston ring lands. Piston renewal is necessary (Chapter 2).
☐ Cylinder head gasket damaged. If a head is allowed to become loose, or if excessive carbon build-up on the piston crown and combustion chamber causes extremely high compression, the head gasket may leak. Retorquing the head is not always sufficient to restore the seal, so a new gasket is necessary (Chapter 2).
☐ Cylinder head warped. This is caused by overheating or improperly tightened head bolts. Machine shop resurfacing or head renewal is necessary (Chapter 2).
☐ Valve spring broken or weak. Caused by component failure or wear; the springs must be renewed (Chapter 2).
☐ Valve not seating properly. This is caused by a bent valve (from over-revving or improper valve adjustment), burned valve or seat (incorrect air/fuel mixture) or an accumulation of carbon deposits on the seat. The valves must be cleaned and/or renewed and the seats serviced (Chapter 2).

1 Engine doesn't start or is difficult to start (continued)

Stalls after starting

- [ ] Faulty fast idle system. Check the operation of the wax unit (see Chapter 4).
- [ ] Engine idle speed incorrect. Turn idle adjusting screw until the engine idles at the specified rpm (Chapter 1).
- [ ] Ignition malfunction (see Chapter 4).
- [ ] Fuel injection system malfunction (see Chapter 4).
- [ ] Fuel contaminated. The fuel can be contaminated with either dirt or water, or can change chemically if the machine has been unused for several months. Drain the tank and fuel system (Chapter 4).
- [ ] Intake air leak. Check for loose throttle body-to-intake manifold connections, loose or damaged AIS vacuum hose or throttle body vacuum hoses (Chapter 4).

Rough idle

- [ ] Idle speed incorrect (see Chapter 1).
- [ ] Ignition fault (see Chapter 4).
- [ ] Throttle body air screws not synchronised. Adjust them as described in Chapter 1.
- [ ] Fuel injection system malfunction (see Chapter 4).
- [ ] Fuel contaminated. The fuel can be contaminated with either dirt or water, or can change chemically if the machine has been unused for several months. Drain the tank and the fuel system (Chapter 4).
- [ ] Intake air leak. Check for loose throttle body-to-intake manifold connections, loose or damaged AIS vacuum hose or throttle body vacuum hoses (Chapter 4).
- [ ] Air filter clogged. Clean the air filter element or replace it with a new one (Chapter 1).

2 Poor running at low speeds

Spark weak

- [ ] Battery voltage low. Check and recharge battery (see Chapter 8).
- [ ] Spark plug caps not making good contact. Make sure that the caps fit snugly over the plug ends.
- [ ] Spark plugs dirty, defective or worn out. Locate reason for fouled plugs using spark plug condition chart on the inside back cover and follow the plug maintenance procedures (see Chapter 1).
- [ ] Incorrect spark plugs. Wrong type or heat range. Check and install correct plugs (see Chapter 1).
- [ ] Ignition coil defective. Test and renew if necessary (see Chapter 4).

Fuel/air mixture incorrect

- [ ] Fuel tank breather hose obstructed.
- [ ] Fuel pump or pressure regulator faulty, or the fuel filter is blocked (see Chapter 4).
- [ ] Fuel hose clogged. Remove the fuel hose and carefully blow through it. Check the fuel filter for damage.
- [ ] Fuel rail or injector clogged. For all of the injectors to be clogged, either a very bad batch of fuel with an unusual additive has been used, or some other foreign material has entered the tank. Check the fuel pump. In some cases, if a machine has been unused for several months, the fuel turns to a varnish-like liquid which can cause an injector needle to stick to its seat. Drain the tank and fuel system (Chapter 4).
- [ ] Intake air leak. Check for loose throttle body-to-intake manifold connections, loose or damaged AIS vacuum hose or throttle body vacuum hoses (Chapter 4).
- [ ] Air filter clogged. Clean the air filter element or replace it with a new one (Chapter 1).

Compression low

Check by performing a compression test (see Chapter 2).
- [ ] Spark plugs loose. Remove the plugs and inspect their threads. Reinstall and tighten securely (see Chapter 1).
- [ ] Cylinder head not sufficiently tightened down. If a cylinder head is suspected of being loose, then there's a chance that the gasket or head is damaged if the problem has persisted for any length of time. The head bolts should be tightened to the proper torque and in the correct sequence (Chapter 2).
- [ ] Improper valve clearance. This means that the valve is not closing completely and compression pressure is leaking past the valve. Check and adjust the valve clearances (Chapter 1).
- [ ] Cylinder and/or piston worn. Excessive wear will cause compression pressure to leak past the rings. This is usually accompanied by worn rings as well. A top-end overhaul is necessary (Chapter 2).
- [ ] Piston rings worn, weak, broken, or sticking. Broken or sticking piston rings usually indicate a lubrication or fuelling problem that causes excess carbon deposits to form on the pistons and rings. Top-end overhaul is necessary (Chapter 2).
- [ ] Piston ring-to-groove clearance excessive. This is caused by excessive wear of the piston ring lands. Piston renewal is necessary (Chapter 2).
- [ ] Cylinder head gasket damaged. If the head is allowed to become loose, or if excessive carbon build-up on the piston crown and combustion chamber causes extremely high compression, the head gasket may leak. Retorquing the head is not always sufficient to restore the seal, so a new gasket is necessary (Chapter 2).
- [ ] Cylinder head warped. This is caused by overheating or improperly tightened head bolts. Machine shop resurfacing or head renewal is necessary (Chapter 2).
- [ ] Valve spring broken or weak. Caused by component failure or wear; the springs must be renewed (Chapter 2).
- [ ] Valve not seating properly. This is caused by a bent valve (from over-revving or improper valve adjustment), burned valve or seat (improper fuelling) or an accumulation of carbon deposits on the seat (from fuelling or lubrication problems). The valves must be cleaned and/or renewed and the seats serviced (Chapter 2).

Poor acceleration

- [ ] Timing not advancing. The crankshaft position sensor (CKP) or the engine control unit (ECU) may be defective (see Chapter 4). If so, they must be renewed.
- [ ] Engine oil viscosity too high. Using a heavier oil than that recommended in Chapter 1 can damage the oil pump or lubrication system and cause drag on the engine.
- [ ] Brakes dragging. Usually caused by debris which has entered the brake caliper piston seals, or from a warped disc or bent axle (see Chapter 6).

3 Poor running or no power at high speed

Firing incorrect

☐ Spark plug caps not making good contact. Make sure that the caps fit snugly over the plug ends and that the wiring is secure.

☐ Spark plugs dirty, defective or worn out. Locate reason for fouled plugs using spark plug condition chart on the inside back cover and follow the plug maintenance procedures (see Chapter 1).

☐ Incorrect spark plugs. Wrong type or heat range. Check and install correct plugs (see Chapter 1).

☐ Ignition coil defective. Test and renew if necessary (see Chapter 4).

☐ Faulty ECU (engine control unit) (see Chapter 4).

Fuel/air mixture incorrect

☐ Fuel tank breather hose obstructed.

☐ Fuel pump or pressure regulator faulty, or the fuel filter is blocked (see Chapter 4).

☐ Fuel hose clogged. Remove the fuel hose and carefully blow through it. Check the fuel filter for damage.

☐ Fuel rail or injector clogged. For all of the injectors to be clogged, either a very bad batch of fuel with an unusual additive has been used, or some other foreign material has entered the tank. Check the fuel pump. In some cases, if a machine has been unused for several months, the fuel turns to a varnish-like liquid which can cause an injector needle to stick to its seat. Drain the tank and fuel system (Chapter 4).

☐ Intake air leak. Check for loose throttle body-to-intake manifold connections, loose or damaged AIS vacuum hose or throttle body vacuum hoses (Chapter 4).

☐ Air filter clogged. Clean the air filter element or replace it with a new one (Chapter 1).

Compression low

Check by performing a compression test (see Chapter 2).

☐ Spark plugs loose. Remove the plugs and inspect their threads. Reinstall and tighten securely (see Chapter 1).

☐ Cylinder head not sufficiently tightened down. If a cylinder head is suspected of being loose, then there's a chance that the gasket or head is damaged if the problem has persisted for any length of time. The head bolts should be tightened to the proper torque and in the correct sequence (Chapter 2).

☐ Improper valve clearance. This means that the valve is not closing completely and compression pressure is leaking past the valve. Check and adjust the valve clearances (Chapter 1).

☐ Cylinder and/or piston worn. Excessive wear will cause compression pressure to leak past the rings. This is usually accompanied by worn rings as well. A top-end overhaul is necessary (Chapter 2).

☐ Piston rings worn, weak, broken, or sticking. Broken or sticking piston rings usually indicate a lubrication or fuelling problem that causes excess carbon deposits to form on the pistons and rings. Top-end overhaul is necessary (Chapter 2).

☐ Piston ring-to-groove clearance excessive. This is caused by excessive wear of the piston ring lands. Piston renewal is necessary (Chapter 2).

☐ Cylinder head gasket damaged. If a head is allowed to become loose, or if excessive carbon build-up on the piston crown and combustion chamber causes extremely high compression, the head gasket may leak. Retorquing the head is not always sufficient to restore the seal, so a new gasket is necessary (Chapter 2).

☐ Cylinder head warped. This is caused by overheating or improperly tightened head bolts. Machine shop resurfacing or head renewal is necessary (Chapter 2).

☐ Valve spring broken or weak. Caused by component failure or wear; the springs must be replaced with new ones (Chapter 2).

☐ Valve not seating properly. This is caused by a bent valve (from over-revving or improper valve adjustment), burned valve or seat (improper fuelling) or an accumulation of carbon deposits on the seat (from fuelling or lubrication problems). The valves must be cleaned and/or renewed and the seats serviced (Chapter 2).

Knocking or pinking

☐ Carbon build-up in combustion chamber. Use of a fuel additive that will dissolve the adhesive bonding the carbon particles to the piston crown and chamber is the easiest way to remove the build-up. Otherwise, the cylinder head will have to be removed and decarbonised (Chapter 2).

☐ Incorrect or poor quality fuel. Old or improper grades of fuel can cause detonation. This causes the piston to rattle, thus the knocking or pinking sound. Drain old fuel and always use the recommended fuel grade.

☐ Spark plug heat range incorrect. Uncontrolled detonation indicates the plug heat range is too hot. The plug in effect becomes a glow plug, raising cylinder temperatures. Install the proper heat range plug (Chapter 1).

☐ Improper air/fuel mixture. This will cause the cylinders to run hot, which leads to detonation. A blockage in the fuel system or an air leak can cause this imbalance (see Chapter 4).

Miscellaneous causes

☐ Throttle valve doesn't open fully. Adjust the throttle cable freeplay (see Chapter 1).

☐ Clutch slipping due loose or worn clutch components (see Chapter 2).

☐ Timing not advancing. The crankshaft position sensor (CKP) or the engine control unit (ECU) may be defective (see Chapter 4). If so, they must be replaced with new ones.

☐ Engine oil viscosity too high. Using a heavier oil than the one recommended in Chapter 1 can damage the oil pump or lubrication system and cause drag on the engine.

☐ Brakes dragging. Usually caused by debris which has entered the brake caliper piston seals, or from a warped disc or bent axle (see Chapter 6).

4 Overheating

Engine overheats

- [ ] Coolant level low. Check and add coolant (see *Pre-ride checks*).
- [ ] Leak in cooling system. Check cooling system hoses and radiator for leaks and other damage. Repair or renew parts as necessary (see Chapter 3).
- [ ] Faulty thermostat. Check and renew as described in Chapter 3.
- [ ] Faulty radiator cap. Remove the cap and have it pressure tested.
- [ ] Coolant passages clogged. Drain, flush and refill with fresh coolant (Chapter 1).
- [ ] Water pump defective. Remove the pump and check the components (see Chapter 3).
- [ ] Clogged or damaged radiator fins (see Chapter 3).
- [ ] Faulty cooling fan, relay or fan switch (see Chapter 3).

Firing incorrect

- [ ] Wrongly connected ignition coil wiring.
- [ ] Spark plugs dirty, defective or worn out. Locate reason for fouled plugs using spark plug condition chart on the inside back cover and follow the plug maintenance procedures (see Chapter 1).
- [ ] Incorrect spark plugs. Wrong type or heat range. Check and install correct plugs (see Chapter 1).
- [ ] Ignition coil defective. Test and replace with a new one if necessary (see Chapter 4).
- [ ] Faulty engine control unit (ECU) (see Chapter 4).

Fuel/air mixture incorrect

- [ ] Fuel tank breather hose obstructed.
- [ ] Fuel pump or pressure regulator faulty, or the fuel filter is blocked (see Chapter 4).
- [ ] Fuel hose clogged. Remove the fuel hose and carefully blow through it. Check the fuel filter for damage.
- [ ] Fuel rail or injector clogged. For all of the injectors to be clogged, either a very bad batch of fuel with an unusual additive has been used, or some other foreign material has entered the tank. Check the fuel pump. In some cases, if a machine has been unused for several months, the fuel turns to a varnish-like liquid which can cause an injector needle to stick to its seat. Drain the tank and fuel system (Chapter 4).
- [ ] Intake air leak. Check for loose throttle body-to-intake manifold connections, loose or damaged AIS vacuum hose or throttle body vacuum hoses (Chapter 4).

- [ ] Air filter clogged. Clean the air filter element or replace it with a new one (Chapter 1).

Compression too high

Check by performing a compression test (see Chapter 2).

- [ ] Carbon build-up in combustion chamber. Use of a fuel additive that will dissolve the adhesive bonding the carbon particles to the piston crown and chamber is the easiest way to remove the build-up. Otherwise, the cylinder head will have to be removed and decarbonised (Chapter 2).
- [ ] Improperly machined head surface or installation of incorrect gasket during engine assembly.

Engine load excessive

- [ ] Clutch slipping due loose or worn clutch components (see Chapter 2).
- [ ] Engine oil level too high. Too much oil will cause pressurisation of the crankcase and inefficient engine operation. Check Specifications and drain to proper level (Chapter 1 and *Pre-ride checks*).
- [ ] Engine oil viscosity too high. Using a heavier oil than the one recommended in Chapter 1 can damage the oil pump or lubrication system as well as cause drag on the engine.
- [ ] Brakes dragging. Usually caused by debris which has entered the brake caliper piston seals, or from a warped disc or bent axle (see Chapter 6).

Lubrication inadequate

- [ ] Engine oil level too low. Friction caused by intermittent lack of lubrication or from oil that is overworked can cause overheating. The oil provides a definite cooling function in the engine. Check the oil level (see *Pre-ride checks*).
- [ ] Low engine oil pressure. Check the pressure (see Chapter 2).
- [ ] Blocked oil filter or oil cooler (see Chapter 2).

Miscellaneous causes

- [ ] Modification to exhaust system. Most aftermarket exhaust systems cause the engine to run leaner, which make them run hotter. When installing an accessory exhaust system, always check with the manufacturer/supplier as to whether the fuel system requires adjustment.

5 Clutch problems

Clutch slipping

- [ ] Insufficient clutch cable freeplay. Check and adjust (see Chapter 1).
- [ ] Clutch plates worn or warped. Overhaul the clutch assembly (see Chapter 2).
- [ ] Clutch springs broken or weak. Old or heat-damaged (from slipping clutch) springs should be renewed (Chapter 2).
- [ ] Faulty clutch release mechanism. Replace any defective parts with new ones (see Chapter 2).
- [ ] Clutch centre or housing unevenly worn. This causes improper engagement of the plates. Replace the damaged or worn parts (see Chapter 2).
- [ ] Incorrect oil used in engine. Oils designed for car engines often contain friction modifiers which if used in an engine with a wet clutch can promote clutch slip. Always use an oil designed for motorcycle engines (see *Pre-ride checks*).

Clutch not disengaging completely

- [ ] Excessive clutch cable freeplay. Check and adjust (see Chapter 1).
- [ ] Clutch plates warped or damaged. This will cause clutch drag,

which in turn will cause the machine to creep. Overhaul the clutch assembly (see Chapter 2).
- [ ] Clutch springs fatigued or broken. Check and renew the springs (see Chapter 2).
- [ ] Engine oil deteriorated. Old, thin oil will not provide proper lubrication for the plates, causing the clutch to drag. Renew the oil and filter (see Chapter 1).
- [ ] Engine oil viscosity too high. Using a heavier oil than recommended in Chapter 1 can cause the plates to stick together. Change to the correct weight oil.
- [ ] Clutch housing bearing seized on the transmission input shaft. Lack of lubrication, severe wear or damage can cause the bearing to seize. Overhaul of the clutch, and perhaps transmission, may be necessary to repair the damage (see Chapter 2).
- [ ] Faulty clutch release mechanism. Renew any defective parts (see Chapter 2).
- [ ] Loose clutch centre nut. Causes housing and centre misalignment putting a drag on the engine. Engagement adjustment continually varies. Overhaul the clutch assembly (see Chapter 2).

6 Gearchanging problems

Doesn't go into gear or lever doesn't return

- ☐ Clutch not disengaging (see above).
- ☐ Gearchange mechanism stopper arm spring weak or broken, or arm roller broken or worn. Replace the spring or arm with a new one (see Chapter 2).
- ☐ Selector fork(s) bent, worn or seized. Overhaul the transmission (see Chapter 2).
- ☐ Gear(s) stuck on shaft. Most often caused by a lack of lubrication or excessive wear in transmission bearings and bushes. Overhaul the transmission (see Chapter 2).
- ☐ Selector drum binding. Caused by lubrication failure or excessive wear. Replace the drum and/or its bearing with a new one (see Chapter 2).
- ☐ Gearchange mechanism return spring weak or broken (see Chapter 2).

- ☐ Gearchange linkage arm broken. Splines stripped out of arm or shaft, caused by a loose linkage arm pinch bolt or from dropping the machine (see Chapter 2).

Jumps out of gear

- ☐ Selector fork(s) worn (see Chapter 2).
- ☐ Selector fork groove(s) in selector drum worn (see Chapter 2).
- ☐ Gear pinion dogs or dog slots worn or damaged. The gear pinions should be inspected and renewed. No attempt should be made to repair the worn parts.

Overselects

- ☐ Gearchange mechanism stopper arm spring weak or broken, or arm roller broken or worn. Renew the spring or arm (see Chapter 2).
- ☐ Gearchange mechanism return spring weak or broken (see Chapter 2).

7 Abnormal engine noise

Knocking or pinking

- ☐ Carbon build-up in combustion chamber. Use of a fuel additive that will dissolve the adhesive bonding the carbon particles to the piston crown and chamber is the easiest way to remove the build-up. Otherwise, the cylinder head will have to be removed and decarbonised (Chapter 2).
- ☐ Incorrect or poor quality fuel. Old or improper grades of fuel can cause detonation. This causes the piston to rattle, thus the knocking or pinking sound. Drain old fuel and always use the recommended fuel grade.
- ☐ Spark plug heat range incorrect. Uncontrolled detonation indicates the plug heat range is too hot. The plug in effect becomes a glow plug, raising cylinder temperatures. Install the proper heat range plug (Chapter 1).
- ☐ Improper air/fuel mixture. This will cause the cylinders to run hot, which leads to detonation. A blockage in the fuel system or an air leak can cause this imbalance (see Chapter 4).

Piston slap or rattling

- ☐ Cylinder-to-piston clearance excessive. Cylinder and/or piston worn, usually accompanied by worn rings as well. A top-end overhaul is necessary (see Chapter 2).
- ☐ Piston ring(s) worn, broken or sticking. Overhaul the top-end (see Chapter 2).
- ☐ Piston pin, piston pin bore or connecting rod small-end worn from high mileage or seized due to lack of lubrication (see Chapter 2).
- ☐ Piston seizure damage. Usually from lack of lubrication or overheating. Replace the pistons and upper crankcase, as necessary (see Chapter 2).
- ☐ Connecting rod big-end clearance excessive. Caused by excessive wear or lack of lubrication. Replace worn parts.

- ☐ Connecting rod bent. Caused by over-revving, trying to start a badly flooded engine or from ingesting a foreign object into the combustion chamber. Replace the damaged parts (Chapter 2).

Valve noise

- ☐ Incorrect valve clearances – check and adjust (see Chapter 1).
- ☐ Valve spring broken or weak. Check and replace weak valve springs with new ones (see Chapter 2).
- ☐ Camshaft or camshaft journals in the cylinder head worn or damaged. Lubrication failure at high rpm is usually the cause of damage due to insufficient oil or failure to change the oil at the recommended intervals. Since there are no replaceable bearings in the head, the head itself will have to be replaced with a new one (see Chapter 2).

Other noise

- ☐ Cylinder head gasket leaking. Check around the joint for blowing with the engine running.
- ☐ Exhaust pipe leaking at cylinder head connection. Caused by incorrect fit of pipe(s), loose exhaust flange or damaged gasket. All exhaust system fasteners should be tightened evenly and carefully to avoid leaks (see Chapter 4).
- ☐ Crankshaft runout excessive. Caused by a bent crankshaft (from over-revving) or damage from an upper cylinder component failure. Can also be attributed to dropping the machine on either of the crankshaft ends.
- ☐ Engine mounting bolts loose – ensure all the bolts are tightened to the specified torque settings (see Chapter 2).
- ☐ Crankshaft bearings worn (see Chapter 2).
- ☐ Cam chain rattle, due to worn chain or defective tensioner. Also worn chain tensioner/guide blades (see Chapter 2).

8 Abnormal driveline noise

Clutch noise

- ☐ Clutch housing/friction plate clearance excessive (Chapter 2).
- ☐ Wear between the clutch housing splines and input shaft splines (Chapter 2).
- ☐ Worn release bearing (Chapter 2).

Transmission noise

- ☐ Bearings worn. Also includes the possibility that the shafts are worn. Overhaul the transmission (Chapter 2).
- ☐ Gears worn or chipped (Chapter 2).
- ☐ Metal chips jammed in gear teeth. Probably pieces from a broken

clutch, gear or selector mechanism that were picked up by the gears. This will cause early bearing failure (Chapter 2).
- ☐ Engine oil level too low. Causes a howl from transmission. Also affects engine power and clutch operation (Pre-ride checks).

Final drive noise

- ☐ Chain not adjusted properly (Chapter 1).
- ☐ Front or rear sprocket loose. Tighten fasteners (Chapter 6).
- ☐ Sprockets and/or chain worn. Fit new sprockets and chain (Chapter 6).
- ☐ Rear sprocket warped. Fit a new sprocket (Chapter 6).
- ☐ Rubber dampers in rear wheel worn (Chapter 6).

9 Abnormal frame and suspension noise

Front end noise

☐ Low fluid level or improper viscosity oil in forks. This can sound like spurting and is usually accompanied by irregular fork action (Chapter 5).

☐ Spring weak or broken. Makes a clicking or scraping sound. Fork oil, when drained, will have a lot of metal particles in it (Chapter 5).

☐ Steering head bearings loose or damaged. Clicks when braking. Check and adjust or replace with new ones as necessary (Chapters 1 and 5).

☐ Fork yoke clamp bolts loose – ensure all the bolts are tightened to the specified torque (Chapter 6).

☐ Forks bent. Good possibility if machine has been dropped. Replace the sliders or tubes with new ones as required (Chapter 5).

☐ Front axle or axle pinch bolts loose. Tighten them to the specified torque (Chapter 6).

☐ Loose or worn wheel bearings. Check and replace with new ones as needed (Chapters 1 and 6).

Shock absorber noise

☐ Fluid level incorrect. Indicates a leak caused by defective seal. Shock will be covered with oil. Replace shock with a new one or seek advice on repair from a suspension specialist (Chapter 5).

☐ Defective shock absorber with internal damage. This is in the body of the shock and can't be remedied. The shock must be replaced with a new one or rebuilt (Chapter 5).

☐ Bent or damaged shock body. Replace the shock with a new one (Chapter 5).

☐ Loose or worn shock absorber mountings. Check and replace with new ones as necessary (Chapter 5).

Brake noise

☐ Squeal caused by pad shim not installed or positioned correctly (where fitted) (Chapter 6).

☐ Squeal caused by dust on brake pads. Usually found in combination with glazed pads. Clean using brake cleaning solvent (Chapter 6).

☐ Pads glazed. Caused by excessive heat from prolonged hard use or from contamination. DO NOT use sandpaper, emery cloth, carborundum cloth or any other abrasive to roughen the pad surfaces as abrasives will stay in the pad material and damage the disc. A very fine flat file can be used, but new pads is the best remedy (Chapter 6).

☐ Contamination of brake pads. Oil or brake fluid can cause the brake pads to chatter or squeal. Fit new pads. Identify the cause of the contamination, especially check the caliper piston seals for leaking fluid. Clean disc thoroughly with brake system cleaner (Chapter 6).

☐ Disc warped. Can cause a chattering, clicking or intermittent squeal. Usually accompanied by a pulsating lever and uneven braking. Replace the disc with new one (Chapter 6).

☐ Loose or worn wheel bearings. Check and replace with new ones as needed (Chapters 1 and 6).

10 Oil level warning light comes on

Engine lubrication system

☐ Engine oil level low. Inspect for leak or other problem causing low oil level and add recommended oil (see *Pre-ride checks*).

☐ Engine oil pump defective, blocked oil strainer gauze or failed pressure regulator. Carry out an oil pressure check (Chapter 2).

☐ Engine oil viscosity too low. Very old, thin oil or an improper weight of oil used in the engine. Change to correct oil (Chapter 1).

☐ Camshaft or crankshaft journals worn. Excessive wear causing drop in oil pressure. Abnormal wear could be caused by oil starvation at high rpm from low oil level or improper weight or type of oil (Chapter 1).

Electrical system

☐ Oil level switch defective. Check the switch according to the procedure in Chapter 8. Replace it with a new one it if is defective.

☐ Oil level warning LED defective. Check for pinched, shorted, disconnected or damaged wiring (Chapter 8).

11 Excessive exhaust smoke

White smoke

☐ Piston rings worn or broken, causing oil from the crankcase to be pulled past the piston into the combustion chamber. Replace the rings with new ones (Chapter 2).

☐ Cylinders worn or scored. Caused by overheating or oil starvation. Install a new upper crankcase (Chapter 2).

☐ Valve stem oil seal damaged or worn. Replace the oil seals with new ones (Chapter 2).

☐ Valve guide worn. Perform a complete valve job (Chapter 2).

☐ Engine oil level too high, which causes the oil to be forced past the rings. Drain oil to the proper level (see Chapter 1 and *Pre-ride checks*).

☐ Head gasket broken between oil return and cylinder. Causes oil to be pulled into the combustion chamber. Replace the head gasket with a new one and check the head for warpage (Chapter 2).

☐ Abnormal crankcase pressurisation which forces oil past the rings, usually caused by a clogged breather.

Black smoke

☐ Air filter clogged. Clean the air filter element or replace it with a new one (Chapter 1).

☐ Fuel injection system malfunction (Chapter 4).

Brown smoke

☐ Air filter poorly sealed or not installed (Chapter 1).

☐ Fuel injection system malfunction (Chapter 4).

12 Poor handling or stability

Handlebars hard to turn

- ☐ Steering head bearing adjuster nut too tight. Check adjustment as described in Chapter 1.
- ☐ Bearings damaged. Roughness can be felt as the bars are turned from side-to-side. Replace the bearings with new ones (Chapter 5).
- ☐ Races dented or worn. Denting results from wear in only one position (e.g., straight ahead), from a collision or hitting a pothole or from dropping the machine. Replace the bearings with new ones (Chapter 5).
- ☐ Steering stem lubrication inadequate. Causes are grease getting hard from age or being washed out by high pressure car washes. Disassemble steering head and repack bearings (Chapter 5).
- ☐ Steering stem bent. Caused by a collision, hitting a pothole or by dropping the machine. Replace damaged part. Don't try to straighten the steering stem (Chapter 5).
- ☐ Front tyre air pressure too low (*Pre-ride checks*).

Handlebar shakes or vibrates excessively

- ☐ Tyres worn or out of balance (Chapter 6).
- ☐ Swingarm bearings worn. Replace the bearings with new ones (Chapter 5).
- ☐ Wheel rim(s) warped or damaged. Inspect wheels for runout (Chapter 6).
- ☐ Wheel bearings worn. Worn front or rear wheel bearings can cause poor tracking. Worn front bearings will cause wobble (Chapters 1 and 6).
- ☐ Fork yoke clamp bolts or handlebar clamp bolts loose. Tighten them to the specified torque (Chapter 5).
- ☐ Engine mounting bolts loose. Will cause excessive vibration with increased engine rpm – ensure all the bolts are tightened to the specified torque settings (see Chapter 2).

Machine pulls to one side

- ☐ Frame bent. Definitely suspect this if the machine has been dropped. May or may not be accompanied by cracking near the steering head, swingarm mountings or engine mountings. Replace the frame with a new one (Chapter 5).
- ☐ Wheels out of alignment. Caused by improper location of axle spacers or from bent steering stem or frame (Chapter 5).
- ☐ Forks bent. Disassemble the forks and replace the damaged parts (Chapter 5).
- ☐ Swingarm bent or twisted. Replace the swingarm with a new one (Chapter 5).
- ☐ Fork oil level uneven. Check and add or drain as necessary (Chapter 5).

Poor shock absorbing qualities

- ☐ Too hard:
  - a) *Rear shock pre-load setting incorrect.*
  - b) *Fork oil level excessive (Chapter 5).*
  - c) *Fork oil viscosity too high. Use a lighter oil (see the Specifications in Chapter 5).*
  - d) *Fork tube bent. Causes a harsh, sticking feeling (Chapter 5).*
  - e) *Fork internal damage (Chapter 5).*
  - f) *Shock shaft or body bent or damaged (Chapter 5).*
  - g) *Shock internal damage.*
  - h) *Tyre pressure too high (Pre-ride checks).*
- ☐ Too soft:
  - a) *Rear shock pre-load setting incorrect.*
  - b) *Fork oil level too low (Chapter 5).*
  - c) *Fork oil viscosity too light (Chapter 5).*
  - d) *Fork springs weak or broken (Chapter 5).*
  - e) *Fork or shock oil leaking (Chapter 5).*
  - f) *Shock internal damage (Chapter 5).*

13 Braking problems

Brakes are spongy, don't hold

- [ ] Low brake fluid level (see *Pre-ride checks*).
- [ ] Air in hydraulic system. Caused by inattention to master cylinder fluid level or by leakage. Locate problem and bleed brakes (Chapter 6).
- [ ] Pad or disc worn (Chapters 1 and 6).
- [ ] Contaminated pads. Caused by contamination with oil, grease, brake fluid, etc. Fit new pads. Identify the cause of the contamination, especially check the caliper piston seals for leaking fluid. Clean disc thoroughly with brake system cleaner (Chapter 6).
- [ ] Brake fluid deteriorated. Fluid is old or contaminated. Drain system, replenish with new fluid and bleed the system (Chapter 6).
- [ ] Master cylinder internal seals worn or damaged causing fluid to bypass (Chapter 6).
- [ ] Master cylinder bore scratched by foreign material or broken spring. Fit a new master cylinder (Chapter 6).
- [ ] Disc warped. Replace disc with new one (Chapter 6).
- [ ] Faulty ABS. Perform ABS operation check (Chapter 6).

Brake lever or pedal pulsates

- [ ] Disc warped. Replace disc with new one (Chapter 6).

- [ ] Axle bent. Replace axle with new one (Chapter 6).
- [ ] Brake caliper bolts loose – tighten the bolts to the specified torque (Chapter 6).
- [ ] Wheel warped or otherwise damaged (Chapter 6).
- [ ] Wheel bearings damaged or worn (Chapters 1 and 6).

Brakes drag

- [ ] Master cylinder piston seized. Caused by wear or damage to piston or cylinder bore (Chapter 6).
- [ ] Lever balky or stuck. Check pivot and lubricate (Chapter 6).
- [ ] Brake caliper piston seized in bore. Caused by corrosion or ingestion of dirt past deteriorated seal (Chapter 6).
- [ ] Caliper sticking on slider pins due to corrosion (front calipers on non-S2 models, rear caliper on all years). Clean and lubricate pins and check dust boots (Chapter 6).
- [ ] Brake pad damaged. Pad material separated from backing plate. Usually caused by faulty manufacturing process or from contact with chemicals. Fit new pads (Chapter 6).
- [ ] Pads improperly installed (Chapter 6).
- [ ] Brake caliper incorrectly installed (Chapter 6).

14 Electrical problems

Battery dead or weak

- [ ] Battery faulty. Caused by sulphated plates which are shorted through sedimentation. Confirm by terminal voltage check (Chapter 8).
- [ ] Broken battery terminal making only occasional contact.
- [ ] Battery leads making poor contact (Chapter 8).
- [ ] Load excessive. Caused by addition of high wattage lights or other electrical accessories.
- [ ] Ignition switch defective. Switch either grounds (earths) internally or fails to shut off system. Renew the switch (Chapter 8).
- [ ] Regulator/rectifier defective (Chapter 8).
- [ ] Alternator stator coil open or shorted (Chapter 8).

- [ ] Electrical system fault. Check for excessive current leakage (Chapter 8).
- [ ] Wiring faulty. Wiring grounded (earthed) or connections loose in ignition, charging or lighting circuits (Chapter 8).

Battery overcharged

- [ ] Regulator/rectifier defective. Overcharging is noticed when battery gets excessively warm (Chapter 8).
- [ ] Battery faulty. Confirm with battery terminal voltage check (Chapter 8).
- [ ] Battery amperage too low, wrong type or size of battery. Install manufacturer's specified amp-hour battery to handle charging load (Chapter 8).

A

ABS (Anti-lock braking system) A system, usually electronically controlled, that senses incipient wheel lockup during braking and relieves hydraulic pressure at wheel which is about to skid.

Aftermarket Components suitable for the motorcycle, but not produced by the motorcycle manufacturer.

Allen key A hexagonal wrench which fits into a recessed hexagonal hole.

Alternating current (ac) Current produced by an alternator. Requires converting to direct current by a rectifier for charging purposes.

Alternator Converts mechanical energy from the engine into electrical energy to charge the battery and power the electrical system.

Ampere (amp) A unit of measurement for the flow of electrical current. Current = Volts ÷ Ohms.

Ampere-hour (Ah) Measure of battery capacity.

Angle-tightening A torque expressed in degrees. Often follows a conventional tightening torque for cylinder head or main bearing fasteners **(see illustration)**.

Angle-tightening cylinder head bolts

Antifreeze A substance (usually ethylene glycol) mixed with water, and added to the cooling system, to prevent freezing of the coolant in winter. Antifreeze also contains chemicals to inhibit corrosion and the formation of rust and other deposits that would tend to clog the radiator and coolant passages and reduce cooling efficiency.

Anti-dive System attached to the fork lower leg (slider) to prevent fork dive when braking hard.

Anti-seize compound A coating that reduces the risk of seizing on fasteners that are subjected to high temperatures, such as exhaust clamp bolts and nuts.

API American Petroleum Institute. A quality standard for 4-stroke motor oils.

Asbestos A natural fibrous mineral with great heat resistance, commonly used in the composition of brake friction materials. Asbestos is a health hazard and the dust created by brake systems should never be inhaled or ingested.

ATF Automatic Transmission Fluid. Often used in front forks.

ATU Automatic Timing Unit. Mechanical device for advancing the ignition timing on early engines.

ATV All Terrain Vehicle. Often called a Quad.

Axial play Side-to-side movement.

Axle A shaft on which a wheel revolves. Also known as a spindle.

B

Backlash The amount of movement between meshed components when one component is held still. Usually applies to gear teeth.

Ball bearing A bearing consisting of a hardened inner and outer race with hardened steel balls between the two races.

Bearings Used between two working surfaces to prevent wear of the components and a build-up of heat. Four types of bearing are commonly used on motorcycles: plain shell bearings, ball bearings, tapered roller bearings and needle roller bearings.

Bevel gears Used to turn the drive through 90°. Typical applications are shaft final drive and camshaft drive **(see illustration)**.

Bevel gears are used to turn the drive through 90°

BHP Brake Horsepower. The British measurement for engine power output. Power output is now usually expressed in kilowatts (kW).

Bias-belted tyre Similar construction to radial tyre, but with outer belt running at an angle to the wheel rim.

Big-end bearing The bearing in the end of the connecting rod that's attached to the crankshaft.

Bleeding The process of removing air from an hydraulic system via a bleed nipple or bleed screw.

Bottom-end A description of an engine's crankcase components and all components contained there-in.

BTDC Before Top Dead Centre in terms of piston position. Ignition timing is often expressed in terms of degrees or millimetres BTDC.

Bush A cylindrical metal or rubber component used between two moving parts.

Burr Rough edge left on a component after machining or as a result of excessive wear.

C

Cam chain The chain which takes drive from the crankshaft to the camshaft(s).

Canister The main component in an evaporative emission control system (California market only); contains activated charcoal granules to trap vapours from the fuel system rather than allowing them to vent to the atmosphere.

Castellated Resembling the parapets along the top of a castle wall. For example, a castellated wheel axle or spindle nut.

Catalytic converter A device in the exhaust system of some machines which converts certain pollutants in the exhaust gases into less harmful substances.

Charging system Description of the components which charge the battery, ie the alternator, rectifer and regulator.

Circlip A ring-shaped clip used to prevent endwise movement of cylindrical parts and shafts. An internal circlip is installed in a groove in a housing; an external circlip fits into a groove on the outside of a cylindrical piece such as a shaft. Also known as a snap-ring.

Clearance The amount of space between two parts. For example, between a piston and a cylinder, between a bearing and a journal, etc.

Coil spring A spiral of elastic steel found in various sizes throughout a vehicle, for example as a springing medium in the suspension and in the valve train.

Compression Reduction in volume, and increase in pressure and temperature, of a gas, caused by squeezing it into a smaller space.

Compression damping Controls the speed the suspension compresses when hitting a bump.

Compression ratio The relationship between cylinder volume when the piston is at top dead centre and cylinder volume when the piston is at bottom dead centre.

Continuity The uninterrupted path in the flow of electricity. Little or no measurable resistance.

Continuity tester Self-powered bleeper or test light which indicates continuity.

Cp Candlepower. Bulb rating commonly found on US motorcycles.

Crossply tyre Tyre plies arranged in a criss-cross pattern. Usually four or six plies used, hence 4PR or 6PR in tyre size codes.

Cush drive Rubber damper segments fitted between the rear wheel and final drive sprocket to absorb transmission shocks **(see illustration)**.

Cush drive rubbers dampen out transmission shocks

D

Degree disc Calibrated disc for measuring piston position. Expressed in degrees.

Dial gauge Clock-type gauge with adapters for measuring runout and piston position. Expressed in mm or inches.

Diaphragm The rubber membrane in a master cylinder or carburettor which seals the upper chamber.

Diaphragm spring A single sprung plate often used in clutches.

Direct current (dc) Current produced by a dc generator.

Decarbonisation The process of removing carbon deposits - typically from the combustion chamber, valves and exhaust port/system.

Detonation Destructive and damaging explosion of fuel/air mixture in combustion chamber instead of controlled burning.

Diode An electrical valve which only allows current to flow in one direction. Commonly used in rectifiers and starter interlock systems.

Disc valve (or rotary valve) A induction system used on some two-stroke engines.

Double-overhead camshaft (DOHC) An engine that uses two overhead camshafts, one for the intake valves and one for the exhaust valves.

Drivebelt A toothed belt used to transmit drive to the rear wheel on some motorcycles. A drivebelt has also been used to drive the camshafts. Drivebelts are usually made of Kevlar.

Driveshaft Any shaft used to transmit motion. Commonly used when referring to the final driveshaft on shaft drive motorcycles.

E

Earth return The return path of an electrical circuit, utilising the motorcycle's frame.

ECU (Electronic Control Unit) A computer which controls (for instance) an ignition system, or an anti-lock braking system.

EGO Exhaust Gas Oxygen sensor. Sometimes called a Lambda sensor.

Electrolyte The fluid in a lead-acid battery.

EMS (Engine Management System) A computer controlled system which manages the fuel injection and the ignition systems in an integrated fashion.

Endfloat The amount of lengthways movement between two parts. As applied to a crankshaft, the distance that the crankshaft can move side-to-side in the crankcase.

Endless chain A chain having no joining link. Common use for cam chains and final drive chains.

EP (Extreme Pressure) Oil type used in locations where high loads are applied, such as between gear teeth.

Evaporative emission control system Describes a charcoal filled canister which stores fuel vapours from the tank rather than allowing them to vent to the atmosphere. Usually only fitted to California models and referred to as an EVAP system.

Expansion chamber Section of two-stroke engine exhaust system so designed to improve engine efficiency and boost power.

F

Feeler blade or gauge A thin strip or blade of hardened steel, ground to an exact thickness, used to check or measure clearances between parts.

Final drive Description of the drive from the transmission to the rear wheel. Usually by chain or shaft, but sometimes by belt.

Firing order The order in which the engine cylinders fire, or deliver their power strokes, beginning with the number one cylinder.

Flooding Term used to describe a high fuel level in the carburettor float chambers, leading to fuel overflow. Also refers to excess fuel in the combustion chamber due to incorrect starting technique.

Free length The no-load state of a component when measured. Clutch, valve and fork spring lengths are measured at rest, without any preload.

Freeplay The amount of travel before any action takes place. The looseness in a linkage, or an assembly of parts, between the initial application of force and actual movement. For example, the distance the rear brake pedal moves before the rear brake is actuated.

Fuel injection The fuel/air mixture is metered electronically and directed into the engine intake ports (indirect injection) or into the cylinders (direct injection). Sensors supply information on engine speed and conditions.

Fuel/air mixture The charge of fuel and air going into the engine. See **Stoichiometric ratio.**

Fuse An electrical device which protects a circuit against accidental overload. The typical fuse contains a soft piece of metal which is calibrated to melt at a predetermined current flow (expressed as amps) and break the circuit.

G

Gap The distance the spark must travel in jumping from the centre electrode to the side electrode in a spark plug. Also refers to the distance between the ignition rotor and the pickup coil in an electronic ignition system.

Gasket Any thin, soft material - usually cork, cardboard, asbestos or soft metal - installed between two metal surfaces to ensure a good seal. For instance, the cylinder head gasket seals the joint between the block and the cylinder head.

Gauge An instrument panel display used to monitor engine conditions. A gauge with a movable pointer on a dial or a fixed scale is an analogue gauge. A gauge with a numerical readout is called a digital gauge.

Gear ratios The drive ratio of a pair of gears in a gearbox, calculated on their number of teeth.

Glaze-busting see **Honing**

Grinding Process for renovating the valve face and valve seat contact area in the cylinder head.

Gudgeon pin The shaft which connects the connecting rod small-end with the piston. Often called a piston pin or wrist pin.

H

Helical gears Gear teeth are slightly curved and produce less gear noise that straight-cut gears. Often used for primary drives.

Installing a Helicoil thread insert in a cylinder head

Helicoil A thread insert repair system. Commonly used as a repair for stripped spark plug threads **(see illustration).**

Honing A process used to break down the glaze on a cylinder bore (also called glaze-busting). Can also be carried out to roughen a rebored cylinder to aid ring bedding-in.

HT (High Tension) Description of the electrical circuit from the secondary winding of the ignition coil to the spark plug.

Hydraulic A liquid filled system used to transmit pressure from one component to another. Common uses on motorcycles are brakes and clutches.

Hydrometer An instrument for measuring the specific gravity of a lead-acid battery.

Hygroscopic Water absorbing. In motorcycle applications, braking efficiency will be reduced if DOT 3 or 4 hydraulic fluid absorbs water from the air - care must be taken to keep new brake fluid in tightly sealed containers.

I

lbf ft Pounds-force feet. An imperial unit of torque. Sometimes written as ft-lbs.

lbf in Pound-force inch. An imperial unit of torque, applied to components where a very low torque is required. Sometimes written as in-lbs.

IC Abbreviation for Integrated Circuit.

Ignition advance Means of increasing the timing of the spark at higher engine speeds. Done by mechanical means (ATU) on early engines or electronically by the ignition control unit on later engines.

Ignition timing The moment at which the spark plug fires, expressed in the number of crankshaft degrees before the piston reaches the top of its stroke, or in the number of millimetres before the piston reaches the top of its stroke.

Infinity (∞) Description of an open-circuit electrical state, where no continuity exists.

Inverted forks (upside down forks) The sliders or lower legs are held in the yokes and the fork tubes or stanchions are connected to the wheel axle (spindle). Less unsprung weight and stiffer construction than conventional forks.

J

JASO Quality standard for 2-stroke oils.

Joule The unit of electrical energy.

Journal The bearing surface of a shaft.

K

Kickstart Mechanical means of turning the engine over for starting purposes. Only usually fitted to mopeds, small capacity motorcycles and off-road motorcycles.

Kill switch Handebar-mounted switch for emergency ignition cut-out. Cuts the ignition circuit on all models, and additionally prevent starter motor operation on others.

km Symbol for kilometre.

kmh Abbreviation for kilometres per hour.

L

Lambda (λ) sensor A sensor fitted in the exhaust system to measure the exhaust gas oxygen content (excess air factor).

Lapping see **Grinding.**
LCD Abbreviation for Liquid Crystal Display.
LED Abbreviation for Light Emitting Diode.
Liner A steel cylinder liner inserted in a aluminium alloy cylinder block.
Locknut A nut used to lock an adjustment nut, or other threaded component, in place.
Lockstops The lugs on the lower triple clamp (yoke) which abut those on the frame, preventing handlebar-to-fuel tank contact.
Lockwasher A form of washer designed to prevent an attaching nut from working loose.
LT Low Tension Description of the electrical circuit from the power supply to the primary winding of the ignition coil.

M

Main bearings The bearings between the crankshaft and crankcase.
Maintenance-free (MF) battery A sealed battery which cannot be topped up.
Manometer Mercury-filled calibrated tubes used to measure intake tract vacuum. Used to synchronise carburettors on multi-cylinder engines.
Micrometer A precision measuring instrument that measures component outside diameters **(see illustration).**

Tappet shims are measured with a micrometer

MON (Motor Octane Number) A measure of a fuel's resistance to knock.
Monograde oil An oil with a single viscosity, eg SAE80W.
Monoshock A single suspension unit linking the swingarm or suspension linkage to the frame.
mph Abbreviation for miles per hour.
Multigrade oil Having a wide viscosity range (eg 10W40). The W stands for Winter, thus the viscosity ranges from SAE10 when cold to SAE40 when hot.
Multimeter An electrical test instrument with the capability to measure voltage, current and resistance. Some meters also incorporate a continuity tester and buzzer.

N

Needle roller bearing Inner race of caged needle rollers and hardened outer race. Examples of uncaged needle rollers can be found on some engines. Commonly used in rear suspension applications and in two-stroke engines.
Nm Newton metres.
NOx Oxides of Nitrogen. A common toxic pollutant emitted by petrol engines at higher temperatures.

O

Octane The measure of a fuel's resistance to knock.
OE (Original Equipment) Relates to components fitted to a motorcycle as standard or replacement parts supplied by the motorcycle manufacturer.
Ohm The unit of electrical resistance. Ohms = Volts ÷ Current.
Ohmmeter An instrument for measuring electrical resistance.
Oil cooler System for diverting engine oil outside of the engine to a radiator for cooling purposes.
Oil injection A system of two-stroke engine lubrication where oil is pump-fed to the engine in accordance with throttle position.
Open-circuit An electrical condition where there is a break in the flow of electricity - no continuity (high resistance).
O-ring A type of sealing ring made of a special rubber-like material; in use, the O-ring is compressed into a groove to provide the sealing action.
Oversize (OS) Term used for piston and ring size options fitted to a rebored cylinder.
Overhead cam (sohc) engine An engine with single camshaft located on top of the cylinder head.
Overhead valve (ohv) engine An engine with the valves located in the cylinder head, but with the camshaft located in the engine block or crankcase.
Oxygen sensor A device installed in the exhaust system which senses the oxygen content in the exhaust and converts this information into an electric current. Also called a Lambda sensor.

P

Plastigauge A thin strip of plastic thread, available in different sizes, used for measuring clearances. For example, a strip of Plastigauge is laid across a bearing journal. The parts are assembled and dismantled; the width of the crushed strip indicates the clearance between journal and bearing.
Polarity Either negative or positive earth (ground), determined by which battery lead is connected to the frame (earth return). Modern motorcycles are usually negative earth.
Pre-ignition A situation where the fuel/air mixture ignites before the spark plug fires. Often due to a hot spot in the combustion chamber caused by carbon build-up. Engine has a tendency to 'run-on'.
Pre-load (suspension) The amount a spring is compressed when in the unloaded state. Preload can be applied by gas, spacer or mechanical adjuster.
Premix The method of engine lubrication on older two-stroke engines. Engine oil is mixed with the petrol in the fuel tank in a specific ratio. The fuel/oil mix is sometimes referred to as "petroil".
Primary drive Description of the drive from the crankshaft to the clutch. Usually by gear or chain.
PS Pfedestärke - a German interpretation of BHP.
PSI Pounds-force per square inch. Imperial measurement of tyre pressure and cylinder pressure measurement.
PTFE Polytetrafluroethylene. A low friction substance.

Pulse secondary air injection system A process of promoting the burning of excess fuel present in the exhaust gases by routing fresh air into the exhaust ports.

Q

Quartz halogen bulb Tungsten filament surrounded by a halogen gas. Typically used for the headlight **(see illustration).**

Quartz halogen headlight bulb construction

R

Rack-and-pinion A pinion gear on the end of a shaft that mates with a rack (think of a geared wheel opened up and laid flat). Sometimes used in clutch operating systems.
Radial play Up and down movement about a shaft.
Radial ply tyres Tyre plies run across the tyre (from bead to bead) and around the circumference of the tyre. Less resistant to tread distortion than other tyre types.
Radiator A liquid-to-air heat transfer device designed to reduce the temperature of the coolant in a liquid cooled engine.
Rake A feature of steering geometry - the angle of the steering head in relation to the vertical **(see illustration).**

Steering geometry

Rebore Providing a new working surface to the cylinder bore by boring out the old surface. Necessitates the use of oversize piston and rings.

Rebound damping A means of controlling the oscillation of a suspension unit spring after it has been compressed. Resists the spring's natural tendency to bounce back after being compressed.

Rectifier Device for converting the ac output of an alternator into dc for battery charging.

Reed valve An induction system commonly used on two-stroke engines.

Regulator Device for maintaining the charging voltage from the generator or alternator within a specified range.

Relay A electrical device used to switch heavy current on and off by using a low current auxiliary circuit.

Resistance Measured in ohms. An electrical component's ability to pass electrical current.

RON (Research Octane Number) A measure of a fuel's resistance to knock.

rpm revolutions per minute.

Runout The amount of wobble (in-and-out movement) of a wheel or shaft as it's rotated. The amount a shaft rotates 'out-of-true'. The out-of-round condition of a rotating part.

S

SAE (Society of Automotive Engineers) A standard for the viscosity of a fluid.

Sealant A liquid or paste used to prevent leakage at a joint. Sometimes used in conjunction with a gasket.

Service limit Term for the point where a component is no longer useable and must be renewed.

Shaft drive A method of transmitting drive from the transmission to the rear wheel.

Shell bearings Plain bearings consisting of two shell halves. Most often used as big-end and main bearings in a four-stroke engine. Often called bearing inserts.

Shim Thin spacer, commonly used to adjust the clearance or relative positions between two parts. For example, shims inserted into or under tappets or followers to control valve clearances. Clearance is adjusted by changing the thickness of the shim.

Short-circuit An electrical condition where current shorts to earth (ground) bypassing the circuit components.

Skimming Process to correct warpage or repair a damaged surface, eg on brake discs or drums.

Slide-hammer A special puller that screws into or hooks onto a component such as a shaft or bearing; a heavy sliding handle on the shaft bottoms against the end of the shaft to knock the component free.

Small-end bearing The bearing in the upper end of the connecting rod at its joint with the gudgeon pin.

Spalling Damage to camshaft lobes or bearing journals shown as pitting of the working surface.

Specific gravity (SG) The state of charge of the electrolyte in a lead-acid battery. A measure of the electrolyte's density compared with water.

Straight-cut gears Common type gear used on gearbox shafts and for oil pump and water pump drives.

Stanchion The inner sliding part of the front forks, held by the yokes. Often called a fork tube.

Stoichiometric ratio The optimum chemical air/fuel ratio for a petrol engine, said to be 14.7 parts of air to 1 part of fuel.

Sulphuric acid The liquid (electrolyte) used in a lead-acid battery. Poisonous and extremely corrosive.

Surface grinding (lapping) Process to correct a warped gasket face, commonly used on cylinder heads.

T

Tapered-roller bearing Tapered inner race of caged needle rollers and separate tapered outer race. Examples of taper roller bearings can be found on steering heads.

Tappet A cylindrical component which transmits motion from the cam to the valve stem, either directly or via a pushrod and rocker arm. Also called a cam follower.

TCS Traction Control System. An electronically-controlled system which senses wheel spin and reduces engine speed accordingly.

TDC Top Dead Centre denotes that the piston is at its highest point in the cylinder.

Thread-locking compound Solution applied to fastener threads to prevent slackening. Select type to suit application.

Thrust washer A washer positioned between two moving components on a shaft. For example, between gear pinions on gearshaft.

Timing chain See **Cam Chain.**

Timing light Stroboscopic lamp for carrying out ignition timing checks with the engine running.

Top-end A description of an engine's cylinder block, head and valve gear components.

Torque Turning or twisting force about a shaft.

Torque setting A prescribed tightness specified by the motorcycle manufacturer to ensure that the bolt or nut is secured correctly. Undertightening can result in the bolt or nut coming loose or a surface not being sealed. Overtightening can result in stripped threads, distortion or damage to the component being retained.

Torx key A six-point wrench.

Tracer A stripe of a second colour applied to a wire insulator to distinguish that wire from another one with the same colour insulator. For example, Br/W is often used to denote a brown insulator with a white tracer.

Trail A feature of steering geometry. Distance from the steering head axis to the tyre's central contact point.

Triple clamps The cast components which extend from the steering head and support the fork stanchions or tubes. Often called fork yokes.

Turbocharger A centrifugal device, driven by exhaust gases, that pressurises the intake air. Normally used to increase the power output from a given engine displacement.

TWI Abbreviation for Tyre Wear Indicator. Indicates the location of the tread depth indicator bars on tyres.

U

Universal joint or U-joint (UJ) A double-pivoted connection for transmitting power from a driving to a driven shaft through an angle. Typically found in shaft drive assemblies.

Unsprung weight Anything not supported by the bike's suspension (ie the wheel, tyres, brakes, final drive and bottom (moving) part of the suspension).

V

Vacuum gauges Clock-type gauges for measuring intake tract vacuum. Used for carburettor synchronisation on multi-cylinder engines.

Valve A device through which the flow of liquid, gas or vacuum may be stopped, started or regulated by a moveable part that opens, shuts or partially obstructs one or more ports or passageways. The intake and exhaust valves in the cylinder head are of the poppet type.

Valve clearance The clearance between the valve tip (the end of the valve stem) and the rocker arm or tappet/follower. The valve clearance is measured when the valve is closed. The correct clearance is important - if too small the valve won't close fully and will burn out, whereas if too large noisy operation will result.

Valve lift The amount a valve is lifted off its seat by the camshaft lobe.

Valve timing The exact setting for the opening and closing of the valves in relation to piston position.

Vernier caliper A precision measuring instrument that measures inside and outside dimensions. Not quite as accurate as a micrometer, but more convenient.

VIN Vehicle Identification Number. Term for the bike's engine and frame numbers.

Viscosity The thickness of a liquid or its resistance to flow.

Volt A unit for expressing electrical "pressure" in a circuit. Volts = current x ohms.

W

Water pump A mechanically-driven device for moving coolant around the engine.

Watt A unit for expressing electrical power. Watts = volts x current.

Wear limit see **Service limit**

Wet liner A liquid-cooled engine design where the pistons run in liners which are directly surrounded by coolant **(see illustration)**.

Wet liner arrangement

Wheelbase Distance from the centre of the front wheel to the centre of the rear wheel.

Wiring harness or loom Describes the electrical wires running the length of the motorcycle and enclosed in tape or plastic sheathing. Wiring coming off the main harness is usually referred to as a sub harness.

Woodruff key A key of semi-circular or square section used to locate a gear to a shaft. Often used to locate the alternator rotor on the crankshaft.

Wrist pin Another name for gudgeon or piston pin.

Note: *References throughout this index are in the form - "Chapter number" • "Page number"*

Haynes Motorcycle Manuals – The Complete List

Title	Book No
APRILIA RS50 (99 - 06) & RS125 (93 - 06)	4298
Aprilia RSV1000 Mille (98 - 03)	♦ 4255
BMW 2-valve Twins (70 - 96)	♦ 0249
BMW K100 & 75 2-valve Models (83 - 96)	♦ 1373
BMW R850, 1100 & 1150 4-valve Twins (93 - 04)	♦ 3466
BMW R1200 (04 - 06)	♦ 4598
BSA Bantam (48 - 71)	0117
BSA Unit Singles (58 - 72)	0127
BSA Pre-unit Singles (54 - 61)	0326
BSA A7 & A10 Twins (47 - 62)	0121
BSA A50 & A65 Twins (62 - 73)	0155
DUCATI 600, 620, 750 and 900 2-valve V-Twins (91 - 05)	♦ 3290
Ducati MK III & Desmo Singles (69 - 76)	◇ 0445
Ducati 748, 916 & 996 4-valve V-Twins (94 - 01)	♦ 3756
GILERA Runner, DNA, Ice & SKP/Stalker (97 - 07)	4163
HARLEY-DAVIDSON Sportsters (70 - 03)	♦ 2534
Harley-Davidson Shovelhead and Evolution Big Twins (70 - 99)	♦ 2536
Harley-Davidson Twin Cam 88 (99 - 03)	♦ 2478
HONDA NB, ND, NP & NS50 Melody (81 - 85)	◇ 0622
Honda NE/NB50 Vision & SA50 Vision Met-in (85 - 95)	◇ 1278
Honda MB, MBX, MT & MTX50 (80 - 93)	0731
Honda C50, C70 & C90 (67 - 03)	0324
Honda XR80/100R & CRF80/100F (85 - 04)	2218
Honda XL/XR 80, 100, 125, 185 & 200 2-valve Models (78 - 87)	0566
Honda H100 & H100S Singles (80 - 92)	◇ 0734
Honda CB/CD125T & CM125C Twins (77 - 88)	◇ 0571
Honda CG125 (76 - 07)	◇ 0433
Honda NS125 (86 - 93)	◇ 3056
Honda CBR125R (04 - 07)	4620
Honda MBX/MTX125 & MTX200 (83 - 93)	◇ 1132
Honda CD/CM185 200T & CM250C 2-valve Twins (77 - 85)	0572
Honda XL/XR 250 & 500 (78 - 84)	0567
Honda XR250L, XR250R & XR400R (86 - 03)	2219
Honda CB250 & CB400N Super Dreams (78 - 84)	◇ 0540
Honda CR Motocross Bikes (86 - 01)	2222
Honda CRF250 & CRF450 (02 - 06)	2630
Honda CBR400RR Fours (88 - 99)	◇ ♦ 3552
Honda VFR400 (NC30) & RVF400 (NC35) V-Fours (89 - 98)	◇ ♦ 3496
Honda CB500 (93 - 01)	◇ 3753
Honda CB400 & CB550 Fours (73 - 77)	0262
Honda CX/GL500 & 650 V-Twins (78 - 86)	0442
Honda CBX550 Four (82 - 86)	◇ 0940
Honda XL600R & XR600R (83 - 00)	2183
Honda XL600/650V Transalp & XRV750 Africa Twin (87 to 07)	♦ 3919
Honda CBR600F1 & 1000F Fours (87 - 96)	♦ 1730
Honda CBR600F2 & F3 Fours (91 - 98)	♦ 2070
Honda CBR600F4 (99 - 06)	♦ 3911
Honda CB600F Hornet & CBF600 (98 - 06)	◇ ♦ 3915
Honda CBR600RR (03 - 06)	♦ 4590
Honda CB650 sohc Fours (78 - 84)	0665
Honda NTV600 Revere, NTV650 and NT650V Deauville (88 - 05)	◇ 3243
Honda Shadow VT600 & 750 (USA) (88 - 03)	2312
Honda CB750 sohc Four (69 - 79)	0131
Honda V45/65 Sabre & Magna (82 - 88)	0820
Honda VFR750 & 700 V-Fours (86 - 97)	♦ 2101
Honda VFR800 V-Fours (97 - 01)	♦ 3703
Honda VFR800 V-Tec V-Fours (02 - 05)	♦ 4196
Honda CB750 & CB900 dohc Fours (78 - 84)	0535
Honda VTR1000 (FireStorm, Super Hawk) & XL1000V (Varadero) (97 - 00)	♦ 3744
Honda CBR900RR FireBlade (92 - 99)	♦ 2161
Honda CBR900RR FireBlade (00 - 03)	♦ 4060
Honda CBR1000RR Fireblade (04 - 07)	♦ 4604
Honda CBR1100XX Super Blackbird (97 - 07)	♦ 3901
Honda ST1100 Pan European V-Fours (90 - 02)	♦ 3384
Honda Shadow VT1100 (USA) (85 - 98)	2313
Honda GL1000 Gold Wing (75 - 79)	0309
Honda GL1100 Gold Wing (79 - 81)	0669

Title	Book No
Honda Gold Wing 1200 (USA) (84 - 87)	2199
Honda Gold Wing 1500 (USA) (88 - 00)	2225
KAWASAKI AE/AR 50 & 80 (81 - 95)	1007
Kawasaki KC, KE & KH100 (75 - 99)	1371
Kawasaki KMX125 & 200 (86 - 02)	◇ 3046
Kawasaki 250, 350 & 400 Triples (72 - 79)	0134
Kawasaki 400 & 440 Twins (74 - 81)	0281
Kawasaki 400, 500 & 550 Fours (79 - 91)	0910
Kawasaki EN450 & 500 Twins (Ltd/Vulcan) (85 - 04)	2053
Kawasaki EX500 (GPZ500S) & ER500 (ER-5) (87 - 05)	♦ 2052
Kawasaki ZX600 (ZZ-R600 & Ninja ZX-6) (90 - 06)	♦ 2146
Kawasaki ZX-6R Ninja Fours (95 - 02)	♦ 3541
Kawasaki ZX-6R (03 - 06)	♦ 4742
Kawasaki ZX600 (GPZ600R, GPX600R, Ninja 600R & RX) & ZX750 (GPX750R, Ninja 750R)	♦ 1780
Kawasaki 650 Four (76 - 78)	0373
Kawasaki Vulcan 700/750 & 800 (85 - 04)	2457
Kawasaki 750 Air-cooled Fours (80 - 91)	0574
Kawasaki ZR550 & 750 Zephyr Fours (90 - 97)	♦ 3382
Kawasaki Z750 & Z1000 (03 - 08)	♦ 4762
Kawasaki ZX750 (Ninja ZX-7 & ZXR750) Fours (89 - 96)	♦ 2054
Kawasaki Ninja ZX-7R & ZX-9R (94 - 04)	♦ 3721
Kawasaki 900 & 1000 Fours (73 - 77)	0222
Kawasaki ZX900, 1000 & 1100 Liquid-cooled Fours (83 - 97)	♦ 1681
KTM EXC Enduro & SX Motocross (00 - 07)	♦ 4629
MOTO GUZZI 750, 850 & 1000 V-Twins (74 - 78)	0339
MZ ETZ Models (81 - 95)	◇ 1680
NORTON 500, 600, 650 & 750 Twins (57 - 70)	0187
Norton Commando (68 - 77)	0125
PEUGEOT Speedfight, Trekker & Vivacity Scooters (96 - 05)	◇ 3920
PIAGGIO (Vespa) Scooters (91 - 06)	♦ 3492
SUZUKI GT, ZR & TS50 (77 - 90)	◇ 0799
Suzuki TS50X (84 - 00)	◇ 1599
Suzuki 100, 125, 185 & 250 Air-cooled Trail bikes (79 - 89)	0797
Suzuki GP100 & 125 Singles (78 - 93)	◇ 0576
Suzuki GS, GN, GZ & DR125 Singles (82 - 05)	◇ 0888
Suzuki 250 & 350 Twins (68 - 78)	0120
Suzuki GT250X7, GT200X5 & SB200 Twins (78 - 83)	◇ 0469
Suzuki GS/GSX250, 400 & 450 Twins (79 - 85)	0736
Suzuki GS500 Twin (89 - 06)	♦ 3238
Suzuki GS550 (77 - 82) & GS750 Fours (76 - 79)	0363
Suzuki GS/GSX550 4-valve Fours (83 - 88)	1133
Suzuki SV650 & SV650S (99 - 05)	♦ 3912
Suzuki GSX-R600 & 750 (96 - 00)	♦ 3553
Suzuki GSX-R600 (01 - 03), GSX-R750 (00 - 03) & GSX-R1000 (01 - 02)	♦ 3986
Suzuki GSX-R600/750 (04 - 05) & GSX-R1000 (03 - 06)	♦ 4382
Suzuki GSX600, 650 & 1200 Bandit Fours (95 - 06)	♦ 3367
Suzuki Intruder, Marauder, Volusia & Boulevard (85 - 06)	♦ 2618
Suzuki GS850 Fours (78 - 88)	0536
Suzuki GS1000 Four (77 - 79)	0484
Suzuki GSX-R750, GSX-R1100 (85 - 92), GSX600F, GSX750F, GSX1100F (Katana) Fours	♦ 2055
Suzuki GSX600/750F & GSX750 (98 - 02)	♦ 3987
Suzuki GS/GSX1000, 1100 & 1150 4-valve Fours (79 - 88)	0737
Suzuki TL1000S/R & DL1000 V-Strom (97 - 04)	♦ 4083
Suzuki GSX1300R Hayabusa (99 - 04)	♦ 4184
Suzuki GSX1400 (02 - 07)	♦ 4758
TRIUMPH Tiger Cub & Terrier (52 - 68)	0414
Triumph 350 & 500 Unit Twins (58 - 73)	0137
Triumph Pre-Unit Twins (47 - 62)	0251
Triumph 650 & 750 2-valve Unit Twins (63 - 83)	0122
Triumph Trident & BSA Rocket 3 (69 - 75)	0136
Triumph Bonneville (01 - 07)	♦ 4364
Triumph Daytona, Speed Triple, Sprint & Tiger (97 - 05)	♦ 3755
Triumph Triples and Fours (carburettor engines) (91 - 04)	♦ 2162
VESPA P/PX125, 150 & 200 Scooters (78 - 06)	0707
Vespa Scooters (59 - 78)	0126
YAMAHA DT50 & 80 Trail Bikes (78 - 95)	◇ 0800
Yamaha T50 & 80 Townmate (83 - 95)	◇ 1247
Yamaha YB100 Singles (73 - 91)	◇ 0474

Title	Book No
Yamaha RS/RXS100 & 125 Singles (74 - 95)	0331
Yamaha RD & DT125LC (82 - 87)	◇ 0887
Yamaha TZR125 (87 - 93) & DT125R (88 - 02)	◇ 1655
Yamaha TY50, 80, 125 & 175 (74 - 84)	◇ 0464
Yamaha XT & SR125 (82 - 03)	◇ 1021
Yamaha Trail Bikes (81 - 00)	2350
Yamaha 2-stroke Motocross Bikes 1986 - 2006	2662
Yamaha YZ & WR 4-stroke Motocross Bikes (98 - 07)	2689
Yamaha 250 & 350 Twins (70 - 79)	0040
Yamaha XS250, 360 & 400 sohc Twins (75 - 84)	0378
Yamaha RD250 & 350LC Twins (80 - 82)	0803
Yamaha RD350 YPVS Twins (83 - 95)	1158
Yamaha RD400 Twin (75 - 79)	0333
Yamaha XT, TT & SR500 Singles (75 - 83)	0342
Yamaha XZ550 Vision V-Twins (82 - 85)	0821
Yamaha FJ, FZ, XJ & YX600 Radian (84 - 92)	2100
Yamaha XJ600S (Diversion, Seca II) & XJ600N Fours (92 - 03)	♦ 2145
Yamaha YZF600R Thundercat & FZS600 Fazer (96 - 03)	♦ 3702
Yamaha FZ-6 Fazer (04 - 07)	♦ 4751
Yamaha YZF-R6 (99 - 02)	♦ 3900
Yamaha YZF-R6 (03 - 05)	♦ 4601
Yamaha 650 Twins (70 - 83)	0341
Yamaha XJ650 & 750 Fours (80 - 84)	0738
Yamaha XS750 & 850 Triples (76 - 85)	0340
Yamaha TDM850, TRX850 & XTZ750 (89 - 99)	◇ ♦ 3540
Yamaha YZF750R & YZF1000R Thunderace (93 - 00)	♦ 3720
Yamaha FZR600, 750 & 1000 Fours (87 - 96)	♦ 2056
Yamaha XV (Virago) V-Twins (81 - 03)	♦ 0802
Yamaha XVS650 & 1100 Drag Star/V-Star (97 - 05)	♦ 4195
Yamaha XJ900F Fours (83 - 94)	♦ 3239
Yamaha XJ900S Diversion (94 - 01)	♦ 3739
Yamaha YZF-R1 (98 - 03)	♦ 3754
Yamaha YZF-R1 (04 - 06)	♦ 4605
Yamaha FZS1000 Fazer (01 - 05)	♦ 4287
Yamaha FJ1100 & 1200 Fours (84 - 96)	♦ 2057
Yamaha XJR1200 & 1300 (95 - 06)	♦ 3981
Yamaha V-Max (85 - 03)	♦ 4072

ATVs

Title	Book No
Honda ATC70, 90, 110, 185 & 200 (71 - 85)	0565
Honda Rancher, Recon & TRX250EX ATVs	2553
Honda TRX300 Shaft Drive ATVs (88 - 00)	2125
Honda TRX300EX, TRX400EX & TRX450R/ER ATVs (93 - 06)	2318
Kawasaki Bayou 220/250/300 & Prairie 300 ATVs (86 - 03)	2351
Polaris ATVs (85 - 97)	2302
Polaris ATVs (98 - 06)	2508
Yamaha YFS200 Blaster ATV (88 - 02)	2317
Yamaha YFB250 Timberwolf ATVs (92 - 00)	2217
Yamaha YFM350 & YFM400 (ER and Big Bear) ATVs (87 - 03)	2126
Yamaha Banshee and Warrior ATVs (87 - 03)	2314
Yamaha Kodiak and Grizzly ATVs (93 - 05)	2567
ATV Basics	10450

TECHBOOK SERIES

Title	Book No
Twist and Go (automatic transmission) Scooters Service and Repair Manual	4082
Motorcycle Basics TechBook (2nd Edition)	3515
Motorcycle Electrical TechBook (3rd Edition)	3471
Motorcycle Fuel Systems TechBook	3514
Motorcycle Maintenance TechBook	4071
Motorcycle Modifying	4272
Motorcycle Workshop Practice TechBook (2nd Edition)	3470

◇ = not available in the USA   ♦ = Superbike

MCL23.12/07

Preserving Our Motoring Heritage

<
The Model J Duesenberg
Derham Tourster.
Only eight of these
magnificent cars were
ever built – this is the
only example to be found
outside the United States
of America

Almost every car you've ever loved, loathed or desired is gathered under one roof at the Haynes Motor Museum. Over 300 immaculately presented cars and motorbikes represent every aspect of our motoring heritage, from elegant reminders of bygone days, such as the superb Model J Duesenberg to curiosities like the bug-eyed BMW Isetta. There are also many old friends and flames. Perhaps you remember the 1959 Ford Popular that you did your courting in? The magnificent 'Red Collection' is a spectacle of classic sports cars including AC, Alfa Romeo, Austin Healey, Ferrari, Lamborghini, Maserati, MG, Riley, Porsche and Triumph.

A Perfect Day Out

Each and every vehicle at the Haynes Motor Museum has played its part in the history and culture of Motoring. Today, they make a wonderful spectacle and a great day out for all the family. Bring the kids, bring Mum and Dad, but above all bring your camera to capture those golden memories for ever. You will also find an impressive array of motoring memorabilia, a comfortable 70 seat video cinema and one of the most extensive transport book shops in Britain. The Pit Stop Cafe serves everything from a cup of tea to wholesome, home-made meals or, if you prefer, you can enjoy the large picnic area nestled in the beautiful rural surroundings of Somerset.

>
John Haynes O.B.E.,
Founder and
Chairman of the
museum at the wheel
of a Haynes Light 12.

<
The 1936 490cc
sohc-engined
International
Norton – well known
for its racing success

The Museum is situated on the A359 Yeovil to Frome road at Sparkford, just off the A303 in Somerset. It is about 40 miles south of Bristol, and 25 minutes drive from the M5 intersection at Taunton.
Open 9.30am - 5.30pm (10.00am - 4.00pm Winter) 7 days a week, *except Christmas Day, Boxing Day and New Years Day*
Special rates available for schools, coach parties and outings Charitable Trust No. 292048